Armed with Sword and Scales

In the mid-eighteenth century, author and magistrate Henry Fielding adjudicated cases of theft, assault, and public disorder from his London home on Bow Street. By the middle of the nineteenth century, Fielding's modest "police office" had expanded to become the most prolific court system in Britain and the cornerstone of criminal and civil justice in the metropolis. Sascha Auerbach examines the fascinating history of this institution through the lens of "courtroom culture" – the combination of formal statute and informal custom that guided everyday practice in the London police courts. He offers a new model for understanding the relationship between law, culture, and society in modern Britain and illuminates how the local courtroom became a crucial part of everyday life and thoroughly entangled with popular representations of justice and morality.

Sascha Auerbach is a lecturer in Modern British and Colonial History at the University of Nottingham. A former Fulbright Scholar, he is the author of *Race, Law and "The Chinese Puzzle" in Imperial Britain.*

See the Studies in Legal History series website at
http://studiesinlegalhistory.org/

Studies in Legal History

Other books in the series:

Alejandro de La Fuente, Ariela J. Gross, *Becoming Free, Becoming Black: Race, Freedom, and the Law in Cuba, Virginia, and Louisiana*
Elizabeth Papp Kamali, *Felony and the Guilty Mind in Medieval England*
Jessica K. Lowe, *Murder in the Shenandoah: Making Law Sovereign in Revolutionary Virginia*
Michael A. Schoeppner, *Moral Contagion: Black Atlantic Sailors, Citizenship, and Diplomacy in Antebellum America*
Sam Erman, *Almost Citizens: Puerto Rico, the US Constitution, and Empire*
Martha S. Jones, *Birthright Citizens: A History of Race and Rights in Antebellum America*
Julia Moses, *The First Modern Risk: Workplace Accidents and the Origins of European Social States*
Cynthia Nicoletti, *Secession on Trial: The Treason Prosecution of Jefferson Davis*

Edward James Kolla, *Sovereignty, International Law, and the French Revolution*
Assaf Likhovski, *Tax Law and Social Norms in Mandatory Palestine and Israel*
Robert W. Gordon, *Taming the Past: Essays on Law and History and History in Law*
Paul Garfinkel, *Criminal Law in Liberal and Fascist Italy*
Michelle A. McKinley, *Fractional Freedoms: Slavery, Intimacy, and Legal Mobilization in Colonial Lima, 1600–1700*
Karen M. Tani, *States of Dependency: Welfare, Rights, and American Governance, 1935–1972*
Stefan Jurasinski, *The Old English Penitentials and Anglo-Saxon Law*
Felice Batlan, *Women and Justice for the Poor: A History of Legal Aid, 1863–1945*
Sophia Z. Lee, *The Workplace Constitution from the New Deal to the New Right*
Mitra Sharafi, *Law and Identity in Colonial South Asia: Parsi Legal Culture, 1772–1947*
Michael A. Livingston, *The Fascists and the Jews of Italy: Mussolini's Race Laws, 1938–1943*

Armed with Sword and Scales

Law, Culture, and Local Courtrooms in London, 1860–1913

SASCHA AUERBACH
University of Nottingham

CAMBRIDGE
UNIVERSITY PRESS

CAMBRIDGE
UNIVERSITY PRESS

University Printing House, Cambridge CB2 8BS, United Kingdom

One Liberty Plaza, 20th Floor, New York, NY 10006, USA

477 Williamstown Road, Port Melbourne, VIC 3207, Australia

314–321, 3rd Floor, Plot 3, Splendor Forum, Jasola District Centre, New Delhi – 110025, India

79 Anson Road, #06–04/06, Singapore 079906

Cambridge University Press is part of the University of Cambridge.

It furthers the University's mission by disseminating knowledge in the pursuit of education, learning, and research at the highest international levels of excellence.

www.cambridge.org
Information on this title: www.cambridge.org/9781108491556
DOI: 10.1017/9781108863711

First published 2021

A catalogue record for this publication is available from the British Library.

ISBN 978-1-108-49155-6 Hardback

For my mother, Margaret Rita Crosby (1942–2018)

"We all coast along
thinking we can take
forever to get down this hill."
from "Ride," by P. H. Crosby

"Justice, justice, you shall pursue."

Deuteronomy 16:20

"Like sailing, gardening, politics, and poetry, law and ethnography are crafts of place: they work by the light of local knowledge."

Clifford Geertz

Contents

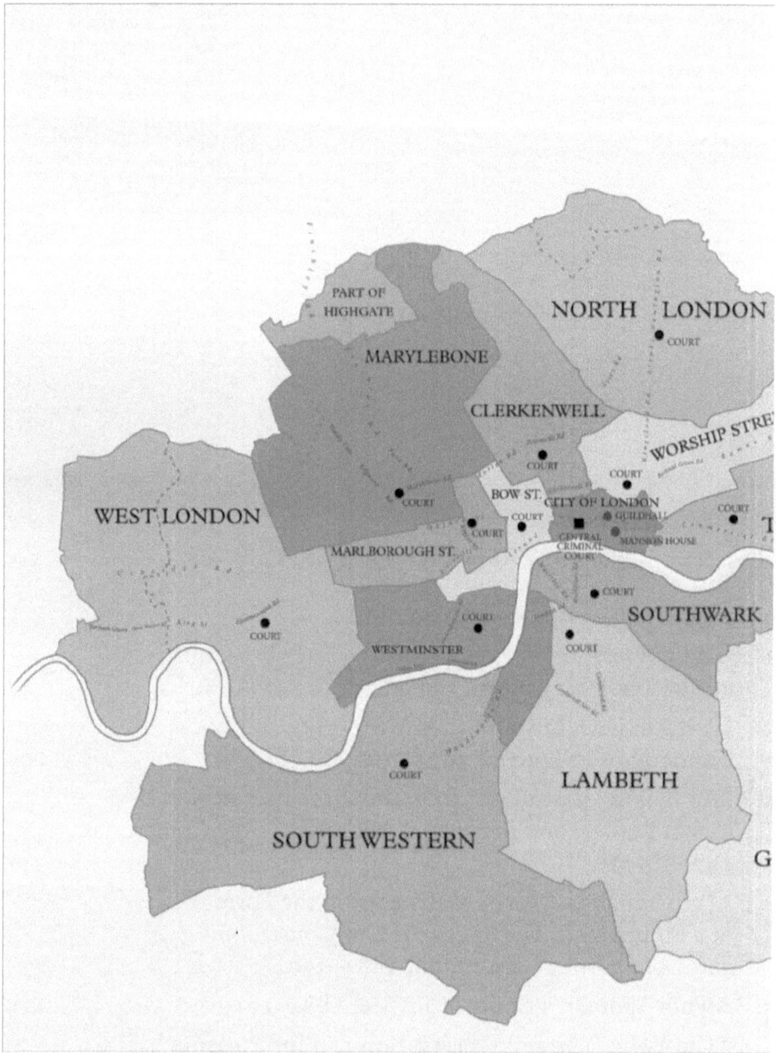

FIG 0.1 London Police Court Divisions, 1904 (by Matilde Grimaldi.)

POLICE COURT DIVISIONS
1904

Division	*Court House*
Bow Street	BOW STREET, COVENT GARDEN, W.C.
Clerkenwell	KING'S CROSS ROAD, W.C.
Worship Street	FINSBURY SQUARE, E.C.
Thames	EAST ARBOUR STREET, STEPNEY, E.
North London	STOKE NEWINGTON ROAD, N.
Marlborough Street	GREAT MARLBOROUGH STREET, W.
Marylebone	SEYMOUR PLACE, W.
West London	VERNON STREET, WEST KENSINGTON, W.
Westminster	VINCENT SQUARE, S.W.
South Western	LAVENDER HILL, S.W.
Lambeth	RENFREW ROAD, LOWER KENNINGTON LANE, S.E.
Southwark	HIGH STREET, BOROUGH, S.E.
Greenwich	BLACKHEATH ROAD, S.E.
Woolwich	TOWN HALL, WOOLWICH, S.E.
City of London Justice Rooms	THE MANSION HOUSE, E.C. GUILDHALL, E.C.

HOURS OF ATTENDANCE

Every day from 10 a.m. until 5 p.m., except Sundays, Christmas Day, Good Friday, and Bank Holidays. NOTE:—The hours of attendance at the Greenwich Court are from 10 a.m. until 1.30 p.m.; and at the Woolwich Court, from 2.30 p.m. until 5 p.m.

At the Mansion House and Guildhall, the hours of attendance are from 10 a.m. until 4 p.m., except on Saturdays, when the hours are from 10 a.m. until 1 p.m.

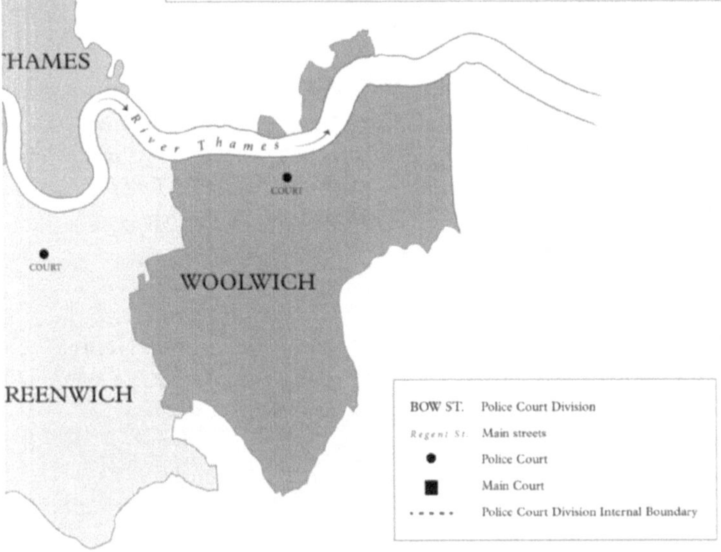

Figures

Acknowledgments

They say it takes a village to raise a child or, in this instance, to designate an idiot. It certainly takes a department and a discipline or, in this instance, departments and disciplines, to produce a monograph. To my colleagues and friends in History, Law, Geography, Politics and English at Oberlin College, Emory University, Mississippi State University, the University of Northern British Columbia, Kings College London, and the University of Nottingham, my gratitude is (almost) beyond words. If you are not named individually in these acknowledgments, it is not because I have forgotten you, but because an exhaustive enumeration would have given a stroke to my editors and a hernia to any reader trying to heft the resulting tome.

My profound gratitude goes also to those whose sacrifice of time and effort made this research possible and the writing experience survivable: my colleagues at the University of Northern British Columbia, in Richmond, and at the University of Nottingham, especially Luke Harris, Sarah Badcock, Nick Baron, Dean "the Dean" Blackburn, Leigh Anne Craig, David Gehring, Anna Greenwood, Onni Gust, David Laven, Spencer Mawby, and Maiken Umbach. You offered me kind hospitality in lands at once both familiar and foreign. Outside of my home institutions, I had the pleasure of working with a marvelous cohort of modern British historians in North America and the UK. Anne Clendinning, always among the best of us, has sadly passed into the footnotes. Her wit and wisdom are sorely missed. Margot Finn's counsel remains beyond exemplary.[1] Essential,

[1] It was Margot who first suggested that I look at local court records. And it was in her British Studies Seminar at Emory University that Paul Menair observed "you talk a lot about magistrates' perceptions of justice, but not much about how working-class

too, was the unstinting support of Antoinette Burton, Jacqueline Holler, Dane Kennedy, Philippa Levine, Susan Pennybacker, Gail Savage, and Bernard Moitt (aka "Dr. Pants"). Their friendship and encouragement have been, in the words of the poet Darren Morris, a little canister of sweet cream that sat resplendent on my lonely desk.

The penultimate writing stages were assisted by the Dean's Research Leave from the University of Nottingham and by the encouragement of Judith Mossman in the School of Humanities and Maiken Umbach in the History Department. The final coda came courtesy of Tamar Garb and a fellowship at University College London's Institute of Advanced Studies.[2] The research itself was completed under the auspices of the Fulbright-King's College London Scholar Award and both an Insight and Standard Grant from the Canadian Social Sciences and Humanities Research Council. Much credit for making these latter feasible goes to Jacqueline Holler at UNBC, where the cold weather was easily outmatched by the warmth of my remarkable colleagues. During my time there, I received invaluable aid from two terrific research assistants, Meghan Horlings and Meg Sterling, who were supported by a collaborative research grant from UNBC. They deserve the highest praise for their meticulous transcription of reams of handwritten pages of court testimony. R. D. Adair also contributed to this effort.

Earlier versions of the manuscript material were offered at various iterations of the North American Conference on British Studies, the Mid-Atlantic Conference on British Studies, and the Pacific Coast Conference on British Studies, as well as at the Social Science History Association annual conference and the Literature and Law annual conference. The other institutions and forums that hosted me included (in rough chronological order) George Washington University, the University of Buffalo, the Institute of Historical Research, Oberlin College, the University of Delaware (Legal Studies Lecture Series), Columbia University, the University of Toronto (via the Osgoode School of Law's exemplary Legal History Workshop, run deftly by David Phillips), Ryerson University, King's College London, Cambridge University, the Institute for Advanced Legal Studies (University of London), City University (Centre for Law, Justice and Journalism), The Open University (International Centre for the History

women viewed things. What were *their* ideas about courtrooms?" That question, in many ways, prompted the book you hold now.

[2] While we were both completing our PhD theses at Emory, Julie Livingston captured the process perfectly when she commented that "no project is ever truly finished, but they are all eventually abandoned."

of Crime, Policing and Justice), the University of Reading, Oxford University, the Institute of Historical Research (University of London), Keele University, the University of Leiden, University College London, Plymouth University, and the University of Adelaide. The Law and Humanities Junior Scholar Workshop held at Columbia University in 2010 was particularly helpful, and my special appreciation goes to Robin West, Willy Forbath, Katherine Franke, and Hilary Shor. The work that they so ably engaged culminated in its recognition by the Sutherland Prize Committee of the American Society for Legal History. Presumably the committee saw the irony of honorably mentioning someone so thoroughly disreputable, but I am grateful nonetheless. I also need to thank the many archivists and research librarians who provided such crucial support, and inexhaustible patience, in my unending requests. The staff at the University of Nottingham's Hallward Library, the London Metropolitan Archives, the National Archives, Emory University's Woodruff Library, the Colindale Newspaper Library, and the British Library were all exemplars of their profession. Particular mention must go to Bev Baker at the Nottingham Galleries of Justice for her meticulous guidance through the (at the time) newly opened Rainer Archive.

My wonderful colleagues in the North American Conference on British Studies and the Mid-Atlantic Conference on British Studies have nurtured this project and its hapless creator from the very first – utterly terrifying – conference delivery at the NYC MACBS in 1999. One of the most enjoyable aspects of working on a book for so long is the pleasure of hearing how other (far better) scholars are approaching similar topics. Although a full tally is not practical, conversations and correspondences with Andy August, Anna Clark, Dina Copelman, Carolyn Conley, Anna Davin, Jennifer Davis, Ginger Frost, Seth Koven, Lara Kriegel, Majorie Levine-Clark, Susan Pedersen, Gail Savage, Judith Walkowitz, and Martin Wiener were all especially helpful. The generosity and intellectual energy of the US-UK Fulbright Commission under the guidance of Penny Egan helped me find a new home across the Atlantic, and both the School of Law and the Department of History at King's College London suffered my residency with admirable patience. For inspirational companionship, one could not have asked for a more brilliant and congenial crowd than the 2011 US-UK Fulbrighters. Their influence explains my continued obsession with the sensorium of bees and contemporary automotive design, as well as my Pavlovian reaction to public announcements on British trains.

In the revision and production of the manuscript itself, foremost thanks must go to Thomas Green and Michael Lobban. Their efforts to bring *Sword and Scales* to fruition were nothing short of herculean (in the sense that the early drafts would have put the Augean stables to shame), and they have earned appropriately heroic stature in my eyes. Debbie Gershenowitz, Rachel Blaifeder, Cecelia Cancellaro, and Ruth Boyes, as well as the rest of the contributing editorial and production staff at Cambridge University Press, the anonymous reviewers, and my copy-editor Jem Langworthy were the epitome of professionalism. Matilde Grimaldi's creative effort brought the book's images to life life and Derek Gottleib did a masterful job on the index and bibliography. Special thanks also to Charles Grench at the University of North Carolina Press, who first showed interest in the original manuscript, and who continued to speak well of the project long after any reasonable person would have forgotten it entirely.

My peerless friends both in and out of the profession played a far greater role than they realize they did. Chief among them are Aaron Fichtelberg, Patrick McDevitt, Paul Deslandes, Len Smith, Kevin Siena, Gregory Feifer, Daniel Ritter, Darren Morris, and Cennydd Bowles. No matter how far I roamed, thanks to you all, I knew I would always find an open door, a full table, a laugh, and a sympathetic ear. Cen needs special recognition for his fantastic cover design, which may be the only part of this volume whose quality is beyond question. Much appreciation goes Hiroshi Forsyth and the rest of the ULU/Regal/Seymour LC basketball crew, who taught me that exhaustion, discouragement, and frustration are no excuses to stop playing, and that loving what you do is victory enough, no matter what the scoreboard says. I have to thank Joseph Bendersky for providing such an apt lesson on injustice, and Camden County Council, which offered equally useful instruction by wrongfully summonsing me for unpaid council taxes during my Fulbright year. I can only hope that my subsequent actions proved, if not my complete innocence, at least my absence of malice.

My brothers, Adam, David, and Martin Auerbach have all followed this saga from beginning to end. Thanks for everything, and feel free to offer suggestions as to your casting in the inevitable film treatment. To my mother, Margaret Rita Crosby, and my father, Norbert Josef Allen-Auerbach, I dearly wish you could have seen the final, happy, conclusion of "that book you are *still* working on?" Well, it is done, and in one way or another, you are on every page. The extended clans Auerbach, Crosby, Saroka, and Vorobieva were always there with support and encouragement.

I am grateful beyond measure for the generosity and patience of Irina Curbelo Vorobieva and for four decades of friendship with the incomparable Colin Burns. Odin, it is said, had a pair of ravens at his shoulders to bring him the wisdom of the world, but Maximus and the Musing Sparrow could give them a run for their money. Last, and certainly not least, two thumbs up for George Curbelo Allen-Auerbach in his many guises as a race-car driver, policeman, fireman, astronaut, and captain courageous of the HMIS *Space Giraffe*. His alternating demands of "papa no work!" and "papa go work!" were constant reminders that the true value of any accomplishment lies in what was sacrificed to the effort. This is, perhaps, the only justice to which we are *all* entitled.

Nottingham and London
2020.

Glossary of Terms and Abbreviations

Assizes or Courts of Assize: Courts held periodically around England and Wales until 1972. Assizes conducted both criminal and civil proceedings, though primarily the former, hearing the most serious cases remanded (see *remand* below) to them in an earlier period by the magistrates sitting alone or in petty sessions, and then later by the police courts.

Application (for summons): An application from a complainant, made in person at the local courtroom, for the issuing of a court summons to a named defendant for a specific offense (see *summons* below).

BLC: Bye-Laws Committee of the London School Board. This committee was responsible for overseeing the enforcement of the mandatory school attendance bye-laws and reported on these efforts to the full Board.

Bound over/bound over on own recognizance: A decision by a judge that required a defendant, in lieu of an immediate fine or imprisonment, to fulfill an obligation, and to pay a significant fine if they failed to do so. In the magistrates' courts, this obligation was typically for "good behaviour" over a set period of time (usually six or twelve months). Recognizances could be further reinforced by *sureties* (see below).

Charge: In contrast to a *summons* (see below), charges were generally employed for more serious crimes, and typically merited immediate arrest and temporary detainment pending trial.

Complainant: The injured party in a summons.

Distress warrant: A distress warrant empowered an officer of the court, should a convicted defendant not have sufficient funds to pay any fine imposed, to seize the property of the defendant and have it sold by a broker to recoup the amount owed.

Home Office: The branch of government, headed by the Home Secretary, responsible for overseeing most domestic policy. Magistrates were appointed and supervised by the Home Office, which held ultimate authority over the entire domestic apparatus of policing and justice.

Indictable offense vs. non-indictable offense: A non-indictable offense was a minor crime that could be punished with a fine instead of imprisonment. For a more serious, indictable offense, a term of imprisonment was mandatory upon conviction.

Informations/the information: A brief description of the circumstances and justification that had to be provided when applying to the magistrate or other court agent for the issuing of a summons. Prior to the mid-Victorian period, "the information" had to be written, but subsequent reforms allowed for verbal informations.

Personal summons vs. institutional summons: The former refers to summonses brought by private individuals, the latter to those brought by representatives of various local and municipal bodies. NB: these are the author's terms, and were not employed by historical subjects.

In camera: Refers to proceedings conducted in the private chambers of the magistrate, most commonly with only the principals and the court clerk present.

LCC: London County Council. The municipal government of London. The LCC succeeded the Metropolitan Board of Works, absorbing all of the latter's powers and some of those previously held by the guardians, vestries, and local boards

LSB: London School Board (or School Board for London).

MBW: Metropolitan Board of Works. The municipal government of London that preceded the London County Council.

Minutes: Written records of magistrates' court testimony recorded and annotated by the court clerk.

MP: Member of Parliament

Old Bailey (Central Criminal Court): The most prominent criminal court in England. Originally, its jurisdiction included only the City and the county of Middlesex (London). In 1834, this was extended to allow the Central Criminal Court to try major crimes committed anywhere in England.

Peer: A member of the House of Lords.

PC: Usually Police Court, on occasion Police Constable (see context).

Police Court Registers: Brief summary records proceedings in the magistrates' courts. They included the name of the informant or complainant and the defendant, the latter's age, the nature of the offense (charge) or matter of complaint (summons), the date of the proceedings, the adjudication, and the name of the presiding magistrate. In the case of charges, the age and occupation of the defendant were often recorded as well.

Public Office: The term used for the original eighteenth-century magistrates courts in London (e.g. "Bow Street Public Office"). The designation "public office" continued to be used through the 1820s, and was phased out with the reforms of the 1830s.

Remand: An order given in a lower court (e.g. a magistrates' court) for a serious offense be tried at a superior court (e.g. the Central Criminal Court).

Sine die: Latin for "without a day." Cases that were adjourned *sine die* were effectively adjourned in perpetuity.

Stipendiary Justice: A paid, professional magistrate assigned to a particular court and sitting in regular rotation.

Summary justice/summary proceedings: Any trial conducted from commencement to conviction solely before a magistrate or magistrates without the participation of a jury.

Summons: (pl. *summonses*): An official order compelling the defendant to attend a certain court on a certain day. Failure to appear could result in the summons escalating to a charge. Police constables could issue a court summons to an alleged offender, while agencies of municipal governance were granted a certain number of summonses annually. Private individuals, in contrast, had to apply in person before the magistrate, who would, if they found the application to have merit, arrange for special constables seconded to the court to deliver the summons document to the defendant's place of residence.

Surety: A surety was an amount of money paid (or promised) to the court and held in trust until certain conditions were fulfilled by the defendant in whose name the surety had been offered. The most common form of surety was provided on the promise that a defendant, once released from imprisonment subsequent to their arrest and charging, would appear in court on the appointed date to face trial. Sureties were also used as a form of suspended fines. A defendant released from a minor charge or summons, most typically for assault, promised "good behaviour" (i.e. no further acts violations) for an allotted period of time (typically six or twelve months), on pain of forfeiting the stipulated amount, which was usually far in excess of the typical fine on conviction (i.e. £1–£5 instead of a few shillings). Smaller sureties (i.e. for court appearance) were paid up front and returned after trial (or used to offset fines on conviction), while larger ones (e.g. suspended fines), were more typically demanded only if the defendant violated their promise of good behavior within the period specified by the magistrate (a very rare occurrence).

Warrant: A document issued by a magistrate to authorize the arrest of a suspect on a particular charge and their conveyance to court to face trial, typically employed in the case of serious crimes. Warrants could also be issued in instances where the offense committed did not ordinarily merit an arrest, but in which the defendant was considered to be a flight risk.

Introduction

Courtroom Culture

In 1891, George P. Ingersoll traveled to London to gather material for the *Yale Law Journal*. Ingersoll belonged to one of Connecticut's most illustrious political families. Like his father, the state's Adjutant General, and his uncle, a former governor, Ingersoll was an alumnus of Yale Law School and a member of the Connecticut Bar Association.[1] When this scion of Connecticut's legal and political elite described England's "temples of justice" in one of the nation's premier law journals, he was not referring to the Old Bailey, the Queen's Bench, or any of England's other renowned judicial venues.[2] Instead, he offered readers a detailed description of the Bow Street Magistrates' Court. The magistrates' courts – or "police courts," as they were commonly called – were the bottom rung of England's criminal justice hierarchy. Their personnel spent much of their time adjudicating petty crime, mediating interpersonal conflicts, and issuing small fines for infractions of various municipal regulations. Lacking high cachet, Bow Street was, nonetheless, the chief venue in London's largest and most prolific court system. Its courtroom, along with the Old Bailey (the Central Criminal Court), was the one most broadly depicted in journalism and popular culture. It was the judicial institution that metropolitan men and women were most likely to

1 *New York Times*, September 14, 1903, 7.
2 George P. Ingersoll, "The London Police Courts," *Yale Law Journal* 2, no.2 (Dec. 1892), 54.

encounter during their daily lives. It was therefore no contradiction for Ingersoll to declare that this locale epitomized English justice even as it constituted the most modest venue of English law. "There is no better place to see the English reverence for the majesty of the law than in a London police court," he wrote, "and this is the more remarkable for the lowest specimens of humanity that one can conceive of are daily brought there to be weighed in the scales of justice."[3]

What is revealing from the perspective of a legal historian is not just what Ingersoll discussed in detail, but also what was altogether absent from his account. At no point did the author mention a single statute or regulation, nor did he outline the limits of the court's purview or of the magistrate's authority. Ingersoll focused instead on the appearance of the courtroom itself, the character of courtroom dialogue, how trial participants approached the proceedings, the bench, the demeanor of the magistrate, and the overall impression conveyed about the nature of law and justice in England. Whatever the issue was at hand and whatever laws might apply, the importance of these elements was readily apparent in the behavior and attitude of plaintiffs, defendants, the audience and, most especially, the adjudicators. "English magistrates," Ingersoll declared, "generally seem to aim to conduct their trials not only to do justice, but also to convince those in attendance that justice is done."[4] Ingersoll was hardly alone in observing that what we would today call the social and cultural aspects of courtrooms were essential to their daily operation. The same opinion was expressed by English magistrates, courtroom journalists, the authors of popular fiction, ancillary agents of the court, and by the legions of ordinary men and women who found themselves before the bench. Much surviving evidence suggests that for all of them, the importance of what was said and done in court, and how those words and actions were portrayed to a broader audience, often matched the significance of formal decisions. Unlike official verdicts, the broader meanings of these social and cultural aspects of the courtroom were often a matter of debate. The interpretations of courtroom events were as diverse as their participants and observers were, and contestation was as common as consensus was from the mid-nineteenth century, when the courts first rose to prominence in public

[3] Ibid., 55. [4] Ibid.

discourse, well into the first decades of the twentieth. In contrast to Ingersoll's admiration for the London police courts and for the deeply respectful demeanor he ascribed to working-class participants, since mid-century, the burgeoning labor press had, for example, been openly contemptuous of magistrates whose decisions seemed counter to the interests of respectable workingmen. In 1865, the editors of the *Bee-Hive*, a prominent trades-unionist newspaper, even dubbed a magistrate of the Lambeth Police Court a "just-ass" in a column bluntly titled "The Stupidity of a Magistrate."[5] Magistrates and other judicial officials themselves often held conflicted views of their roles and the function of their courtrooms in everyday society, praising them as the "poor man's court of justice" at one moment and deriding them as burlesque or grotesque the next.[6]

Although contemporaries articulated widely varying interpretations of the police courts, the surviving evidence attests to three core features: their engagement with everyday life, their depiction in a broad variety of media, and their significance as one of the primary points of contact between the state and the individual. In 1831, the London magistrates delivered one summary verdict for approximately every sixty-five people recorded in that year's metropolitan census.[7] Between 1834 and 1845, they dealt with an average of 64,500 cases a year.[8] This deluge of adjudications would continue to increase in tandem with the growth of urban society in England and the expansion of the modern state. By the second half of the nineteenth century, across the country, there would be one summary trial annually for roughly every fifty men

[5] *Bee-Hive*, April 8, 1865, 2.

[6] Cecil Chapman designated them as such in the title of his interwar memoir, *The Poor Man's Court of Justice: Twenty-Five Years as a Metropolitan Magistrate* (London: Hodder and Stoughton, 1925). The significance of the burlesque and the grotesque as nineteenth-century genres was brought to my attention by Kurt Newman at the May 2010 Columbia Law and Humanities Interdisciplinary Junior Scholar Workshop.

[7] In 1831, London magistrates "summarily disposed of or held to bail" defendants in 21,843 cases. Joseph Fletcher, "Statistical Account of the Constitution and Operation of the Criminal Courts of the Metropolis," *Journal of the Statistical Society of London* 9, no. 4 (Dec. 1846), 303(information originally from the Returns of the Metropolitan Police for 1842). The 1831 census recorded a London population of 1,474,069. It should be noted, however, that this latter statistic included the population of the City of London, over which the police courts did not have jurisdiction, hence the approximation.

[8] Fletcher, "Statistical Account," 303.

and women counted in the census.[9] In 1880, summary justice in England and Wales accounted for over 660,000 cases, with nearly 126,000 in London alone.[10] These official tabulations, striking though they are, represented merely the tip of the iceberg. Hundreds of thousands more men and women appeared every year in court to apply for summonses, to give witness testimony, or simply to observe the proceedings. And greater still were the multitudes who encountered these courtrooms vicariously through the writings of flâneurs, memoirists, popular literary authors, and the ubiquitous "Police Intelligence" columns that became a central feature of both local and national newspapers. As Charles Dickens Jr. observed in 1890, "to make the acquaintance of a police-court is, at some time or other, the common lot of most of those who bear the burden of life within the limits of the great metropolis."[11]

Magistrates' courts intersected the everyday life of their local communities at more points, and with greater frequency, than any other legal venue in England did. The only comparable institution in terms of scale were the County Courts, which issued almost as many judgments yearly, but held far fewer full hearings.[12] Whereas the latter dealt primarily with civil matters, most commonly the recovery of debt, the magistrates' courts engaged a wide variety of concerns both civil and criminal, including family relations, employment, property, sexual reputation, child-rearing, citizenship,

[9] This does not, however, mean that 1 out of every 50 individuals recorded in the census faced a summary trial, since with certain violations (drunk and disorderly most especially), it was not uncommon for the same individual to be charged twice or more in the same year.

[10] 663,404 in England and Wales. *Judicial Statistics, 1880, England and Wales, Pt. I, Police – Criminal Proceedings – Prisons* (PP 1881, C. 3088) [hereafter *Judicial Statistics, 1880*], 32. London 125,911, ibid., 28. This constituted the vast majority of criminal proceedings in England and Wales, the remaining being trials for indictable offenses. These numbered 22,231 in 1880, ibid., xiii.

[11] Charles Dickens Jr., "A London Police-Court," *All the Year Round: A Weekly Journal* 4 (3rd series) (Jan.–Jun. 1899), 349. Peter King has made a similar assertion with regards to the eighteenth century and summary justice nationwide, asserting that "summary courts were the arena in which the vast majority of the population experienced the law." Peter King, "The Summary Courts and Social Relations in Nineteenth-Century England," *Past & Present* 183 (May 2004), 128.

[12] In 1880, the County Courts across England and Wales determined actions in 658,695 instances, but only half of these instances required a full hearing, the remainder being decided by consent, admission, or default. *Judicial Statistics, 1880*, xli.

social competition, interpersonal violence, and public safety.[13] Of equal importance, with their discretionary powers, magistrates helped set the standards of public morality. They determined which violations and which offenders were dangerous to the community and therefore to be treated severely, and which actors and acts deserved leniency. The London police courts were also among the most widely portrayed of all legal venues in Britain. The drama, tragedy, and farce that typified much of their newspaper reports made them a popular topic across a broad readership, and particularly among the growing cohort of working-class and lower-middle-class readers. Editors and journalists alike commented on the public's hunger for courtroom stories, and their success in attracting readers helped make them a staple of the popular press that developed following the reduction of the Stamp Tax in the mid-1830s.[14] In the words of newspaper pioneer and Radical politician Henry Heatherington, who co-founded the *Twopenny Dispatch* in 1834, they were "the sort of devilment that will make it sell."[15] By the second half of the nineteenth century, magistrates' courtrooms were being depicted daily in newspapers from the venerable *Times* to sensationalist broadsheets and local borough papers. In all of these functions and in all of these portrayals, whether any given defendant was deemed guilty or innocent was only one of many considerations. The experience of a courtroom was far more than the verdict of a trial, and the public portrayals of trials were far more than a catalog of punishments. Courtrooms offered opportunities for all involved to make public statements about some of the most important issues of the time. Even those who had no official role in the proceedings could contribute to ongoing dialogues about morality, public order, and

[13] As Margot Finn observes, "magistrates were the day-to-day face of criminal law in the Victorian era." Margot Finn, "The Authority of the Law," in Peter Mandler, ed., *Liberty and Authority in Victorian Britain* (Oxford: Oxford University Press, 2006), 162.

[14] The tax on British newspapers was reduced from fourpence to one penny in 1836, prompting a nearly fourfold increase in newspaper circulation in the subsequent two decades. Brian Lake, *British Newspapers: A History and Guide* (London: Sheppard Press, 1984), 213.

[15] Henry Hetherington quoted in Ivor Asquith, "The Structure, Ownership and Control of the Press, 1780–1855," in George Boyce, James Curran, and Pauline Wingate, eds., *Newspaper History from the Seventeenth Century to the Present Day* (London: Constable, 1978), 107.

social norms well beyond the boundaries that law officially defined. Courtroom events and their public depictions, in short, did not just reflect social relations and express the authority of the state over the individual, they also helped constitute their very nature.

Magistrates' courtrooms were part of a constellation of state entities that, across the nineteenth century, were playing an increasingly prominent role in everyday life, and in the lives of London's working class in particular. They joined public health inspectors, Poor Law Guardians, London School Board Visitors (i.e. truant officers), child protection agents, the Metropolitan Police, and the various iterations of London municipal governance to constitute the "everyday state" in the metropolis.[16] This was a state that changed significantly across the nineteenth century as two traditional institutions of English governance, the Anglican Church and the Monarchy, continued their steady, albeit uneven, retreat in power and influence. The Church of England lost its near-monopoly on education and the provision of charity and social welfare with Nonconformist interests, especially strong in London, engineering a transfer of these responsibilities to ostensibly secular municipal bodies under elected or appointed leadership.[17] Ecclesiastical courts, which had once adjudicated a wide variety of morally inflected legal issues, from sexual slander to divorce, likewise ceded such matters to secular jurisdiction.[18] Nineteenth-century municipal governance in London underwent a series of iterations, the most important of which were the Metropolitan Board of Works (MBW) and the London County Council (LCC), that reflected the changing social, political and demographic character of the city. The MBW constituted the metropole's primary instrument of governance from 1855 to 1889 and consisted of members nominated by local vestries (which themselves were not democratically elected until 1894). In 1889, the MBW was succeeded by the LCC, an elected body that assumed all of its predecessor's duties and more besides.[19]

[16] George Behlmer, *Friends of the Family: The English Home and Its Guardians, 1850–1940* (Stanford: Stanford University Press, 1998), 76.

[17] The classic account of this process is David Roberts's *Victorian Origins of the British Welfare State* (New Haven: Yale University Press, 1960).

[18] R. B. Outhwaite, *The Rise and Fall of the English Ecclesiastical Courts, 1500–1860* (Cambridge: Cambridge University Press, 2010).

[19] John Davis, *Reforming London: The London Government Problem, 1855–1900* (Oxford: Oxford University Press, 1988), 96–114.

The transformation of metropolitan government reflected the changing character of national politics. Successive expansions of the franchise in 1834, 1867, and 1884 brought more political power to the middle-class and Nonconformists, accelerating the secularization of law and social welfare, but did little to satisfy the growing demands for working-class votes.[20] The failure of Chartism after the turbulence of the 1840s ushered in a period of relative political stability where the rivalry between Tories and Liberals, who alternated terms in power, was tempered by the long reign of Queen Victoria and Britain's preeminent position in industry, trade, finance, and imperial dominion.[21] This lasted well into the last quarter of the century, when the economic depression of the 1880s and the growing influence of the working-class leaders and moderate Socialists, expressed most visibly through the wide membership of the Trades Union Congress, culminated in the foundation of Labour Party in 1900.[22] Even on the eve of the First World War, however, the British franchise included less than half of all adults, excluding many men and all the women of the working class.[23] Throughout this period of transition at both the metropolitan and national levels, the magistrates' court operated as arguably the most democratic and inclusive venues of the local state, open to all men and women for the price of a summons (set at two shillings by mid-century). That these courts could, on any given day, serve as tools of coercion in

[20] For a critical perspective on the process of secularization and modernization, see J. C. D. Clark, "Secularization and Modernization: The Failure of a 'Grand Narrative'," *The Historical Journal* 55, no. 1 (Mar. 2012), 161–94.

[21] The "Age of Equipoise," as assessed in W. L. Burns, *The Age of Equipoise: A Study of the Mid-Victorian Generation* (London: George Allen & Unwin, 1964) was not without its own serious internal tensions and disruptions, however, as recent scholars have emphasized. See Martin Hewitt, *An Age of Equipoise: Reassessing Mid-Victorian Britain* (Aldershot and Burlington: Ashgate, 2000).

[22] Conservatives and Liberals (the latter in alliance with Labour in the prewar years) retained much of the loyalty of the popular electorate until the post-war reorganization of the Labour Party in response to the Representation of the People Act 1918. Chris Wrigley, "The Labour Party and the Impact of the 1918 Reform Act," *Parliamentary History* 37, no. 1 (Feb. 2018), 64–80; Paul A. Readman, "The 1895 General Election and Political Change in Late Victorian Britain," *The Historical Journal* 42, no. 2 (Jun. 1999), 467–93.

[23] Mari Takayanagi, "The Representation of the People Act 1918: A Democratic Milestone in the UK and Ireland" (OxHRH Blog, February 6, 2018), http://ohrh.law.ox.ac.uk/the-representation-of-the-people-act-1918-a-democratic-milestone-in-the-uk-and-ireland.

the hands of the Metropolitan Police, municipal agents, or magistrates themselves; empower workers to claim unpaid wages from their employer; and be harnessed by a local housewife to seek relief from an abusive husband goes far in explaining why they came to occupy such prominent roles in both their communities and the popular imagination.

In contrast with the new institutions of municipal governance such as the MBW and LCC, courts of summary justice, where minor trials were adjudicated by magistrates without a jury, enjoyed well-established precedents. Although the exponential growth of the magistrates' courts and their legal remit in the nineteenth century was accompanied by a commensurate expansion of their impact on their community's daily affairs, this type of court had existed for centuries already in the guise of that presided over by the unpaid Justices of the Peace (JPs).[24] The most important elements that distinguished the London police courts from those of the JPs were the legal qualifications of the respective benches, the former's rise in tandem with the regulatory state and the popular press, and the rapid expansion of the police courts' involvement in the everyday life of their communities.[25] The ranks of JPs, so central to rural governance in the seventeenth and eighteenth centuries, experienced a transition in social composition similar to that of magistrates in the late eighteenth century as landed gentlemen were replaced by middle-class professionals, manufacturers, and even tradesmen.[26] In contrast to

[24] Norma Landau, *The Justices of the Peace, 1679–1760* (Berkeley and London: University of California Press, 1984). For some of the other contrasts and continuities between the London magistrates and their amateur predecessors, the Justices of the Peace, see Jennifer Davis, "A Poor Man's System of Justice: The London Police Courts in the Second Half of the Nineteenth Century," *The Historical Journal* 27 (1984), 313–15.

[25] The Justices of the Peace have been a perennial topic of scholarly study, most notably in Landau's magisterial (no pun intended) *The Justices of the Peace*. See also Cynthia Herrup, *The Common Peace: Participation and the Criminal Law in Seventeenth-Century England* (Cambridge: Cambridge University Press, 1987); James Sharpe, "'Such Disagreement Betwyx Neighbours,' Litigation and Human Relations in Early Modern England," in John Bossy, ed., *Disputes and Settlements: Law and Human Relations in the West* (Cambridge: Cambridge University Press, 1983), 167–88; Robert Shoemaker, *Prosecution and Punishment: Petty Crime and the Law in London and Rural Middlesex, c.1660–1725* (Cambridge: Cambridge University Press, 1991).

[26] Douglas Hay, "England, 1562–1875: The Law and Its Uses," in Douglas Hay and Paul Craven, eds., *Masters, Servants, and Magistrates in Britain and the Empire, 1562–1955* (Chapel Hill: University of North Carolina Press, 2004), 105; Landau, *Justices*, 318.

their professionalized successors, however, JPs arrived at the bench without specialized training in law and typically handled a few hundred cases each year in local, *ad hoc* courts. Their proceedings were not widely reported in the metropolitan press, and their interface with the burgeoning edifice of municipal governance was limited. The passage of 1792 Middlesex Justice Act, which replaced the unpaid JPs throughout the metropolis with stipendiary magistrates, was a watershed moment in the transition from an amateur, decentralized system to a centralized and professionalized one. The exceptions to this judicial overhaul were the two summary courts of the City of London, Guildhall and Mansion House. With their relative accessibility and array of modest petitioners, the City courts foreshadowed the roles that the police courts would play in the nineteenth century. The City of London Justices, who have been examined closely by Daniel Grey, reached their heyday in the late eighteenth century, however, and never enjoyed the broad social and cultural influence that the magistrates' courts did in nineteenth-century London.[27]

The argument made here is not that the magistrates' dispensation of justice to the lower orders and popular interest in the courtroom were entirely new phenomena in nineteenth-century London. Rather, it is that the considerable increase in the scale and impact of magistrates' work in the metropolis was a crucial aspect of the changing relationship between the government and the governed and of modern urban culture more generally in this period. Storied figures such as Henry and John Fielding, Patrick Colquhoun, Claud Mullins, J. A. R. Cairns, Montagu Williams, and a host of other magistrates became synonymous with popular justice. Their venues would achieve renown and attract equally vociferous criticism. Bow Street Police Court, home to London's Chief Magistrate, reigned as the most prominent and influential magistrates' court in England for much of its existence.[28] London magistrates were sought after by the Home Office for their legal expertise, consulted closely in national reforms of the criminal justice system, and praised (or condemned) by name in

[27] Daniel Grey, *Crime, Prosecution and Social Relations: The Summary Courts of the City of London in the Late Eighteenth Century* (Basingstoke and New York: Palgrave Macmillan, 2009).

[28] Alan Lambert, "650 years of the office of Justice of the Peace/Magistrate," *Amicus Curiae* 88 (Winter, 2011), 8.

Parliament. Allen S. Laing, of the Hatton Garden Police Court, was even immortalized by Charles Dickens as the infamous "Mr. Fang," the epitome of cruel and arbitrary justice in *Oliver Twist*. The police-court columns were instrumental in the rise of the popular newspapers, helping shape the tastes of a burgeoning mass readership for "real life" stories from the courtroom.[29] And the London magistrates were influential in the practices of summary justice throughout Britain.[30] They were even the source of significant commentary and consideration from across the Atlantic by both journalists and their North American corollaries, the police-court magistrates of Canada and the United States.[31] All of these elements lent the London magistrates a national and international significance exceeding that of the Justices of the Peace. Police courts assumed the former remits of the JPs in both criminal and civil affairs, and expanded upon them. While sustaining some of the key traditions established by their rural predecessors – paternalism, moral authority, and responsiveness to community need most especially – the police courts were distinctly modern institutions. They were staffed with the legal expertise and ancillary agents necessary to handle the array of increasingly complex and numerous statutes that characterized urban governance in the nineteenth century. The County Courts, established in the mid-Victorian period (1846), matched the police courts in their prolific activity and wide press coverage, but were limited in scope to civil and commercial concerns such as debt recovery.[32] Although they played a crucial role regulating economic matters, they never achieved the cultural prominence, integration into working-class social relations, or role in mediating the relationship between the state and the individual that the police courts – as the lynchpins of criminal justice, public order, morality, and regulatory measures – did.

[29] Marjorie Jones, *Justice and Journalism* (London: Barry Rose, 1974), 54.

[30] Much of this influence was informal, with the chief professional journal, the *Justice of the Peace*, frequently citing London magistrates' decisions as guidance for similar cases in other locales.

[31] Emily Murphy, *The Black Candle* (Toronto: Thomas Allen, 1922), 202–5.

[32] Margot Finn, "Working-Class Women and the Contest for Consumer Control in Victorian County Courts," *Past and Present* 161, no. 1 (Nov. 1998), 120–21, 144. Among the other issues initially handled in the County Courts were claims for damages, claims for the administration of estates, and foreclosures.

Unlike the central institutions of metropolitan governance such as the London School Board or the London County Council, however, magistrates' courts were not explicitly institutions of social reform. Though unofficially, magistrates saw the moral uplift of the working class as one of their primary *raisons d'être*. In further contrast to other elements of London's burgeoning municipal edifice, Progressives, such as those who dominated the London County Council from 1889 to 1907, were not a major animating influence of the police courts.[33] Magistrates instead advocated a more traditional form of paternalism, emphasizing the power of personal persuasion and often expressing doubt or opposition to the involuntary intervention of the state in social affairs where legal violations were absent.[34] They had to reconcile their self-promoted image as representatives of a "benevolent state" with their equally strong commitment to their particular vision of justice and to the hostility expressed towards the police, regulatory agencies, and the magistrates themselves from any number of quarters.[35] Not least among the latter was a cohort that was, at best, ambivalent towards the state's growing role in daily life, the working-class men and women that made up the bulk of magistrates' courtroom clientele.[36] Such claims to paternalism, made frequently and publicly by magistrates, were undermined by a number of courtroom practices and by the changing social composition of the bench. As the magistracy, in London and elsewhere, became less the provenance of lesser gentry and more that of urban professionals, their association with the paternalism of the country gentleman atrophied as well, despite the efforts of the magistrates themselves.

The courtroom's role in reshaping the relationship between the state and the individual extended to the governors as much as it did to the governed. Municipal agents, police, and judicial officials all saw their authority both enhanced through the courtroom's expanded legal

[33] The Progressive Party was linked to the Liberal Party at the national level, and remained a majority on the LCC until the ascendency of the Municipal Reform Party (MRP, formerly the Moderate Party) in 1907. This was a significant blow to the Liberals, as the MRP was linked to the Conservative Party, and held sway until Labour gained control of the LCC in 1934.

[34] Davis, "Poor Man's System," 331.

[35] Henry Turner Waddy, *The Police Court and Its Work* (London: Butterworth, 1925), 2.

[36] Davis, "Poor Man's System," 310, 315.

reach and constrained by its growing cultural visibility and commensurate public accountability. Courtroom conflicts also helped determine the balance of power between different elements of the state, most visibly between judicial authorities, who had a long history of community influence, and relative newcomers such as the police, regulatory agents, and the London School Board. Magistrates influenced both the ideological discourse that justified the state's expanded reach and the practical capacity of police and municipal agents to implement new laws and regulations. Their courtroom statements and public commentary incorporated the paternalism of their eighteenth-century forefathers, the JPs and storied Bow Street magistrates, the Liberal individualism and moral reformism of the mid-Victorian period, and the bureaucratic positivism and regulatory interventionism of the late Victorian years.[37]

Magistrates' ambivalence towards coercive reform and their assertion of paternalist principles reminds us that older ideologies had a remarkably long and influential lifespan, and that the implementation of newer models of governance remained incomplete and contested, both externally by the targets of reform and internally by its implementers, well into the early twentieth century.[38] Seen through the local courtroom, the Victorian state emerges as a fractured entity. It was fraught with internal tension, vulnerable to challenge by even the most modest court clientele, and played host to a variety of competing viewpoints, all of which jostled for space in the crowded dockets of the magistrates' courts. Such ideological complexity was only to be expected in an institution that found its spiritual and formal origins in the mid-eighteenth century, but whose rapid expansion coincided with both the Victorian reform movement and the advent of Chartism in the post-Napoleonic period, and which achieved its greatest social and cultural authority in the latter decades of the nineteenth century.[39] Embedded though they were in other

[37] Alfred Chicele Plowden, *Grain or Chaff? The Autobiography of a Metropolitan Police Court Magistrate* (London: T. F. Unwin, 1903), 237.

[38] On the reconciliation of newer, Positivist models of penal reform with older, "classical" perspectives, see Sascha Auerbach, "Beyond the Pale of Mercy, Victorian Penal Culture, Police Court Missionaries, and the Origins of Probation in England," *Law and History Review* 33, no. 3 (Aug. 2015), 621–23.

[39] Joanna Innes and Arthur Burns, "Introduction," in Innes and Burns, eds., *Rethinking the Age of Reform: Britain 1780–1850* (Cambridge: Cambridge University Press, 2003), 46–56.

aspects of London governance, magistrates enjoyed a level of direct authority that other municipal agents did not. Whereas the latter could bring violators to court, only the magistrates, like their JP predecessors and County Court contemporaries, retained the power of adjudication *and* punishment. They could not legislate or dictate policy, but by acting as the lynchpin for the enforcement of the wide array of laws passed in the nineteenth century, magistrates shaped the impact of these laws on their communities and the public perception of new laws for those most affected by them.

The considerable influence of magistrates on social policy in London was due both to their occupations and to their social position. Their official authority was reinforced by their membership in a professional elite that exerted a powerful influence on urban philanthropy and municipal reform.[40] Magistrates often shared the class and gender biases of this cohort. As Jennifer Davis has argued, magistrates' expression of these views in their public behavior and self-portrayal, however, was constrained by their sense of mission as the patrons of the poor and by their dependence on working-class cooperation to maintain the authority and efficacy of their courts.[41] In the second half of the nineteenth century, as the execution of social welfare in London became largely the remit of centrally administered charities and impersonal, professionalized bureaucracies, police-court magistrates tried to maintain both their independence and the tradition of the courts as bulwarks of personal advice and service to the poor.[42] Their claims to sympathy for and expert knowledge of working-class districts were both powerful rhetorical tools that magistrates wielded to justify their expanding authority and to encourage voluntary employment of their courtrooms by the local

[40] Gareth Stedman Jones, *Outcast London: A Study in the Relationship between Classes in Victorian Society* (London: Clarendon Press, 1971), 239–40.

[41] Davis, "Poor Man's System," 331.

[42] For changes in voluntary and state provision of social welfare, see Behlmer, *Friends of the Family* and Lynn Hollen Lees, *The Solidarities of Strangers: The English Poor Laws and the People, 1700–1948* (Cambridge: Cambridge University Press, 1998). For the bureaucratization and professionalization of local governance, see Susan Pennybacker, *A Vision for London 1889–1904: Labour, Everyday Life, and the LCC Experiment* (London: Routledge, 1995); Roy Macleod, ed., *Government and Expertise: Specialists, Administrators, and Professionals, 1860–1919* (Cambridge: Cambridge University Press, 1988); Harold Perkin, *The Rise of Professional Society: England Since 1880* (London: Routledge, 1989).

community. The problematic nature of these assertions, the limits of paternalism, and the complex relationship between the magistrates, the working-class targets of reform, and agents of municipal governance in nineteenth-century London are all explored in the chapters that follow.

Considering the significance of these courtrooms in modern British society, it is not surprising that scholars have employed them as a lens to examine a broad variety of subjects, from law and criminal justice reform to Victorian culture and identity. Assessments of the relationship between law and society, and how policing, adjudication, and other aspects of the legal process reflected patterns of social relations and authority have been a central concern of historians and legal scholars for many decades.[43] Recently, the Central Criminal Court (the Old Bailey), which handled many of the most serious crimes committed in Britain, has been a topic of particularly intense study.[44] What has been missing is a concerted engagement with London's nineteenth-century magistrates' courts in their many dimensions; local courtrooms in the metropolis and elsewhere have been fitted into different frameworks of analysis without becoming the focus of analysis themselves.[45] Both Jennifer Davis and Shani D'Cruze, for example, have made excellent use of local courtrooms as an avenue to explore modern British social and gender history. Davis, while emphasizing the myriad uses made of the magistrates' courts by the working class, has drawn largely on local newspaper reports to argue that these venues inevitably served class interest and proved "essential to

[43] Natalie Zemon Davis, *Fiction in the Archives: Pardon Tales and Their Tellers in Sixteenth-Century France* (Stanford: Stanford University Press, 1990); V. A. C. Gatrell, *The London Hanged: Crime and Civil Society in the Eighteenth Century* (London: Allen Lane, 1991); Shoemaker, *Prosecution and Punishment*; Carolyn Conley, *The Unwritten Law: Criminal Justice in Victorian Kent* (New York and Oxford: Oxford University Press, 1991).

[44] The Old Bailey Proceedings Online, a project directed by Clive Emsley, Tim Hitchcock, and Robert Shoemaker has provided a wealth of information that will inform investigations into the nature of British criminal justice for many decades to come (https://www.oldbaileyonline.org/).

[45] Two noteworthy exceptions are Paul Craven, "Law and Ideology: the Toronto Police Court, 1850–80," in David H. Flaherty, ed., *Essays in the History of Canadian Law*, vol. 2 (Toronto: The Osgoode Society, 1983), 248–307; and Shani D'Cruze, *Crimes of Outrage: Sex, Violence and Victorian Working Women* (Dekalb: Northern Illinois University Press, 1998).

the effective maintenance of the social order by the nineteenth-century state."[46] While both magistrates and court clientele could contest the authority of the police or municipal agents on a case-by-case basis, in her view, the courts served primarily as a mechanism for co-opting the working class into accepting the rule of law and, in doing so, the legitimacy of state authority.[47] D'Cruze, taking a more culturally inflected approach towards law and domestic assault, has demonstrated how local courtrooms such as those of the Lancashire and Cheshire Petty Sessions could operate as both theaters for the public articulation of gender norms and as venues in which women's voices were circumscribed by both formal legal protocols and the more nebulous dynamics of genre and narrative.[48]

The legal records of the London police courts and the broad sweep of their cultural portrayals across the nineteenth century confirm their findings in some ways, but challenge them in others. These venues did, indeed, disseminate and reinforce standards of middle-class morality both through adjudication and as a public platform for magistrates' opinions. And women's roles within them were often limited both by their lack of legal status and by the wider matrix of gender bias in Victorian society. At the same time, however, magistrates, too, were constrained by the public nature of their courtrooms, their inability to control speech within it or portrayals beyond it, and the myriad ways in which working-class clientele adapted to new laws and employed the courts to achieve their own ends. Working-class women, meanwhile, found ways to turn their lack of legal status into an advantage. Magistrates could, and often did, decide against them, but could not prevent them from using the courts as they saw fit. Nor could magistrates punish women for defying regulations to which, though they appeared in court to challenge them, they were not legally accountable. Just as the London police courts themselves have only fleetingly been the focus of analysis, the tensions that existed between the courts' daily operation and their common public portrayals, and the multiple perspectives and agencies that drove courtroom events and their subsequent depictions have all received very limited

46 Davis, "Poor Man's System," 310. See also Davis, "Prosecutions and Their Context," in Douglas Hay and Francis Snyder, eds., *Policing and Prosecution in Britain, 1750–1850* (Oxford: Clarendon Press, 1989).

47 David, "Poor Man's System," 315.

48 D'Cruze, *Crimes of Outrage*, 169–70.

attention.[49] On closer examination, neither legal records, nor statistical accounts, nor newspaper portrayals provide a full picture of the courts' role in the community or in wider metropolitan society. It is only by considering them in conjunction, by carefully tracing the evolving *relationship* between local courtrooms' daily operation and their widespread depictions, and by assessing the broad sweep of courtrooms' roles, from interpersonal conflict and marital strife to police prosecution and regulatory enforcement, that a clearer view of the police courts' significance in metropolitan law, culture, and social relations emerges.

While addressing law and crime with careful attention, my central concern is with the space of the courtroom itself and the dynamics that linked courtrooms to their local communities. This study builds on previous studies of law and society in early-modern and modern England, extending them conceptually and chronologically, and bringing the neglected topic of the London magistrates' courts into sharper focus. Until recent decades, many historians of law and society in the British context had confined their scope largely to crime, penal ideology, pretrial and trial, verdict, and punishment as they were experienced by those with the power to shape them and by those who were the targets of such authority.[50] Scholars of modern British criminal justice, working primarily in the nineteenth and "long eighteenth" centuries, have amassed a staggering amount of information on crime, policing, and trials.[51] A watershed moment came in the late 1960s and early 1970s, when the pioneering work of

[49] The most well-cited work on the London police courts remains, with good reason, Davis's brief but insightful article, "A Poor Man's System."

[50] The classic, and still very relevant, scholarship in this vein is that of Leon Radzinowicz. One of the most-referenced works in the field remains his magisterial five-volume series, co-authored with Roger Hood, *A History of English Criminal Law and Its Administration from 1750*, the fifth and final volume, *The Emergence of Penal Policy in Victorian and Edwardian England* (Oxford: Clarendon, 1990), being a particular milestone. See also his *Ideology and Crime: A Study of Crime in Its Social and Historical Context* (New York: Columbia University Press, 1966).

[51] Douglas Hay, "Prosecution and Power: Malicious Prosecution in the English Courts, 1750–1850," in Douglas Hay and Francis Snyder, eds., *Policing and Prosecution in Britain, 1750–1850* (Oxford: Clarendon Press, 1989), 347. This sustained historiographical focus on the formal expression of law remains apparent in Hay's review of recent work in British and imperial legal history. Douglas Hay, "Women, Men, and Empires of Law," *Journal of British Studies* 44, no. 1 (Jan. 2005), 204.

E. P. Thompson, Douglas Hay, and Peter Linebaugh offered a new direction for British legal history. Employing class as their primary lens, they explored how criminal law and the ideology of "rule of law" replaced older institutions of social control such as the Church and the Monarchy as the primary means by which English property-holders managed the lower orders.[52] A second wave of British legal historians has built on this foundation, further expanding our understanding of law and ideology in modern British society.[53] Those in this highly prolific cohort have argued that the law can be best understood through a combination of statistical analysis and an examination of the social relations that underpinned the execution of arrests, trials, and punishments – in other words, the legal, social, and economic circumstances of the case.[54] Their work has also explored how a broader segment of British society, including working-class men, employed the law as a tool for governing social and economic relations. Another common topic of focus has been how gender influenced court cases and how non-elite women made use of legal forums.[55]

[52] E. P. Thompson, "Patrician Society, Plebian Culture," *Journal of Social History* 7 (1974), 382–405 and *Whigs and Hunters: the Origin of the Black Act* (New York: Pantheon, 1975); Douglas Hay *et al.*, *Albion's Fatal Tree: Crime and Society in Eighteenth Century England* (London: Allen Lane, 1975).

[53] John Langbein, "Albion's Fatal Flaws," *Past and Present* 98, no. 1 (Feb. 1983), 96–120; Landau, *The Justices of the Peace*; J. M. Beattie, *Crime and the Courts in England, 1660–1800* (Oxford: Oxford University Press, 1986); Clive Emsley, *Crime and Society in England, 1750–1900* (London and New York: Longman, 1987); Hay and Snyder, eds., *Policing and Prosecution in Britain*, 1750–1850; Shoemaker, *Prosecution and Punishment*; Peter Linebaugh, *The London Hanged: Crime and Civil Society in the Eighteenth Century* (London: Allen Lane, 1991); David Philips, "Crime, Law and Punishment in the Industrial Revolution," in Patrick O'Brien and Roland Quinault, eds., *The Industrial Revolution and British Society* (Cambridge: Cambridge University Press, 1993), 156–82; Peter King, *Crime, Justice, and Discretion in England, 1740–1820* (Oxford: Oxford University Press, 2000) and *Crime and Law in England, 1750–1840: Remaking Justice from the Margins* (Cambridge: Cambridge University Press, 2006); John Beattie, *Policing and Punishment in London, 1660–1750* (Oxford: Oxford University Press, 2001).

[54] This empiricist approach reflects the profound impact of criminology on British legal history, an approach that has kept the majority of studies firmly grounded in formal trial records and the measurable impact of changes in policy.

[55] A. James Hammerton, *Cruelty and Companionship: Conflict in Nineteenth-Century Married Life* (London: Routledge, 1992); Josephine Hoegaerts, "Legal or Just? Law, Ethics, and the Double Standard in the Nineteenth-Century Divorce Court," *Law and History Review* 26, no. 2 (Summer 2008), 259–84. The work of early-modern English historians has been especially important here, see

This criminological bent notwithstanding, historians have long recognized that the implementation of law in eighteenth- and nineteenth-century England was a cultural affair as well. The current interest among British historians in the interaction between law, society, and culture traces back to the original work of Thompson, Hay, and Linebaugh. For them, law's public manifestations amplified and reinforced the power of the propertied elite in a myriad of ways. And yet, the courtrooms' *generative* role in the social and cultural realms remained highly constrained. Law's meaning was determined exclusively by the law-givers and it could express or reflect ideas already in circulation, but its everyday operation in the courtroom did not give more modest participants an opportunity to shape these ideas. "Justice" and "mercy," for example, in Douglas Hay's seminal essay on the eighteenth-century Assizes, were part of an "ideological instrument," determined by those with formal authority and used a means of social control; those on the receiving end had little say in the matter.[56] This equation, in which law served as a tool of the elite to enforce the status quo and in which only those with formal authority could shape the overarching concepts of law and governance, in which law's daily operation expressed culture but did not constitute it, has been challenged in recent years. Responding to the "cultural turn," historians of law and crime have become more interested in how the ideas and practices that circulated outside the realm of formal law interacted with legal concepts and their concrete enforcement.[57] The

Jenny Kermode and Garthine Walker, eds., *Women, Crime and the Courts in Early Modern England* (Chapel Hill: University of North Carolina Press, 1994).

[56] Douglas Hay, "Property, Authority, and the Criminal Law," in Douglas Hay *et al.*, *Albion's Fatal Tree: Crime and Society in Eighteenth Century England* (London: Allen Lane, 1975), 26.

[57] Martin Wiener, *Reconstructing the Criminal: Culture, Law, and Policy in England, 1830–1914* (Cambridge: Cambridge University Press, 1990); Carolyn Conley, *The Unwritten Law: Criminal Justice in Victorian Kent* (Oxford: Oxford University Press, 1991); George Behlmer, "Summary Justice and Working-Class Marriage in England, 1870–1940," *Law and History Review* 12, no. 2 (Fall, 1994), 229–76; Finn, "Consumer Control," 116–54; Gail Savage, "'The Magistrates Are Men': Working-Class Marital Conflict and Appeals from the Magistrates' Court to the Divorce Court after 1895," in George Robb and Nancy Erber, eds., *Disorder in the Court: Trials and Sexual Conflict at the Turn of the Century* (New York and Basingstoke: Palgrave Macmillan, 1999), 231–49; Ginger Frost, *Promises Broken: Courtship, Class, and Gender in Victorian England* (Charlottesville and London: University of Virginia Press, 1995).

cultural turn has also destabilized historical understanding of the social context in history, revealing the limitations of any explanation that rests on supposedly objective categorizations of social groups in modern society.[58] In the broader context, those relying on sociological or anthropological analyses of law's function have questioned traditional legal theorists' approach to law as either a formal entity operating autonomously from other social relations, or as a tool by which elites maintain social control over non-elites.[59] The incorporation of cultural theory and literary criticism into the examination of criminal and civil law has led to original and significant insights into the relationship between law, culture, and society.[60] Such studies – especially when focused on gender – have often interpreted the law and court cases as unstable texts whose meanings varied according to the observer and their context.[61] The development of "law and society" histories in the British context has been intertwined with larger debates about the nature and evolution of the British state and its relationship to social identity and relations in the eighteenth and nineteenth centuries. Of particular importance here is the divergence between earlier historians who employed a class-based

[58] Victoria E. Bonnell and Lynn Hunt, "Introduction," in Victoria E. Bonnell and Lynn Hunt, eds., *Beyond the Cultural Turn: New Directions in the Study of Society and Culture* (Berkeley and Los Angeles: University of California Press, 1999), 6–7; Dana Rabin, *Identity, Crime and Legal Responsibility in Eighteenth-Century England* (New York and Basingstoke: Palgrave Macmillan, 2004), 3–5. V. A. C. Gatrell's *The Hanging Tree: Execution and the English People* (Oxford: Oxford University Press, 1996) stands as one of the most comprehensive, and most controversial, explorations of law and culture in modern Britain.

[59] Pierre Bourdieu, "The Force of Law: Toward a Sociology of the Juridical Field," *Hastings Law Journal* 38 (1987), 814–15; Barbara Yngvesson, "Inventing Law in Local Settings: Rethinking Popular Legal Culture," *Yale Law Journal* 98, no. 8, Symposium: Popular Legal Culture (Jun. 1989), 1689–709; Sally Engle Merry, "Legal Pluralism," *Law and Society Review* 25, no. 8 (1988), 869–96.

[60] For a broad analysis of this impact, see Amy Gilman Srebnick, "Does the Representation Fit the Crime? Some Thoughts on Writing Crime History as Cultural Text," in Amy Gilman and René Lévy, eds., *Crime and Culture: A Historical Perspective* (Aldershot: Ashgate, 2005), 3–19.

[61] D'Cruze, *Crimes of Outrage*; Hal Gladfelder, *Criminality and Narrative in Eighteenth-Century England: Beyond the Law* (Baltimore: Johns Hopkins University Press, 2001). See also Gillian Spraggs, *Outlaws and Highwaymen: The Cult of the Robber in England from the Middle Ages to the Nineteenth Century* (London: Pimlico, 2001); and Donna T. Andrew and Randall McGowan, *The Perreaus and Mrs. Rudd: Forgery and Betrayal in Eighteenth-Century London* (Berkeley: University of California Press, 2001).

Marxist approach and their successors who argued that the state was more variegated in its interest groups, more driven by internal dynamics and tensions, more participatory and, in consequence, less adaptable to a Marxist historiographical framework.[62]

Following in these historiographical footsteps, the chapters of this book bring the local courtroom into focus as the nexus of where law and state authority met social practice and cultural norms. I have hewed to the guidelines set by Stuart Hall and the Birmingham Centre for Contemporary Cultural Studies in defining culture as the ways in which "meaning is constructed, conveyed, and understood" and Patrick Joyce in seeing this process as located "*in* practice, and in material forms."[63] By extension, "courtroom culture," a persistent theme throughout this book, refers to how meaning is constructed, conveyed, and understood through the practices of the courtroom and their public representations. These definitions guide my framing of the relationship between law, local courtrooms, culture, and metropolitan society across the nineteenth century and the beginning of the twentieth within one particular set of legal venues, the London magistrates' courts, and several cohorts who were pivotal to their evolving roles. The result is an in-depth examination of the magistrates, municipal agents, working-class men and women, and other members of the community who frequented the London police courts from the early Victorian period until the First World War. The most important reasons for this choice of focus are first, that the police courts are particularly revealing about the nature of the "everyday state" as it operated at the local level and about the agency of those who tried to navigate and negotiate its growing authority in London. And secondly, in the period under study, the police courts rose to occupy a central position in the evolving relationship between the daily operation of law and its public depictions. The late Victorian and Edwardian years were crucial in both regards. The ascent of these venues was driven simultaneously by the expanding realm of activity

62 In the first cohort, key historians include E. P. Thompson, Douglas Hay, and Peter Linebaugh. In the latter, among the most significant are John Brewer, Linda Colley, Joanna Innes, and John Styles.

63 Peter Jackson, *Maps of Meaning* (London and New York: Routledge, 1989), 2; Patrick Joyce, *The Rule of Freedom: Liberalism and the Modern City* (London and New York: Verso, 2003), 7.

regulated by law, courts' key roles in adjudicating these laws, the increasing accessibility of local courtrooms to plebian men and women, and the proliferation of the courts' public portrayals in the burgeoning popular press.

The magistrates' courtrooms of nineteenth-century London offer valuable insights into several topics of intense interest among modern British historians. Foremost among them is the trajectory of state power with regards to the individual.[64] In particular, the history of the police courts can help us refine our understanding of the tripartite relationship between judicial institutions, the local communities in which they were embedded, and how working-class men and women understood and engaged with law and the state. Most previous examinations of the Victorian criminal justice system have typically treated criminal charges brought by the police, either by their initiative or at the behest of the wronged party, and personal summonses as the dominant (if not sole) activity of summary courtrooms.[65] This, in part, has been due to the focus on crime (as a legal, statistical, historiographical, and discursive entity) and a general reliance on government reports or magistrates' accounts for qualitative analysis and criminal statistics for quantitative assessments. The work of Peter King and Barry Godfrey, for example, has made great strides in revealing the intricate details of prosecution and punishment in modern England through a meticulous investigation of criminal justice practice within their institutional, ideological, and social contexts.[66] Examined from the perspective of the magistrate's courtroom, and the court records in particular, the trials and verdicts that are central to these

[64] For a broad summary of views on this issue, see S. J. D. Green and R. C. Whiting, "Introduction: The Shifting Boundaries of the State in Modern Britain," in S. J. D. Green and R. C. Whiting, eds., *The Boundaries of the State in Modern Britain* (Cambridge: Cambridge University Press, 1996); Mandler, *Liberty and Authority*. This has also become a key question in the study of "modernism" and the emergence of modern governance in nineteenth-century Britain. Joyce, *Rule of Freedom*, 2–11.

[65] For a keen assessment of crime research, see Clive Emsley, "Crime and Punishment: Ten Years of Research (1) – Filling In, Adding Up, Moving On: Criminal Justice History in Contemporary Britain," *Crime, Histoire & Sociétiés/Crime, History & Societies* 9, no. 1 (2005), 2–19.

[66] Peter King, *Crime and Law in England, 1750–1840: Remaking Justice from the Margins* (Cambridge: Cambridge University Press, 2006); Barry Godfrey, Stephen Farrall and Susan Karstedt, "Explaining Gendered Sentencing Patterns for Violent Men and Women in the Late-Victorian and Edwardian Period, *British Journal of Criminology* 45 (2005), 696–720.

studies come into sharper focus as a crucial aspect of a varied and complex relationship between local courts and their communities. This relationship was conducted through a number of activities, many of which were absent from the records typically employed to study the history of law and crime. Trials operated alongside applications for summonses, regulatory cases, the provision of advice and charity, marriage counseling, informal conflict mediation, public entertainment, and a myriad of other common functions. It is important to note here that magistrates occupied a dual role. They remanded those accused of serious offenses to be tried by juries at assizes and quarter sessions and adjudicated an expanding array of summary (non-jury) cases. Public attitudes towards the magistracy were governed by magistrates' actions in both roles, but this volume will focus on the latter, as it saw the most rapid and dramatic change across the nineteenth century.

In this wider context of courtrooms' roles as a key local resource and one of the primary points of contact between the state and the community, the constraints and challenges to police were every bit as noticeable as their authority was. Given such restrictions, the limitations on other agents of the state, and the extensive voluntary engagement with the police courts through personal summonses, the picture of courtrooms and working-class communities that emerges is one of slow integration, despite considerable tension. What developed over the course of the nineteenth century was as much, if not more so, a "court-going community" as it was what V. A. C. Gatrell has called a "policeman-state."[67] The intervention of the state into the daily life of working-class communities and the hostility of those communities towards unwonted police intrusion were both palpable across the Victorian and Edwardian periods, as Gatrell argues. But the increasing willingness of ordinary men and women to summon constables for aid, their widespread and varied employment of court summonses, and their determination, in both practices, to engage these resources on their own terms were equally evident.[68] In many ways, the relationship between the working class and

[67] V. A. C. Gatrell, "Crime, Authority and the Policeman-State," in F. M. L. Thompson, ed., *The Cambridge Social History of Britain*, vol. 3: *Social Agencies and Institutions* (Cambridge: Cambridge University Press, 1990), 244.

[68] Nancy Tomes, "A 'Torrent of Abuse': Crimes of Violence between Working-Class Men and Women in London, 1840–1875," *Journal of Social History* 11, no. 3 (Spring, 1978), 336.

local courtrooms set the precedent for the large-scale intrusion of municipal authorities and regulatory measures into everyday life by several decades, a point often elided in studies that focus on the rapid increase of regulatory measures in the late Victorian period.[69] The rise of magistrates to prominent positions in urban communities similarly antedated the introduction of modern policing by a considerable margin. And although the expansion of the police-court system was concurrent with the establishment of the Metropolitan Police (both dating to the Metropolitan Police Act 1829), and despite both institutions' keen concern with public order, the roles of courtrooms and constables in the community were very different. As Jennifer Davis has argued, magistrates themselves were especially eager to maintain the distinction between themselves, the police, and other, more coercive agents of the state.[70] Too close an association, they feared, would earn them the ire of a community whose cooperation was essential to maintaining both public order and their own moral influence. Consequently, constables faced unique challenges, and enjoyed particular advantages, in the courtroom. The dynamics of the police courts thus emphasize the complex relationship between policing, the communities they policed, and the courtrooms where the consequences of this policing were determined.

This tripartite dynamic of communities, courtrooms, and police bears on a long-running debate over the ideological role of law and legal institutions in social relations.[71] Jennifer Davis has asserted that convincing the lower class to accept the authority of the law "and, thus, implicitly, of the social order," was a central purpose of the police

69 Such is the case, for example, in George Behlmer's excellent study of English domestic reform. While making some mention of the period prior to the 1870s, the majority of analysis commences with the formal expansion of the courts' role in working-class marital relations following the passage of the Matrimonial Causes Act 1878 and the establishment of the juvenile court system in 1908. Behlmer, *Friends of the Family*, 192–271.

70 Davis, "Poor Man's System," 331.

71 The extent to which eighteenth-century English legal institutions acted as tools of ideological as well as social control was at the heart of John Langbein's trenchant refutation of Hay's article "Property, Authority, and the Criminal Law," which appeared as the opening piece in the Warwick School's now-canonical volume, *Albion's Fatal Tree*. Langbein argued that the eighteenth-century criminal law and its procedures, far from being a "'ruling-class conspiracy' against the lower orders," as Hay had claimed, "existed to serve and protect the interests of the people who suffered as victims of crime, people who were overwhelmingly non-elite." Langbein, "Albion's Fatal Flaws," 96–98

courts.[72] But whether or not magistrates "were always going to serve the *status quo* and not the lower classes" has different implications when one realizes that they were not always able to manage the uses to which their courtrooms were put.[73] Within the courts' wide gamut of daily activities, providing daily justice and, at the same time, offering a public forum to contest the meaning of both justice and morality were not easily reconciled.[74] There were significant limits to magistrates' ability to control both courtroom speech in personal summonses, one of the courtroom's most common activities, and the public portrayals of their courts in any capacity. Those who appeared in these public venues, be they magistrates or police, prosecutors or defendants, were subject to constant scrutiny by journalists and the attending public. Just as magistrates' discretion could undermine the intentions of policymakers or police officials, the wide play of courtroom action and its subsequent portrayals could undermine magistrates' ability to send a consistent moral message. This made the local courtroom a highly problematic tool for consistently reproducing paternalist ideology and reinforcing the social status quo, no matter what the intentions of those wielding authority were.

Even when acquiescence was expressed by working-class petitioners, it was usually to the local court and the person of the magistrate rather than to the relative abstraction of the law or the larger entity of the state that underpinned it. For those who found themselves before the bench, voluntarily or involuntarily, recognition of the courtroom's utility or respect for the magistrate's judgment was not necessarily a submission to the authority of the law. Nor did an appeal for the magistrate's assistance invariably indicate adherence to his to his moral standards. This common contrast between working-class *presence* in the courtroom – whether as complainant, defendant, witness, or audience – and their *acceptance* of the moral norms espoused here has long been

72 Davis, "Poor Man's System," 315. 73 Ibid., 333.

74 John Brewer and John Styles have argued that, in order to legitimize the principles of English law, elites were willing to allow a lessening of their own control over its processes, a movement that prompted voluntary engagement with legal institutions by a host of groups and individuals, from rural villagers to Kingswood colliers to Wilkesite radicals. "The room for manoeuvre may have been limited," they assert, "but it was exploited to the full." John Brewer and John Styles, "Introduction," in John Brewer and John Styles, eds., *An Ungovernable People: The English and Their Law in the Seventeenth and Eighteenth Centuries* (New Brunswick: Rutgers University Press, 1980), 20.

recognized by historians.[75] But the consequences of this for the courtroom's broader relationship to the community and the influence of working-class expectations and standards on courtroom practice, magistrates' attitudes, and the efficacy of state authority more generally remain obscured. The instances when participants in local courtrooms challenged the very right of magistrates, police, or other state agents to govern their lives are some of the most revealing moments in this study. They illuminate both the possibilities and the limitations of individual agency in relation to law and culture in metropolitan society. Magistrates' perennial complaints that working-class men and women employed the courtrooms for their own purposes and according to their own visions of justice rather than deferring to the law or magistrates' authority attested to this. Ideologically, magistrates straddled an ambivalent position between *laissez-faire* anxieties over a powerful state apparatus, a desire to maintain public order and contain a potentially disruptive and demoralized urban working-class, and a Liberal commitment to fostering moral self-governance through a visible and didactic system of policing and public justice. These contradictory impulses help to account for their eagerness to see working-class men and women in the courtroom, voluntarily or involuntarily, and their consternation at how such clientele chose to employ the venue and conduct themselves there.

Examining such interactions in the courtroom illuminates working-class agency vis-à-vis the law at a granular level. By contrast, taking a wider angle of view over the course of the nineteenth century, the evolution of courtrooms' roles in metropolitan society and culture reveals important changes in the British state, the evolution of Liberal ideology, the nature of governance, and individualism. The local courtroom was a vital locale in which all of these elements coalesced and were publicly defined and contested by magistrates, journalists, social commentators, and even ordinary court clientele. The involvement of the latter group, in particular, is key to understanding the development of the courtroom's role in governing metropolitan society.[76] Across the nineteenth century, appearing in a local courtroom,

[75] Davis, "Prosecutions," 413–14; Behlmer, *Friends of the Family*, 187.

[76] Even the laboring poor, the one group that was largely excluded from regular employment of the law in the seventeenth and eighteenth centuries, could afford the two-shilling cost of a private court summons in the nineteenth century. On their exclusion from courtrooms in the earlier period, see Brewer and Styles, *An Ungovernable People*, 20.

voluntarily or involuntarily, changed from an unusual experience to a common one. This entanglement of the courts and everyday life had a longer lifespan than has been previously acknowledged. Contrary to Jennifer Davis's argument otherwise, local courtrooms remained a vital resource for London's working-class communities until the interwar period, when the increasing opacity of summary procedure, monopolization of the courts' mornings with expensive and lengthy motoring cases, closer integration between local courts and policing, and the shame associated with the venue all combined to make the magistrates' venues either unappealing or inaccessible to most working-class complainants.[77]

In order to understand the evolution of London's local courtrooms and their roles in metropolitan society and culture, the periodization of this study encompasses the courts' reform and rise to public prominence in the late eighteenth and early nineteenth century, their developing relationship with the regulatory state in the mid-Victorian period, and their integration with working-class life in the decades preceding the First World War. This period entailed significant changes in both the formal structure of the state and in its roles in British society, especially with regards to class and gender relations. The late eighteenth to mid-nineteenth century witnessed intense reform in British criminal justice as flexible adjudication and exemplary punishments were steadily shed in favor of a more bureaucratic, impersonal, and predictable system.[78] This corresponded with a shift in official attitudes about the nature of criminality and the broader relationship of the individual, and working-class individuals in particular, to the law and the state. The desire of policymakers to keep the worst instincts of the lower orders in check through stern adjudication never evaporated, but it was slowly replaced with the promotion of moral self-governance on the one hand and a more extensive array of institutions for policing and punishment on the other. Such changes have prompted historians to examine how older

77 "Solicitor" (Henry Loveridge Hodgkinson), *English Justice* (London: Penguin Books, 1932), 9. Jennifer Davis has asserted that it was the focus on criminal cases alone that prompted the decline in working-class use in the twentieth century (Davis, "Poor Man's System," 334). Although this was certainly the general trend, the causes were more complex, and the courts remained an important resource, especially for working-class women seeking to address marital and affiliation issues, well into the interwar period.

78 Wiener, *Reconstructing the Criminal*, 49.

institutions of governance adapted to these changes, how new entities developed, and how key ideas about class relations, the rule of law, and the role of the state changed over time. These historians can be divided roughly into two overlapping groups: those most interested in institutions and policies and those most interested in the social and cultural impact of governance. Class has been of longstanding interest to both cohorts, as has gender, in recent decades. This volume addresses the concerns of both groups in that it follows the history of one particular institution, employing it as a lens to better comprehend how broader changes in law and policy shaped ground-level interactions and how those interactions could, in turn, influence broader ideas and even foster concrete changes in the law. My approach owes much to the work of Peter King, whose *Crime and Law in England, 1750–1840* demonstrated how crucial decisions made in individual courts "on the margins" could help shape and remake English justice as a whole.[79] It also draws on Joanna Innes's ideas about "inferior politics," how a more dispersed system of political authority adapted to social issues in English society, and the crucial role played by local information in shaping governance.[80] These historians work primarily in the "long eighteenth century," but their observations about the changing nature of state and society in England remain highly relevant for the magistrates' courts, an eighteenth-century institution that adapted effectively to the nineteenth and twentieth centuries.

In the nineteenth-century history of the metropolitan state, the scholarship of John Davis and Susan Pennybacker has laid the groundwork for my examination of the courts as a continually evolving institution of governance. These authors have established how new ideas about rationalized municipal reform and a new "vision" of class identity and metropolitan society helped reshape the relationship between the state and the people in London.[81] John Davis, in particular, has revealed how the power of local institutions and community identity persisted even as metropolitan authorities struggled to centralize and integrate systems of city-wide management.[82] The social and cultural impact of nineteenth-century governance is also the central theme in the

[79] King, *Crime and Law in England*, 2.

[80] Joanna Innes, *Inferior Politics: Social Problems and Social Policies in Eighteenth-Century Britain* (Oxford: Oxford University Press, 2009), 142–43.

[81] Davis, *Reforming London*, 121; Pennybacker, *Vision for London*, 23–25.

[82] Davis, *Reforming London*, 8–9.

work of Ellen Ross, Lynn Hollen Lees, and George Behlmer. All three have examined how gender and class issues were encoded into the state's deepening involvement in the everyday lives of urban English men and women, and in working-class life most especially. Their careful attention to the multitude of responses this intervention elicited, and to the ways in which working-class men and women developed and deployed their own ideas about the role of the state and the limits of its authority, informs my analysis of how courtrooms and their communities interacted.[83]

Building on the work of these scholars, my examination of local courtrooms as formal institutions and as spaces constructed and represented through public dialogue and media portrayal, and the interplay of both realms in generating the meaning of courtroom events, invites a reconsideration of the state itself and its relationship to the individual in the nineteenth century. Here, Patrick Joyce's concept of the "omniopticon, the many viewing the many," is particularly apt.[84] While magistrates handed down formal judgments and the law determined the ultimate parameters of state action, a wide array of participants contributed to public discussions of state authority, justice, and the relationship of courts and the law to moral norms. They did so through courtroom statements, newspaper portrayals, and through the daily use (or alleged misuse) of the courts' various resources. Courtroom speech and courtroom representations were not necessarily political, in the sense that they did not invariably reference wider political structures or depend on coherent ideological stances for their meaning. But they were nonetheless part of the process by which individuals from magistrates to working-class petitioners participated in the wider discussions about state power and its limits, and through which they defined their own status and role in this milieu.

The steady expansion of middle-class and working-class participation in municipal and national politics formed a compelling backdrop to this participation and to the expansion of summary justice and courtrooms' consonant roles in their communities. For men and especially for women

[83] Ellen Ross, *Love and Toil: Motherhood in Outcast London, 1870–1918* (New York and Oxford: Oxford University Press, 1993), 15–17; Behlmer, *Friends of the Family*, 182–229; Lees, *Solidarities of Strangers*, 166–69.

[84] Joyce, *Rule of Freedom*, 16.

from the ranks of artisans, shopkeepers, publicans, lesser landlords, and laborers both skilled and unskilled, the local courtroom was the vehicle by which many of the changes in the state were made manifest. The wide range and publicity of courtroom encounters, their potential consequences, the flexibility of courtroom language, and the movement of the latter beyond the courtroom and into social interaction all encourage greater attention to the historical significance of courtroom speech in *constituting* the relationship between the state and the individual.[85] In speaking of language, class, and culture, the overarching influence of Gareth Stedman Jones's work on this study comes into focus. Stedman Jones describes how three waves of anxiety among the propertied classes – in the 1840s, 1866–72, and 1883–88 – prompted the "use of legislation to create a physical and institutional environment in which undesirable working-class habits and attitudes would be deterred, while private philanthropy would undertake the active propagation of a new moral code."[86] This process required the police courts' participation, since the enforcement of reform legislation (e.g. sanitary legislation, the Education Act 1871) funneled through them. But this neat equation of governance as a way of "civilizing" the working-class has been challenged on a number of fronts in recent decades, most notably by scholars of law and society such as Anna Clark, Shani D'Cruze, and A. J. Hammerton. The latter have all noted how plebian men and women incorporated legal institutions into their interpersonal conflicts in much the same way that artisans and middle-class cohorts did in the early-modern period.[87] Margot Finn, similarly,

85 For the significance of language in shaping social identity and political relations in modern Britain, see Gareth Stedman Jones, "Rethinking Chartism," in *Languages of Class: Studies in English Working Class History, 1832–1982* (Cambridge: Cambridge University Press, 1983), 92–97.

86 Stedman Jones, *Languages of Class*, 191.

87 Hammerton, *Cruelty and Companionship*, 118–33; Shani D'Cruze, "Sex, Violence and Local Courts: Working-Class Respectability in a Mid-Nineteenth Century Lancashire Town," *British Journal of Criminology* 39, no. 1 (1999), 41, 51–52; Anna Clark, *The Struggle for the Breeches: Gender and the Making of the British Working Class* (Berkeley: University of California Press, 1995), 42–87. For women's active employment of the courts in the early-modern context, see Laura Gowing, "Language, Power and the Law: Women's Slander Legislation in Early Modern London," in Jenny Kermode and Garthine Walker, eds., *Women, Crime and the Courts in Early Modern England* (Chapel Hill: University of North Carolina Press, 1994), 26–47.

has examined the ways that plebian married women employed their liminal legal status to mount effective courtroom challenges against debt collection.[88]

The model of civilizing legislation is further problematized by the contested atmosphere of local courtrooms, where working-class defendants and magistrates alike often challenged not only the practical implementation of reform measures but the moral precepts that underpinned them. The willingness of ordinary men and women to work through the courts was itself an acquiescence to the authority of the state, but only to a very specific manifestation of it (i.e. the local courtroom and the presiding magistrate). The ability of modest petitioners to challenge state agents at the local level, albeit from within a state structure, emerged from a relationship between the working-class and the courts that predated the waves of civilizing legislation that began in the mid-Victorian period. It was a relationship that responded to the needs of local men and women, to their moral standards, and to their visions of justice, as well as to those of magistrates, reformers, and policymakers.

Like the civilizing mission of Victorian discourse and moral reform, class itself has been continually revised and reinterpreted as a category of analysis in recent years, a process that Stedman Jones accelerated with his critique of social explanations for Chartism and his emphasis on language, culture, and ideology.[89] Given its prevalence in official discourse about law, in public portrayals of courtrooms, and in the self-perception of magistrates and court clientele alike, class remains a crucial concept to engage in any study of London's local courtrooms. Class is treated here as a category that interacts with other facets of social identity such as gender, and as one that is constructed through language and social experience as well as through public contestation.[90] Courtrooms were locales not merely where preconceived notions of class and class relations played out, but where their meaning in relation to law and the state were defined. The active construction of class identity and relations vis-à-vis the state was evident, for example, when magistrates asserted that the

[88] Finn, "Consumer Control," 128. [89] Stedman Jones, *Rethinking Chartism*, 93–94.

[90] On the continued relevance of class as an analytical category in the study of modern British history, see Selina Todd, "Class, Experience and Britain's Twentieth Century," *Social History* 39, no. 4 (2014), 489–90.

misuse of assault summonses was the distinct provenance of working-class women, or when working-class mothers insisted that their economic circumstances justified their defiance of compulsory school attendance bye-laws on both legal *and* moral grounds.[91]

In addition to their roles in class and gender dynamics, local courtrooms and their public portrayals were mediums for the articulation and clash of ideological concepts such as personal liberty, individualism, paternalism, patriarchy, domestic morality, and a host of others.[92] To a degree not often found in Victorian society, the longstanding relationship between courtrooms and their communities allowed for a multitude of views about law, the state, the governors, and the governed to be expressed by an array of historical actors. This relatively free play of language in the courtroom was counterbalanced by the limitations of formal legal authority, the rules and traditions of courtroom conduct, and the persistence of a paternalistic mindset among the majority of Victorian magistrates. This contrast lends further weight to the arguments of James Vernon and others who have examined the halting and uneven progress of democratic culture and political modernization in Britain.[93] The counterpoise of freedom and constraint offered by local courtrooms also reminds us how Liberalism in Victorian Britain could operate as an "antidote to democracy rather than an inducement."[94] The mediation of the courts between the agents of social reform and the targets of it was part of the broader Victorian compromise described by Ross McKibbin, wherein working-class integration into civil society was achieved through their willingness to accept the legitimacy of a state whose interventions into private life remained relatively restrained.[95] Such integration was hardly achieved

[91] On the key role of gender in the introduction and governance of compulsory schooling in Victorian London, see Dina M. Copelman, *London's Women Teachers: Gender, Class and Feminism, 1870–1930* (London: Routledge, 1996).

[92] On the ideological function of buildings in this milieu, see Deborah Weiner, *Architecture and Social Reform in Victorian London* (Manchester: Manchester University Press, 1994).

[93] James Vernon, *Politics and the People: A Study in English Political Culture c.1815–1867* (Cambridge: Cambridge University Press, 1993), 8–9, 207–51.

[94] Nicholas Rogers, "Review of James Vernon, *Politics and the People: A Study in English Political Culture, c.1815–1867*," *Histoire Sociale/Social History* 29, no. 57 (1996), 231–32.

[95] Ross McKibbin, *Ideologies of Class: Social Relations in Britain, 1880–1950* (Oxford: Oxford University Press, 1991), 27–28.

without contest, however, and just as magistrates would only tolerate so much in their courtrooms, working-class complainants and defendants, as much as they were able, engaged the court on their own terms, insisting that their ideas of justice and fairness take precedence.

Paternalist and conservative in some aspects, egalitarian and democratic in others, the historical development of courtroom culture in London encourages a reexamination of the relationship between law, the individual, the state, social relations and identity, and cultural precepts. Rather than law constraining popular custom, an equation of coercion and resistance, a concerted campaign of social control, or awkward efforts by courtroom clientele to transform social problems into legal ones, we see instead the reciprocal movement of practice, ideal, and expectation between the courtroom and the community. Following this line of reasoning, the evolution of courtroom practice over time and of courts' roles in their communities were driven less by external social conflict and more by the steady adaptation – on the part of magistrates, courtroom clientele, and municipal agents – of established courtroom custom and its integration with social identity and relations. This adaptation could include both collaboration and contestation between the groups involved. Close attention to testimony, for example, demonstrates how specific courtroom terms (e.g. "I shall summons you") could operate powerfully in the street and in the home as well as in court. Assessing how such terms were deployed and the chronology of their use in relation to the evolution of the law can help us understand the impetus and character of change over time. In some instances, the adoption of new courtroom tactics (e.g. the employment of a spouse's drinking habits as grounds for judicial separation) followed quickly on the heels of the legislation that made them efficacious. In others, the reverse was true, such as when the cost and procedure of applying for summonses were reduced and simplified in response to popular demand.

Examining the history of state and society through the lens of the magistrates' courts helps reveal how local courtrooms played a particularly important role in the evolution of women's status vis-à-vis the law. By the beginning of the Victorian era, women's use of the law to address a variety of issues, familial and sexual matters most prominently, had been an aspect of European legal institutions for centuries. But expense, low rates of literacy, and the gendered balance of power against them had limited the range and frequency of such use, particularly among women of the lower orders.[96] Although patriarchal authority remained pervasive in summary justice, by the late nineteenth century, the affordability and accessibility of the courtroom, combined with women's adaptability and agency, had significantly altered the gender dynamics of local courtrooms.[97] Cases brought by women from the working class and lower-middle class rose to become among the most numerous and significant functions of the magistrates' courts. By the late nineteenth century, women were bringing personal summonses at roughly twice the rate that men were, and at the busier venues in east and north London, this could amount to 200 or more summonses a month per court.[98] Women's engagement with this very public forum – as complainants, defendants, and witnesses – influenced both the relationship between the courts and their communities and wider discourses on gender roles, morality, and the limits of state authority. The expansion of summary justice did not introduce such "close encounters" between working-class women and the state, nor had it been impossible for women of modest means to access the court system prior to the early nineteenth century.[99] Rather, the advent of the police-court system in tandem with the expanding municipal government and program of social reform significantly increased the frequency, variety, and public prominence of such encounters in London.

The role of local courtrooms in mediating social relations and generating cultural meanings, and their widespread portrayal as a key facet of the modern state, are relevant to the ongoing historical

[96] Peter King, "Summary Courts and Social Relations in Eighteenth Century England," *Past and Present* 183 (2004), 143; Geoffrey Hudson, "Negotiating for Blood Money: War Widows and the Courts in Seventeenth-Century England," in Jenny Kermode and Garthine Walker, eds., *Women, Crime and the Courts in Early Modern England* (Chapel Hill: University of North Carolina Press, 1994), 146–69. For the history of women's use of summonses in London, see Jennine Hurl-Eamon, *Gender and Petty Violence in London, 1680–1720* (Columbus: Ohio University Press, 2005).

[97] As Margot Finn has written, "working-class women of the Victorian era were enmeshed in legal processes, rather than positioned in clear and unequivocal opposition to them." Finn, "Consumer Control," 120.

[98] See Chapter 4, 191–2.

[99] My thanks to Marjorie Levine-Clark for providing this very apt description of Victorian reform as the title of our panel at the Annual Meeting of the North American Conference on British Studies in October 2003 (Portland, OR).

debate over what constitutes "society" and "culture." Amongst their many other functions, local courtrooms were continually mined for information that was subsequently incorporated into debates and reports conducted by Parliament, the Home Office, the Metropolitan Police, and other state entities. The statistics and anecdotes gleaned from them were integral to efforts by reformers and policymakers to define the character of metropolitan life, to justify or oppose state intervention and, in the broadest sense, to delineate "the social" as a realm distinct from the spheres of politics and economics.[100] The latter was evident, for example, in the Home Office's extensive employment of summary prosecution data to define crime as a social problem that could be addressed without reexamining the fundamental tenets of Victorian economic or political culture.

As one would expect from an institution with such longevity and range of activity, the documentation on the London magistrates' courts is voluminous. The nature of this historical record dictates that in Chapter 1, which deals with the late-eighteenth-century origins of the police courts and their development until the mid-nineteenth (when the *Annual Statistics* become available), any examination must proceed from other sources. Fortunately, the key position of these courts in metropolitan law and culture ensured that the material dealing with them in this period was rich and varied. Regular coverage of the police courts in newspapers such as *The Times*, the *Morning Post*, the *Morning Chronicle*, and *The Standard* began in the 1820s. By the mid-Victorian period, court reports had become a dominant segment of both the half-penny press and the London borough papers. Remaining as one of the most ubiquitous sections of many newspapers well into the early twentieth century, their legacy would indeed be enduring; both the "crime" and "human interest" segments of modern news reporting trace their origins to police-court journalism.[101] In the most general sense, official court records are more reliable than press accounts are, but that does not necessarily make the former more

[100] Mary Poovey, *Making a Social Body: British Cultural Formation, 1830–1864* (Chicago and London: University of Chicago Press, 1995), 8–10. See also Patrick Joyce, "What Is the Social in Social History?" *Past and Present* 206 (Feb. 2010), 221–22.

[101] "Historical Representations of Crime and the Criminal," *Oxford Research Encyclopedia of Criminology* (Aug. 2017), criminology.oxfordre.com/view/10.1093/acrefore/9780190264079.001.0001/acrefore-9780190264079-e-205?print=pdf, 19–20.

valuable for understanding the historical significance of local courtrooms or their role in metropolitan society. Minutes of testimony can tell us much about what happened to the few individuals involved in a case, but a nationally distributed newspaper story of the same case might have shaped its meaning for readers numbering in the thousands or even tens of thousands. Examining the contrast between how such cases were described in official sources and how they were portrayed in newspapers, moreover, reveals much about how legal processes were reinterpreted as moral lessons for the burgeoning newspaper readership and how public expressions of authority can enhance, conceal, or even undermine the power of the state.[102]

My core source material in the second half of the book consists of two types of official records – police-court minutes and registers – both of which have received limited attention previously. Police-court minutes encompass testimony by all the principals in a case, including the prosecutor/complainant, the defendant, any witnesses called by either party, and, in the case of charges, the statements by the arresting constable and any other officers on the scene. This dialogue, often conducted in the vernacular, reveals how those involved in a case represented themselves and their actions in the courtroom. The second core source, London police-court registers, offers a comprehensive view of local courtrooms' daily activities. These are short-form records that include the name of the prosecutor or complainant and that of the defendant, the nature of the charge or summons, the verdict, what punishment was imposed, and who the adjudicating magistrate was. In some registers of charges, the occupation of the defendant was also listed. These records allow for greater precision in assessing a courtroom's activities than police statistics do. Unlike the latter, which only indicate the end result of each type of charge in any given year in the entire metropolis (i.e. discharge or conviction, and if the latter, punishment imposed), court registers allow one to make a careful accounting of exactly what types of cases any given court heard, and the progression of various adjudications (i.e. how many adjournments prior to resolution). Most crucially, these registers provide a detailed picture of

[102] James Scott, *Domination and the Arts of Resistance: Hidden Transcripts* (New Haven: Yale University Press, 1990), 1–15, 45–69. On the "performance" of power more generally, see Clifford Geertz, *Negara: The Theatre State in Nineteenth-Century Bali* (Princeton: Princeton University Press, 1980), 98–109.

summonses brought by institutions and private individuals. Police-court minutes and registers thus open up for detailed examination a broad array of courtroom activities that have previously been obscured from historical view.[103]

These court records do place three serious limitations on analysis. First, the voices of courtroom principals come to us secondhand through a certain level of filtering by the court clerks who recorded testimony. The detail and precision of police-court minutes varied from court to court and from clerk to clerk. Some clerks were meticulous, apparently recording testimony nearly verbatim. Others were less painstaking, tending to abbreviate or condense testimony, though not to the point that the salient elements were lost entirely. We cannot know what speech or action they chose *not* to record, nor are we privy to the rich visual lexicon of appearance and gesture that was often described in journalistic accounts. Secondly, the speakers involved could hardly have been unaware that they were in a courtroom. With this in mind, I have taken great pains to assess their utterances within this context, and to try to account for their sensibility to their circumstances. This consciousness of their locale was especially clear when principals directly addressed the courtroom audience.[104] Courtrooms, then and now, are performative spaces as well legal and social ones.[105] Thirdly, the amount of material available, which includes tens of thousands of long-form minutes and hundreds of thousands of short-form register entries, means that a comprehensive assessment would have been impractical. It was only with the generous efforts of several dedicated research assistants that I was able to process a substantive fraction of it.

A database of approximately 10,000 entries from the police-court registers constitutes the primary evidence base for my broader

[103] Since these summonses did not require apprehension of the defendant and did not result in a charge, beyond their total number each year, they were absent from the statistical records amassed by the Commissioner of Police for the Metropolis for his annual report to the Home Office.

[104] Though it is worth noting that magistrates actually encouraged court clientele to relate the language of any given exchange as precisely as possible so that the implications of it on subsequent actions could be best understood. Courtroom testimony was rife with colorful invectives, which clerks recorded by abbreviating all but the first and last letter, in most instances.

[105] Pat Carlen, "The Staging of Magistrates' Justice," *British Journal of Criminology* 16, no. 1 (Jan. 1976), 48.

conclusions about courtroom activity in the period from 1882 to 1915. This database is particularly valuable for two reasons. First, it provides the material from which one can draw conclusions about the general character of courtroom activities and to compare that with how other, more subjective sources such as magistrates' memoirs or newspaper portrayed the courts. And secondly, it provides a record of activities that, although they are significant to any assessment of courts' roles in their communities, are either difficult to glean from annual statistics or absent altogether from them. Empty summonses, those applied for and granted but never conducted due to the failure of the complainant or of both parties to appear on the appointed date, are one example of this. For the analysis of courtroom dialogue, my primary sources are the minute books of one of London's busiest legal venues, the Clerkenwell Police Court in Islington. These are supplemented with the statistical records of court charges and convictions found in the Parliamentary *Judicial Statistics* and the *Annual Reports of the Commissioner of Police for the Metropolis*. The last and most significant limitation to the registers and minutes is that they are available only for certain courts, and the earliest surviving records date to the final quarter of the nineteenth century.

Although this study uses new sources and employs familiar ones in innovative ways, it is nonetheless predicated on the well-established concept of legal culture. This holds that the operation of the law in modern society is best understood as a set of codified regulations that are located in a wider array of contested ideas and relations – social, political, economic, and cultural – through which power is expressed.[106] The ultimate limits of the law and the significance of its operation in society over time lie not just in the evolution of its legal statutes, but also in the manner by which they are employed and in the public perception of and response to them.[107] Drawn from Anglo-American legal theory, the concepts of "legal pluralism," the multiple sites and manifestations of law's forms both within and beyond formal legal settings, and "popular legal culture," which encompasses the contribution of non-elites to the processes and meanings of legal

[106] Erhard Blankenburg, "Civil Litigation Rates as Indicators for Legal Cultures," in David Nelken, ed., *Comparing Legal Cultures* (Aldershot: Routledge, 1997), 41.

[107] Barbara Yngvesson, "Inventing Law in Local Settings: Rethinking Popular Legal Culture," *Yale Law Journal* 98, no. 8, Symposium: Popular Legal Culture (Jun. 1989), 1693.

discourse, have further refined our understanding of the social and cultural dimensions of law and legal institutions.[108] By examining law in the context of culture and social relations, I am following a long tradition of historians, legal anthropologists, sociologists, and cultural theorists.[109]

My investigation into this complex mélange of practice and representation is guided by the analytical lens of "courtroom culture." This can be understood most simply as the social and cultural dimensions of courtroom interactions in the police courts of nineteenth- and early-twentieth-century London. By referring to it as a culture, I am suggesting that events in these courtrooms, discussions of those events in the public sphere, and the experiences of individuals in these instances had both a formal element (e.g. laws, testimony, verdicts) and a conceptual one (i.e. meanings and interpretations of laws, testimony, and verdicts) that enjoyed a unique relationship in the courtroom itself. The dynamics of local courtrooms and their meanings for those who experienced and described them therefore lay at the confluence of several distinct social and cultural realms, each with their own patterns of practice and their own shifting dynamics of authority. At the same time, the magistrate's courtroom was a distinct space. Whether described, imagined, or physically occupied, it was a place in which concepts

[108] This approach draws heavily on anthropological and sociological perspectives. Sally Engle Merry describes the "new" legal pluralism as "[rejecting the] law-centeredness of traditional studies of legal phenomena, arguing that not all law takes place in the courts (e.g. Nader and Todd, 1978; Arthurs, 1985). The concern is to document other forms of social regulation that draw on the symbols of the law, to a greater or lesser extent, but that operate in its shadows, its parking lots, and even down the street in mediation offices." Sally Engle Merry, "Legal Pluralism," *Law and Society Review* 25, no. 8 (1988), 874. Of "popular legal culture," Barbara Yngvesson writes, "from this perspective, the 'spirit of law,' while embodying the concerns of a powerful and dominant professional elite, is not simply invented at the top but is transformed, challenged, and reinvented in local practices that produce a plural legal culture." Yngvesson, "Popular Legal Culture," 1693. See also Lauren Benton, "Beyond Legal Pluralism: Towards a New Approach to Law in the Informal Sector," *Social & Legal Studies* 3 (Jun. 1994), 223–42.

[109] For a concise survey of how interdisciplinary perspectives, and those of cultural theory and literacy criticism in particular, have shaped the study of crime, see Amy Gilman Srebnick, "Does the Representation Fit the Crime? Some Thoughts on Writing Crime History as Cultural Text," in Amy Gilman Srebnick and René Lévy, eds., *Crime and Culture: An Historical Perspective* (Aldershot: Ashgate, 2005), 3–19.

and the language associated with them prevailed, such as summonses, charges, and verdicts; where certain distinct practices occurred, trials being the most distinctive, since they could not take place anywhere *outside* of a courtroom; and where individuals engaged a distinct set of roles and identities, most common among them being complainant, defendant, or witness. This volume takes as its premise that by studying the *interaction* between law and legal institutions such as courts, social relations and identities, and cultural norms (e.g. morality), we can best understand the meaning of courtroom events to those who participated in them.

The concept of "courtroom culture" describes a reciprocal dynamic that operated between courtroom events, the formal structures of law, the depictions of both in printed media, and the contested meanings that emerged from all three. This dynamic was most clearly expressed as the nineteenth century wore on in the relationship between public portrayals of courtrooms and the everyday experience of them, how this relationship fostered local ideals and expectations, and how these ideals and expectations, in turn, fostered substantive changes in courtrooms and their practices. One example of this is magistrates' reformation of the physical layout of their courtrooms to reflect a more hierarchical and ordered society that they hoped to encourage beyond the courtroom itself. Another is how working-class men and women used the forum of the public courtroom to offer their own ideas about what constituted justice, as was apparent in their vehement protests over Education Act prosecutions and their contestation of constables' assault charges. This reciprocal relationship between institutional operation, social power, and beliefs or expectations about courtrooms also had significance in public discourse more broadly. Courtroom encounters, both immediate and vicarious, shaped conceptions of the law and the state, individual identity, social relations, and moral norms. Of particular importance was the role that courtrooms and their portrayals played in reconciling (or exacerbating) the dissonances between what was illegal and what was considered morally wrong. This became an increasingly vital and visible aspect of local courtrooms as the state dramatically expanded its regulation of daily life in the second half of the nineteenth century.

Both the formal power of courtrooms and their social influence privileged certain voices and silenced others. But they did so in a way that drew simultaneously on the realm of legal processes, social hierarchy and identity, and cultural ideas and dynamics. Working-class women, for example, were able to employ local courtrooms to achieve something otherwise denied to them, a public platform for their views on morality and the limits of government authority. At base, however, though a summons was incorporated into social conflict and only employed in the first place because it was imbued with cultural meaning, it was nonetheless a legal process. The simultaneity of courtrooms' daily operation in the realms of law, social relations, and popular perception was at the core of courtroom culture. At times, the social dynamics were predominant, as in an "empty summons" where the complainant had no intention of entering the courtroom itself, but wished merely to embarrass, bluff, or leverage the defendant. Here, the legal process of the summons was relevant, but it was not what made the courtroom significant to those who employed it to convey a distinct moral message. Instead, the cultural facet of the local courtroom came to the fore, while the social element receded and the law itself was downplayed or even ignored. In other instances, the legal parameters of courtrooms were the key to their social impact and cultural significance. Changes in the laws on separation and maintenance, for example, fundamentally shaped both how local courtrooms influenced working-class social relations and how husbands and wives understood the role of the courtroom in their marital affairs. The marginalization of magistrates' courts by higher legal authorities, the courts' frequent employment by those with little or no specific understanding of laws, and the absence of those elements so prominent in other aspects of England's legal infrastructure (e.g. juries, barristers) also contributed to maintaining courtroom culture as a distinct realm for the construction of meaning and the operation of power in metropolitan communities. In the process, courtroom culture generated its own customs, expectations, and myths that helped shape the significance of courtroom events for those who experienced or portrayed them.

Lastly, the specific type of courtroom culture under discussion here has a historical dimension that distinguishes it from legal culture and legal discourse. The latter concepts are generally employed by legal scholars to either assess the workings of one specific aspect of law in a given society or to compare the myriad operations of law in its social and cultural context across different societies.[110] Courtroom culture as it operated in the London magistrates' courts was born in a specific time and place where awareness of, access to, and public portrayals of summary courtrooms all coalesced, namely, the mid- and late Victorian years. It only lasted until the ongoing bureaucratization and professionalization of the magistrates' courts in the interwar period drastically reduced access to the public courtroom and the ability of local clientele to employ the arena for their own social purposes. By the 1930s, the courts had changed dramatically in the range of cases they handled, how those cases were processed, and the degree of public access to their proceedings. The increasing predominance of regulatory and motoring cases, the greater complexity and opacity of summary justice, the professionalization of trials through the involvement of solicitors, and the recusing of domestic cases to adjudication *in camera* all reduced the cultural and social footprint of local courtrooms. Summonses, which had once facilitated modest petitioners' voluntary engagement with the courts, became largely a tool for regulatory bodies and police to employ against minor offenses. At the same time, newspaper portrayals of local police courts were almost entirely decoupled from their everyday activities, though with no commensurate decline in their popular appeal.[111] What form and relevance courtroom culture, in a broader sense, occupied in this later period or in other societies where police courts or their analogs were common lies beyond the scope of this study.[112]

110 This tendency stems from the strong sociological vein that informs the study of legal culture. G. Bierbrauer, "Toward an Understanding of Legal Culture: Variations in Individualism and Collectivism between Kurds, Lebanese, and Germans," *Law & Society Review* 28, no. 2 (1994), 243–45; David Nelken, "Disclosing/Invoking Legal Culture: An Introduction," *Social & Legal Studies* 4 (1995), 435–36.

111 As Richard Hoggart observed, "crime stories" remained perennially popular among working-class readers well into the twentieth century. Richard Hoggart, *The Uses of Literacy: Aspects of Working-Class Life with Special Reference to Publications and Entertainment* (London: Penguin, 1957), 91.

112 There are certainly indications to be found in previous scholarship that local courtrooms did operate as distinct realms for the generation and contestation of meaning and social relations in other times and places. In the historical record, see Mary Roberts Smith, "The Social Aspect of New York Police Courts," *The American Journal of Sociology* 5, no. 2 (Sep. 1899), 145–54. In historical analysis, see Paul Craven, "Law and Ideology: The Toronto Police Court 1850–80," in David Flaherty, ed., *Essays in the History of Canadian Law*, vol. II (Toronto: Osgoode Society for Canadian Legal History by University of Toronto Press, 1983); Michael Willrich, *City of Courts: Socializing Justice in Progressive Era*

The organization of the book's chapters is roughly chronological. It begins with the origins of the London police courts and the introduction of courtroom scenes as a literary and journalistic subject in the later eighteenth century. In the absence of an official police force, an orderly, hierarchical courtroom was necessary to sustain magistrates' public legitimacy and to justify the considerable expansion of the summary court system. In the reformation of summary justice amidst its widening public portrayals, the courtroom's legal authority to punish disorder became indelibly linked to its cultural capacity to define, in popular discourse, what *constituted* public order itself and the putative threats to it. This linkage of legal and cultural power emerged from the efforts of the first generation of courtroom reporters and the magistrates working in the early decades of the nineteenth century. Both cohorts employed their privileged positions within the venue to propose, through their writing and public speech, distinct visions of moral and social order in the metropolis. They set many of the precedents that would continue to define local courtrooms and their portrayals in subsequent decades. Among the most important and persistent of these precedents were the installment of press representatives as permanent fixtures in local courtrooms, the expansion of the roles of local courtrooms in civil and criminal matters, magistrates' sensitivity and responsiveness to local demand, and the creation of a ready market for courtroom stories among a burgeoning newspaper readership.

Chapter 2 examines how public portrayals of local courtrooms changed in the latter half of the nineteenth century. As the advertisements that crowded the pages of the new popular press broadcast the expanding availability of products and services, columns of "Police Intelligence" broadcast the expanding roles of courtrooms and the authority of magistrates, police, and municipal agents. In doing so, they emphasized the courts' authority in the public eye, commented on its expression, and assessed the morality of individual responses to it. By portraying these daily encounters between the state and the people, police-court columns offered

Chicago (Cambridge: Cambridge University Press, 2003); Carol Smart and Selma Sevenhuijsen, *Child Custody and the Politics of Gender* (London and New York: Routledge, 1989), 138.

readers a common standard for defining morality, for determining victims and villains, and for measuring justice and injustice in the courtroom. One of the key shifts in both legal authority and its depictions during this period was the increasing power of municipal bodies and their representatives in the courtroom and the concurrent decline of the voice of the individual defendant. In these processes, local courtrooms emerged as a key locale where tensions between older ideas of Liberal individualism and moral choice on the one hand and the growing trend towards mass society and environmental explanations for crime and immorality on the other played out in public view.

To understand the full spectrum of police courts' activities in metropolitan society, and the full dimensions of courtroom culture, we must establish both the quantitative and qualitative contours of the courts' daily adjudications. This is the focus of Chapter 3. Police prosecutions accounted for part of the rapid proliferation of summary prosecutions across the second half of the nineteenth century. This increase, however, was dwarfed by the meteoric rise in summonses involving regulations on health and public safety, social reform, minor disruptions of public order, and the collection of various fees and debts to municipal, commercial, and corporate bodies. These cases raised crucial questions about the relationship between the state, the individual, and the community. They also revealed key fractures in the principles and methods that guided different facets of metropolitan governance. What were the limits of state authority versus individual autonomy? Where was the line to be drawn between public order and private liberty? What violations represented a genuine hazard to the "public good," and how was the latter to be defined? And did courtroom authority in these matters ultimately lie with the municipal representatives who levied summonses or with the magistrates who adjudicated them? London School Board officials, for example, consistently advocated a coercive approach towards working-class parents, while magistrates doggedly hewed to paternalistic persuasion. This chapter also demonstrates how, in the context of the local courtroom, the state remained vulnerable to contestation and public defiance by even the poorest of defendants.

The frequent and varied use of private court summonses is one of the most significant, and least understood, aspects of metropolitan summary justice. It offers compelling evidence that the evolving social and cultural roles of the courtroom in the community and the agency of local men and women guided daily court practice. Accordingly, Chapter 4 examines the wide array of daily activities that became the subject of police court contests in the decades before the First World War. The ease of access and broad participation of the local community as principals and witnesses helped make the police-court summons process the most egalitarian aspect of metropolitan law. As courtrooms incorporated an ever-wider segment of the urban population in a diverse array of operations, courtroom language and its implications also became integrated into personal contests outside the court. And just as particular phrases or concepts changed their meanings when used in a courtroom, their employment outside the courtroom carried distinct meanings. The final section of the chapter examines not just what it meant for men and women to summons one another, but what it meant to use the language of summonses in different contexts. With such practices, men and women brought the courtroom, as an imagined space, into an interpersonal contest well before they brought their contests into the courtroom. This oscillation of conflicts between the home, the street, and the court demonstrated the reciprocal influence of practices and norms in each milieu, rather than the predominance of one over all.

Chapter 5 examines how, via the daily parade of summonses, a variety of actors employed local courtrooms to shape the social and cultural contours of marriage and affiliation. As in other aspects of metropolitan life, the courtroom was not merely a venue for the expression of law or norms that were constituted elsewhere or a space for the enforcement of middle-class standards of morality.[113] Legal structures originally developed to protect patriarchal privilege could, to some degree, be co-opted by women instead.[114] Several decades before working-class women could directly shape the terrain of formal politics, they were effectively navigating the terrain of local courtrooms and influencing both their daily practices and the meanings that emerged from them. And they did so on a scale that far exceeded women's employment of courtrooms in the eighteenth or early

[113] Savage, "The Magistrates Are Men," 240–41.

[114] Margot Finn, "Working-Class Women and the Contest for Consumer Control in the County Courts," *Past & Present* 161, no. 1 (1998), 188–200; Behlmer, *Friends of the Family*, 200–201.

nineteenth century. Their frequent engagement with local courts demonstrates how vital working-class women were to recasting the nature of urban law and governance in the later nineteenth century. The expansion of the police and judicial apparatus in the prewar decades, however, was a double-edged sword. Even as working-class women were capitalizing on more than a generation of steady contact with the police courts, they were increasingly becoming the targets of surveillance and regulation. Thus, the adaption of the courtroom to address familial matters occurred in tandem with the adaption of women to the mechanisms of the courtroom. This was particularly visible in the varied and creative ways that women employed the laws on judicial separation and affiliation to hold men to account.[115] In this process, the venues of summary adjudication were less a "poor man's court of justice," as the magistrate Cecil Chapman would assert in his interwar memoir, and more a poor *woman's*.[116]

The topics of Chapter 6 are constables, charges, and how magistrates and defendants alike were able to mediate police authority in the courtroom. Specifically, the chapter examines the character of daily prosecution, the contrast between how constables and magistrates handled charges, and the changing patterns of charges in the decades preceding the First World War. In these years, the relationship between policing, adjudication, and punishment was continually being redefined not only for those who were it targets, but for its wielders as well. Police authority in the courtroom, though strengthened by expertise and training, was hardly uncontested. Magistrates and police constables were under constant public scrutiny, and the former were keen to avoid the widespread hostility expressed towards the latter in working-class communities. Regardless of the increasing intrusion of policing into everyday life, it lay in a magistrate's hands to decide if any given defendant deserved leniency or severity and which laws merited rigorous enforcement. Magistrates and journalists challenged the reputation of constables,

115 As Margot Finn observes, "local magistrates . . . were among the first representatives of the Victorian criminal law to confer limited legal autonomy on that most long-lived legal and contractual non-entity, the married woman." Finn, "The Authority of the Law," 164.

116 Cecil Chapman, *A Poor Man's Court of Justice: Twenty-Five Years as a Metropolitan Magistrate* (London: Hodder and Stoughton, 1925).

while defendants opted for summary jurisdiction of indictable offenses or guilty pleas to mediate the consequences of arrest and prosecution. Through these and other practices, local courtrooms proved important in reshaping the legal, social, and moral dimensions of criminal justice in this period. The final section of this chapter assesses how the late Victorian magistracy grounded their claims to authority in the courtroom and traces the eventual decline of the police courts' public roles and voluntary usage by the local community in the interwar period. A brief conclusion summarizes what the study of the nineteenth-century police courts can contribute to our historical understanding of London, the state, and culture in modern Britain, and suggests some potential directions for future research.

1

"Many-Coloured Scenes of Life"

The Police Courts in Metropolitan Culture and Society, 1758–1860

This first chapter traces the early development of the London magistrates' courtroom during the second half of the eighteenth century and the first half of the nineteenth. In this period, local courtrooms of summary justice became one of the key institutions for maintaining public order in the metropolis, and essential to the propagation of a distinct vision of social order and morality. For the early magistrates and reformers, the practice of law and its public portrayals were intended to operate in tandem, reinforcing one another in metropolitan society. Those with authority in the courtroom were just as keen to control the latter as they were the former. The reform and expansion of the police-court system, however, opened the door for a widened array of portrayals and much greater access by both reporters and the local community. The more public and accessible courtrooms became, the more difficult it was for magistrates to control their depictions. By the early nineteenth century, the reciprocal influence of courtroom practice, public representation, and personal participation had been firmly established.

This entanglement of public dialogue, dissemination through newspapers and other media, and courtroom practice constituted the core of courtroom culture. The origins of it lie in the simultaneous expansion of the latter's role in criminal justice administration in the late eighteenth century, on the one hand, and in the popularization of courtroom scenes in late eighteenth and early nineteenth-century newspapers, on the other. The first development was largely the work of two sibling magistrates, the Fieldings. Building on the efforts of his older brother, the famed novelist and playwright Henry Fielding, John Fielding worked in the 1750s and 1760s to make his Bow Street "public office" the most important venue for the daily prosecution of crime in the metropolis.[1] His program of reforming the magistrates' role and the Bow Street court's remit had three main goals. First, he wished to see Bow Street and its staff, be they magistrates or the newly inaugurated "runners" (the prototype of the modern detective), become the centerpiece of the state's response to crime and disorder in the metropolis.[2] Secondly, John Fielding wanted to widen the availability and increase the affordability of the courts. He would dispense with expensive fees and replace privately funded pursuit and arrest with a system of publicly funded investigation by his runners and prosecution by a permanent, rotating staff of magistrates. The latter would convene their trials and examinations in spaces dedicated specifically to that purpose (in contrast to the part-time court spaces more typical of England in that period).[3] Lastly, both Fieldings were committed to a wide public dissemination of the courts' activities. They would accomplish this via their own publications, by encouraging an audience to witness the magistrates conducting their various duties, and by making special arrangements for the attendance of newspaper reporters at trials.[4]

The Bow Street public office, in addition to being among the earliest locales in Britain to be devoted solely to the administration of justice, was also among the first where trials and other public judicial processes took place continuously and at set times. John Fielding reorganized his court temporally as well as spatially by ensuring that at least one magistrate was on duty for both a morning session that ran from 10 a.m. to 2 p.m. and an afternoon session that was conducted from

1 J. M. Beattie, *The First English Detectives: The Bow Street Runners and the Policing of London, 1750–1840* (Oxford: Oxford University Press, 2012), 96. The Fieldings came from the ranks of the Somerset gentry, their father being Lt. Gen. Edmund Fielding.

2 For a comprehensive account of the Bow Street Runners, see ibid.

3 J. M. Beattie, "Sir John Fielding and Public Justice: The Bow Street Magistrates' Court, 1754–1780," *Law and History Review* 25, no. 1 (Apr. 2007), 63; Anthony Babbington, *A House in Bow Street* (London: Macdonald, 1969), 93.

4 Beattie, "Public Justice," 70. This "public" character of English courtrooms in the eighteenth century is also discussed by James Epstein in "Spatial Practices/Democratic Vistas," *Social History* 24, no. 3 (Oct. 1999), 299.

5 to 9 p.m.[5] This was justice that, like the new rhythms of industrial labor, ran according to specific allotments of time.[6] Thus Fielding's "public office," which was depicted repeatedly across a significant range of publications in the last half of the eighteenth century, helped introduce and popularize the modern conception of a courtroom as a space specifically designed for, and permanently dedicated to, the conduct of justice, where trials are held on a regular basis, and where the public is encouraged to witness (and legitimize) important decisions. The formal ordering of the courtroom in both space and time was integral to John Fielding's stated purpose of maintaining good order among the metropolitan populace. He well aware of the increasing value of time in his society, and argued that a primary goal of law should be to ensure that the "lower orders" did not waste their time in idleness and vice, but rather that they dedicated it to useful pursuits.[7] The magistrate, like his brother and many of his contemporaries, was deeply concerned with the apparent breakdown of deference among the lower orders (in which Fielding included shopkeepers, artisans, and laborers).[8] The elder Fielding was particularly alarmed by the unwonted assertiveness of this cohort in the face of local judicial authority. His solution to such "wild Notions of Liberty," was to increase the power of the metropolitan magistrates, and it was to address the fears of those who opposed such a measure that Fielding directed much of his initial arguments in his famous 1751 public treatise, *Enquiry into the Causes of the Late Increase of Robbers*.[9]

John Fielding took a similar tack in his own 1758 treatise supporting his brother's plan to introduce formal policing in London.[10] Like their contemporary, Edmund Burke, both Fieldings espoused a view of society that only functioned in an orderly and moral fashion when those lower

[5] Babbington, *Bow Street*, 123.

[6] Clare Graham, *Ordering Law: The Architectural and Social History of the English Law Court* (Aldershot: Ashgate, 2003), 106.

[7] John Fielding, *Account of the Origin and Effects of a Police Set on Foot by His Grace the Duke of Newcastle in the Year 1753, upon a Plan Presented to His Grace by the Late Henry Fielding* [hereafter *Account of the Origins and Effects of a Police*] (London: A. Millar, 1758), viii.

[8] V. A. C. Gatrell, "Crime, Authority, and the Policeman-State," in F. M. L. Thompson, ed., *The Cambridge Social History of Britain 1750–1950*, vol. 3: *Social Agencies and Institutions* (Cambridge: Cambridge University Press, 1990), 248–50.

[9] H. Fielding, *Enquiry into the Causes*, xxvlii.

[10] J. Fielding, *Account of the Origins and Effects of a Police*, viii.

down on the social scale expressed deference and respect, and when those with rank and authority exercised their power sternly but responsibly. The late 1760s and 1770s were a particularly crucial period for those who wished to mold society in this hierarchical, patriarchal vision. In addition to rising concerns about crime in the metropolis and its region, which seemed to be overrun with highwaymen and robbers, the city was alive with Radical agitation by John Wilkes and his allies.[11] In an atmosphere of license and profligacy by both the high and the low of Hanoverian England, with agrarian riots, a weavers' strike, and Wilkesite disturbances abounding, the magistracy was to be "an Object worthy of the Acceptance, nay, meriting the Study of the Best of Men."[12] John Fielding reorganized his court to both embody a stable social order – through its spatial and temporal organization along clearly demarcations of rank, role, and purpose – and to maintain public order directly through the administration of criminal law. The Bow Street courtroom, under Fielding's direction, was meant to epitomize an orderly society that contrasted with the disruption and antagonism that allegedly pervaded outside its walls. Fielding's reforms and the portrayals of Bow Street also articulated a vision of order based on the interaction between categories specific to the courtroom and its attendant legal parameters rather than being wholly predicated on divisions in the preexisting social hierarchy.

The Fieldings' goal was a courtroom that combined coercion with mediation, bringing order both through imposed authority and through voluntary co-optation. On the one hand, the brothers supported the Bow Street public office as a mechanism for, quite literally, policing the "lower orders." And the typical cases of larceny and other property felonies reported in the papers were in accord with this. In these instances, stern civic authority was the order of the day. On the other hand, they also desired a courtroom where decisions were not tainted by mercenary proclivities to make "Gain of the paltry Quarrels of the Poor," as had been the case with the so-called "trading justices" who demanded fees for adjudication.[13] Their broader vision of a courtroom accessible to the public, where the

[11] Frank McLynn, *Crime and Punishment in Eighteenth-Century England* (Oxford: Oxford University Press, 1989), 231.

[12] J. Fielding, *Account of the Origins and Effects of a Police*, 37. [13] Ibid., 36.

lower orders could also find advice and affordable justice, offered a much wider segment of society an opportunity to engage the court's resources rather than merely becoming its targets. This was true at least in theory if not necessarily in practice.[14] The Fieldings' changes to the conduct and character of the police courts in the metropolis left a profound legacy. They set the precedent for the magistrates' expanded discretion in summary justice, while at the same time incorporating a broader segment of the metropolitan population into legal processes.[15] By the last quarter of the eighteenth century, what was once an obscure, informal venue of minor criminal administration now occupied a much larger space in the consciousness, and the conscience, of politicians, journalists, newspaper readers, and the men and women who found themselves before "the beak" at Bow Street.

In creating a courtroom that was public and accessible, and one that could only remain so with the constant involvement and attention of the community, the Fieldings simultaneously enhanced and undercut their own authority within it. Public justice was not justice at all if it was not perceived to be such by observers. This change required a magistracy that was in tune with the moral expectations and social circumstances of its audience.[16] As with the dissemination of Bow Street newspaper reports beyond the direct control of the Fieldings, opening up the court to public use and observation made the orderly courtroom world they envisioned more vulnerable to interference and criticism. This could originate from the local community, the London press, or the magistrates' own superiors in government. Maintaining

[14] Again, the paucity of magistrates' court records from this period makes it impossible to determine, with any degree of accuracy, the social composition of Bow Street complainants. Judging this from the character of published reports is, for reasons already described, quite problematic. The accessibility of the Essex Quarter Sessions to Fielding's "lower orders" in assault cases, on the other hand, is certainly apparent. From 1760 to 1799, tradesmen and artisans comprised 36–46% of all assault prosecutors there, and laborers comprised 24–30%. Peter King, *Crime and Law in England, 1750–1840: Remaking Justice from the Margins* (Cambridge: Cambridge University Press, 2006), 239.

[15] Much of John Fielding's reforms, it should be noted, concerned pretrial proceedings such as preliminary hearings.

[16] This awareness was similarly crucial among Justices of the Peace in the same period. Douglas Hay, "The Criminal Prosecution in England and its Historians," *Modern Law Review* 47, no. 1 (Jan. 1984), 15–16.

the delicate balance between a court that enforced the law in a manner approved of by the Home Office, administered "justice" in the public's eye, and made itself responsive to the needs and expectations of the community would remain a perennial issue for the next century and a half. The frequency with which men and women on the lower end of the social scale would find themselves on both the giving and receiving end of summary justice, as prisoners and petitioners, would make this task even more challenging. The result was an urban magistracy that, far from becoming "disinterested and distanced," was instead becoming increasingly enmeshed in the culture of courtroom practice and portrayal that they themselves were helping to fashion, but could not entirely control.[17]

Summing up the first three decades after Henry Fielding's death, Bow Street's success in his stated goals of embodying and maintaining public order, encouraging deference to social hierarchy, and fostering respect for magistrates and the "civil power" they wielded was mixed. John Fielding was able to reconstruct his courtroom as a permanent space for the conduct of justice, and one in which a visible order prevailed. There, law was administered in the public eye, and the magistrates' knowledge and discretion were paramount. With these reforms, the Bow Street "public office" joined the Guildhall and the Old Bailey as prototypes of courtrooms that occupied a distinct and permanent space in the legal landscape of the metropolis. The Fieldings' legacy would loom large in the dialogue of their successors, and in the general discussion of metropolitan summary justice across the decades that followed. Successive magistrates would frequently frame their roles and their courts in the context of their illustrious predecessors, albeit in ways that suited their own purposes. But this legacy was not without blemish. The Fieldings' bequest to judicial posterity was colored by controversy, which those who later

[17] Peter King, *Crime, Justice, and Discretion in England, 1740–1820* (Oxford: Oxford University Press, 2000), 122 (citing Norma Landau, *The Justices of the Peace, 1679–1760* (Berkeley and Los Angeles: University of California Press, 1992), 3–5, 328–62). Landau, in turn, is building on E. P. Thompson's arguments about the alleged transition from patriarchal to patrician rule, "Patrician Society, Plebian Culture," *Journal of Social History* 7, no. 4 (Summer 1974), 382–405. As King points out, this "was not a sudden or complete transformation ... the two models overlapped and the change in judicial styles did not occur by the simple displacement of one model by another," (King, *Crime, Justice, and Discretion*, 122).

referenced them either did not know of or chose not to mention. John Fielding had encountered strong opposition, and the Lord Chief Justice (William Murray, the Earl of Mansfield) himself had publicly condemned his practices for undermining respect for the law and perverting the very justice that the magistrate had claimed to promote.[18] This harangue and the warnings that accompanied it had been enough to drive would-be chroniclers from Bow Street, at least temporarily. Such opposition to the court's methods was hardly confined to official channels. Bow Street soon became the target of a direct assault by displeased members of the local community. At the height of the Gordon Riots, on June 5, 1780, a crowd of demonstrators turned their fury on the Bow Street house, wrecking and pillaging it for several hours.[19] It was one of several prominent London homes, some which were similarly connected to the administration of law in the metropolis, to be looted and partially destroyed over the course of the next few days. Just as press attention and magistrates' commitment to a particular vision of order would remain perennial aspects of summary justice in the metropolis, so too would controversy, public opposition, and communal anger. Notoriety has its price, and this would not be the last time that magistrates and their courts bore the brunt of public outrage.

The destruction wrought in June of 1780 was a setback for John Fielding and his fellow magistrates, and Mansfield's fierce chastisement pushed the court out of the public eye for a short while. Fame (or infamy) wide enough to make Bow Street a target for rioters, however, was not to be undone by evanescent mayhem, nor by a Lord Chief Justice beating the tocsin of judicial misconduct and newspaper mischief. The court's importance in the metropolitan legal landscape was too great, and its appeal too broad for it to languish long. Bow Street's continued evolution as a forum for legal administration would occur in tandem with its rising popularity as a didactic amusement for newspaper readers. Less than a decade after the Gordon Riots, these

[18] John Beattie, *The First English Detectives: The Bow Street Runners and the Policing of London, 1750–1840* (Oxford: Oxford University Press, 2012), 102. Lord Mansfield was hardly alone in such criticisms. Lance Bertelsen, "Committed by Justice Fielding: Judicial and Journalistic Representation in the Bow Street Magistrates' Office, January 3–November 24, 1752," *Eighteenth-Century Studies* 40, no. 4 (1997), 342.

[19] Babbington, *Bow Street*, 160–61.

columns began to multiply once again. *The Times* began covering Bow Street in 1787, and added Hatton Garden (Clerkenwell) to its purview in 1792. By 1810, the paper had devoted more than 750 columns to trials at Bow Street, and a few dozen to trials at Hatton Garden.[20] Other papers with notable coverage of the "public offices," as the magistrates courts were called at the time, included the *Morning Post*, *The Oracle*, *The Argus*, the *London Chronicle*, and several papers that had reported on the courts in the 1750s and 1760s, among them *The Gazetteer* and *The Advertiser*. The *Morning Herald*, whose columns would be instrumental in the next major development of courtroom journalism, began its courtroom coverage in the late 1780s. This period of revived press interest in the late eighteenth and early nineteenth century encompassed several important milestones in the development of the magistrates' courts as legal and literary terrain. It culminated in a powerful reframing, via the most popular and extensive series of courtroom press vignettes yet, of the relationship between the courts, their depictions, and their communities.

The Middlesex Justices Act 1792 was the first of these major milestones. It employed Bow Street as a model for a city-wide system of public offices, which were to be administered by a rotation of professional magistrates under the direct supervision of the Home Secretary. Henceforth, the metropolis would have, in addition to Bow Street, seven public offices – two in Westminster (Queen's Square and Great Marlborough Street), and one each in Hatton Garden, Shoreditch, Whitechapel, Shadwell, and Southwark.[21] Two years later, another court was established at Wapping. In succeeding decades, all of them would either be renamed or succeeded as the Westminster, Marylebone (which replaced the Shadwell court in 1821), Clerkenwell, Old Street, Tower Bridge, Lambeth, and Thames Magistrates' courts, with only the Marlborough Street Court remaining on its original site into the twentieth century, albeit in rebuilt form.[22] Four additional "junior" courts – North London, West London, Hammersmith, and South-

[20] These numbers are based on a survey of the Gale Digital Archives, *Eighteenth-Century British Newspapers* and *Nineteenth-Century British Newspapers*.

[21] Middlesex Justices Act 1792 (32 Geo. 3 c. 53 ss. 15, 16). Beattie, *First English Detectives*, 165. Henry Turner Waddy, *The Police Court and Its Work* (London: Butterworth, 1925), 199.

[22] Waddy, *Police Court*, 200.

Western (the latter a fusion of the Greenwich and Woolwich courts) – would eventually follow in 1840. Each of the original courts would be staffed by three stipendiary magistrates and six constables.[23] The former would receive an annual salary of £400. The constables would be paid twelve shillings weekly plus expenses for their duties of investigation and arrest. The eightfold expansion of the system, which now officially combined the powers of policing and prosecution in a single locale, exponentially increased its significance in the judicial landscape of the metropolis. Four decades after the Fieldings first began their project to put Bow Street at the center of the state's response to daily crime and disorder in London, few would argue that the newly expanded system of magistrates' courts had not become just that. The explicit constraint of each office's jurisdiction to a specific area further increased their local impact and notoriety.

But what of the Fieldings' broader goals? Specifically, what of their vision of a courtroom whose activities were disseminated to a wide audience, where the magistrates' authority and discretion were paramount, and where members of the community could seek redress for grievances both great and small? It was in the early nineteenth century that we first find evidence that local magistrates' courtrooms, following the precedents of rural Justices of the Peace and the Guildhall and Mansion House sessions, were becoming more integrated into the daily life of the metropolis.[24] As they were employed on a wider scale by the lower-middle class and working class of the metropolis, the social dimensions of courtroom culture would become exponentially wider. Local courtrooms would become places where social relations between individuals, and between individuals and the state, were negotiated and contested through legal processes. They would also become the means by which, through frequent public portrayals, the growing cohort of middle-class newspaper readers would learn about the law's daily duties in London's teeming districts. Lastly, local courtrooms would continue, in the vision of the Fieldings, to convey distinct moral messages to those who experienced and observed them, though how the intended audience

[23] Clive Emsley, *Crime and Society in England, 1750–1900* (London and New York: Longman, 1986), 176.

[24] Drew Grey, *Crime, Prosecution and Social Relations: The Summary Courts of the City of London in the Late Eighteenth Century* (Basingstoke and New York: Palgrave Macmillan, 2009), 29–31.

interpreted those messages is difficult to determine. Parliamentary inquiries offer some insight into how and when these developments progressed. The most typical method of assessing the impact of the magistrates' courts' operation and the potential or observable consequences of proposed or implemented reforms was through parliamentary committees, which were sub-legislative bodies composed of small numbers of MPs and Peers. Organized by the governing party to meet across a set timescale and concluding with a formal report and recommendations, such committees were tasked with considering policy issues, evaluating government conduct and expenditure and examining proposed legislation. Their deliberations could extend over days, weeks. or even months. They were empowered to seek extensive and detailed testimony from any individuals they deemed relevant to the matter at hand, and their list of witnesses, ranging in size from a handful to scores, could encompass the most modest of local residents and the highest officials in government. Over the course of the nineteenth century, the workings of the magistrates' courts and the role of summary justice in British society would be a common topic of investigation in parliamentary committees as they considered the broad impact that even minor changes in law and procedure there had brought or might bring to the communities they served.

During one such inquiry in 1816, magistrates and clerks from police offices across the city testified that, in the two decades since the expansion of the system, the new courts of summary justice had become an oft-employed resource by their local communities. The private prosecutions that had prompted so many trials prior to the Middlesex Justices Act remained common, but the reduced cost of warrants had made them feasible for a much broader segment of the population. Thomas Evance, a magistrate at Union Hall in south London, had the unenviable task of trying to maintain public order with a mere seven constables overseeing a population estimated at 127,000.[25] The dearth of policing personnel, however, was more than made up for by the zeal with which those under his jurisdiction employed his court. The "lower orders" in his district were so eager to

[25] Testimony of Thomas Evance, *Minutes of Evidence Taken Before a Select Committee Appointed by the House of Commons to Inquire into the State of the Police of the Metropolis* (London: Sherwood *et al.*, 1816), 110.

access his courtroom, he told the committee, that they would "pawn their clothes to take out warrants."[26] Such "parochial work," Evance estimated, in which he included cases brought by local authorities against delinquent rate-payers, took up "as much time as felonies and other criminal matters."[27] Workplace disputes "between masters and labourers, labourers and apprentices" also appeared in local courtrooms in great number.[28]

In the absence of reliable court records, we cannot verify that London magistrates were responding to local initiative and practicing such mercy as they preached in the 1816 inquiry. Such lacunae notwithstanding, magistrates of the early nineteenth century, like the Fieldings before them, continued to insist that their courts were responsive to the local community. In these duties, they were guided by their moral precepts and their vision of justice as much, if not more so, as they were by the demands of policymakers and the general climate of anxiety about crime and immorality in the metropolis. Magistrates were generally unwilling to admit that the latter was justified, and when asked directly about the alleged increases in crime and vice, either equivocated or responded to the contrary.[29] The degree to which the needs of the local community, particularly members of the shopkeeping and laboring classes, and the magistrates' vision of their courts were shaping the public character of courtroom interactions was even more evident in the next major parliamentary commission on justice and policing in the metropolis, which issued its report in 1828. Maurice Swabey, a magistrate at the Union Hall public office, explained to the committee that much of the work in that court consisted of hearing "hackney-coach disputes, pawnbrokers cases, apprentice cases, summonses about the engines, disputes between man and wife, which we endeavor to settle without warrants, applications for summonses of all descriptions for the detention of property where it does not amount to a felony."[30] Were they not

[26] Ibid., 112. [27] Ibid. [28] Ibid., 109.

[29] Testimony of Sir Nathanial Conant, ibid., 40.

[30] Testimony of Maurice Swabey, *Report from the Select Committee on the Police in the Metropolis 1828* (PP 1828 (533) VI), 148. Union Hall was responsible for adjudicating cases in a district that encompassed much of Lambeth and Southwark. In 1845, the responsibility for summary justice in this area was split between two courts, Lambeth PC and Southwark PC. In 1905, the latter was relocated and again renamed, this time to Tower Bridge PC (PS/TOW) (LMA).

given considerable aid by the county magistrates, he continued "those particular cases I have mentioned would take up our time fully, without attending to one single instance of criminal business." But on the state of crime in the metropolis, the general tone of the magistrates' evidence in the 1828 inquiry was very different from 1818. In their testimony, Chief Magistrate Sir Richard Birnie and other London magistrates insisted that serious crime against persons and property had indeed been increasing steadily in the preceding years.[31] Birnie, like his predecessor had in 1816, went on to assert that much of the rise in commitments to prison was attributable to the greater willingness of individuals to prosecute "since there has been greater liberality in allowing expenses."[32] On the eve of the reforms that would create London's first centrally administered police force and would permanently segregate magistrates' duties of adjudication from the supervision of policing, the "public offices" of the city were a popular resource employed by a wide spectrum of residents for a vast array of purposes. They were courtrooms whose roles were indeed shaped by magistrates' visions of morality and justice and by the needs of local authorities in the enforcement of key regulations. But the demands of the local population for convenient and speedy redress of their common grievances had also played a crucial role in their development.

By the 1820s, three key groups were involved in constructing the daily roles of magistrates' courtrooms in their communities. Contributing to both their concrete character and their public interpretations, these cohorts were setting the foundations of courtroom culture as it would develop across the following decades. John Wight and other courtroom reporters formed one group, the magistrates a second, and the

[31] Testimony of Sir Richard Birnie, Chief Magistrate of the Bow Street Police Office, in *Report from the Select Committee on the Police in the Metropolis 1828*, 34. Birnie, a native of Scotland, had begun his professional life as a saddler's apprentice. He was appointed to succeed Sir Arthur Conant as Chief Magistrate, and remained a respected and oft-consulted figure by government ministers until his death in 1821. T. F. Henderson, "Birnie, Sir Richard (*c.*1760–1832)," rev. Catherine Pease-Watkin, *Oxford Dictionary of National Biography* (Oxford: Oxford University Press, 2004).

[32] *Report from the Select Committee on the Police in the Metropolis 1828*, 48. Peter King has proposed a similar explanation for the apparent rise in juvenile crime during the same period. Peter King, "The Rise of Juvenile Delinquency in England 1780–1840: Changing Patterns of Perception and Prosecution," *Past and Present* 160, no. 1 (1998), 151.

courtroom clientele a third. Of these, only the first two had the means to shape public portrayals. The magistrates possessed, by far, the greatest authority to realize their visions in daily courtroom practice. Despite this power, however, they could neither dictate legal policy nor force the community to employ their venues and their attendant personnel. Even as the Fieldings and their successors sought greater authority and wider publicity, they also became more accountable in the eyes of policymakers and middle-class newspaper readers. With the issue of crime and public order becoming increasingly prevalent in the press and in parliamentary debates, and with the explosion of courtroom coverage in national newspapers, the *image* of justice in the courtroom was more important in the 1820s than it ever had been before.[33] The inauguration of regular courtroom columns in the early nineteenth century, however, cost magistrates' their ability to directly manage the portrayals of their venues. Gone were the days when men like John Fielding or Patrick Colquhoun could issue bold tracts on the meaning of justice, the role of magistrates in preserving social hierarchy, and the nature of public order both within and beyond the courtroom. Having lost control of the avenues of dissemination, accommodating local expectations of justice and what the courts could do to address individual grievances on a daily basis became increasingly important.

The public image of their courtrooms was certainly in the minds of the London magistrates who testified in the 1828 inquiry, where they asserted that this maintenance of legitimacy in the eyes of the local community was absolutely essential to the courts' continued viability. Henry Merton Dyer, a magistrate of the Marlborough Street court, explained to the committee that this could be accomplished by three complementary efforts. The first was making operation of the courts more comprehensible, and their employment more feasible, to the community (and to the poor in particular). The second was managing the expectations of the community with regards to what the courts could and could not do. And the last was bringing the visible operation of the courts more in line with the expectations of those who sought

[33] Whereas *The Times*, for example, had only carried a little more than a 100 Bow Street columns in the period 1811–20, they printed nearly six times that many in the subsequent decade, and nearly 300 more from the Marlborough Street court.

their aid. Dyer proposed one relatively simple reform that would further all three goals. This was to dispense with the submission of formal "written information" to initiate a case, and instead substitute a simpler summons process relying on a verbal attestation. This would provide complainants with the relatively speedy and straightforward prosecutions that they desired. As things stood, Dyer explained, the detailed legal requirements of written informations caused many cases to either "fail for want of form," or to simply not proceed at all past the initial complaint.[34] The result was that justice was being denied to many of those whom the courts were meant to serve.[35] Dyer proposed that this change be applied across the board, to every case covered by summary jurisdiction, excepting those that already proceeded (by current statute) on the basis of summonses rather than written informations. The simple change of protocol advocated by the magistrate would have amounted to a fundamental transformation of summary justice from a documentary process that often required considerable familiarity with the law, a solicitor, or both, into a verbal process that required neither. Dyer's proposal was included prominently among the committee's suggested reforms, though it would be some time before it became official policy.[36] As much as Dyer and other magistrates sought to make the courts both accessible and comprehensible to a wide audience, it is clear from their statements that, like their famous predecessors, they still saw themselves as the arbiters of justice and the ultimate determiners of the courts' roles.[37] On the other hand, the same testimony suggests that many who sought the courts' intervention proceeded from the *other* direction. They came to the courtroom seeking their own vision of justice and expected it to be met. Dyer used the frequent cases brought by the "poor and ignorant persons" against pawnbrokers as one prominent example the distance

[34] Testimony of Henry Merton Dyer, March 28, 1828, *Report from the Select Committee on the Police in the Metropolis 1828*, 173.

[35] Ibid., 174.

[36] Ibid. It is unclear exactly when the requirement of written information was officially dispensed with, but it was certainly no later than the Summary Jurisdiction Act 1848. Thomas William Saunders, *The Practice of the Magistrates' Courts*, 2nd ed. (London: The Law Times Office, 1858), 10–12.

[37] As Sir Richard Birnie, the chief Bow Street magistrate, put it bluntly, "magistrates are not in the habit of being controlled." Testimony of Sir Richard Birnie, March 10, 1828, *Report from the Select Committee on the Police in the Metropolis 1828*, 46.

between expectations and experience.[38] Poor petitioners' inability to properly assemble written informations (e.g. by hiring a solicitor to aid them) "wholly precludes them from taking any benefit from the law," he wrote.[39] This discrepancy was part a much more fundamental problem, in Dyer's view. The current protocols used in the London courts, he declared, "amounts to an absolute denial of justice to the poorer or the busy classes of life." His proposed reform, the wholesale replacement of written informations with summonses, was therefore imperative if the summary justice system was to provide for the "just rights and attainable remedies of the public."[40] Where the expectations and needs of the public for justice conflicted with the law, Dyer insisted, it was the latter that required adjustment.

The 1828 inquiry offered several other insights into how members of the local community employed the magistrates' courtrooms and what they perceived to be justice. In addition to the abovementioned cases against pawnbrokers, Chief Magistrate Birnie told the committee that assault cases, mainly attributable to drunkenness, occupied a considerable portion of the courts' time.[41] In response, the committee member conducting the interview suggested that this was due not to a general rise in violence, but rather to an increased willingness of the public to employ the courts instead of resolving disputes on their own.[42] Assault cases had become so common, one East End resident (Richard Gregory) told the committee, that some magistrates in the area, instead of incarcerating otherwise respectable and orderly men, were resorting to an informal system of recognizances. In such cases, a defendant released under the conditions that he not commit a breach of the peace in the following months was held "*in terrorem* by the warrant hanging over his head," and could still support his family.[43] This system served the goals of all involved. The victim received justice, the magistrates maintained order, respectable men were not degraded by incarceration with common criminals, and families were not thrown onto the parish for relief. In the absence of court records, it is impossible to determine how frequently magistrates across London adopted this course, but there are indicators that it was quite common in other jurisdictions where records

[38] Testimony of Henry Merton Dyer, March 28, 1828, ibid., 174.
[39] Ibid. [40] Ibid., 173. [41] Testimony of Sir Richard Birnie, March 10, 1828, ibid., 45.
[42] Ibid. [43] Testimony of Richard Gregory, March 17, 1828, ibid., 98.

are accessible. By the later nineteenth century, when registers of metropolitan summary jurisdiction become available, binding over one or both parties on their own recognizance had become among the most frequent outcomes of assault cases proceeding from summonses.

Beyond the tendency of the local community to bring various petty cases before the magistrates, witnesses testified that London residents were, in general, becoming more adept at employing courtroom protocols to their advantage. Opposing parties, one magistrate explained, commonly employed a progressive series of summonses, convictions, and appeals as a pathway to a negotiated compromise, with no fines ever being collected by the court at all.[44] Many of these strategies, recognizances and courtroom mediation in particular, had long been common in the courts of county justices and in the Middlesex Sessions.[45] Their increasing employment in London PCs represented a change in the scale of implementation and the breadth of usage rather than a novel innovation in courtroom practice. The expansion of the police-court system and the reduced cost of employing it, along with the rising familiarity of local residents with its operation, made the adoption of such tactics more popular. The local court could be used, quickly and relatively cheaply, by a wider socioeconomic range of residents in a broader number of circumstances. Would-be court clientele were further encouraged by magistrates who saw the value in providing justice that met the expectations of participants and observers alike. Seventy-five years after Henry Fielding first took his seat in the magistrate's chair, Bow Street and its sister courts had gone from relative obscurity to center stage in the daily execution of law in London. Exactly what part the magistrates' courts would play in the legal and social canvas of the metropolis remained a matter of debate. There was no consensus even among magistrates, let alone between magistrates, parliamentary authorities, and the myriad men and women who found themselves before the bench, by the tens of thousands, each year. The contest over what roles courtrooms would occupy in their local communities and how they would be portrayed to the public would continue throughout the nineteenth century.

[44] Testimony of Henry Merton Dyer, March 28, 1828, ibid., 178.

[45] Robert Shoemaker, *Prosecution and Punishment: Petty Crime in London and Rural Middlesex, c.1660–1725* (Cambridge: Cambridge University Press, 1991), 25–27, 55.

"The Public Are the Jury": The Evolving Social and Cultural Roles of Local Courtrooms in London, 1829–57

The proliferation and popularization of courtroom events in regular newspaper columns, serialized fiction, popular journalistic accounts of London, and other venues coincided with two fundamental changes in the authority and role of the London magistrates' courts. The first, driven by Robert Peel's reforms as Home Secretary, was the inauguration of the Metropolitan Police and the subsequent transfer of almost all executive powers of policing from the magistrates to this new institution. The courts retained a few constables on staff, and they continued to work in close cooperation with "the Met." In the years that followed the passage of the Metropolitan Police Act 1829, however, London magistrates, often against their expressed desire, conceded their previous supervision over daily law enforcement to the new professional force. The latter operated under the auspices of the Metropolitan Police Commissioners and the Home Office. The summary justice system, and the London magistrates' courts in particular, would remain a key focus in Parliament's ongoing campaign to rationalize and consolidate the criminal justice system in the 1830s. Even as London magistrates lost their power to dispatch constables and were forced share the legal limelight with the new police, their roles in courtrooms, and the roles of their courts in their communities, became broader and more powerful. New legislation, along with the magistrates' adaptation of older regulations, brought an increasing number of criminal and civil issues within their purview.[46] Police-court judges also secured the ability to inflict longer terms of imprisonment and higher fines. The inception of the new police force and the enhanced authority of the magistrates' courts brought ever-greater numbers of Londoners into contact with both institutions. An

46 Ruth Paley, "An Imperfect, Inadequate and Wretched System? Policing London before Peel," *Criminal Justice History* 10 (1989), 95–130; Stefan Petrow, "The Rise of the Detectives in London, 1869–1914," *Criminal Justice History* 14 (1993), 91–108; David Philips, "A New Engine of Power and Authority: The Institutionalization of Law Enforcement in England, 1780–1830," in V. A. C. Gatrell, Bruce Lenman, and Geoffrey Parker, eds., *Crime and the Law: The Social History of Crime in Western Europe since 1500* (London: Europa Publications, 1980); Elaine Reynolds, *Before the Bobbies: The Night Watch and Police Reform in Metropolitan London, 1720–1830* (Stanford: Stanford University Press, 1998).

appearance before the magistrate, by coercion or by choice, became an increasingly common occurrence, particularly among those at the lower end of the socioeconomic spectrum. These developments, along with the tremendous multiplication of newspapers and their audiences, are the keys to comprehending how the social and cultural roles of the police courts in London changed in the three decades following the passage of the 1829 Act.

The general procedure of the magistrates' courts was largely standardized by the mid-Victorian period. There were several overlapping circumstances that determined how a defendant was first brought to court and their treatment subsequently. The first was whether or not they were appearing on a summons or a charge. A summons was the most flexible and broadly employed means by which one individual, either as a private person or as a representative of a larger organization, could compel someone to appear in court. A magistrate could grant a summons during a court sitting, in his private chambers, or even in his own home. He could also refuse to grant one, but only on judicial grounds (i.e. the complaint made did not constitute a legal violation), not on his personal views of the matter.[47] The process of requesting a summons was known as an "application," the individual seeking it was designated as the "complainant," and the justification they offered for their request was "the information." Prior to the mid-Victorian period, the information had to be written, which severely hampered the accessibility of summonses. The allowance of verbal information removed this obstacle.

A summons, once granted, was delivered to the address of the putative defendant by special constables seconded to the courts. The document indicated a court date and location, and on what grounds they were being summonsed. Summonses were the primary means by which individuals brought one another to court. Over time, summonses increasingly became the prerogative of municipal institutions such as the London School Board, the Metropolitan Board of Works, and the London Country Council. The police also became frequent employers of summonses beginning in the prewar years, as they found them to be a less intrusive means for bringing minor offenders to court. Regardless of this slow incorporation into the remit of state authorities, private

[47] F. T. Giles, *The Criminal Law* (Harmondsworth: Penguin, 1954), 74.

summonses for marital issues remained a key aspect of London courts' activity well into the mid-twentieth century. Such summonses, which the magistrates' clerk F. T. Giles described as "a more gentlemanly weapon," were hardly without a coercive aspect.[48] In instances where the summons was "served" (i.e. reliably delivered) to the defendant and they nonetheless failed to appear on the appointed court date, the case was typically adjourned and a second summons issued. If this next measure failed, magistrates' general recourse was to issue a warrant to compel their attendance on pain of arrest.[49]

The bringing of charges in court, regardless of who lodged the initial complaint, was a more puissant measure. The prosecution of a charge was preceded by an arrest, and the latter could be the result either of a constable witnessing the commission of a crime or of a magistrate's issuance – and the ensuing police execution – of a warrant. In the latter case, private initiative still played an important role, since the alleged victim of the crime in question had to make a sworn statement before a magistrate to justify the warrant and subsequent arrest, and the relevant information had to be written and signed.[50] Summonses, the lesser measure, required no such affirmation.[51] As discussed in more detail in Chapter 6, one of the most common ways by which a defendant found themselves facing a charge was when, subsequent to an alleged assault, the victim fetched a constable to effect an arrest. The prosecutor (or prosecutrix), would then need to visit the court and make their sworn statement ("the information") before a magistrate so that the charge could be leveled and the defendant tried in court on a subsequent date. In the interim, the defendant would either be held in the cells attached to the court (which was almost invariably adjacent to the police station) or released on a surety (i.e. bail) to appear later.[52]

Once charged, the next major procedural question was whether the offense was indictable or non-indictable. For an offense to be classified as non-indictable, it had to be one for which the relevant Act of

48 F. T. Giles, *The Magistrates' Courts* (London: Pelican Books, 1949), 58. 49 Ibid., 59.

50 Constables used warrants to make arrests, but this had been the law for centuries prior to the creation of the new police, when constables were typically private citizens serving for a year. Even after the reforms of the 1830s, the police were not granted any prosecutorial powers that were not already held by private citizens.

51 Ibid., 54; Giles, *Criminal Law*, 76–77.

52 Although typically the defendant had to provide a surety, the Bail Act 1898 permitted magistrates to grant bail without it, at their discretion. Giles, *Magistrates' Courts*, 67.

Parliament expressly directed summary trial. The overwhelming majority of criminal offenses across the second half of the nineteenth century fell into this category. Indictable offenses, on the other hand, consisted of felonies, treasons, and other serious criminal offenses. Murder, abduction, manslaughter, burglary, and robbery with violence were all prominent examples. In the initial decades of the nineteenth century, cases where defendants were charged with an indictable offense could not be resolved by the magistrates. Following a preliminary hearing in the police court, where the charges were read and the evidence summarized, they had to be committed for trial ("remanded") in a higher court such as the Assizes, Quarter Sessions, or (most commonly) the Central Criminal Court (i.e. The Old Bailey).[53] And yet, despite this stipulation, by the prewar decades, more than three-quarters of all defendants charged with indictable offenses would be tried summarily.[54] Among the most common indictable offenses dealt with in this manner were assault, larceny, and malicious damage. This was possible because successive reforms from the 1820s onwards permitted an increasingly wide array of offenses to be tried summarily if the defendant consented.

These circumstances gave defendants a considerable amount of leeway to determine, in the broadest strokes, their own potential fate when charged with an indictable offense. Faced with the choice of either a longer sojourn in prison and the possibility of much heavier punishment in a jury trial, or a speedy summary trial with a much milder range of consequences upon conviction, small wonder that so many defendants opted for the latter.[55] Considering the expense of long-term, pretrial imprisonment and jury proceedings, the flexibility afforded by summary justice found favor with magistrates, legislators, and judicial reformers alike. From the perspective of courtroom culture in London, the steady shift of prosecutions for indictable crimes from jury trials to summary proceedings increased the significance of public

[53] Ibid., 47.

[54] 80% from 1911 to 1913, by V. A. C. Gatrell's estimate. V. A. C. Gatrell, "The Decline of Theft and Violence in Victorian and Edwardian England," in V. A. C. Gatrell, Bruce Lenman, and Geoffrey Parker, eds., *Crime and the Law: The Social History of Crime in Western Europe since 1500* (London: Europa Publications, 1980), 274.

[55] The list of indictable offenses that, by consent of the defendant, could be tried summarily continued to grow across the first half of the twentieth century. Giles, *Criminal Law*, 92.

interactions between defendants and police-court magistrates in the public discourse on crime and punishment. By the early twentieth century, this trend was visible enough to attract the attention of legal experts across the Atlantic, prompting one prominent American scholar of jurisprudence to assert that the rise of summary jurisdiction was the single most significant change to occur thus far in modern English criminal law administration.[56]

The increasing popularity of the courts for the resolution of minor local conflicts and the implications of their growing visibility in the community were both major issues in the first official inquiry into law and policing that followed the Metropolitan Police Act 1829. Appearing before a parliamentary committee in 1833, magistrates and police officials argued that the establishment of the Metropolitan Police and the hiring of full-time constables who worked under police superintendents rather than the authority of the magistrates had not fundamentally transformed the daily operation of the courts. Rather, according to the Commissioners of the Metropolitan Police, the local population was employing this new policing infrastructure largely as a mechanism for engaging the magistrates' courts, and was doing so for the purposes that had taken them directly to the courts themselves in the past.[57] Since police station houses were open for longer hours than the courts were, and constables were much more frequently at hand, the number of individuals attempting to "bring a charge" had increased substantially. The statistical information available, albeit incomplete, attested this continued importance of private initiative in triggering police involvement.[58] In 1830s Lambeth, private citizens brought roughly 20 percent of all charges that resulted in a prisoner being taken into custody, the balance being made up largely of charges brought by constables, and a smaller proportion of those brought by representatives of various municipal bodies. In 1833, the former

[56] Pendleton Howard, "The Rise of Summary Jurisdiction in English Criminal Law Administration," *California Law Review* 19, no. 5 (Jul. 1931), 486.

[57] Testimony of Lt. Col. Rowan and R. Mayne, July 2, 1833, *Report from the Select Committee on the Police of the Metropolis 1834*, 302.

[58] In contrast, Bruce Smith has argued that public officials in the Old Bailey were playing an increasingly important role in prosecution during this period. Bruce Smith, "The Myth of Private Prosecution in England, 1750–1850," in Drew Gray, ed., *Crime, Prosecution and Social Relations: The Summary Courts of the City of London in the Late Eighteenth Century* (Basingstoke: Palgrave Macmillan, 2009), 153.

("private" charges) amounted to roughly thirty-five cases a month.[59] Although hardly a massive caseload overall, this number did not include attempts to bring charges that were refused, charges brought that did not result in detention of the accused, or charges brought in the sixteen other police divisions. Nor was one of the most common circumstances of police involvement through private initiative, the number of people detained on charges brought by a constable *after* the latter's intervention was requested by the alleged victim (e.g. by fetching a constable), specifically recorded.[60]

In the midst of this increased usage, C. K. Murray, a magistrate at the busy Union Hall court, argued that the needs of working-class petitioners must take precedence over other considerations. If the law did not accommodate their current practices, it must be changed to suit. In this context, Murray insisted, the magistrates must be prepared to inhabit a diverse and influential set of roles. "The value of his office does not consist more in the strict legal performance of his judicial duties," he asserted, "than in his exercise of sound discretion, and in the considerate application of his feelings of humanity, as an advisor, an arbitrator, and a mediator."[61] Here, the magistrate offered a formulation of the local courtroom's role similar to that articulated by the Fieldings in the middle of the eighteenth century. It was a mechanism for influencing the morality and behavior of the community, certainly through the punishment of specific transgressions, but more so through the judicious application of a magistrate's experience and authority in a wide variety of capacities. According to Murray and others, this vision of the courtroom's function, the magistrate's role, and the relationship of both to the people in the community was not merely imposed upon a recalcitrant populace with no morality of their own and no agency in the process. Murray and his colleagues recognized that those who used local courtrooms brought to them their own ideals and opinions on matters legal and moral, ideals that had to be accommodated both visibly and substantively if the courts were

59 Letter from James Traill, Magistrate of the Union Hall court, *Report from the Select Committee on Metropolis Police Offices 1838* [hereafter *Metropolis Police Offices 1838*], 217.

60 For the prevalence of this, see Chapter 6.

61 Testimony of C. K. Murray, Magistrate of the Union Hall Police Office, June 4, 1833, *Report from Select Committee on Metropolitan Police 1833* [hereafter *Metropolitan Police 1833*], 189.

to maintain any degree of influence at all.[62] The courtroom itself, insisted the magistrates, was where this accommodation must take place.

This could all be read as nothing more than the magistrates' attempt to protect their own authority and discretion in the midst of encroachment by the powerful new institution of legal enforcement, the Metropolitan Police. More broadly, it could be interpreted in the same way that historians have previously assessed the operation of daily justice in the eighteenth and early nineteenth century. Scholars working in this context have argued that the *appearance* of being a forum open to the working class was merely a tool to further the impression of the rule of law and to secure the cooperation of the majority with a system that maintained the social status quo and protected the power and property of the elite.[63] And the need to preserve their discretion over the daily administration of justice was a strong motivator for the magistrates' statements. Nonetheless, there was more at stake here than who had the authority to determine what charges were legitimate and where the line was to be drawn between police initiative and magisterial oversight. In these discussions and those that followed, the meaning of "the public," justice, morality, and a host of other concepts central to Victorian society were being shaped and deployed either within the courtroom itself or through reference to the courtroom as the site of their composition. The timing of the public discussions came at a crucial period in the history of the Victorian state as it attempted to deal with the impetus for reform from a number of quarters, the need to maintain public order in Britain's growing cities, and concerns over the costs of government and the concurrent burden on ratepayers. The expansion of summary justice was an integral part of wider wave of law reform.[64]

[62] They arrived with a "sense of justice or shame," according to Murray. Ibid., 189. See also Testimony of R. E. Broughton, Magistrate of the Worship-Street Police Office, May 20, 1833, ibid., 116.

[63] John Brewer and John Styles, "Popular Attitudes to the Law in the Eighteenth Century," in Mike Fitzgerald, Gregor McLennan, and Jennie Pawson, eds., *Crime and Society: Readings in History and Theory* (London: Routledge, 1981), 32–35; Jennifer Davis, "A Poor Man's System of Justice: The London Police Courts in the Second Half of the Nineteenth Century," *The Historical Journal* 27 (1984), 315.

[64] Michael Lobban, "Old Wine in New Bottles': The Concept and Practice of Law Reform, *c.*1780–1830," in Arthur Burns and Joanna Innes, eds., *Rethinking the Age of Reform: Britain 1780–1850* (Cambridge: Cambridge University Press, 2003), 133.

It coincided with a widening of the franchise, a move prompted, in part, by the desire on the part of the political elite for a Parliament that was more responsive to its constituency.[65] The 1830s also witnessed the rise of the Chartist movement and the demands by its adherents that the working-class receive a greater voice in their own governance. In the midst of debates over the role and responsiveness of the state, the magistrates' courts offered the benefits of being receptive to the needs of local clientele, adaptable to legal reforms and, despite the costs of expansion and operation, affordable on a per-case basis when compared to the more protracted proceedings of the higher courts.

Although magistrates were in the most advantageous position to define the courts' purpose in the years following the expansion of the system, the growing social and cultural role of their courtrooms was not merely imposed from above. The local users of these venues, through both direct action and the impact of their expectations and demands, were shaping their development as well. The significance of local agency in the courtroom was increasing in tandem with the legal power and range of matters with which they dealt. As frequent employers of the courts and keen observers of them, the local community was a key concern for the witnesses called by the parliamentary committees convened in 1837 and 1838 to inquire into the operation of summary justice in the metropolis. The impact of local initiative was particularly evident in magistrates' articulations of their roles. Although they retained the moralizing paternalism of their eighteen-century predecessors, community accountability and responsiveness to local demand was a much greater concern for them than it had been for the Fieldings and their immediate successors. The magistrates who testified in 1837 and 1838, like their colleagues who appeared in the 1833 committee proceedings, argued that their courts must set a moral example for their communities. But they also insisted that they were acutely answerable to those whom their courts served, and that the public's view of *justice* was constantly on their minds. This consideration, according to both witnesses and the committee members, who included Robert Peel himself, had to remain central in any reform of current practices in magistrates' courtrooms and of the laws themselves. The most serious and potentially controversial of the

65 Arthur Burns and Joanna Innes, "Introduction," ibid., 46.

changes under consideration were the extension of summary jurisdiction to cover a wide variety of lesser offenses, chief among them petty larceny; whether magistrates could preside singly, rather than in pairs (as was the current practice); and the overall merits of summary jurisdiction as compared to trial by jury. James Traill, a magistrate of the Union Hall court, whose testimony would be quoted extensively by the committee in their recommendations, was questioned closely on what, if any, objection there would be "in the public mind" to the extension of summary jurisdiction in cases where the accused party either pled guilty or consented to be tried in this manner. Traill was unequivocal in his response. For the magistrate, the central issue was not a legal one, but rather one of principle and the public perception of fairness.[66] Traill's colleagues were likewise questioned repeatedly on issues of "the public feeling" and what the general response would be to proposed changes. They replied, to almost every inquiry, that the public favored the proposed extensions of summary jurisdiction and that such changes would bring the authority of the courts more in line with the expectations of those who brought cases or were tried there.

Although the focus on public perceptions of justice and the broad roles of the magistrates' courts were a common thread in parliamentary inquiries across the decade, on several important points, the testimony magistrates offered in 1837 formed a striking contrast with the discussions of policing that had taken place in 1833. The first of these contrasts concerned the role of class in the administration of criminal justice. The 1833 witness testimony on policing emphasized the dangers to publicorder posed by the immoral and indigent elements of the lower orders. This concern prompted extensive discussion of how to best prosecute juvenile delinquency, drunk and disorderly behavior, and various dimensions of vagrancy (e.g. begging and sleeping out of doors).[67] The claims by police

66 Testimony of James Traill, Magistrate of the Union Hall Police Office, *Report from the Select Committee on Metropolis Police Offices 1837* [hereafter *Metropolis Police Offices 1837*], 39.

67 The identification of "juvenile delinquency" as a key issue in English law and culture has prompted considerable historical debate. John Gillis, "The Evolution of Juvenile Delinquency in England, 1890–1914," *Past and Present* 67, no. 1 (1975), 96–126; Peter King, "The Rise of Juvenile Delinquency in England, 1780–1840: Changing Patterns of Perception and Prosecution," *Past and Present* 160 (Aug. 1998), 116–66; Heather Shore, *Artful Dodgers: Youth and Crime in Early Nineteenth-Century London* (Rochester: Royal Historical Society, 1999).

officials that these were escalating problems in the metropolis were supported with the growing panoply of statistical evidence available on arrests, prosecutions, and imprisonment.[68] In police efforts to address these issues, a moral hierarchy based on class was an explicit guiding principle – the poor were the problem, and therefore, to combat crime and disorder, efforts must be concentrated there.[69] This line of reasoning, that immorality among the working class nurtured crime, had been propounded in the eighteenth century by both John Fielding and Patrick Colquhoun. By the middle of the nineteenth century, it would evolve into the theory that a hardened "criminal class" embedded in this social stratum was to blame for much of the serious crime in the metropolis.[70] In this formulation, the working class was divided into the "rough" and the "respectable." The latter were largely law-abiding, while the former were an inherently immoral and disorderly group who required policing to prevent more dangerous disorder and a firm, authoritative judicial system that clearly delineated specific punishments for specific acts. A combination of policing and punishment, according to policymakers, would both keep the criminal class in check and help foster moral accountability among the working class more generally.[71] The public discourse on crime and responses to it in this period has prompted modern historians of the "social control" model to integrate the expansion of summary justice into the larger "civilizing mission" of Victorian social reform.[72] Chief among these interpretations has been V. A. C. Gatrell's argument that the new regimes of law and policing constituted a "disciplinary state" that "was not only an earlier but a more

[68] King, *Crime and Law in England*, 73. See also Margaret May, "Innocence and Experience: the Evolution of the Concept of Juvenile Delinquency in the Mid-Nineteenth Century," *Victorian Studies* 17 (Sep. 1973), 7–29; Susan Magarey, "The Invention of Juvenile Delinquency in Early Nineteenth-Century England," *Labour History* 34 (May 1978), 11–27.

[69] For a more detailed assessment of the Metropolitan Police's role in social control and moral reform, see Robert Storch, "The Policeman as Domestic Missionary: Urban Discipline and Popular Culture in Northern England, 1850–1880," *Journal of Social History* IX (1975–76), 481–509.

[70] Clive Emsley, *Crime and Society in England, 1750–1900* (London and New York: Longman, 1986), 54–57.

[71] Martin J. Wiener, *Reconstructing the Criminal: Culture, Law, and Policy in England, 1834–1914* (Cambridge: Cambridge University Press, 1990), 61–67.

[72] Barry Godfrey, *Crime in England, 1880–1945: The Rough and the Criminal, the Police and the Incarcerated* (Abingdon and New York: Routledge, 2014), 34.

power powerful presence in working-class life" than the institutions of reform that followed by mid-century would become.[73] Recent historiography, in contrast, has posited a more ambiguous relationship between judicial institutions and the working class in the Victorian period, despite the apparent hostility of the latter towards the police. In this revised assessment, as the reach of the criminal law extended into more social spaces, its moral power to stigmatize lessened.[74] The increase in regulatory offenses, which could fall on the shoulders of rough and respectable alike, meant that a courtroom appearance was hardly a reliable indicator of membership in the former, regardless of the sustained association between the police courts and general moral turpitude. The increasing numbers of working-class petitioners to the court, particularly for assault cases, also undermines any argument that magistrates' justice was imposed from above with the goal of social control.[75]

Although these developments were more characteristic of the second half of the nineteenth century, examining the debates over summary justice in the 1830s can help clarify why the relationship between the working class and the magistrates' courts evolved along its own unique path. Mid-Victorian magistrates were certainly committed to the moral uplift of their charges, but they lacked the Progressive zeal and self-assurance that would animate subsequent cohorts of municipal reformers. London magistrates were acutely aware that the expansion of summary justice was an experiment that could fail for lack of popular support and community engagement. One clear path to success that they identified was the expansion of voluntary court usage to a broad swath of the working class. In this, distinctions of "rough" and "respectable" were less important than a willingness to employ the courts and to respect their authority and the magistrates' decisions. Both this awareness of their courts' entanglement with the local community and their, at best, ambivalent relationship with Progressivism helps explain why magistrates would clash so frequently with the agents of social reform in final decades of the century. Whereas the latter predicated much of their effort on the assumption that their targets required

[73] Gatrell, "Crime, Authority, and the Policeman-State," 259.

[74] Wiener, *Reconstructing the Criminal*, 263.

[75] Jennifer Davis, "Prosecutions and Their Context: The Use of the Criminal Law in Later Nineteenth-Century London," in Douglas Hay and Francis Snyder, eds., *Policing and Prosecution in Britain* (Oxford: Clarendon, 1989), 417.

coercive intervention to achieve any moral or social progress, magistrates asserted from early on the working class already possessed a sense of justice that could be harnessed for mutual benefit through careful cultivation in local courtrooms.

This picture of the evolving relationship between local courtrooms and the working class accords with the one presented by many magistrates and other judicial authorities to Parliament in the late 1830s. For them, the local working-class community formed an essential aspect of the public to whom they were accountable in their venues. Their inherent "sense of justice or shame," as one prominent magistrate put it, was integral to the operation of the expanding metropolitan court system.[76] Maintaining public order and moral development was not primarily a matter of policing and punishment, but of moving the conduct and resolution of conflicts from the street to the courtroom, fostering respect for courts and magistrates in the eyes of the community, and bringing the decisions made therein closer to accord with popular ideas of justice and fairness. The extension of summary jurisdiction, explained William Empson, a professor of law and one of the first witnesses called by the 1838 committee, was suited to meet popular needs because it was both affordable and speedy.[77] Securing public approval was also essential, he asserted, because the law "will not work well if there is a strong prejudice against it."[78] The key to effectiveness, contrary to the advice of police officials and the Home Office, was not more reliable convictions accompanied by stern and consistent sentences, but rather a lighter sentencing policy. In Empson's arguments, trust in the mechanisms of justice would come from bringing courtroom decisions in line with popular expectations, rather than through strict adherence to formal statutes or an abstract vision of morality and order. This accountability to public opinion, and the necessity of accommodating the public's vision of justice, was stated even more plainly by Sir Peter Laurie, a City magistrate, who told the committee simply that "the public are the jury."[79]

[76] Testimony of C. K. Murray, Magistrate of the Union Hall Police Office, June 4, 1833, *Metropolitan Police* 1833, 189.

[77] Testimony of William Empson, Professor of Law at East India College, December 7, 1837, *Metropolis Police Offices* 1838, 16.

[78] Ibid., 17.

[79] Testimony of Peter Laurie, Magistrate of Mansion-House and Guildhall, March 19, 1838, ibid., 122.

Was this approach merely an attempt by magistrates to preserve their autonomy and co-opt the working class into the fiction of a legal system that accommodated some of their needs (as defined by the magistrates themselves)? There are good reasons to believe otherwise. Magistrates were acutely aware that they were being observed and reported on, and were sensitive to public opinion. Their strongest concern, however, was with a newspaper-reading audience that was largely middle and upper class. This cohort was most closely informed about the magistrates and their affairs both within the court and beyond it, and wielded influence in municipal affairs thanks to their income and social position. Magistrates, given their public prominence, could hardly avoid entanglement in municipal politics, with all the attendant risks. They were appointed by the Home Secretary and, should they fall out of favor, they could be removed by him as well. Such instances were rare, but at no time was the hazard more obvious than in June 1837, while testimony was still underway for the first of the two parliamentary commissions discussed above. It was then that the Hatton Garden magistrate Allan S. Laing became embroiled in a scandal over a physical confrontation with well-connected doctor (Paine) on the Strand.[80] The messy affair finally concluded in January of 1838, when, shortly before the trial was due to commence, Laing agreed to pay Paine £50 and cover his legal costs.[81] Although it was far from certain that a jury would have found for the complainant, and Laing claimed he had been a deliberate target of Paine's antipathy from the outset, the damage to the magistrate's public reputation was irreparable. Laing's vituperation against defendants was already well-known around London, and he had done little to further the positive image of his profession. This was, after all, a magistrate whose vitriol and harsh treatment of defendants had earned him public opprobrium in the press and portrayal as an exemplar of judicial tyranny in Parliament. In 1832, one newspaper report of Laing's courtroom bullying had even prompted the "Great Liberator," Irish MP Daniel O'Connell, to raise the issue before the House of

80 Allyson May, "Fiction or 'Faction'? Literary Representations of the Early Nineteenth-Century Criminal Courtroom," in David Lemmings, ed., *Crime, Courtrooms and the Public Sphere in Britain, 1700–1850* (London: Ashgate, 2012), 175.

81 *The Times*, January 16, 1838, 4.

Commons.[82] Adding further fuel to the flame of scandal was the publication, in the July 1837 issue of *Bentley's Miscellany*, of Charles Dickens's *Oliver Twist* chapter introducing Laing's literary *doppelganger*, the infamous "Mr. Fang." This was the only known occasion on which Dickens explicitly modeled a character on a real-life individual.[83] As he had on previous occasions, despite this raft of negative commentary and growing public clamor, Laing remained steadfast in his declarations that he was beyond reproach. Lord John Russell, the Home Secretary, was unconvinced. He removed Laing from the magistracy, and the unabridged correspondence on the issue was subsequently published in *The Times*.

The dismissal of Laing was a nadir in the magistrates' campaign to improve their public image. There could have been no better object lesson on the precipitous use of judicial authority or the consequences of a sustained reputation for spleen in the courtroom.[84] Laing may have been the first metropolitan magistrate brought down by scandal and negative press, but he would not be the last.[85] The timing could not have been worse, since his removal coincided with the expansion of press coverage, Parliament's consideration of widening the courts' civil and criminal authority, and their prospective authorization of magistrates to preside alone (rather than in pairs, as had been the established practice). Small wonder, then, that the magistrates who testified before successive parliamentary committees were eager to emphasize their responsiveness to public opinion, their concern with working-class grievances, their accommodation with popular notions of justice and fairness, and their positive engagement in the roles of "an advisor, an arbitrator, and a mediator" in their local communities.

Magistrates' apprehension about the opinions of newspaper readers formed a compelling backdrop to the more pressing concern of their standing in their respective communities, where the impact of local opinion was more immediately visible. Their attention to the local

[82] House of Commons, Jun. 15, 1832, *Hansard's Parliamentary Debates*, Third Series, vol. XIII (London, 1833), 738.

[83] John Forster, *The Life of Charles Dickens*, vol. III (Boston, 1876), 25.

[84] See also the brief discussion of Laing in Marjorie Jones, *Justice and Journalism* (London: Barry Rose, 1974), 27–28.

[85] According to the journalist James Greenwood, this was the first instance in recent memory of a London magistrate being removed from office (James Grant, *Sketches in London* (1838), 195). Joan Lock, *Tales from Bow Street* (London: Hale, 1982), 94–99.

reputation of their courts emerged from the increasing integration of their courtrooms with everyday affairs rather than as a response to the political power of their most common court clientele. The ranks of workers, artisans, and shopkeepers, still lacking the franchise, could not directly influence municipal politics. Both popular literacy and the press that catered to it and would shape public opinion in these quarters remained decades in the future. This did not mean, however, that their views could be ignored if public order was the goal. Amidst increasing popular political discontent, in a city known for social tension and disorder, and with some of the busiest courts located in what were, historically, the most turbulent districts, magistrates were anything but dismissive of working-class needs and expectations with regards to their local courtrooms.[86] In order to support this distinct view of local, consensual justice that emphasized the working-class employment of, and respect for, the courtroom, magistrates offered alternative statistics to those measuring arrests, prosecutions, and convictions. The 1837 committee drew particular attention to those provided by Mr. James Traill of the Union Hall court, who estimated that there were 12,000–15,000 applications each year for matters over which the courts currently had no jurisdiction.[87] Chief among them were "unlawful detention of property," "masters and servants," "abusive language or insulting behavior," "injuries by the bite of dogs," and "complaints between landlords, tenants and [pawn] brokers." Traill supported his claim with the unofficial record he had kept of such complaints in his own court across a three-month period. Even taking into account the hazy nature of the magistrate's extrapolations from his monthly totals, the implied scale of local demand for the courts' services in these instances was staggering.[88] They exceeded, by a significant margin, many of the most common causes of police charges. In

86 For how such discontent played out in the metropolitan context in this period, see David Goodway, *London Chartism, 1838–1848* (Cambridge: Cambridge University Press, 1982), 12–53; Edward Royle, *Chartism*, 3rd ed. (London: Routledge, 1996 [1980]), 23–30.

87 *Metropolis Police Offices 1838*, 28.

88 Traill arrived at this total by calculating that each of the three magistrates at Union Hall received between 200 and 800 such applications yearly, and that his court, estimating by its comparative number of trials to others in the metropolis (along with Worship Street, it was one of the most-used), encompassed between a fifth and a sixth of the total business conducted by all nine courts each year (Letter from James Trail, *Metropolis Police Offices 1838*, 217).

comparison to Traill's estimate of 12,000–15,000 applications annually by working-class petitioners, there were just over 3,100 arrests for disorderly prostitution in the metropolis and just under 4,000 for vagrancy in 1837.[89] The case made by C. K. Murray in 1834, Traill in 1837, and by their colleagues throughout the 1830s found a receptive audience in the 1838 committee. The latter argued vociferously that the authority of the magistrates' courts must encompass the multitude of small grievances brought by plaintiffs of modest means. In this, they repeated with even greater urgency the call of the 1837 committee to introduce "that which has long been required in this country . . . a system of poor man's justice."[90] They also affirmed the crucial role that the magistrates' courts had played, and would continue to, in the lives, minds, and moral compasses of the common people. It was essential that these venues address the profound need for affordable justice, and that they fulfill the absolute requirement of "good government" to protect the "civil rights" of the lower classes.[91] Failure to do so, the committee asserted, would undermine the moral legitimacy of the state and threaten the very stability of the nation.

Although magistrates' desire to co-opt their local communities into their vision of law and order was evident, there were other, equally powerful dynamics at work. Members of the 1838 Committee, presenting their report just a few weeks after the first publication of *The People's Charter*, put their recommendations in a particularly dire context by employing the rising tide of Radicalism to justify the urgent

[89] *Returns from the Commissioners of Metropolitan Police*, excerpted in the *Journal of the Statistical Society of London*, vol. 1 (London: Charles Knight, 1839), 96–97.

[90] Appendix 1, *Metropolis Police Offices 1837*, 186. NB: this passage, ubiquitously cited in studies of nineteenth-century summary justice and criminal procedure, has been repeatedly mislabeled as appearing in "Appendix 5." No such appendix exists in the actual report, which contains only three appendices. Appendix 1, where it does appear, consists of the specific recommendations made by the committee, and is divided into "proposed clauses" and "reasons for clauses." The longer section in which this passage appeared stands out because it is the sole section that does not appear in this format, and is offered rather as a context for the five proposed clauses that followed, which were expressly aimed at facilitating "a great part of the community" in "obtaining redress for many petty grievances which, though trifling in value of money, are of vital importance to a poor man" (ibid., 185). The cases specifically enumerated were those dealing with landlords and tenants, willful damage to property, unlawful detention of goods, disputes between masters and servants, and injuries incurred by dog bites.

[91] *Metropolis Police Offices 1838*, 28.

need for reform.[92] Speaking ominously of alienation, disaffection, and discontent, they elevated the police courts from legal venues to locales "closely allied with the happiness and morality" of an entire class.[93] In their arguments, the much-needed expansion of these courts' purview to define and dispense justice provided an opportunity to reshape the relationship of the working class to the law, to the courtrooms in which it was executed, and to the nation whose stability rested upon both. By accommodating their demands for accessible justice and recompense in a multitude of small matters, they could be shown that the local magistrate's court was a far better resort than taking "the law into their own hands."[94] The latter often led, through "penal consequences or litigation, to the ruin of their property or their prospects."[95] The assumption was that working-class men and women would accept both the rule of law and the authority of courtrooms in their daily life, and that the moral standards of the magistrates would spread accordingly. As subsequent chapters will discuss, however, this would prove a two-way street. Just as the demands and expectations of the local community had shaped the reform of the courts and the expansion of summary justice from the outset, their vision of justice, morality, and the courtrooms' roles would continue to exert a powerful influence on courtroom practice in the decades that followed. So, too, would the threat of public disorder.

With the case for reform so convincingly made, Parliament was quick to respond. The Metropolitan Police Act and the Metropolitan Police Courts Act, both passed in August 1839, implemented almost all of the major changes advocated by the 1837 and 1838 committees.[96] These statutes authorized the magistrates, sitting singly, to give summary judgments in a broad variety of civil and criminal issues, including assaults, willful damage, prostitution, unlawful detention of goods, insulting or threatening words, illegal pawning, furious (i.e.

[92] These concerns, much evident among the propertied classes, had been instrumental in animating the earlier overhaul of policing in the metropolis orchestrated by Robert Peel in 1829. Philips, "A New Engine," 182–83.

[93] Similar arguments were being made by reformers with regards to the prosecution of criminal offenses in the higher courts as well. Randall McGowen, "Images of Justice and Reform of the Criminal Law in Early Nineteenth-Century England," *Buffalo Law Review* 32, no. 1 (1983), 113.

[94] *Metropolis Police Offices 1838*, 28. [95] Ibid.

[96] 2 & 3 Vict. c. 47 and 71, respectively.

reckless) driving, drunk and disorderly behavior, loitering, and dog bites. They also widened magistrates' discretion to issue summonses and warrants based on the accounts of complainants, and to release on their own recognizance those taken into custody by constables, with or without sureties for their subsequent appearance to stand trial. In addition, the Metropolitan Police Court Act 1839 delineated the formal parameters for the courts' personnel and practice. It established the magistrates as a professional class to be drawn from the cohort of experienced barristers, with a salary befitting their status (£1,200 per annum).[97] In the decades that followed, the bench would fill with men of high professional standing who would enjoy a significant voice in the legal and political affairs of the metropolis.[98] The 1839 Act also set the standard hours of the courts operation (10 a.m.–5 p.m.) and provided for the retention of an administrative structure consisting of a receiver, and two clerks (chief and secondary) at each of the courts (paid £500 and £300 per annum, respectively). Finally, by standardizing the fees for the most common court actions, the Act made summary justice affordable if not to all, then to a much wider array of would-be participants. The cost of a summons to court was fixed at two shillings, as was that of a warrant and of a recognizance to keep the peace or for good behavior.[99]

The Metropolitan Police Act 1839 also significantly enhanced the powers of the police, most especially by granting them authority to arrest, without a warrant, anyone they personally witnessed committing a wide array of common offenses (including the aforementioned insulting or threatening words, public prostitution, and furious driving). Beyond that, they could take into custody "all loose, idle, and disorderly Persons whom he shall find disturbing the public Peace, or whom he shall have good cause to suspect of having committed or being about to commit any Felony, Misdemeanour, or Breach of the Peace."[100] Much hay has been

[97] Solicitors would not become eligible as candidates until more than a century later. J. R. Spencer, ed. *Jackson's Machinery of Justice*, 6th ed. (Cambridge: Cambridge University Press, 1972), 232.

[98] Davis, "Poor Man's System," 311.

[99] The fee for a recognizance to appear before a magistrate was set slightly higher, at two shillings and sixpence.

[100] An Act for Further Improving the Police in and Near the Metropolis 1839, 2 & 3 Vict. c. 41 (aka the "Metropolitan Police Act 1839"), 516.

made of the latter in previous analyses of the growth of Metropolitan Police authority, but the magistrates' courts remained the lynchpin of the system, as policemen quickly learned. In the case of "disorderly persons," for example, after a brief apex from 1840 to 1843, in which arrests exceeded 12,000 yearly, the numbers dropped rapidly to under 5,500 by 1844.[101] The new contingent of professional magistrates ensured high discharge rates for these and other social or moral crimes, serving as a brake on more aggressive policing.[102] For magistrates keen to maintain an image of a court that was not wholly unsympathetic to the needs of working-class residents, it was a sensible move. The range of common activities forbidden by the 1839 was so impractical that it prompted the law's public mockery in two 1841 George Cruikshank cartoons (see Figs. 1 and 2). Whether the very small police force of mid-Victorian London could have ever effectively policed such ubiquitous practices remains a matter of considerable debate.[103]

Neither the frequency with which those of modest means employed the courts, nor the magistrates' strong emphasis on the influence of "the public" and the need to accommodate working-class views of justice, nor the 1838 committee's elevation of the courts as a locale where the relationship between the working class and the state could be defined, nor the passage of the 1839 Act directly contradict the widely accepted historical interpretations of metropolitan justice and society in the 1830s. These either posit a new Metropolitan Police that was coercive in its methods and keen on moral regulation (with varying degrees of success), or portray magistrates as committed to maintaining social status quo by winning working-class acceptance of the law.[104] These

101 Stephen Inwood, "Policing London's Morals: The Metropolitan Police and Popular Culture, 1829–1850," *London Journal* 15, no. 2 (1990), 136. This highpoint coincided with the depression of 1842. The decline that followed tracked with the ebbing of the first wave of Chartist demonstrations.

102 Ibid., 143. 103 Inwood, "Policing London's Morals," 129–30.

104 See Gatrell, "Crime, Authority, and the Policeman-State," 282–84 and Stefan Petrow, *Policing Morals: The Metropolitan Police and the Home Office, 1870–1914* (New York: Clarendon Press, 1994) for the former; and Davis, "Poor Man's System," 315 for the latter. This second argument suggests continuity between the ideological function of eighteenth-century criminal justice and its nineteenth-century developments (see John Brewer and John Styles, eds., *An Ungovernable People: The English and Their Law in the Seventeenth and Eighteenth Centuries* (New Brunswick: Rutgers University Press, 1980), 35).

FIGURE 1.1 "Commentary upon the late 'New Police Act.'" George Cruikshank, 1841 (*George Cruikshank Collected Plates*, vol. II: *Collection of Prints from Drawings by George Cruikshank c.1841–1843, Nos. 2130–2239*. ISG AF741.942 CRU. *George Cruikshank's Omnibus* (1842). Courtesy of the Guildhall Library.)

FIGURE 1.2 "Commentary upon the 'New Police Act'" (no. 2). George Cruikshank, 1841 (*George Cruikshank Collected Plates*, vol. II: *Collection of Prints from Drawings by George Cruikshank c.1841–1843, Nos. 2130–2239.* ISG AF741.942 CRU. *George Cruikshank's Omnibus* (1842). Courtesy of the Guildhall Library.)

latter interpretations are compatible with a process of expansion and reform that took careful account of public opinion, local demand, and popular expectations. The debates and reforms of the 1830s nonetheless reveal important divergences between magistrates and the prevailing attitudes of the municipal institutions that would develop in subsequent decades. The first, discussed earlier, was magistrates' belief that the popular vision of justice and their own views of law and order had be reconciled if the expanded police-court system was to survive the harsh light of public scrutiny. The magistrates had to be seen as stern and impartial enforcers of law and order to justify the costs of their venues and satisfy the demands of judicial reformers. This prioritization of effectiveness and value would be shared with late Victorian municipal bodies such as the London School Board and the London County Council. The latter, as "experiments" in governance, would be much more subject to the vagaries of urban politics than magistrates were, and would face the daunting task of having to satisfy both Liberals and Conservatives.[105] In contrast with the municipal institutions whose regulatory prosecutions they handled, however, magistrates would face increasing pressure from below as well as from above. Tradition, practicality, and their overriding concern with reputation all required them to maintain an image as sympathetic purveyors of fair and speedy justice in line with the popular expectations of their local clientele. The public character of summary proceedings was therefore of paramount importance to their continued support from both their superiors and their communities, since it was through the lens of the courtroom that the magistrates would themselves be judged by an increasingly broad array of observers and critics. Thanks to the growth of newspaper coverage and general interest in the courts, this audience now included a public comprised, at least in part, of the local community whose participation in and respect for the courts were essential to their success.

Observation and accountability were also integral to the second important difference between the magistrates' courts and other

[105] John Davis, *Reforming London: The London Government Problem, 1855–1900* (Cambridge: Clarendon Press, 1988).

institutions of Victorian governance – the courtroom itself. More so than any other state entity at the time, magistrates' courtrooms operated simultaneously in the social space of the neighborhood, the legal space of statutes, and the cultural space of public observation and newspaper portrayals. Other elements of metropolitan governance only operated in the third context to a limited degree, and even then most commonly by bringing cases to the courts. Some level of negotiation was almost always possible between reformers, both state and private, and their charges, but it was very rarely public and when it was, the courtroom was the typical venue.[106] The character of magistrates' justice, on the other hand, required, in principle if not always in practice, that *all* voices must be heard and acknowledged, even if they were hardly accorded equal weight in either the final legal judgments or the public's assessment.[107] As such, local courtrooms were uniquely suited to reconciling (or exacerbating) competing ideas about of justice and morality, whether they were held by magistrates, local petitioners, police, or other agents of the Victorian state. They fulfilled this function both in the immediacy of courtroom interactions and subsequently in the construction of official and unofficial courtroom stories. Courtroom events, whether in court records, newspaper accounts, parliamentary debates and inquiries, or personal memoirs, were continually reconstituted as *narratives* of justice that helped define the relationship between law and morality and between the state and the individual for an increasingly literate and, by century's end, enfranchised population. The coercive elements of London's new police notwithstanding, the relationship that evolved between courtrooms and local communities was thus characterized by the integration of competing ideals and demands. The local clientele, both as individual court-users and a more nebulous "public," exerted a significant influence on the evolution of the police courts, and their sense of justice and expectations of courtroom redress were keenly observed and incorporated by legal reformers in their policies and by local magistrates in their practices.

In these courts, as the committee of 1838 had insisted, the relationship between the "lower orders" and the state was being personally

[106] On private negotiations between paupers and Poor Law Guardians, see Lynn Hollen Lees, *The Solidarities of Strangers: The English Poor Laws and the People, 1700–1948* (Cambridge. Cambridge University Press, 1998), 166–69.

[107] Magistrates then, as now, routinely cut off defendants and plaintiffs when their speech was deemed irrelevant.

experienced and publicly fashioned.[108] They were the very stuff of justice for shopkeepers, artisans, and laborers. In this light, we can revise the statement made by V. A. C. Gatrell in his seminal 1990 article on the "policeman-state." In Victorian London, it was often specifically through the magistrates' courts that "the expansion and meaning of the modern state was first made palpable" to the lower classes.[109]

"Justice Doled Out in Small Parcels": Portrayals of Local Courtrooms and Their Communities in the Mid-Victorian Period

Given the magistrates' courts' key roles in mediating between local communities and the expanding state, it is vital to determine what meanings were communicated through their activities, as well as how and by whom they were constructed and construed. The most revealing insights were not to be found in the realm of parliamentary committees and legal reform but rather in how courtrooms were portrayed in newspapers and literary media. The key relationship here was that between the local courtroom as a conceptual space in metropolitan culture – as a publicly depicted stage on which the tension between the state and the individual played out and where the law was made manifest – and the concrete operation of the local courtroom as a space where individuals encountered the state on a daily basis. In this equation, the goals of those with legal authority to govern courtrooms and those with the cultural authority to portray them were often at cross-purposes. Even as reformers and legislators were, with magistrates' support, attempting to rationalize the law and through it, to foster public order and collective recognition of legal authority, journalistic accounts were promoting the dramatic and emotional dimensions of courtrooms.[110] This contrast between how

108 This was more recently asserted by Peter King with regards to the eighteenth century as well, "The Summary Courts and Social Relations in Eighteenth-Century England," *Past and Present* 183, no. 1 (2004), 128.

109 Gatrell, "Crime, Authority, and the Policeman-State," 259.

110 For the rationalization of criminal justice, see Emsley, *Crime and Society*, 157; Wiener, *Reconstructing the Criminal*, 64–67; R. McGowan, "The Image of Justice and Reform of the Criminal Law in Early Nineteenth-Century England," *Buffalo Law Review* 32 (1983), 89–125, 116. For the significance of emotion in the administration of capital punishment, see V. A. C. Gatrell, *The Hanging Tree: Execution and the English People* (Oxford: Oxford University Press, 1996), v–vii.

courts were portrayed and how they were being reformed, between depictions and experiences, would remain a central feature of courtroom culture well into the early twentieth century. It would be a source of frustration to magistrates and complainants alike, as courtroom accounts, over time, would reach an ever-wider audience and were far more comprehensible to the laymen than law and courtroom procedure were.[111]

The reforms of 1839 fed into the dramatization of courtroom events by making the decisions therein more immediate and crucial, and by incorporating into summary justice a much broader scope of behaviors. With the advent of cheap, summary jurisdiction over a wide range of issues, many more cases could be decided in a single sitting, by a lone magistrate in dialogue with the principals, and without legal representation or recourse to complex legal technicalities. The broad and informal adjudication of summary trials was easily translated into emotional and impressionistic tales for a public audience. The latter could assess "justice" in any given instance through loaded language and carefully selected dialogue rather than through the technical and procedural aspects of law, which were described sparsely, if at all. Despite the ongoing standardization of punishments, what happened every day in local courtrooms *besides the sentence* became less predictable and regularized as the types of cases and courtroom clientele diversified.[112] This combination of unpredictable dialogue, moral implications, and rich social detail made the police court a setting highly amenable to entertaining reconstruction in the burgeoning popular press. Scholars have consistently placed the rapid increase and broad dissemination of courtroom reporting in the context of perceptions of crime and its relation to popular morality, policing, and criminal policy.[113] That these stories were based largely on reporters' observation of police-court trials (and trials in the Old Bailey) has rarely been

[111] Magistrates, in their attempts to "rebuild respect for the law" in the 1830s and 1840s, played their own part as well in encouraging the hopes of working-class complainants that they would find justice in their local courtrooms. Hay, "The Criminal Prosecution in England and Its Historians," 10–11. See also King, *Crime, Justice, and Discretion*, 109.

[112] Weiner, *Reconstructing the Criminal*, 61.

[113] Most recently, one sees this approach in the SOLON volume of essays edited by Judith Rowbotham and Kim Stevenson, *Criminal Conversations: Victorian Crimes, Social Panic, and Moral Outrage* (Columbus: Ohio State University Press, 2005).

acknowledged. More importantly, no serious attention has been given to what this evolution reveals about the changing roles of local courtrooms in Victorian society and culture. It is crucial to recognize that the demand for courtrooms and the demand for their portrayals were related phenomena. Just as courtroom practice had expanded to accommodate a popular demand as framed by the magistrates, so too did the widespread portrayal of them adapt to popular demand as it was interpreted by courtroom reporters and newspaper editors.[114]

Seen through this relationship between operation and depiction, the picture of the courtrooms' evolution that emerges is one different from the focus on rising judicial and police authority that has predominated in historical interpretations of nineteenth-century summary justice. From this perspective, the portrayal of courtrooms, much like the initiation of criminal prosecutions, appears as an arena in which the ideals and authority of different groups, both elite and non-elite, have to be taken into historical account.[115] In contrast to their authority in the framing and execution of summary justice, magistrates and policymakers exercised very limited authority over the reporting of it. The authority of law was tangential in shaping these depictions – there is no indication that reporters frequenting the police courts were drawn from the legal profession, as those who penned stories of the higher courts for *The Times* sometimes were.[116] There were many instances, no doubt, where magistrates and reporters shared moral norms in their interpretations of courtroom events, norms held in common with middle-class newspaper readers as well. The idea of "respectability," a key issue in cases involving sexual and marital issues, had resonance across class boundaries, encompassing readers of the *Morning*

[114] Judith Rowbotham and Kim Stevenson, "Introduction," ibid., xxvi.

[115] Whether criminal law and summary jurisdiction served the interests of the property-holding elite or whether plebeians to could harness its power effectively and undermine elite authority in the process remains one of the most hotly contested issues among historians of criminal justice in the late eighteenth and nineteenth centuries. Bruce P. Smith, "English Criminal Justice Administration, 1650–1850: A Historiographic Essay," *Law and History Review* 25, no. 3, 609–15.

[116] Judith Rowbotham and Kim Stevenson, "Causing a Sensation," in Judith Rowbotham and Kim Stevenson, eds., *Behaving Badly: Social Panic and Moral Outrage – Victorian and Modern Parallels* (Aldershot, Hants, and Burlington, VA: Ashgate, 2003), 42.

Chronicle, *Lloyd's Weekly*, and *Cleave's* alike.[117] Beyond these shared norms, however, the commentary and criticism of magistrates, the selective reporting of cases, the diversity of issues covered, and the variety of papers in which they appeared all suggest that the possible interpretations of courtroom portrayals were indeed broad.[118] The combination of the considerable dialogue excerpted in these early court columns and their focus on privately initiated prosecutions also offered an image of the courtroom in which individual men and women, even those of the most modest means, played significant roles.

Whereas the cases were personally experienced by very few, these reports could be read by hundreds or even thousands of individual readers and shared, through the tradition of communal reading and recounting, with many more.[119] Examining, in these constructed accounts, who was given a voice and how this either illuminated or occluded the changing legal and social roles of the courts in their communities reveals much about the historical development of London courtrooms. From looking at these portrayals, we can also divine the general tenor of public discourse on the changing relationship between the state, the community, and the individual in early Victorian London. 1811–12 was an early milestone. It witnessed the *Morning Herald*'s inauguration of John Wight's Bow Street Police Court reports. Following the introduction of Wight's tales of farce and folly, sales of the *Herald* rose exponentially. According to one account, the paper became one of the most widely circulated of its time.[120]

117 Kim Stevenson, "The Respectability Imperative: A Golden Rule in Cases of Sexual Assault?" in Ian Inkster, Judith Rowbotham, and Colin Griffin, eds., *The Golden Age: Essays in British Social and Economic History, 1850–1870* (Aldershot and Burlington, VT: Ashgate, 2000), 237–48. Rowbotham and Stevenson, "Causing a Sensation," 38.

118 Peter King, "Newspaper Reporting and Attitudes to Crime and Justice in Late-Nineteenth- and Early-Twentieth-Century London," *Continuity and Change* 22, no. 1 (2007), 76.

119 For evidence of this latter practice, which had a long tradition, see Rosalind Crone, *Violent Victorians: Popular Entertainment in Nineteenth-Century London* (Manchester: Manchester University Press, 2012), 246; Shani D'Cruze, *Crimes of Outrage: Sex, Violence and Victorian Working Women* (Dekalb: Northern Illinois University Press, 1998), 177; Robert K. Webb, *Higher Education Quarterly* 12, no. 1 (Nov. 1957), 24–44.

120 The circulation of the paper reportedly rose from 600 before the introduction of Wight's columns to over 7,000 subsequently (J. Passmore, *Lives of the Illustrious (the Biographical Magazine)*, vol. 3 (London: Partridge, 1856), 110). Helen Hughes, in contrast, reports that the circulation of the paper merely tripled. Helen MacGill Hughes, *News and the Human Interest Story* (Chicago: University of

A collected edition of Wight's columns, published in 1824 under the title *Mornings at Bow Street*, was accompanied by illustrations from the realm's foremost caricaturist, George Cruikshank. *Mornings at Bow Street* was replete with the altercations of drunken working-class men, the comically exaggerated accents of Irish immigrants, fickle women and their hapless suitors, the misadventures of rakes and the petty presumptions of the lower-middle class. These stereotypes were conveyed and reinforced with a particular attention to dialect and idioms of speech, which often resulted in amusing contradictions or unintentional witticisms. Wight also asserted that the stories articulated basic truths about British society and, in particular, about its amusing side, which was "genuine only among the uncultivated."[121] These claims, that the courtroom scenes described were genuine, that they offered a window into the "real life" of the city, and that, in doing so, they revealed a fundamentally authentic picture of British society that was unavailable elsewhere, would remain the cornerstones of courtroom reporting throughout the century. Like the accounts penned by the Fieldings and Patrick Colquhoun, Wight's descriptions of the magistrates' courts were intrinsically linked with the author's view of their key role in the social and moral order of the metropolis.[122]

John Wight's success was profoundly influential in shaping the dynamics of the British newspaper industry, the character of future police-court journalism, and how comic newswriting was defined as a whole. His impact even extended to the USA, where editors of the burgeoning penny dailies of New York, Boston, and Philadelphia all inaugurated police-court columns as a central feature.[123] By the 1830s, newspaper coverage of the London police courts was substantial,

Chicago Press, 1940; reprinted New Brunswick: Transaction, 1981), 188. The *Herald* was the first paper for which Charles Dickens obtained regular work as a reporter.

121 John Wight, *Mornings at Bow Street: A Selection of the Most Humourous and Entertaining Reports Which Have Appeared in the Morning Herald* (London: Charles Baldwyn, 1824), iv.

122 Those who read his stories, Wight insisted, should "rightly appreciate the advantages they enjoy, and the value and importance of these particular institutions of their country." Ibid., v.

123 As new papers were founded in US cities, their staff often consisted of only three members, one of which was the police reporter (Hughes, *News and the Human Interest Story*, 10).

though still nowhere near as pervasive as it would become later in the century. The same papers that had devoted considerable column space to them in the 1820s – principally *The Times*, *Morning Post*, and *Morning Chronicle* – continued to do so, publishing thousands of individual case accounts across the course of the decade. Bow Street, Marlborough Street, and Hatton Garden remained the primary foci of courtroom reporting. The circumstances of the courts' most prominent coverage give further weight to the 1838 Committee's warning that the conduct of justice in the magistrates' courts had significant implications for popular politics and public attitudes towards law and governance. The only paper that devoted its front page to police-court coverage, *Cleave's Weekly Police Gazette*, was also the most popular of the penny newspapers that were so central to the articulation of Radicalism. After leaving his work on the *Poor Man's Guardian*, the London printer John Cleave would go on to found (along with William Lovett and Henry Hetherington), the London Working-Man's Association, and would play an active role in the National Charter Association, serving briefly as its treasurer.[124] In the turbulent political climate of the 1830s, the editorial staff he led during brief but prolific publication run of *Cleave's* (1834–36, circulation of 40,000 at its peak) vehemently declared their commitment to exposing any abuse of power by magistrates. This, they insisted, was one of the most significant roles occupied by the "public press," and it was most effective when such reporting was specific to the paper's own local community.[125]

Such interest in the courts and the doings of magistrates was hardly confined to the Radical penny press. As was clear from sustained coverage in *The Times* and a host of other newspapers, courtroom accounts maintained a wide appeal across the political and social spectrum. Shortly after *Cleave's* ceased its run, James Grant, a prolific columnist for the *Morning Chronicle,* published his fourth book. Like the *Chronicle*, which was a Whig paper, Grant's book, *Sketches in London* (1838), was aimed largely at a reading audience of the merchant and professional classes, along with the propertied elite.[126] In it, he devoted one of the most substantial chapters to the

[124] Goodway, *London Chartism*, 21–22. [125] *Cleave's*, May 14, 1836.
[126] Dennis Griffiths, ed., *The Encyclopedia of the British Press: 1422–1992* (London: Macmillan, 1992), 422.

London police courts. Throughout this period, the *Morning Herald* also continued to publish its popular courtroom accounts. In 1845, George Hodder, who had inherited John Wight's mantle as the *Herald*'s chronicler of the London police courts, published an expanded anthology of his columns under the title *Sketches of Life and Character Taken at the Police Court, Bow Street*. These three sources demonstrate the range of ways that police-court accounts could portray identity, morality, justice and the role of courtrooms in their local communities. Despite their contrasts, their content and structure reveal underlying congruencies in portraying everyday life among the lower end of the metropolitan social spectrum. In these depictions, courtroom accounts helped set the precedents for the next generation of urban journalists and social investigators, the "flâneurs." The writings of the latter would, in turn, publicly portray the laws and social policies that would preoccupy magistrates' and their courtrooms in the second half of the nineteenth century.

Cleave's offered police-court affairs front and center in every issue, and its coverage elevated the dialogue of courtroom participants to unprecedented prominence. The accounts therein gave much the same impression of the courtrooms' typical affairs as magistrates themselves had in their parliamentary testimony. Most of the cases described involved disputes over small amounts of property, petty larceny, minor assaults between familiars, landlord and tenant disputes, vagrancy, drunkenness, and workplace quarrels.[127] When the police were involved, it was almost always at the initiative of the principals, and the crimes were rarely serious ones. This had also been true of reports from the earlier decades of the nineteenth century that appeared in the *Chronicle*, *Times*, *Post*, and elsewhere. These similarities aside, the *Cleave's* accounts were distinct in several significant ways. For one thing, they were considerably longer and more detailed, often running to several paragraphs or substantial columns that took up half a page. Whereas earlier police-court columns had been largely narrative and, in the case of the *Herald*, highly stylized narrative at

[127] On the prosecution of vagrancy in this period, see M. J. D. Roberts, "Public and Private in Early Nineteenth-Century London: The Vagrant Act of 1822 and Its Enforcement," *Social History* 13, no. 3 (1988), 273–94.

that, at least half of the typical *Cleave's* courtroom account consisted of directly quoted testimony from the cases themselves. It was the voices of the principals, witnesses, and magistrates that constituted the bulk of the reports, and their words were clearly distinguished from the background narrative. Unlike Wight's original stories for the *Herald*, this dialogue was not colored with comically exaggerated accents or peppered with authorial *bon mots* attributed to the participants' (often unintentional) wit. Lastly, *Cleave's* occasionally provided the gallery's reaction to testimony in the form of single-word parenthetical statements (e.g. "A laugh").[128]

The courtroom accounts printed in *Cleave's* constituted one of the earliest sustained attempts in British culture to portray the voice and behavior of working-class men and women to a substantial reading audience not as caricature or satire, but in a more realistic fashion.[129] They were also one of few instances where the poorest of the London poor were publicly depicted as distinct individuals and identified by their real names. This might seem, at face value, to have been close to the authenticity claimed by John Wight in his Bow Street columns for the *Morning Herald*. In the sense that the *Cleave's* accounts presented courtroom events and dialogue in a relatively unadorned fashion and with minimal narrative embellishments, this was true. These stories were detailed but somewhat austere, they consisted largely of testimony, they recounted the types of trials that magistrates had claimed were common in this period, and they did not openly replicate the stereotypes of class, gender, and ethnicity that earlier courtroom columns had.[130] So, were the *Cleave's* stories what they implicitly claimed to be, accurate reports of what had happened in London courtrooms? This is an essential question to answer, since courtroom reporting in the mid-Victorian period, as it became a pervasive feature in local and national newspapers, would tend to follow the model set by *Cleave's*.

[128] The inclusion of this element likely originated with parliamentary reporting, which followed a similar convention.

[129] The other most prominent early example is, of course, Charles Dickens's writing, though it should be remembered that his training and original employment was as a courtroom reporter (Jones, *Justice and Journalism*, 25).

[130] They did occasionally include accents to indicate ethnicity or class, but not to the level of ridicule practiced by Wight.

The simple answer is no. They were certainly *more* representative than any type of courtroom reporting that had preceded them. But they remained thoroughly and deliberately constructed, although not to the same degree as the Fieldings' or Wight's accounts had been. *Cleave's* courtroom stories were condensed versions of events, the magistrates' voices often predominated over those of the principals and the witnesses, and certain groups of people and types of cases were drastically overrepresented. To read *Cleave's*, one would think the entire metropolis was overrun by begging widows, uproariously drunken Irishmen, con artists of various sorts, and litigious Jews. In contrast, the great number of requests for magistrates' intervention in minor everyday conflicts, which had been a key issue in parliamentary inquiries throughout the decade, received very limited coverage. The deliberate construction of these courtroom stories was amplified by the editor's addition of titles to each report. Such designations could range from the poignant (e.g. "Melancholy Case of Seduction") to the humorous (e.g. "A Dog-Day Rumpus") to the shocking and sensational (e.g. "Horrors of Gin Palaces").[131] Regardless of their diverse subject matter, they shared elements that made them suitable for presentation as dramas, comedies, tragedies, or morality tales. Which of those genres any given story belonged to was clearly indicated by the title, and often reinforced by the first line, which typically gave a physical description of the principle character. One could predict, from the title "The Poor Law Bill. Distressing Case" that what followed would be a sympathetic account of a vagrancy case. And the first line, which described "Bridget M'Carthy, a wretched-looking young female, with a squalid infant in her arms that appeared in a starving and dying state," removed all doubt.[132] Readers could rightly anticipate a demonstration of ethnic peculiarities from the stories titled "Paddy in a Dilemma" and "MacBeth in Trouble," an impression confirmed by the initial description of the first defendant as "a tall, slovenly-looking Irishman," and the second as an "ugly, big-whiskered Scotchman."[133] Though, happily, the mayhem was confined to mere drunkenness in the latter's version of "the Scottish

[131] These titles appeared in *Cleave's Weekly Police Gazette*, August 13, 20, and 30, 1836, respectively.

[132] *Cleave's*, July 30, 1836. [133] *Cleave's*, December 26, 1835 and May 14, 1836.

play." The titles, descriptions of the defendants, and selectively excerpted dialogue, in conjunction with the verdicts, all conveyed the impression that those who appeared in court were treated fairly. This fairness was to be assessed relative to the individual and their particular circumstances, as described in the column, and not to the technicalities of applicable statutes, which were never discussed. So the piteous young widow M'Carthy was let off with a warning, and "a repentant thief" who sought advice was given a shilling by the magistrates and some money by courtroom onlookers.[134] The defiant urchin who stole an egg and then lied about it, in contrast, was sent to the house of corrections for six weeks.[135]

The reports of trials that filled the front page of *Cleave's* were thus concerned not with law, but with *justice*. In this, they were of the same vein as magistrates' statements to Parliament. In the latter, magistrates had insisted that what mattered in the local community was justice far more so than the law, and the key to increasing the courtroom's influence on the public was to bring the two closer in accord.[136] Such arguments about justice had dealt with specific complaints to be addressed and the convenience of obtaining redress. *Cleave's* columns, on the other hand, portrayed justice as something defined through the genre of a courtroom tale, the depiction of its characters, and the emotional congruence of both with the final verdict. Justice, in its pages, meant the violent or immoral receiving serious punishment, the amusing and colorful being patiently chastised, and the sympathetic or piteous being treated with compassion. In the pages of *Cleave's*, justice was dependent on individual character and morality, not legality. The increasing prominence of such courtroom portrayals as a mechanism by which the growing newspaper readership encountered images of justice, morality, and the relationship between the state and the individual came at a crucial time for Victorian society. The 1830s and 1840s witnessed a rising concern among the middle class, who formed the bulk of these papers' readership, with the conditions of life among the metropolitan multitudes. The 1832

134 *Cleave's*, July 2, 1836. 135 *Cleave's*, June 4, 1836.

136 Carolyn Conley, in her discussion of summary justice in rural Kent in the 1860s–1880s, has similarly argued that, in *informal* practice, a similar dynamic applies. Carolyn Conley, *The Unwritten Law: Criminal Justice in Victorian Kent* (Oxford: Oxford University Press, 1991), 41.

Royal Commission into the Operation of the Poor Laws, and the reform of the system catalyzed by its findings, was the beginning of a trend towards philanthropic intervention. This trend would continue, albeit somewhat unevenly, until various state institutions claimed this role in the last quarter of the nineteenth century.[137] Although the principles of economic Liberalism, individual moral accountability, and limited government encouraged the replacement of traditional paternalism with private philanthropy and voluntarism in the first half of the century, some institutions of state nonetheless expanded their purview over life in Britain's rapidly growing cities. The inauguration of the Metropolitan Police, prompted by growing fears of public disorder, was one aspect of this trend.[138] The expansion of the summary jurisdiction system, partly in the hopes of channeling the grievances of the poor into local courtrooms, was another.

In an environment of growing interest in the lives of poor Londoners, it should come as no surprise that courtroom reporting, which promised readers accessible and entertaining windows into this world, multiplied exponentially. In the 1840s, the *Morning Post* alone printed nearly 3,000 reports on cases heard in London's courts of summary justice, and the *Morning Chronicle* nearly as many. Other papers that carried considerable numbers of courtroom reports, though on nowhere near the scale of the *Post* or the *Chronicle*, included *The Times*, *John Bull*, *Lloyd's Illustrated Newspaper*, *Reynolds's Weekly Newspaper*, and *The Standard*, to name but a few. Such reports appeared alongside the accounts from social investigators, most notably those of Henry Mayhew, whose work was also distributed primarily through the *Morning Chronicle*. Like

137 The growth of Victorian social reform, a major topic of Victorian historiography, has been assessed in works too numerous to list in full. Some seminal titles include Mary Poovey, *Making a Social Body: British Cultural Formation 1830–1864* (Chicago: University of Chicago Press, 1995); Lynn Hollen Lees, *The Solidarity of Strangers: the English Poor Laws and the People, 1700–1948* (Cambridge: Cambridge University Press, 1998); George K. Behlmer, *Friends of the Family: the English Home and Its Guardians, 1850–1940* (Stanford: Stanford University Press, 1998); F. David Roberts, *The Social Conscience of the Early Victorians* (Stanford: Stanford University Press, 2002).

138 V. A. C. Gatrell, "The Decline of Theft and Violence in Victorian and Edwardian England," in V. A. C. Gatrell, Bruce Lenman, and Geoffrey Parker, eds., *Crime and the Law: The Social History of Crime in Western Europe since 1500* (London: Europa Publications, 1980), 271.

Mayhew's investigations into the intimate details of everyday life among the poor, courtroom stories offered a constantly varying tableau of conflict, crime, and drama in London's teeming districts.

At the same time that both public interest in the daily life of the poor and the reporting of their courtroom encounters were expanding, the purview of the courts themselves continued to widen. Acts in 1848, 1850, and 1855 brought a range of new offenses and new offenders into the milieu.[139] Both juvenile crime and larceny figured largely in these new reforms, and they were covered in courtroom columns with great frequency. The overall congruency between reporting and practice, however, remained questionable. "Police Intelligence" sections could often take up a full broadsheet page in the *Chronicle*, *Post*, *Lloyd's*, or *Reynolds's*, constituting the largest coherent news space in some of the most widely circulating papers of the time. They continued, however, to correspond poorly with the incidence of any given crime in the metropolis. Compared to its frequency as a charge in police courts themselves during the 1850s, murder occupied a vastly disproportionate space in court columns, as did attempted suicides, elaborate frauds, false marriage proposals, and indecent assaults on women.[140] Open defiance by defendants in the courtroom, which had been a favorite topic of police-court chroniclers since their beginnings, was much-reported. So, too, were sexual peccadillos, from licentious women to working-class Don Juans to hapless, cuckolded husbands.

There was even less correspondence between what was printed in newspapers and what magistrates, policymakers, and police officials considered to be important cases. Magistrates' frequently expressed frustration with the daily parade of personal squabbles, tangential testimonies, and personal summonses for non-existent offenses – all

[139] The Juvenile Offenders Act 1847, Summary Jurisdiction Act 1848, Juvenile Offenders Act 1850, Larceny Act 1850, and Criminal Justice Act 1855.

[140] The most thorough assessment of the stark contrast between the incidence of violent crime, and murder in particular, and its disproportionate reporting in Victorian newspapers can be found in Christopher A. Casey, "Common Misperceptions: The Press and Victorian Views of Crime," *Journal of Interdisciplinary History* 41, no. 3 (Winter, 2011), 376–81. Rosalind Crone has provided some welcome statistical analysis on newspaper coverage of crime and its correspondence with trials in the Central Criminal Court. But it is of limited utility in assessing police-court coverage and the two newspapers, the *Post* and the *Chronicle*, that provided it most extensively. Crone, *Violent Victorians*, 223–31.

great fodder for newspaper columns – attested to this. In contrast, prosecutions for drunkenness, disorderly behavior, vagrancy, and disorderly prostitution, which collectively constituted roughly half of all arrests by mid-century, and which were widely considered to be essential to public order and morality in the metropolis, occupied only a small fraction of the "Police Intelligence" columns in these papers.[141] Taken as an aggregate, the patterns of policing and prosecution bore very little correspondence to the content of courtroom reporting. The latter catered to the tastes of the readers, and were composed by reporters who were either assigned specifically by a newspaper for that purpose, or belonged to a roving coterie that produced pieces "on spec" for whatever paper chose to print them.[142] Courtroom reporters, like many others in their profession, were paid by the line, hence their nickname of "penny-a-liners." Exaggeration and embellishment were intrinsic to their writing.[143] So, to the various dimensions courtroom culture already established, we must add another by the mid-Victorian period, that of providing a daily stream of entertainment to the burgeoning audience of newspaper readers across a broad political and social spectrum. These reports, embellished and selective as they were, offered a highly skewed picture of courtroom practice. They remain very useful, nonetheless, for understanding the expectations and tastes of readers and the relationship between courtrooms as legal venues, courtrooms as a lens into "real life," and courtrooms as spaces constructed in cultural milieu.

The Fieldings' original goal with the admission of reporters to Bow Street had been to emphasize the authority of the law and, in doing so, to help foster a more moral and orderly society. According to James Richie, one of the most prolific chroniclers of Victorian life in the metropolis, however, by mid-century, the intimate access to the courtroom afforded by these columns was undermining the courts'

141 Inwood, "Policing London's Morals," 136.

142 By mid-century, *Reynolds's Newspaper* alone had assigned eight to ten reporters in "the various courts of justice" on a daily basis. *Reynolds's Newspaper*, February 23, 1851.

143 James Ewing Richie, *The Night Side of London*, 2nd ed. (London: William Tweedie, 1858), 209–10. Richie authored some three-dozen books between 1847 and 1898, including biographies and travelogues. London was, by far, his most common topic, and the focus of nine of his titles.

authority instead. "In such matters," he asserted, "it is especially true [that] familiarity breeds contempt."[144] Regardless of its overall effect on increasing or decreasing respect for the law in London, the growth and development of newspaper coverage represented another vital evolution of magistrates' courtrooms as public spaces accessible to an ever-broader range of participants and observers. The legal reforms of mid-century made the courts available to a wider social spectrum, and in doing so, narrowed the distance between daily conflict and contest outside the courtroom and that within it. The expansion of police-court columns, by broadcasting a wide range of courtroom tales to a growing readership, further weakened that boundary and made what happened in the courtroom even more relevant beyond it, breaking down the barrier between participation and observation, and between courtrooms and everyday life in general.

The rapid expansion of police-court columns and their particular appeal for working-class and lower-middle-class readers, as evidenced by their proliferation in the weekly Sunday papers and the Radical press, also offers at least a partial answer to a vital question in the study of nineteenth-century law and society. Namely, how did the metropolitan population develop their own understandings of law and the courts, and their definitions of justice? Although it would be impossible to prove definitively that they emerged from engagement with police-court columns, such accounts were, by far, the most extensive, compelling, and readily available sources on the subjects of law, courts, and justice.[145] This had been the case since the late eighteenth century.[146] The popularity of police-court columns by mid-century, however, does not imply a consensus among either their writers or their readers on the lessons to be learned from them. "Justice" remained among the most contested of all the words that could be heard in a police court. The power of different individuals to define it depended upon their authority in the courtroom, their ability to disseminate their views, and the circumstances in which they deployed the concept. Newspaper reporters could frame certain cases as being just or unjust through a variety of methods, and most

[144] Through seeing the courts in action, he wrote, "the criminal class get an initiation in the secrets of the law, which robs it of its terrors." Ibid., 217.

[145] Rowbotham and Stevenson, "Causing a Sensation," 41.

[146] King, "Newspaper Reporting," 73–74.

frequently did so through the use of column titles, the selective quoting of testimony or dialogue, the evocation of particular emotions, or the adherence to particular narrative genres (e.g. comedy, tragedy, or melodrama). The multiplication and rising prominence of courtroom columns invited a growing reading public to witness the presence, or absence, of justice in the courtroom. Despite magistrates' comments to the contrary, however, the public did not become the jury that was so conspicuously absent from summary proceedings. Beyond the limited class of those with political influence, readers of courtroom columns had power only to the degree that magistrates and other legal reformers granted it in their consciousness of an amorphous cohort of vicarious observers who could be moved to condemnation by negative reporting. Instead, police-court columns offered readers the opportunity to join the audience of the courtrooms, and to witness the conduct of trials without the authority and accountability that accompanied adjudication.

It would seem, then, that middle-class readers were largely content to interpret courtroom events through their portrayals rather than visiting them in person. This boundary was both desirable and, in most instances, easily maintained. The mid-Victorian police court, described as crowded, dirty, and thoroughly disrespectable, a haunt of the debauched, the criminal, and the hopeless, was not a locale that a typical middle-class reader would wish to frequent in person.[147] For those of the working class and lower middle class, the circumstances were different. As the primary targets of the Metropolitan Police, the intended clientele for the newly affordable and expanded powers of summary justice, and the majority of local courtroom audiences, the barrier for them was much more porous. The new penny press eagerly courted their readership by publishing dramatic or humorous police court tales. In contrast to middle-class readers, what the working class and lower middle class read about had more direct relevance to their lives – they were much more likely to find themselves crossing the line into participation through a summons, facing a charge leveled by a constable,

[147] Fear of contagion, attributable to the cholera epidemics of 1831 and 1849, as well as the rising awareness of epidemic diseases more generally, was a "dominant theme and organizing impulse of urban description." Deborah Epstein Nord, "The City as Theater: From Georgian to Early Victorian London," *Victorian Studies* 31, no. 2 (Winter, 1988), 185.

or giving witness testimony in either instance. The Old Bailey, where more serious crimes were tried, may have received much greater press coverage for individual cases, but largely addressed acts well outside the norm of ordinary experience. The lessons of justice they taught and image of the law and the state they offered were much less immediately relevant than the more modest fare of police-court columns. Trials for murder and other felonies were unlikely to provide information that would be helpful in harnessing the courts to deal with a troublesome tenant, and rent-racking landlord, an abusive husband, a larcenous servant, an employer who withheld wages, or the host of other daily tribulations faced by the growing readership of the popular press.[148]

Although the development of summary justice and newspaper coverage were opening courtrooms up to broader participation and observation, and even softening the boundary between the two, the same cannot be said of the police courts' physical reorganization in the mid-Victorian period. Segregation and hierarchy were increasingly the order of the day. The relatively open courts that had crowded audiences and petitioners together in the late eighteenth and early nineteenth century were becoming a thing of the past. Just as the second half of the eighteenth century had witnessed the creation of venues permanently dedicated to the hearing of summary cases (e.g. the Bow Street Police Office), the mid-nineteenth century saw the further subdivision and specialization of summary courtrooms and of the larger court buildings that contained them. The courtroom of the new Clerkenwell Police Court, built in 1841–42 to replace Hatton Garden, incorporated all the elements that, according to one reporter for the *Illustrated Police News*, constituted the "usual Police Court arrangements." These consisted of "the judicial armchair" which was "faced and flanked" by a series of "particular boxes" that accommodated, separately, "Clerks, Police, Inspectors, Reporters, Barristers, and, not least, Culprits."[149] There was also a separate space for the public. In the surrounding building, even greater effort was made to segregate the various cohorts who came within the police

148 For the Victorian interest in the former, see Martin Wiener, *Men of Blood: Violence, Manliness and Criminal Justice in Victorian England* (Cambridge: Cambridge University Press, 2004), 154–55.

149 Angus Reach, "The Police Offices of London," *Illustrated London News*, May 22, 1847.

court's remit, either voluntarily or involuntarily. A separate room, adjacent to the courtroom, was assigned to deal with the processing of warrants and summonses. Defendants were kept apart from all others present throughout their trial process. They could be led directly from the courtyard or the cells into the courtroom without passing through any of the spaces reserved for the magistrates, the clerks, witnesses, or the public.[150] The spaces that defendants occupied, before, during, and after their trial were even organized so that they moved on the same plane throughout, with no requirement to go up or down steps. The intention was to enable a trial process as smooth and free from interruption as possible, and to better accommodate the increasingly busy schedule of the courts.[151]

The Clerkenwell model would be replicated in even more detailed and monumental fashion in the flagship of London's summary justice system, the new Bow Street Police Court. Planned and built in the period 1876–81 at an estimated cost of over £100,000, the imposing edifice was described in *The Graphic* as "a model institution," even though the courtroom's acoustic properties were less than ideal.[152] The courtroom itself was meticulously subdivided into areas for the magistrates, witnesses, police witnesses, solicitors, chief clerk, subsidiary clerks, counsellors, inspectors, public, and prisoners (Figure 1.3). There were no less than five discrete entrances, one each for magistrates, police and prisoners, solicitors, witnesses, and the public. These entrances also corresponded with four separate routes of access that connected the courts to the appropriate offices (for officials) or waiting rooms (for the prisoners and public) of those who would be occupying the courtroom. The principle of gender segregation operated as well, with separate waiting rooms for male and female prisoners. The courtroom and its various offices, waiting rooms, and passages formed half of the court complex, the other being a police station. The latter was similarly divided into the offices of various police officials and a suite of cells for prisoners (Figure 1.4).

The physical space of the courts had been a longstanding concern among policymakers, magistrates, and journalists. Their disquiet

[150] Clare Graham, *Ordering Law: The Architectural and Social History of the English Law Court to 1914* (Aldershot: Ashgate, 2003), 179.

[151] Ibid. [152] Ibid., 183.

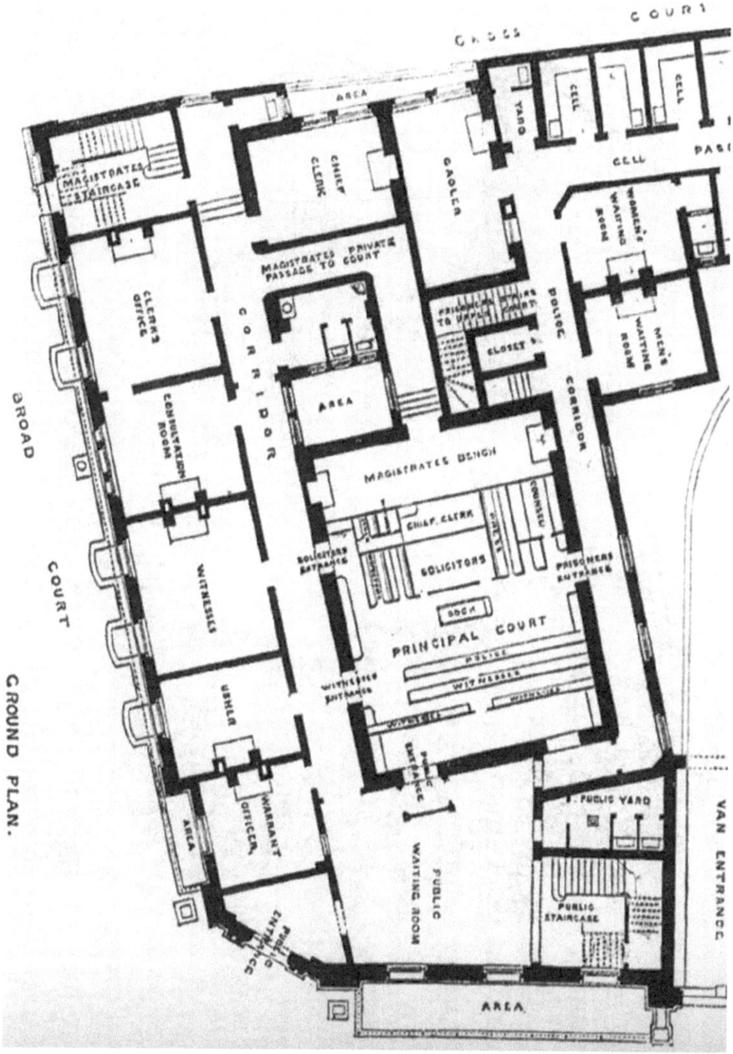

FIGURE 1.3 Bow Street Police Court – detail of courtroom and offices, *The Builder*, 1879, 689 (From Clare Graham, *Ordering Law: The Architectural and Social History of the English Law Court to 1914* (London and New York: Routledge Press, 2003). Courtesy of Routledge Press.)

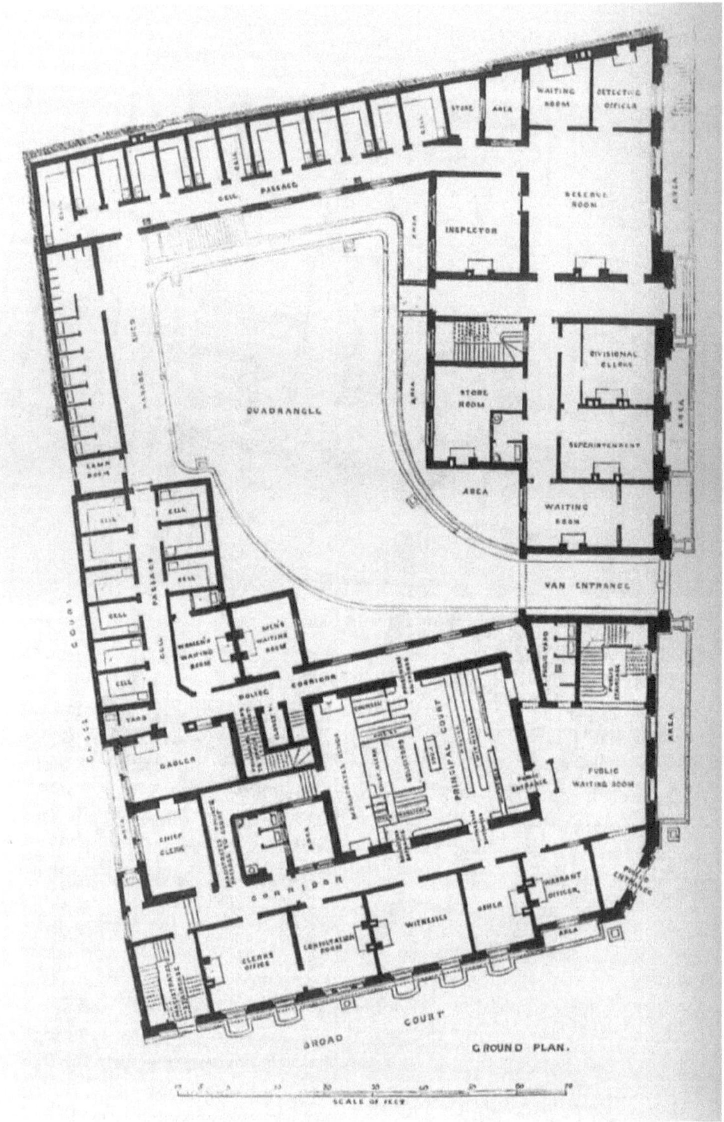

FIGURE 1.4 Ground plan of the Bow Street Police Court, *The Builder*, 1879, 689 (From Graham, *Ordering Law*. Courtesy of Routledge Press.)

became even more acute as the courtrooms rose in popularity and had to accommodate more trials covering a wider array of complaints and offenses, as well as a public eager to observe them. The focus of attention was almost invariably on the interior space of the courts.[153] The filth of the public waiting room and passages was a frequent source of commentary among journalists, as was crowding, the mixing of genders, and the co-mingling of the demoralized and respectable. These matters were raised by magistrates and other officials in their testimonies before Parliament as well.[154] One noticeable trend in the mid-Victorian period, as courtrooms and court buildings became more modernized and specialized, was a growing distance between descriptions of the areas that the public frequented – the passages and waiting rooms – and the courtrooms proper. Angus Reach, describing the new Clerkenwell court for readers of the *Illustrated London News*, contrasted the passages traversed by the "disreputable public of the Police Court" with the courtroom itself.[155] The former, he wrote, was "a long dirty passage: the passages leading to Police Courts are always dirty – the walls are always greasy – glazed, so to speak, by the constant friction of frowsy rags." While the courtroom, in comparison, was "a handsome, airy, wainscoted apartment."

Like the police-court columns, such descriptions engaged police courts from the perspective of the reporters. Ignored was the vast majority of space in both court annexes and the larger buildings around them, which reporters either did not have access to or chose not to portray. Even though a great deal of vital information was exchanged and decisions made in the various offices that comprised the bulk of the court annexes, and most of the prisoners' time was spent in the cells rather than in the court itself, the courtroom remained the overwhelming focus of attention.[156] As with the decisions about which cases to report and which to ignore, reporters' focus reflected the desires of a reading public whose taste was for the courtroom contest, not for the organizational minutiae that underpinned it.

153 On the state's organization of space and light to make subjects more amenable to governance, see Patrick Joyce, *The Rule of Freedom: Liberalism and the Modern City* (London and New York: Verso, 2003), 128–37.

154 Testimony of John Hardwick, Magistrate of the Lambeth Street Court, *Metropolis Police Offices 1838*, 18; Testimony of James Traill, Magistrate, *Metropolis Police Offices 1837*, 40.

155 *Illustrated London News*, May 22, 1847, 322.

156 Julienne Hanson, "The Architecture of Justice: Iconography and Space Configuration in the English Law Court Building," *Architectural Research Quarterly* 1, no. 4 (Summer 1996), 55–56.

Intentionally or not, this further heightened the public significance of the courtroom by conveying the impression that it was there and there alone where a defendant's fate was determined. This tendency served largely to conceal the operation of authority from the reader, while emphasizing both the magistrates' discretion and the public's role in witnessing and legitimizing justice in the courtroom.

The segregation of courtrooms and court buildings into specialized subspaces and reporters' continued focus on action and dialogue in the courtroom itself were in accord with broader trends in Victorian criminal justice. The former fit with the desire of policymakers to rationalize and depersonalize the trial process. Both tendencies accentuated individuals' moral accountability for their actions and the social isolation they incurred through immoral choices.[157] Courtrooms and their rapidly multiplying portrayals, however, were more than merely reflections of policy goals, Liberal-individualist ideology, or the tastes of newspaper readers. Like the evolution of summary justice, courtroom space and police-court columns evolved in constant dialogue and interaction with the men and women that experienced courtrooms, read about them, wrote about them, and expressed their ideas and demands through a number of avenues. The reform and specialization of courtroom space certainly reflected the priorities of magistrates and other officials who sought more efficient processing of cases and a strict segregation of prisoners from the public. This was at the same time a response to the increasing demand of the public for employment of the courts and their interest in its activities – hence the specialized warrant and summons room of the Clerkenwell Court, the substantial public waiting room of the Bow Street Police Court, and the frequent descriptions of individuals and crowds gathered outside the courtroom doors either seeking justice or a glimpse of the latest occupants.[158]

Indications of the increasing participation of the local population in shaping the courtroom and its operation multiplied across the mid-Victorian period. They could be found in magistrates' reports of the widening range of petty complaints brought before them. They were

[157] For the reform of criminal policy in this direction, see Weiner, *Reconstructing the Criminal*, 64–65.

[158] William Pitt Byrne, *Undercurrents Overlooked* (London: Richard Bentley, 1860), 52.

also apparent in magistrates' frustration with "idle charges" brought by complainants merely to temporarily rid themselves of a troublesome person, charges that were "abandoned immediately after the person is taken into custody."[159] The growing number of onlookers who attended court, and the rapid proliferation of courtroom stories in newspapers across the political and social spectrum similarly demonstrated a rising interest in and awareness of the courts.[160] In police-court columns themselves, albeit through a highly distorted lens of reporters' priorities and editors' interpretations, we find, over and over again, signs that individuals entered local courtrooms not just to receive what was offered, but to declare their intentions and demand accommodation. We cannot know exactly how Bridget Donovan, "a tall big-boned Irishwoman of decent appearance," learned that she could apply in the Clerkenwell Police Court for a warrant to arrest her unnamed adversary, which she did in October 1848.[161] Her belief in the rightness of her cause was strong enough that, when she was refused, she hurled a brick at the recalcitrant magistrate, Mr. Tyrwhitt. Charged with assault at the Worship Street Police Court – due to the obvious conflict of interest that prevented her being tried in Clerkenwell – Donovan remained steadfast in her convictions. When asked by the presiding magistrate if she had anything to say for herself, she responded emphatically, "well, I did throw the brick at him because he would not give me law and justice, and he sneered at me, and so do you." Donovan could have familiarized herself with warrants through the "Police Intelligence" columns. If she was illiterate, such knowledge could just as easily have been acquired through conversations with friends, family, and neighbors who either read about or experienced the local courtroom. She herself could conceivably have attended another trial as a witness, defendant, complainant, or an audience member. What is clear is that she was at least passingly familiar with her local courtroom, and that she entered it with some consciousness of law, justice, and her rights.

The diversity of roles and portrayals that characterized magistrates' courtrooms in the mid-Victorian period suggests that they were not

[159] *Metropolis Police Offices 1837*, 37.
[160] Rowbotham and Stevenson, "Causing a Sensation."
[161] *Morning Post*, October 28, 1848.

merely reflective of broader ideas about law, morality, and everyday life in the metropolis. The expansion of summary justice and the proliferation of police-court columns helped fashion the courtrooms as locales where these concepts were generated and disseminated for a growing cohort of participants and observers. The desires of magistrates and policymakers that the courts expand their role in the resolution of minor neighborhood conflict intersected with a growing local demand for the prompt address of a variety of minor grievances. The popular "Police Intelligence" reports, while providing a skewed vision of daily justice, not only brought the courtroom into the purview of a broad audience, but weakened the barrier between observation and participation. A self-reinforcing cycle of demand for courtroom services, readers' tastes, popular expectations, and magistrates and officials' consciousness of an observing public had a powerful impact on the reform of summary justice and the daily operation of courtrooms. These effects were readily apparent in a variety of milieus, from parliamentary reports to journalistic accounts to the language of those who attended the courts themselves.

Neither the provision of detailed court reports that allowed for multiple interpretations by readers nor the portrayal of police courtrooms as locales where ordinary individuals could influence the meaning of events, however, persisted long past mid-century. As the purview of summary justice expanded to a broader range of laws and a greater spectrum of activities, the content of public portrayals would contract. Newspaper reporters and editors, contending with a changing commercial and legal landscape, would increasingly adopt a style of court reporting that was concise rather than detailed, that emphasized the authority of magistrates and the state over individuals, and that discarded humor and satire for realism and a coherent moral message. As police-court columns, through the popular press, became an element of mass culture for an enfranchised and literate public, the images they offered about law, the state, and morality would change significantly. Once tales meant to amuse and divert, courtroom stories were about to become "news."

2

"A Ruffian Rightly Punished"

Morality and Local Courtrooms in Practice and Portrayal, 1860–80

The steady rise in summary proceedings and the widening array of statutes attest to the growing prominence of police courts in the legal landscape of nineteenth-century London. The courts' social and cultural importance, and how events there influenced popular understandings of law, justice, and morality, must be traced via other avenues. The rapid proliferation of newspaper police-court columns in the second half of the nineteenth century offer one such point of access. As dramatically as the police courts' legal remit expanded, these public portrayals expanded more dramatically still. The image of courtrooms offered there, however, did not accord with the wider trends in courtroom usage itself. Despite the crucial role of individual petitioners and the flexibility of courtroom usage, newspapers continued to present courtrooms as places where magistrates' voices dominated and where the moral interpretations of cases were coherent and clear. Courtrooms may have been locales of contested and contingent meaning, but courtroom newspaper columns, after mid-century, were not. Departing from the focus of previous historians and cultural theorists on crime and sensationalism, this chapter will examine the images of law and morality these stories offered and demonstrate how those images were stabilized in the latter part of the nineteenth century.[1] The broad

[1] For a summary of how this topic has been studied in the eighteenth century, see Peter King, "Newspaper Reporting and Attitudes to Crime and Justice in Late-Nineteenth- and Early-Twentieth-Century London," *Continuity and Change* 22, no. 1 (2007), 76–77; and Simon Devereaux, "The Fall of the Sessions Paper: The

dissemination of courtroom portrayals had significant implications for the popular understandings of the Victorian state, the communities most affected by the expansion of municipal governance, and the relationship between law and morality. Police-court columns in this period did not merely reflect and disseminate moral norms and help notify the public of what was legal and illegal. As the advertisements that crowded the pages of the new popular press broadcast the expanding availability of products and opportunities for employment, columns of "Police Intelligence" broadcast the expanding roles of courtrooms and the authority of magistrates, police, and municipal authorities. In doing so, they served to delineate that authority in the public eye and to either condone or condemn – largely the former – its expression and individual responses to it. The absence of explicit references to law and the portrayal of cases as adhering to moral boundaries rather than legal ones only served to further naturalize the authority of the police, magistrates, and agents of public authority as a part of everyday life in London.[2]

This naturalization occurred in the midst of vociferous public debate and political contest over the limits of a rapidly expanding municipal government structure. Disagreements over the remit of such authority would plague the Metropolitan Board of Works, which was the main instrument of metropolitan administration in the period 1855–89.[3] In addition to long-running arguments over the limits of police authority and the right of state agents to dictate "private" activities such as child-rearing and marital treatment, two key issues occupied reformers. These were whether or not municipal governance should centralize or maintain its decentralized structure, and to what extent those who administrated should be directly elected and therefore accountable to the growing cohort of voting ratepayers.[4] The multiplying portrayals

Criminal Trial and the Popular Press in Late Eighteenth-Century London," *Criminal Justice History* 18 (2003), 57–59.

[2] Its impersonal conduct, "with the character of a market," operating in conjunction with a modernized penal regime and in contrast to the discretionary and patriarchal system of the eighteenth century, would serve to reform individual character through systematic and predictable criminal justice. Martin Wiener, *Reconstructing the Criminal: Culture, Law, and Policy in England, 1830–1914* (Cambridge: Cambridge University Press, 1990), 66.

[3] John Davis, *Reforming London: The London Government Problem, 1855–1900* (Oxford: Clarendon, 1988), 16–18.

[4] Ibid., 60.

of local courtrooms implicitly legitimized the state's involvement in everyday life, but under the direction of unelected magistrates and largely in circumstances where moral wrongdoing was clearly evident. In doing so, they paved the way for the more interventionist incarnations of the state that would follow with the rising influence of Progressives in London governance during the 1880s, but they did so in a way that reinforced the courts' position as the moral arbiter of working-class behavior. Just as local courtrooms themselves made the state palpable to the working class, police-court stories made the presence of the state in the local community visible, comprehensible, and, to a certain degree, justifiable to the burgeoning audience of Victorian newspaper readers.

The integration of the state and everyday life at the cultural level via courtroom stories occurred at the same time that courtrooms of summary justice became among the most common and public sites of personal, concrete contact between ordinary citizens and the state in its various guises. Between 1860 and 1880, there would be, on average, one summary trial each year for roughly every forty-eight men and women in England and Wales. In the final decades of the century, hundreds of thousands more appeared in these courtrooms annually to face or pursue summonses, to give witness testimony, or to observe the proceedings.[5] The police courts of London, having joined the Central Criminal Court and the Queen's Bench as the most publicized courtrooms in the nation, began to play a commensurately larger role in shaping the public discourse on morality as well as legality. Police-court columns offered a common standard for defining right and wrong, for identifying victims and villains, and for

[5] This calculation is based on the official judicial statistics, discussed more below, and census data for those years. More precisely, there was one summary trial for about every 50 individuals recorded in the census. With certain violations (drunk and disorderly most especially), however, it was not uncommon for the same individual to be charged twice or more in the same year. In 1860, there were 384,918 summary proceedings in a recorded population of 20,066,224 (*Census Records for 1861*; *Judicial Statistics, 1860, England and Wales, Pt. I, Police – Criminal Proceedings – Prisons* (PP 1861, 2860), xii), i.e. 1/52. In 1870, there were 526,869 summary proceedings in a recorded population of 22,712,266, i.e. 1/43 (*Census Records for 1871*; *Judicial Statistics, 1870, England and Wales, Pt. I, Police – Criminal Proceedings – Prisons* (PP 1871, C. 442) [hereafter *Judicial Statistics, 1870*], xv). In 1880, there were 517,373 summary proceedings in a recorded population of 25,974,436, i.e. 1/50 (*Census Records for 1881*; *Judicial Statistics, 1870*, xvii).

assessing justice and injustice.[6] To whom voice and authority was granted within these columns, and to what degree it coordinated with authority within the courtroom itself, are therefore crucial considerations.[7] The essential role played by gender and class in courtrooms and stories written about them will be dealt with in later chapters. Here, the focus will be the structural changes in courtroom reporting, most particularly the shifting balance from private to public authority, and how these changes worked together with the expanding legal purview of local courts to shape the moral meaning of courtroom events for a burgeoning newspaper readership.

The circulation of newspapers across Britain, and among working-class audiences most notably, continued to grow in the wake of the 1855 repeal of the Stamp Act.[8] The general effect of reduced newspaper costs, rising literacy rates, and franchise reform (respectively providing means, method, and motive for newspaper consumption) was a broadening of the audience of daily papers.[9] These could now turn more to advertising and readership for income as opposed to being dependent on the support of a political party and its constituency, as had previously been the case. Whether one looked to the daily press and

[6] As Roland Barthes has argued, the intersection of literature, broadly conceived, and courtrooms was characterized by a generative interchange between the various groups who contributed to both milieus. Roland Barthes, "Dominici, or the Triumph of Literature," in *Mythologies* (Les Lettres Nouvelles, 1957), 44–45.

[7] On the importance of narrative in according agency in Victorian culture, see Judith Walkowitz, *City of Dreadful Delight: Narratives of Sexual Danger in Late-Victorian London* (Chicago: University of Chicago Press, 1992), 83–84. On multi-vocality and the ambiguous character of early crime reporting, see King, "Newspaper Reporting."

[8] By 1890, *Lloyd's* would enjoy a circulation of 600,000 weekly, and *Reynolds's*, 300,000. George Boyce, James Curran, and Paul Wingate, eds., *Newspaper History from the Seventeenth Century to the Present Day* (London: Constable, 1978), 257.

[9] Martin Conboy, *The Language of Newspapers: Socio-Historical Perspectives* (London: Continuum, 2010), 79; Ivor Asquith, "The Structure, Ownership and Control of the Press, 1780–1855," in Boyce, Curran and Wingate, eds., *Newspaper History*, 107. Literacy rates are notoriously difficult to assess, and the size of the newspaper-reading public even more so. Raymond Williams, through a very rough calculation, estimated that in 1860, the daily newspaper reading public was about 3% of the population, and the Sunday public 12% (Raymond Williams, "The Press and Popular Culture: An Historical Perspective," in George Boyce, James Curran, and Paul Wingate, eds., *Newspaper History from the Seventeenth Century to the Present Day* (London: Constable, 1978), 42). There is evidence that, like literacy itself, this rate was increasing rapidly over the last half of the nineteenth century, and the rising circulation figures certainly support this conclusion.

established papers of record such as the *Times*, which were aimed at a middle and upper-class audience, to the Sunday weekly papers and their lower-middle-class and working-class readership, to dailies such as the *Morning Chronicle* or *Morning Post*, to provincial papers such as the *Liverpool Mercury*, or to the new crop of local London papers, columns covering the metropolitan police courts, to judge by their profusion and ubiquity, clearly enjoyed wide appeal. Dramatized stories that involved individuals from all walks of life, they bridged the gap between the familiar and the exotic, between the private and the public, and between "elite and popular knowledge," linking the new press to traditional forms of popular culture.[10] The columns' broad appeal, and the free access to their sources, also made them ideal subject matter for an industry that was increasingly guided by commercial concerns.[11] The marketability of court reports had been clear to newspaper owners and editors alike well before the Stamp Act's repeal. In the words of Henry Hetherington, co-founder of the London Working Men's Society, on the eve of his launching the *Twopenny Dispatch* in 1834, "Police Intelligence" was the "sort of devilment that will make it sell."[12]

If the commercial success and popular appeal of newspaper police-court columns is easily apparent, determining to what degree these stories shaped morality and conceptions of justice is a far trickier proposition. One indicator of their moral significance is the extraordinary concern expressed by magistrates in various parliamentary commissions over the negative effects that coverage would have on public morals. Magistrates were particularly keen that tales of indecent assault did not receive too wide or detailed an

10 Conboy, *The Language of Newspapers*, 79; Williams, "The Press and Popular Culture," 44; Anne Baltz Rodrick, "'Only a Newspaper Metaphor': Crime Reports, Class Conflict, and Social Criticism in Two Victorian Papers," *Victorian Periodicals Review* 29, no. 1 (Spring, 1996), 2.

11 Michael Harris and Alan Lee, "Introduction" (to pt. 2: "The Nineteenth Century"), in Michael Harris and Alan Lee, eds., *The Press in English Society from the Seventeenth to Nineteenth Centuries* (London: Associated University Presses, 1986), 108–9.

12 Henry Hetherington quoted in Ivon Asquith, "The Structure, Ownership and Control of the Press, 1780–1855," in Boyce et al., *Newspaper History*, 107. As mentioned in Chapter 1, Hetherington's fellow-founders were William Lovett and John Cleave.

exposition.[13] In terms of the role of courtroom columns in shaping popular ideas of justice, the explicit commitment of both local reporters and editors to this task is telling. In a system that was rife with prosecution but sparse on any manner of public defense, journalists were the first figures in Victorian society to assume the mantle of judicial watchdogs, a role they adopted with relish after 1848, when the law mandated that all magistrates' proceedings be public.[14] Most courtroom reporters' legal expertise, however, was limited. Magistrates prioritized the law and its procedures, but were concerned with whether or not their decisions would be recognized as just. Their explicitly stated goal of providing moral guidance to the working-class community depended more on the latter than it did on the former. Journalists, by comparison, were more keen to assess a case's moral content than its strict adherence to legal principles. As with those writing such accounts, those who read them, lacking any expertise to judge a case's legal dimension, developed a standard for assessing their moral aspects that inevitably drew, in no small part, on the context of previous accounts. Thus, courtroom stories, while drawing on the wider frame of Victorian morality, also contributed to its construction.

The growing interest of magistrates, journalists, and a widening public readership in the legal and moral role of local courtrooms was precipitated by a significant extension of summary jurisdiction itself, and with it, the prominence of magistrates' courtrooms in the lives of London's working class. The most rapid expansion came in the late 1840s and early 1850s with the passage of laws concerning petty theft and domestic violence. Key pieces of legislation included the Juvenile Offenders Act 1847, Summary Jurisdiction Act 1848, Larceny Act 1850, and Criminal Justice Act 1855.[15] By 1855, the police courts could deal summarily with any person under the age of 16 charged with larceny, and with any defendant charged with simple larceny (i.e. for goods of less than five shillings' worth), provided the accused

[13] As discussed in Chapter 5, towards the end of the century, they would protest with equal vehemence (though little result) against the broad publication of separation and divorce proceedings.

[14] Marjorie Jones, *Justice and Journalism* (London and Chichester: Barry Rose, 1974), 26–27.

[15] 10 & 11 Vict. c. 82; 11 & 12 Vict. c. 43; 13 & 14 Vict. c. 37; and 18 & 19 Vict. c. 126.

consented.[16] In 1860, the metropolitan courts of summary justice alone dealt with over 80,000 cases, the most frequently prosecuted being drunkenness and "drunk and disorderly" (21,340), common assault (13,090), and various stealing offenses (10,453).[17]

In contrast to their increasing involvement in crimes of harm against persons or property, the intervention of the Metropolitan Police and the police courts in "social crimes" declined in the 1840s and 1850s. There were more proceedings under the laws regulating public roads and waterways (4,820), than there were for either prostitution (3,223) or begging (2,037) under the Vagrancy Acts.[18] On the other hand, the police were hardly passive when it came to arresting and charging those they found suspicious, even when they lacked the evidence for a more serious violation – London's summary courts in 1860 prosecuted nearly 11,000 cases under the Police Acts, the largest single category being unlawful possession of goods (3,092), with another 6,716 charges for various offenses punishable as misdemeanors.[19] The Police Acts also gave the courts authority to punish, most commonly with fines, activities associated with the street-life of working-class children. Especially in the latter decades of the century, respectable rate-payers associated these activities with hooliganism if they disturbed bystanders, caused minor damage to property, or obstructed public spaces (e.g. streets, alleys, or pedestrian thoroughfares).[20] Among the most common of these juvenile diversions were playing ball in the road, knocking on doors, throwing stones, and games such as "tip-cat" and "pitch-and-toss."[21]

The changing dockets of the police courts, in turn, influenced the types of cases covered in police-court columns and therefore the messages on morality and justice conveyed through them. The

16 David Bentley, *English Criminal Justice in the Nineteenth Century* (London: Hambledon, 1998), 19–20; Jones, *Justice and Journalism*, 34–35.

17 *Judicial Statistics, 1860*, 28. The third category of offenses included larceny (8,240), larceny by offenders under 16 years (1,740), and stealing or attempts to steal trees, shrubs, etc. (27).

18 Ibid.

19 Another 1,413 charges were brought under a catch-all Police Acts category of "other offences." Ibid.

20 John Gillis, "The Evolution of Juvenile Delinquency in England, 1890–1914," *Past & Present* 67, no. 1 (1975), 98.

21 Carolyn Conley, *The Unwritten Law: Criminal Justice in Victorian Kent* (Oxford: Oxford University Press, 1991), 128.

prosecution of children's street behavior, unless classified as more serious crime such as larceny or assault, was unlikely to make it into local newspapers, though the occasional case did appear.[22] This was not true, on the other hand, of the laws intended for the protection of women and children from violence, private or public, at the hands of men. The passage of new laws to address wife-beating and violence against children, still seen by many in Victorian culture – including magistrates themselves – as legitimate methods of patriarchal discipline, brought such actions into both the police courts and the pages of national, provincial, and local newspapers.[23] An Act passed in 1853 authorized summary trials for all assaults against females and against males under the age of 14, and designated them as a special class of offense punishable by a maximum £20 fine or six months' imprisonment with hard labor.[24] The Society for the Protection of Women and Children, by assisting with prosecutions, further increased the employment of this law and its commensurate reporting in the press.[25] The new definition of aggravated assault encompassed sexual assault as well, and these cases, too, began appearing in much greater numbers in the "police intelligence" columns, albeit often in euphemized form.[26] All told, in 1860, of the 323,551 men and 86,229 women who were proceeded against for criminal violations in England and Wales, 305,507 (94 percent) of the former and 79,411 (92 percent) of the latter faced summary justice.[27] For some of the most common

[22] Most commonly when it either involved a large group of children or was accompanied by defiant, rowdy, or abusive behavior.

[23] Nancy Tomes, "A 'Torrent of Abuse': Crimes of Violence between Working-Class Men and Women in London, 1840–1875," *Journal of Social History* 11, no. 3 (1978), 336; Montagu Williams, *Round London: Down East and Up West* (London and New York: Macmillan, 1893), 25–26

[24] 16 & 17 Vic. c. 30., Act for the Better Prevention of Aggravated Assault on Women and Children. Martin Wiener, *Men of Blood: Violence, Manliness, and Criminal Justice in Victorian England* (Cambridge: Cambridge University Press, 2004), 157.

[25] Ben Griffin, *The Politics of Gender in Victorian Britain: Masculinity, Political Culture, and the Struggle for Women's Rights* (New York: Cambridge University Press, 2012), 70.

[26] Susan Edwards, "'Kicked, Beaten and Jumped On Until They Are Crushed,' All Under Man's Wing and Protection: The Victorian Dilemma with Domestic Violence" in Judith Rowbotham and Kim Stevenson, eds., *Criminal Conversations: Victorian Crimes, Social Panic, and Moral Outrage* (Columbus: The Ohio State University Press, 2005), 254–55.

[27] *Judicial Statistics, 1860*, xiv.

offenses, this percentage was even higher. Among men and women prosecuted as habitual drunkards, for example, over 98 percent were tried summarily.[28] Among the most numerous employments of summary prosecution that year were for drunkenness and drunk and disorderly (88,361 total proceeded against summarily and indicted, the vast majority the former); assaults (77,290); the vagrant laws (23,748); local acts and bye-laws (25,831); the laws regulating roads and transportation (20,561); licensing laws and Beer Acts (11,602); and the laws relating to servants, apprentices, and masters (11,938).[29]

The 1860s witnessed a further legal reform that brought even more cases to the police courts. The Offences Against the Person Act 1861 consolidated a number of earlier laws covering crimes of physical harm.[30] Among the most common of these that would be prosecuted summarily and later reported in newspapers were assaults, threats to murder, wounding, and causing bodily harm through reckless driving of a carriage. Almost without exception, the actions encompassed by the Act had been offenses prior to its passage, but the standardizing of a wide range of procedures, in conjunction with the "Jervis Acts" passed in 1848, meant that these cases would both be more commonly tried in police courts and that the trials would be open to representatives of the press.[31] In many instances, the maximum sentence for those convicted was increased, heightening the drama of such trials and their appeal for newspaper editors and readers. The Malicious Damages Act 1861 had much the same significance for crimes against property.[32] By 1870, the number of summary proceedings held annually across England and Wales had risen by over 37 percent from 1860,

[28] 19,200 out of 19,471 total men and 5,149 out of 5,210 total women. Though it should also be noted that, in some offenses, this percentage was slightly lower. For example, only 91.5% of those designated as prostitutes by police were tried summarily (18,907 out of 20,666). Ibid., xiv.

[29] Ibid., xiii. [30] 24 & 25 Vict. c.100.

[31] One stipulation of these acts, which regularized and modernized summary procedure, was that all summary trials must be held publicly.

[32] 24 & 25 Vict. c. 97. Collectively, the Offences Against the Person Act, the Malicious Damages Act, and the Acts concerning forgery, counterfeiting coin, and general criminal procedure are referred to as the "Criminal Law Consolidation Statutes." James Edward Davies, *Criminal Law Consolidation Statutes of 24 & 25 Victoria, Chapters 94 to 100, Edited with Notes, Critical and Explanatory* (London: Butterworths, 1861).

increasing at nearly double the rate of the population. That year, 427,546 cases against men and 99,323 against women came before police magistrates and Justices of the Peace.[33] Two-thirds resulted in convictions.[34] The combination of expanding summary jurisdiction over property offenses (both larceny and damage) and over minor acts of violence and intimidation would make the courts an even more commonly employed resource for shopkeepers and artisans seeking recompense in interpersonal conflicts.[35] This group comprised a significant proportion of the readership for local newspapers and the Sunday papers where police-court reporting was expanding so rapidly.[36] In conjunction with the courts' widened authority over domestic violence, this meant that formerly private conflicts in the home or neighborhood that translated into police court trials were much more likely to become news in the local paper. Bringing one's husband or neighbor to court had long been a public act, in the sense that it was conducted before a courtroom audience. By the 1860s and 1870s, the potential size of this audience had grown exponentially. A trial could attract a local readership of a few hundred to a few thousand, and any story submitted by a local reporter could potentially be picked up by the national press and reprinted across the country.

Across the 1850s and 1860s, national newspapers such as *The Times*, *Morning Post*, *Morning Chronicle*, *Reynolds's*, and *Lloyd's* reported trials in a range of venues, including the Central Criminal Court (the Old Bailey), the County Courts, the Queen's Bench, and the Middlesex Sessions. Reports from the London police courts were the most numerous, though they were often less detailed than accounts of cases in the higher courts were. Beginning in this period, police courts stories also became a staple item in local and provincial papers.[37] The lowered costs of newspaper production and rising literacy rates among the lower-middle class, in conjunction with continuing demand among the commercial and professional middle class, encouraged the establishment of papers that catered specifically to readers in the

[33] *Judicial Statistics, 1870*, xv. [34] 322,792 men and 66,920 women. Ibid.

[35] Jennifer Davis, "A Poor Man's System of Justice: The London Police Courts in the Second Half of the Nineteenth Century," *The Historical Journal* 27, no. 2 (1984), 321–25.

[36] Harris and Lee, "Introduction," 108. [37] Griffin, *Politics of Gender*, 69.

various boroughs of London.[38] These local papers, though their circulation numbers were small compared to national dailies or Sunday weeklies, appealed across a broad social spectrum within their communities precisely because they contained *local* news.[39] The breadth of readership was reflected in their content, which could range from parliamentary and financial news to announcements about important new regulations for shopkeepers and accounts of the meetings of working-men's associations. It was in this new cohort of urban weeklies, and in metropolitan borough papers in particular, that police-court reports would rise rapidly in both number and prominence. Dynamics of both production and consumption encouraged this, since local reports on local courtrooms offered editors and reporters cheap access to column material and a high likelihood, if presented correctly, of broad interest and relevance to their readership.

Prominent among the borough papers that featured considerable police-court coverage in the second half of the century were the *East London Observer*, the *West London Observer*, the *Bethnal Green Times*, and the *Marylebone Mercury*. One of the oldest of the borough papers, the *Islington Gazette*, also offered police-court reports almost from its inception. A halfpenny paper, the *Gazette* was founded in September 20, 1856, above a pie-shop on Islington High Street.[40] Each issue, published on Fridays, covered the meetings of local municipal committees and councils, political news, editorials, readers' correspondence, book reviews, cultural pieces (e.g. poetry), at least a full page of advertisements (for revenue), and a "Law Intelligence" column. The latter focused on the Clerkenwell Police Court, but could include stories from other metropolitan courts and

[38] For a detailed assessment of how literacy grew among these cohorts in the second half of the nineteenth century, and among the working class in the wake of 1870 Education Act and the advent of compulsory school attendance (though the responsibility of this legislation for rising literacy rates is much-debated), see David Mitch, *The Rise of Popular Literacy Rates in Victorian England: The Influence of Private Choice and Public Policy* (Philadelphia: University of Pennsylvania Press, 1992); Alan J. Lee, *Origins of the Popular Press in England, 1855–1914* (London: Rowman & Littlefield, 1976), 29–34.

[39] Lee, *Popular Press*, 38; Andy Croll, "Street Disorder, Surveillance and Shame: Regulating Behavior in the Public Spaces of the Late Victorian British Town," *Social History* 24, no. 3 (Oct. 1999), 260–61.

[40] http://www.islingtongazette.co.uk/home/about-the-islington-gazette.

the Old Bailey as well. The *Gazette* would have had a significant number of middle-class readers, but was aimed just as much – to judge from its letters, content and advertising – at the lower-middle-class of shopkeepers, publicans, and tradesmen that would have followed local affairs with interest. It would have had some readers among the respectable working-class as well, given its regular and favorable coverage of the meetings of local workingmen's associations.[41] In the opening issue, the founding editor explicitly (and optimistically) rejected any overt class interest, while his cries against "party strife among men who should be united in a bond of brotherhood" gave readers a taste of the Radical shading that would remain part of the paper's *oeuvre* in subsequent decades.[42] Founded a half-decade before the Liberal Party, the *Gazette* would soon become a strong advocate of its cause, staunchly supporting Liberal candidates and platform from the 1860s onwards.

As examples of the new local press, the police courts that received their attention, and the communities that were the focus of both, the *Gazette*, the Clerkenwell Police Court, and Islington all merit historical examination on a number of counts. Although not as prominently featured in the press as Bow Street or Marlborough Street were, the Clerkenwell court had been the object of press attention for some time prior to mid-century. One of the original cohort of magistrates' courts established by the Middlesex Justices Act 1792, it commenced its judicial life as the Hatton Garden Police Court. In the early nineteenth century, Hatton Garden's notoriety had come first through the vitriol of the magistrate Allen S. Laing, which had been frequently commented on by the press, and subsequently through Laing's literary incarnation as Charles Dickens's "Mr. Fang" in *Oliver Twist*.[43] The *Islington Gazette* was likewise significant in setting precedents, being one of the earliest and most prominent of the London borough papers, as well as one of the longest surviving (it is still being published today). The *Gazette*'s coverage is also a useful lens into courtroom reporting because many of the patterns evident there corresponded well with those found in other papers, both national and

[41] Circulation figures from the nineteenth century have not survived from the *Gazette*, but a paper of its type typically printed between 1,000 and 3,000 copies weekly.

[42] http://www.islingtongazette.co.uk/home/about-the-islington-gazette.

[43] As discussed in Chapter 1.

local. Its manner of London courtroom reporting was in particularly close accord with those of the *Morning Post*, which led the national dailies in London police-court coverage, and of the *Liverpool Mercury*, which had the most prolific accounts among the provincial papers. This is hardly surprising in the case of the *Mercury*, since their courtroom stories had to be either reprinted from the London papers or drawn from the pool of work submitted by freelancers working in the London courts. The *Post* supplemented its own court reporters' stories from the same sources.

Islington, the *Gazette*'s locality, was bounded by the City in the south, St. Pancras in the west, and Hackney and Shoreditch in the east and south east, and its northern edge constituted the border of the metropolitan boroughs. Islington encompassed a wide socioeconomic spectrum of occupants and a variety of neighborhoods, from the slums of Somers Town and Campbell Bunk – the latter dubbed by London historian Jerry White as "the worst street in North London" – and the rookeries of Clerkenwell and St. Luke's, to the more salubrious climes of St. Mark's and Tufnell Park.[44] In both its diversity and its rapid growth, the area reflected broader demographic trends in the metropolis during the second half of the nineteenth century, when Islington's population swelled from approximately 55,000 in 1841 to over 300,000 by 1891.[45] This period saw a rapid decline of the southern part of the borough, where the Clerkenwell Police Court lay, from a genteel green suburb into an area characterized by overcrowding, poverty, and rising crime rates.[46] The court itself was in one of the busiest and most densely populated sections of the borough, King's Cross Road, to where it had been relocated from Hatton Garden in 1841.[47] To the northwest, King's Cross railway station was an entry point for all manner of visitors and transients from parts northwards, while a mile to the north was the notorious

[44] Jerry White, *Campbell Bunk: The Worst Street in North London Between the Wars* (London: Pimlico, 2003).

[45] Exact figures, according to the *Statistical Abstract for London*, vol. IV (1901), were 55,690.

[46] A. P. Baggs, Diane K. Bolton, and Patricia E. C. Croot, "Islington and Stoke Newington Parishes," in T. F. T. Baker and C. R. Elrington, eds., *History of Middlesex*, vol. 8 (London: Victoria County History, 1985), http://www.british-history.ac.uk/report.aspx?compid=6734.

[47] The road at the time had been called Bagnigge Wells, and was renamed in 1861.

FIGURE 2.1 Detail map of Clerkenwell Police Court (at center) and environs, *c.*1870. To the southeast is Coldbath Fields Prison (aka the Middlesex House of Correction, Clerkenwell Gaol, or "the Steel," closed permanently in 1877) and King's Cross station is in the northwest corner. (*The A to Z of Victorian London* (London Topographical Society, 1987).) "The Steel" is a Cockney rhyming slang for Paris's Bastille, the infamous fortress and state prison of the Bourbon monarchs.

Pentonville Prison, the next stop for more than a few visitors to the Clerkenwell courtroom.[48]

In the 1850s and early 1860s, the *Gazette's* courtroom coverage was relatively sparse, though it was rare for an issue to be without at least one report from the Clerkenwell Police Court. This changed rapidly. By 1870, the *Gazette*, now a bi-weekly paper appearing on Tuesdays and Fridays, was often devoting as much of half a page of a four-page issue to "Law and Police Intelligence." Since as much as a quarter of the paper was devoted to advertising, court reports could, in more than

[48] The area around the court was particularly notorious for prostitution. An 1857 Metropolitan Police report counted 349 street-walkers on Clerkenwell Road, Pentonville Road, and City Road alone. *Crime and Punishment in Islington* 1, no. 1 (2009), https://rebelhand.files.wordpress.com/2015/05/crime-punishment-in-islington.pdf.

a few issues, constitute the single largest "news" (i.e. non-advertising) section. The significantly expanded police-court coverage of the Clerkenwell and Worship Street courts appeared alongside reports from the Clerkenwell County Court, Highgate Petty Sessions and, on occasion, other police courts, the Old Bailey, Guildhall and Mansion House, the Bail Court, and the Bankruptcy Court. It would have been impossible for the limited reporting staff of the *Gazette* to consistently cover all of these courts simultaneously, and this same mix of court reports was a pattern across the London borough papers. We know that reporters could sell the same stories to several different newspapers, and that newspapers reprinted court accounts from one another. It is reasonable to conclude that the *Gazette*'s own reporting resources were concentrated on the courts within its borough or immediately adjacent (i.e. Clerkenwell and Worship Street police courts, the Clerkenwell County Court, and the Highgate Petty Sessions).[49] Both from the memoirs of magistrates and from the content of the reports themselves, which included audience reactions and snippets of dialogue absent from the testimony recorded by the court clerks, it seems that the core of every original version of a police-court report was produced largely from firsthand observation.

The coherence of moral messages offered in these accounts, and the consequent narrowing of possible interpretations by readers, was apparent in the increasing focus on magistrates' authority rather than on competing testimony by the principals. In the pages of the *Gazette* and throughout the growing crop of police-court reports in both local and national newspapers, the preeminence of magistrates' voices matched the widening legal remit of summary justice itself. Magistrates' statements, particularly those accompanying their verdicts, stood out as prominent elements in the majority of individual case descriptions. Their closing comments were reported in much more detail, even though they were directly quoted with less frequency than they had been in previous decades. The Clerkenwell magistrate Robert Philip Tyrwhitt's pronouncements were often reported at length in the *Gazette*, likely because of his tendency to thunder at defendants, sometimes with quite dramatic results. Following the magistrate's vehement condemnation in a June 1860

[49] Rodrick, "Crime Reports," 3.

case, one defendant, brought before the bench for attempting suicide, fainted at the dock and had to be carried from the courtroom.[50] This practice of closely reporting magistrates' pronouncements on morality, the character of defendants, and the implications of any given case for the state of affairs in London could be found in other local newspapers and in the *Gazette's* reporting of other courts as well. The titles of stories in the *Gazette* were also often in accord with magistrates' statements, and were sometimes drawn directly from them.[51] This bookending, with a magistrates' commentary at the end and a title reflecting that commentary at the beginning, served to reinforce one particular interpretation of the case to readers.

The focus on magistrates' voices was a common element across national, metropolitan, and local newspapers that were otherwise diverse in their courtroom coverage. As Anne Rodrick has pointed out in her brief comparison of police-court reports from the *Illustrated London News* and the *Northern Star*, papers speaking from different positions on the political spectrum could vary considerably in the types of cases they reported and how they reported them.[52] They could also carry different messages depending upon the presumed class of the readership. In contrast to these variations, the pattern of declining testimony and increasing magisterial voice held true across the gamut of police-court reporting, even in papers that were, at best, ambivalent about the authority of the magistrates themselves.[53] The privileging of magistrates' voices in newspaper courtroom coverage, however, did not transform these stories into accounts of the magistrates themselves. Their pronouncements served as moral signposts, but as individuals, they were not the focus. The spotlight of court columns remained firmly on the local men and women who passed before the dock, and on the various agencies, individuals, and circumstances that brought them there. The police-court columns stood at the intersection between the expanding reach of police, the authority of the regulatory state, volunteer organizations, and courtrooms on one

[50] For Victorian views on suicide, see Olive Anderson, *Suicide in Victorian and Edwardian England* (Oxford: Clarendon, 1987); Barbara T. Gates, *Victorian Suicide: Mad Crimes and Sad Histories* (Princeton: Princeton University Press, 1988).

[51] Both *Lloyds's* and *Reynolds's* signposted their police-court stories with titles. The *Morning Post*, in contrast, did not.

[52] Rodrick, "Crime Reports," 3–5, 13.

[53] *Bee-Hive*, March 8, 1865.

hand and the burgeoning readership of newspapers on the other.[54] Courtroom accounts were rapidly becoming the primary means by which the growing press industry sought to gain new readers and sustain the interest of their audience. One sign of the intertwining of the press and London courtrooms in this period was the increasing frequency with which the two were discussed in tandem by prominent commentators. In their 1872 satirical work, *Two Idle Apprentices*, Thomas Wemyss Reid, a reporter for various provincial papers and later the editor of the *Leeds Mercury*, and William Henry Cooke, a prominent London barrister, catalogued and compared the foibles of each profession.[55] W. H. Watts, John Wight's successor as the police-court reporter for the *Morning Herald*, likewise intimately linked the parallel development of local courtrooms and the press that covered them.[56] Watts's career itself demonstrated how closely entwined courts and press had become by mid-century. Prior to taking up his post at the *Herald*, he had served as the chief clerk of the Marylebone Police Court.[57]

Watts, however, was writing nostalgically in 1864, when he penned his popular retrospective, *London Life at the Police Courts*.[58] He lamented the decline of "literary matter" in court reporting even as he acknowledged the "vast power" that the press constituted by the mid-1860s. The true culprit, he explained, was not parsimonious editors who were no longer willing to pay for "the 'humourous' delineation of *real* life," and favored, instead, "the heaviness of politics and criminal charges."[59] It was the social and cultural transformation of the country itself, and of the working class in

[54] For the growth of the state in the mid-Victorian period, see F. David Roberts, *The Social Conscience of the Early Victorians* (Stanford: Stanford University Press, 2002), 396–413.

[55] Two Idle Apprentices, *Briefs and Papers: Sketches of the Bar and the Press* (London: Henry King, 1872).

[56] W. H. Watts, *London Life at the Police Courts* (London: Ward and Lock, 1864), 17. Watts also published some of this material in *St. James Magazine*. W. H. Watts, "Records of an Old Police Court," no. IV, *St. James Magazine* 12 (Nov. 1864), 444–52.

[57] Henry Turner Waddy, *The London Police Court and Its Work* (London: Butterworth, 1925), 200.

[58] In 1834, Watts had replaced John Wight as the *Morning Herald*'s "'comic' police-reporter" in the Marlborough Street court. Watts, *London Life*, 4.

[59] Ibid., 8.

particular, that was to blame. "The march of education, the spread of cheap knowledge, the nearer approximation of classes, have worn away old broad distinctive lines," Watts explained, "and have obliterated or destroyed much of that rough originality which once constituted so large and so conspicuous a portion of what may be called the *individuality* of the lower orders of English society."[60] Writing in the mid-1860s, with 1848 and the Chartist movement decades past, the economic disruptions of the late 1880s still to come, and the working-class Radicalism of the 1830s and 1840s having largely given way to a new focus on respectability, it is easy to see why a newsman might pine for more interesting times.[61] Watts was hardly the only one, then or now, to describe the mid-Victorian period as one of economic progress, social stability, and relative political calm.[62] The Education Act of 1870 lay in the future, but increasing Sunday school attendance and the rising popularity of Sunday papers all pointed to the "march of education" and the "spread of cheap knowledge" that Watts blamed for the loss of class distinctions.[63] This latter claim was the most problematic, however, and jibed poorly with the growing public concern over demoralization and slums in London's East End.[64] Problematic or not, in Watts's view, the changing character of courtroom accounts was a barometer of the changing character of Victorian society itself, for where else could one hope to find such a broad and detailed account of everyday life than in the police courts?

As their humor and melodrama faded, the police-court columns' wide popularity grew, and with it, the authority of their implicit claim

60 Ibid., 9.

61 F. M. L. Thompson, *The Rise of Respectable Society: A Social History of Victorian Britain, 1830–1900* (Cambridge, MA: Harvard University Press, 1988), 197–205.

62 This period has been critically reexamined in Martin Hewitt, ed., *An Age of Equipoise?: Reassessing Mid-Victorian Britain* (Aldershot and Burlington, VT: Ashgate, 2000); and Ian Inkster, Judith Rowbotham, and Colin Griffin, eds., *The Golden Age: Essays in British Social and Economic History, 1850–1870* (Aldershot and Burlington, VT: Ashgate, 2000).

63 On working-class literacy and education, see Jonathan Rose, *The Intellectual Life of the British Working Classes* (New Haven: Yale University Press, 2001), 146–86.

64 See Gareth Stedman-Jones, *Outcast London: A Study in the Relationship between Classes in Victorian Society* (Oxford: Oxford University Press, 1971); Ellen Ross, *Love and Toil: Motherhood in Outcast London* (Oxford: Oxford University Press, 1994); Seth Koven, *Slumming: Social and Sexual Politics in Victorian London* (Princeton: Princeton University Press, 2004).

to depict life as it really was in London's poorer districts. The changes in style and content, much bemoaned by Watts and echoed by other court chroniclers of the period, encouraged the transition of police-court reports from sensationalist fodder for a privileged audience of upper- and middle-class newsreaders in the 1830s and 1840s to a popular readership in which the lower middle class and working class were well represented by the 1860s and 1870s. Newspaper customers, whether from the older or newer cohorts, demanded stories that both informed and entertained, and their taste for courtroom accounts had been well primed by decades of editorial practice. Police-court reports appealed across this spectrum, and sensationalist cases of murder and scandal were still prominent. But particularly for the borough papers that multiplied across London in the wake of the Stamp Act's repeal, and for which local police-court reports provided the commercial advantage of easy access and broad interest, such cases were few and far between. Annually, the metropolitan courts adjudicated only a handful of charges for murder, attempted murder, attempted suicide, and manslaughter.[65] And though a long case, as murder trials often were, could fill multiple columns across the course of days or weeks, sensational or dramatic courtroom stories were vastly outnumbered by the daily or weekly run of "Police Intelligence." These regular columns dealt with a wide panoply of cases, from assaults and burglary to dog bites and cab-fare dodging.

At first glance, such reports, which were printed and reprinted by the tens of thousands each year, seemed to have had little in common. In the aggregate, however, they depicted the increasing integration of courtrooms and daily life in the metropolis. In conjunction with the continued expansion of both summary jurisdiction and the host of regulations that governed urban life, they helped shape the significance and popular understandings of what happened in a courtroom for newspaper readers and court clientele alike. The loss of individuality

[65] In 1860, the Metropolitan Police District reported 3 murders, 1 attempted murder, 34 cases of manslaughter, and 54 cases of "shooting at, wounding, stabling" or other attempts to inflict grievous bodily harm. In addition, they reported 4 attempts to commit suicide. The City of London, it should be noted, reported only 1 murder and 1 case of manslaughter, but 34 attempted suicides (likely due to the ease of access to the Thames River and the popularity of the major bridges for such acts). *Judicial Statistics, 1860*, 16.

bemoaned by Watts was one of the most notable aspects of this change. Across the range of reported cases, from the brutal to the banal, the role of the private individual in initiating prosecutions, which had been a central feature of the older, humorous vein of police-court reporting, diminished dramatically. The theme of personal redress for wrongs was increasingly superseded by a more depersonalized and amorphous process of punishing wrongdoers not only for acts against individuals or their property, but for social transgressions, abuses of public space, or alleged threats to the general wellbeing of local communities. Gone were the days when police-court reports could depict magistrates patiently explaining to petitioners that their complaint might be morally valid, but had no legal basis. The newer portrayals of courtrooms as locales where, through the person of the magistrate and at the initiative of municipal or voluntary organizations, a largely rational and impersonal justice was dispensed were in accord with broader revisions of the criminal code. The intention in the latter, whether through fines or imprisonment, was not merely to punish violators, but to morally reform them in the process, to maintain public order, and to serve the public good.[66] The magistrate, in these equations, remained the arbiter of morality as well as the dispenser of law. His decisions, along with the language employed to describe individual cases, left little room for alternate interpretations on the part of the reader. The contrast between individual defendants, who were described through physical appearance and character, and magistrates, who operated only as disembodied voices of law and morality, only served to emphasize the distance between the authority of the state and the agency of the individual in courtroom interactions.

A more consistent picture of magistrates as the guardians of the public weal was matched in the *Islington Gazette*'s police-court columns with a sharper moral division between victims and villains. Nowhere was this more evident than in the portrayal of women and children in courtrooms. The moral ambiguity that had attended the tales of Wight and the court stories of the 1830s–1850s was nowhere to be found. Instead, the language employed both by the reporters and those they quoted became unequivocal in painting women and children as either the perpetrators of moral iniquity or the sufferers from it. Children who stole without reason

[66] Wiener, *Reconstructing the Criminal*, 61.

or reluctance were "uncontrollable urchins," and examples of "youthful depravity" who were "dishonest ... utterly beyond parental control."[67] Even something as seemingly innocuous as playing street-games, if done on a large enough scale, could prompt a magistrate, in May 1880, to publicly label dozens of teenage and adolescent boys "rogues and vagabonds" and to threaten them with long terms of imprisonment.[68] Though the threat was not carried out in this case (they received only a day's imprisonment, without option of a fine), the large number of defendants and the magistrate's tirade merited two separate news stories totaling more than a full column of print.[69] This matched the level of coverage ordinarily reserved for murders, vicious neglect, daring frauds, or other crimes either serious or scandalous. In contrast, a "ragged-looking boy" who committed similar crimes out of desperation was "a sad case."[70] In the paper's description, it was appropriate that the defendants in the former case were destined for prison or a reformatory. In contrast, the "ragged" boy, though he was "often guilty of dishonesty," "would not go to school or work," and had even robbed his own ailing mother, deserved mercy and generosity. He would receive twenty shillings, coal, and food, all paid for from donations to the police court's "poor box."

This drawing of stark moral divisions between the neglected and the delinquent was a prominent aspect of Victorian debates over the role of children in the household. These debates reached a particularly high pitch in the decade following the passage of the Education Act 1870 and the subsequent implementation of compulsory school attendance.[71] The rising public concern with the physical neglect or abuse of children, and the attendant segregation of those involved into villains or victims, was also much in evidence in police-court columns.[72] The content of these columns, however, was a very poor reflection of the courts' involvement in the child-reform movement. As

[67] *Gazette*, April 21, 1880, April 16, 1880. [68] Ibid., May 17, 1870.

[69] Ibid., May 10, 1880, May 17, 1870. [70] *Gazette*, April 21, 1880.

[71] Sascha Auerbach, "'The Law Has No Feeling for Poor Folks Like Us!': Everyday Responses to Legal Compulsion in England's Working-Class Communities, 1871–1904," *Journal of Social History* 45, no. 2 (Spring 2012), 686–708 and "'Some Punishment Should Be Devised': Parents, Children, and the State in Victorian London," *The Historian* 71, no. 4 (Winter, 2009), 757–79.

[72] George Behlmer, *Child Abuse and Moral Reform in England, 1870–1908* (Stanford: Stanford University Press, 1982) and *Friends of the Family: The English Home and Its Guardians, 1850–1940* (Stanford: Stanford University Press, 1998), 104–6.

discussed in the following chapters, the most common types of regulatory summonses, such as those brought by the London School Board against parents who violated the compulsory school attendance bye-laws, were vastly underreported in newspapers. Unlike School Board cases themselves, where magistrates often expressed sympathy for the parents and were ambivalent about enforcement, police-court columns emphasized the kindly treatment of good children and the stern disciplining of bad ones. In these representations, particularly when parents failed in their duties of care and protection, magistrates, municipal authorities, or volunteer agents appeared as vigilant and compassionate. Patterns of reporting, rather than accurately depicting courtroom practice, instead reflected the public's interest in seeing those who victimized the helpless brought to justice.[73] In such stories, the perfidy of unredeemable defendants was sharply contrasted with the stern and measured imposition of punishment by magistrates.

In newspaper stories, along with the increasing use of moral archetypes, class and gender stereotypes, and the general decline of verbatim testimony, the valorization or villainization of plaintiffs and defendants undermined the individuality of those who were portrayed in local courtrooms. Although the cultural autonomy of the individual was waning in police-court columns as the century progressed, the public were not excluded altogether. The multiplication and wide publication of these columns encouraged *passive* encounters with courtrooms, inviting a broad cross-section of the population to vicariously experience events in London's courts of summary justice. The passively participating public was also incorporated more prominently into published descriptions of these courtrooms. According to James Greenwood, one of the most prominent of the late Victorian *flâneurs*, both readership and

[73] In 1870, aggravated assaults on women and children (as defined in 24 & 25 Vict. s. 43) combined for a total of 295 cases in London's courts of summary justice, making them among one the *least* prosecuted crimes of violence and damage. They were exceeded by prosecutions for maliciously destroying walls, gates, vegetable and fruit patches, and trees and shrubs (303 total), and equal with prosecutions for mutiny under the Army Acts (292). *Criminal Statistics, 1870*. As Shani D'Cruze and others have emphasized, however, this certainly does not mean they were among the least *committed* crimes, since women and children often failed to report such acts, for a variety of reasons. Shani D'Cruze and Louise A. Jackson, *Women, Crime and Justice in England since 1660* (Basingstoke: Palgrave Macmillan, 2009).

audience attendance were essential features of the police courts. Like his brother, who was the founding editor of the *Pall Mall Gazette*, James was committed to bringing the tribulations of life in the poorer districts to light, and in his descriptions of these areas, the police courts played a key role.[74] Greenwood's widely read *Mysteries of Modern London* (1883) included a chapter on each of the busiest Islington courts, Clerkenwell and Worship Street, as well as another devoted to the Lambeth court. The "general public," he wrote, derived their knowledge of the courts from newspaper reports.[75] A more immediate experience was sought at the Worship Street court, which was "every morning beset by just such a crowd as pack the gallery door of a cheap theatre on a pantomime night."[76] Mixed in with the accompanying illustrations, which caricatured various defendants, were drawings of attentive crowds attempting entry to the courts, women seeking summonses from the court officers, and onlookers responding to the proceedings with a wide gamut of emotions.[77]

This portrayal of courtrooms as integrated with the daily life of the community, whose members could be found both before the bench and observing it from the gallery, granted further reinforcement to the alleged authenticity of police-court columns and to their presentation as realistic depictions. It also offered support to the image of the courtroom as being transparent, accessible, and operating in accord with consensual standards of justice and morality. In this way, newspapers and state action worked in tandem to generate a common taxonomy of morality that operated alongside the other vectors of communicating moral standards such as the church, the family, and measures of respectability. This taxonomy drew on definitions of right and wrong shaped by these more established, though far from static, milieus. Public accounts of the police courts and cases tried there also incorporated a more novel dimension to moral assessment. In such portrayals, moral rectitude was consonant with obedience to the host of new regulations and respect for the authorities that enforced them, be they police, Poor Law Guardians,

[74] James was the younger brother of Frederick Greenwood. Koven, *Slumming*, 31.

[75] James Greenwood, *Mysteries of Modern London, by One of the Crowd* (London: Diprose & Bateman, 1883), 84.

[76] Ibid., 19. [77] Ibid. 18, 84, and 19, respectively.

representatives of the RSPCA, or ticket-collectors on the London omnibuses.[78] Considering the highly selective and constructed nature of police-court reports, we cannot take the frequent accounts of prosecutions for resistance to – or physical assaults on – state or voluntary agents as clear signs of popular opposition. Conflict with the agents of law enforcement in particular, to judge by the number of prosecutions each year for obstruction, resisting, and assaults on peace officers, was certainly not uncommon in London.[79] The reports themselves, however, are more accurately read as an effort by the editors of the *Gazette* to publicly label such acts as inherently immoral as well as illegal. The magistrates' cited statements hammered the point home further. The latter were hardly unanimous or unwavering in their support of constables, parish officers, or volunteer agents, all of whom were appearing in increasing numbers to prosecute cases. In contrast to police-court practice, no such ambiguity was apparent in the *Gazette*'s police-court reports. In the paper's published accounts, magistrates publicly castigated men and women who interfered directly with the conduct of their duties and were often severe in their sentencing of those who physically abused them.[80]

In contrast to the increasing press coverage of individuals' legal and moral accountability to state authorities (the courts themselves not least among them), municipal bodies, volunteer social reformers, and the potentially dire consequences of unruly behavior in urban communities more generally, the voice of defendants in declaring or contesting justice diminished rapidly. The steady elimination of

[78] According to Mary Poovey, Edwin Chadwick, in his 1830s advocacy of the New Poor Laws in the *Edinburgh Review*, was performing a similar ideological function by presenting specific social arrangements that were in accord with the market economy by being universal and of self-evident virtue. Mary Poovey, *Making a Social Body: British Cultural Formation, 1830–1864* (Chicago: University of Chicago Press, 1995), 108–9.

[79] In 1860, these crimes were prosecuted 2,374 times; in 1870, 2,454 summary proceedings were initiated on these charges; 2,434 in 1875; 3,140 in 1880; 3,446 in 1885 and 4,343 in 1890. *Judicial Statistics, England and Wales, Pt. I, Police – Criminal Proceedings – Prisons, 1860* (PP 1861, 2860), *1870* (PP 1871, C. 442), *1875* (PP 1876, C. 1595), *1880* (PP 1881, C. 3088), *1885* (PP 1886, C. 4808), and *1890* (PP 1890–1, C. 6443).

[80] *Gazette*, May 3, 1880.

defendants' verbatim testimony from police-court columns ensured this. It often left magistrates, or occasionally solicitors, as the sole contributors to the courtroom dialogue on the merits of any given charge or sentence. The impetus to broadcast such dialogue did not lie with courtroom officers or trial principles in any case, but with reporters and editors. By the late 1870s, the most frequent reference to defendants' views on the fairness of unfairness of any given sentence was confined to their derisive exit lines following conviction.[81] Exclusive of magistrates' courtroom declarations, commentary on the legal or moral implications of specific trials moved from the courtroom reports themselves into other sections of newspapers, most notably editorials and letters to the editor. This commentary, in contrast to magistrates' pronouncements, was prompted by the police-court reports rather than by firsthand participation or observation of courtroom events. In December 1880, the only direct criticism of the Metropolitan Police to appear that year in the *Gazette* came via editorial commentary on a previously reported case rather than defendants' courtroom dialogue.[82] But the magistrate himself was not censured, and even in their harshest declamation of "petty tyranny" by police, the editors questioned neither judicial authority nor judicial wisdom.[83] The movement of discussions of justice and fairness from reported courtroom dialogue to letters and editorials was a corollary of the police-court columns' gradual transformation from stylized accounts offered in explicitly comic or melodramatic form to more realistic and unadorned stories of local, metropolitan, or even national significance. Unlike the former, the latter was explicitly news, and therefore appropriate subject matter for serious discussion and further engagement by readers and editors.

The cases that appeared with greatest frequency in the *Gazette*'s police intelligence columns in the 1870s and 1880s were those concerning public drunkenness. In these reports, the major trends of police-court portrayals in the second half of the nineteenth century

[81] The most common being "I can do that bit standing on my head," or some variation on this theme.

[82] *Gazette*, January 14, 1880.

[83] In the December incident, for example, the same editorial that castigated the police reaffirmed the authority of the magistrate to issue the warrant for arrest (due to a missed second summons) and applauded his judgment in the case (dismissal).

were all clear, as was the contribution of police courts and their representations in definitions of public morality more generally. Specifically, they emphasized the growing predominance of state and voluntary agents in police-court prosecutions and positively depicted their interventions in everyday life while negatively depicting those who defied them. Such stories also were devoid of all but brief defendants' testimony, a practice that further amplified the role of the magistrates as the embodiment of uncontested moral authority. The portrayal of morality and authority as a one-sided affair coincided with the rising concrete execution of summary jurisdiction in these matters. Prosecutions for public drunkenness, which had been on the decline since their high point in the early 1830s, began to rise again after 1848, which is also the year when the law mandated that all magistrates' prosecutions had to be conducted in open court.[84] In this case, an increase in the portrayal of the magistrates as moral arbiters in everyday life coincided perfectly with the increasing visibility of these prosecutions to the local community. By 1865, such prosecutions comprised nearly a quarter of all summary prosecutions in the metropolis, reaching a peak of 31,013 in 1875 and remaining near that level throughout the final decades of the nineteenth century.[85] The pattern in London tracked well with national trends.[86] Although drink had been a frequently mentioned topic in police-court columns from their inception, it was not until the 1870s that prosecutions for public drunkenness began to be published as a segregated category of police-court reports. In that period, what one provincial paper referred to as the "Drunkard's List" began to appear

[84] In 1831, there were 31,353 arrests for drunkenness in the metropolis. They decreased steadily, along with arrests for other social and moral crimes such as vagrancy and disorderly prostitution, until reaching a nadir in 1848, when there were only 8,392 arrests for drunkenness and 8,069 for drunk and disorderly behavior. After that year, arrests for both began to rise once again. Stephen Inwood, "Policing London's Morals: The Metropolitan Police and Popular Culture, 1829–1850," *London Journal* 15, no. 2 (1990), 136.

[85] 20,684 of 91,579 total summary prosecutions. *Judicial Statistics, 1865, England and Wales, Pt. I, Police – Criminal Proceedings – Prisons* (PP 1866, 3726), 71. In 1870, 20,819; in 1875, 31,013/106,237; in 1880, 32,710; in 1885, 26,614; and in 1890, 30,514 (*Judicial Statistics, 1870*, 28; *1875*, 90; *1880*, 88; *1885*, 86; *1890*, 94).

[86] Paul Jennings, "Policing Drunkenness in England and Wales from the Late Eighteenth Century to the First World War," *Social History of Alcohol and Drugs* 26, no. 1 (Winter, 2012), 89.

in the *Gazette* and other local and provincial papers.[87] In national dailies and the Sunday weeklies that covered multiple London police courts, such cases became more frequent, though they were not usually reconstituted as a distinct news section.

Drunkenness trials and their regular penalties appeared by the score every month in the *Gazette*. For a local newspaper with limited material available to fill the standard run of courtroom columns, they were indeed useful if no more substantial or compelling cases were heard on the day in question. The *Gazette* made a particular point of covering the "Monday charges," when the dozens of men and women arrested over the weekend had their moment before the bench. In reporting these cases, the paper was following a long-established tradition of police-court reporting; trials for public drunkenness had been common fare since the time of John Wight and his *Mornings at Bow Street*. But the stories of Wight and his immediate successors had been embellished with comic dialogue and narrative flourishes, little of which remained in the modern form of realistic courtroom reporting that prevailed by the 1870s. Yet another in a seemingly endless cavalcade of inebriated artisans found helpless on the high street, too insensible to make their own way home, did not excite undue interest from reporters, editors, or readers. Nor was there any deeper moral or legal meaning to be offered or construed from any single case, since it was rare to encounter one that had not been reported *ad nauseam* before and would not be repeated countless times subsequently. At first glance, the only significance their proliferation seems to offer is as testimony to the prevalent concern over intemperance in late Victorian society.[88]

The message conveyed in the aggregate, however, was more noteworthy. In a paper that catered to the respectable readership of shopkeepers, literate artisans, and middle-class Islington residents with an interest in local affairs, the steady stream of reports that began with the defendant's name and address reminded readers that public inebriation posed significant hazards, if not to finance or freedom, then certainly to reputation. Harsh punishment was highly unlikely,

87 Ibid., 72.

88 The various arguments made by Brian Harrison, F. M. L. Thompson, V. A. C. Gatrell and others as to whether or not alcohol consumption itself was actually on the rise in this period, and the effect that prosecution figures had on perception, are outlined in Jennings, "Policing Drunkenness," 82–83.

unless the defendant compounded their intemperance with further misbehavior. The risks of embarrassment before a courtroom audience, on the other hand, were much higher, and the possibility of a public shaming before the cohort of *Gazette* readers could hardly be ignored. There was even the potential, as with any other local report, that the story might be picked up by the provincial, daily, or Sunday press as well, causing humiliation on a national scale. It should be noted, though, that some defendants reveled in the process, and a small number achieved a measure of local celebrity from their plethora of appearances before the bench.[89] In this way the "Drunkard's List," like other categories of police-court reports, worked in tandem with prosecutions themselves to make courtrooms a locale where both legal boundaries *and* moral norms were publicly drawn. The individuals could be judged by magistrates, whose moral pronouncements would be duly reported, uncontested, for affirmation by the broader community of local newspaper readers. The strongest deterrent these reports offered to would-be violators, especially to those who were unlikely to assault constables or operate a horse and cart, lay not in the fines (a discharge being by far the most common outcome), but in the potential for public humiliation.[90]

The consistent moral lessons and orderly, predictable punishments apparent in the police-court reports, while corresponding well with larger cultural trends in Victorian society, contrasted with the development of the courtroom environment itself. In the latter, magistrates continued to exercise a high degree of discretion and could impose harsh punishments for minor violations in some instances, while letting those charged with a panoply of transgressions go free in others.[91]

[89] Among the most notorious in the North London courts was Jane Cakebread, allegedly arrested over 200 times, whose courtroom antics in the late 1880s were reported in the *Morning Post* (September 11, 1888), *Reynolds's* (October 12, 1890), *Lloyds's* (August 31, 1890), *Illustrated Police News* (February 12, 1887), *Pall Mall Gazette* (April 20, 1887), *Leeds Mercury* (October 11, 1890), and even *The Times* (August 26, 1890). The most famous and widely published incident was an October 1890 trial when Cakebread claimed relation to an Anglican Bishop ("Jane Cakebread Once Again," *Gazette*, October 13, 1890). Also noted in Jennings, "Policing Drunkenness," 84.

[90] Croll, "Street Disorder," 262–64.

[91] As discussed in Chapter 6, the court records themselves revealed much greater variation in sentences granted, with magistrates exercising a high degree of discretion. Violations associated consistently with harsh punishments in the police-court columns were not infrequently dismissed, and significant fines or even imprisonment

Both the "naming and shaming" element and the contrast between the formulaic reports and the diverse court practice further emphasize the importance of seeing the writing and reading of these courtroom tales as processes of cultural construction and consumption, rather than as unproblematic windows onto courtroom events. As the most common type of courtroom report, the accounts of trials for drunkenness or drunk and disorderly behavior demonstrated how the greatest significance of a police court trial could lay in its public perception rather than in its practical outcome. Their import for both the individuals involved and the witnessing community resided in the courtrooms' cultural and social operation rather than in its legal and concrete dimensions.

Although increasingly uniform in their moral content, police-court reports nonetheless epitomized a fundamental tension in a society that was transitioning towards modernity. Whether they were discussing assault or drunkenness, vaccination or furious driving, the police-court columns of the later nineteenth century starkly illuminated the contradiction between older ideas of Liberal individualism and moral choice on the one hand and the growing trend towards mass society, determinism, and environmental explanations for crime and immorality on the other.[92] Mid-Victorian criminal policy revolved around moral accountability, reforming character, and demonstrating the clear and consistent consequences for those who chose to break the law. It was dependent on the idea of the individual as being free to make choices for good or ill. In these aspects, criminal justice assumed the character of a market, with the concurrent emphasis on rationality, self-discipline, and impersonal arbitration.[93] The disappearance of individual defendants' voices from police-court columns of the late Victorian period communicated the opposite message. Those who faced trial were still named and described, and their choices up until the time they appeared in court were recounted, but once in that

could be inflicted on those convicted of being solely drunk and disorderly. On multiple occasions at the Hammersmith PC in January 1880, those convicted of the latter received fines of 40 shillings or 14 days in in prison, while those convicted of being drunk, disorderly and using obscene language or being drunk and fighting were fined only 5 shillings or discharged. Register of Charges, Hammersmith Police Court, January 12 and 13, 1880 (PS/WLN/A1/6) (LMA).

92 Weiner, *Reconstructing the Criminal*, 224–32.

93 Ibid., 66.

environment, they were increasingly stripped of choice, voice, and agency as individuals. Watts's "rough originality" and "individuality" were replaced with a predictable and consistent moral and social typology.

These changes were reflected in the style of reports as much as they were in their content. As police-court columns became more numerous, they also became more concise and condensed. Dialogue between the principles contracted to brief snippets. With this reduction of reported testimony, the explicit moral pronouncements of magistrates, constables, municipal representatives, and voluntary agents passed uncontested, as did the implicit moral assessments offered by reporters and editors through story titles and selective citing of dialogue. Earlier in the century, overzealous magistrates or intrusive new laws could receive rough treatment or even caricature in the press. But by the last quarter of the century, magistrates were increasingly portrayed as the veritable voice of justice, narrowing the distance between what was illegal and what was immoral in press portrayals. This, in turn, reduced the need for defendants' speech to be extensively reported in court columns, despite its continued presence in courtrooms themselves. Those accused of crimes were placed in easily identifiable categories, their moral status as victims or villains clearly communicated through column titles, descriptive language, and other journalistic devices. Gone was the rogue's gallery of humorous characters that had typified early police-court reporting, characters that, although embodying archetypes, nonetheless remained as individuals capable of dialogue and contestation. Readers, too, were denied enough detail to arrive at their own conclusions. A story that promised "YOUTHFUL DEPRAVITY," "POLICE VIGILANCE," "A VIRAGO," "A BRUTAL FATHER," "DISSOLUTION AND DRUNKENNESS," or "A SAD CASE" was bound to deliver precisely that.[94] Every defendant found guilty was, by definition, deserving of punishment, and every urchin acquitted was blameless. Readers could still choose what newspapers they bought, and might get different perspectives on a prominent case as a result. The ability to reinterpret individual reports was highly constrained nonetheless, since almost all these columns hewed to the

[94] *Gazette* (depravity) April 16; (police) April 7; (virago) May 5; (father) May 10; (dissolution) March 29; and (sad case) May 19, 1880, respectively.

same basic structure of reduced dialogue and concise narrative. The dynamics of police-court reporting itself, in which single reports were reproduced and reprinted in multiple papers, strengthened this homogenization of meaning.

As a result of these trends, the opportunity of individual plaintiffs and defendants to shape the public meaning of courtroom events declined precipitously in the second half of the nineteenth century. The typical police-court report provided a single, coherent moral message reinforced through the title, magistrates' pronouncements, and absence of verbatim dialogue. The widened role of constables and other agents of state and voluntary reform also diminished the authority of private individuals in published courtroom narratives. The multiplication and dissemination of these accounts across the local, regional, and national press undercut further the very idea that individuals unconnected to larger authorities – such as the criminal justice system or municipal government – could shape the outcome of police-court cases at all, let alone their moral meanings. In contrast to individual plaintiffs and defendants, who were becoming less important elements of police-court reports, the reports themselves were becoming more significant in the wider context of newspaper production and consumption, occupying a liminal space between serious news and sensationalized entertainment. Their variety and content offered the appeal of the latter, from an editors' or readers' point of view, while their realism and engagement with issues of note distinguished them from mere amusements.

Here, then, was the dominant public image of what happened in a London magistrates' courtroom on a daily basis. The vast majority of police-court reports covered charges, usually initiated by the police – though increasingly by agents of municipal or voluntary institutions as well – to deal with a largely unruly and uncooperative community who had little understanding of how the law worked. Punishment, in the form of imprisonment or fines, was the most typical outcome of an appearance in court, and the magistrates were the sole arbiters of law *and* morality. The men and women who found themselves in court did so involuntarily, and had little role in shaping either the concrete outcomes, the daily practices, or the meaning and significance of what was said and done in a courtroom. In these reports, justice was declared, legality determined, and morality pronounced. Negotiation played no role, unless conducted by solicitors, and the voice of the individual defendant was heard faintly, if at all. This was the image, and the messages it communicated – about the state, the law, the individual, and the role of the courtroom in mediating between them – were powerful ones.

In contrast, daily conduct in local courtrooms remained a complicated and contested affair, as the surviving police-court records demonstrate. Newspaper stories were vastly unrepresentative of the types of cases that came before magistrates, the likely outcome of those cases and, most especially, the character of courtroom interactions. This does not lessen the powerful role that newspapers played in shaping courtroom culture, but it does fundamentally undermine any effort to draw a direct correlation between what was reported in "Police Intelligence" columns and what happened in these courtrooms. The communication of basic information, such as the principals and the verdict, was generally correct. Beyond that, these stories hewed to moral narratives and the changing dynamics of newspaper production and consumption rather than accurate portrayals of what was said and done. Police-court columns helped reproduce an image of legal and moral authority that accorded with the growing reach of summary justice, but contrasted with the persistent flexibility of police-court practice and the agency of individuals within it. Newspaper readers were rarely offered enough context or contrary testimony to reinterpret the story of "A RUFFIAN RIGHTLY PUNISHED."[95] In the courtroom, the ruffian himself might have expressed a very different view on the matter.

[95] *Gazette*, March 29, 1880.

3

"An Evil Quarter of an Hour about the Precincts"

Urban Reform and Municipal Authority in the Courtroom, 1870–1902

The previous chapters have traced the evolution of the police courts as an institution in London's legal apparatus, their widening remit and role in local communities, and how their activities and their portrayals shaped discussions of morality. Until the final quarter of the nineteenth century, in most respects, police courts loomed larger in metropolitan culture than they did in metropolitan social life, though their importance in the latter, especially in working-class communities, had risen steadily. Portrayals of the courts, a staple in both the local and national press, were widely read and much commented on. Likewise, the reform and expansion of summary justice in the years following the Peel Acts was a key concern to legislators, magistrates, police officials, social reformers, and public commentators. Nonetheless, the courts remained more widely viewed from the outside than from the inside. In the late Victorian period, however, even as public portrayals of courtrooms and their daily duties began to diverge ever more widely, the roles of courtrooms in their communities began to expand considerably.[1] To understand the role played by local courtrooms in shaping social relations, moral norms, and the relationship between the state and the individual in London, we must

[1] As Charles Dickens Jr. explained at the turn of the century, only a "very small portion" of police-court business found its way into the newspapers. Charles Dickens Jr., "A London Police-Court," *All the Year Round: A Weekly Journal* 4 (3rd series) (Jan.–Jun. 1899), 349.

examine this rapid expansion of activity, whose initiative prompted it, and what the consequences were for all involved.

By 1870, in London alone, the newspaper reports of police-court cases numbered in the many thousands annually. Cases themselves far exceeded this, totaling over 100,000 each year. The general trajectory over the second half of the nineteenth century was a widening of enforcement or behaviors being policed rather than an increasing severity of punishment.[2] The rise in summary prosecutions for violent crime, theft, and other offenses against property and person was dwarfed by a meteoric growth in summonses involving regulations on health and public safety, social reform, minor violations of public order statutes, and the collection of various fees and debts to municipal, commercial, and corporate bodies. As Charles Dickens Jr. rightly observed, it was these minor summonses that would make "enjoying an evil quarter of an hour about the precincts of a London police-court ... the common lot" of metropolitan residents by century's end.[3] Despite their vast number, neither commentators then nor scholars of law, crime, and the press more recently have taken much time to examine these relatively banal prosecutions. Their relationship to public discussions and portrayals of the courts was different from the more dramatic tales of vice and violence, but it was hardly inconsequential. Summonses for minor offenses, prosaic though they may appear to be, played an influential role in shaping interactions between individuals, communities, and the state. The focus of media attention in this period on dramatic violations of the law has been mirrored in historiography. Largely ignored by historians of crime and policing, the operation of the ubiquitous, but less dramatic, laws regulating daily urban life has been left to scholars of Victorian government and social reform. Current explanations can be divided into three interrelated categories, those that focus on discourses of class

[2] Chapter 6 deals with this in greater detail. And it should be noted at the outset that declines were as common as increases. In the period 1859–1900, for example, the summary prosecution of common assault declined in relation to the population (13,874 persons prosecuted in 1859 versus 13,530 in 1900). *Judicial Statistics, 1859, England and Wales, Pt. I, Police – Criminal Proceedings – Prisons* (PP 1860, 2692), 65; *Judicial Statistics, 1900* (PP 1902, Cd. 953), 68. Martin Wiener, *Reconstructing the Criminal: Culture, Law, and Policy in England, 1830–1914* (Cambridge: Cambridge University Press, 1990), 66–67.

[3] Dickens Jr., "A London Police-Court," 349.

and gender, those that focus on social geography and the regulation of urban space, and those that focus on Liberalism and "governmentality."[4] The courtroom itself, when it has appeared at all in this scholarship, has been an inert field of engagement, a stage on which larger dramas of power and authority played out.

Regardless of what laws Parliament passed and what regulations the agents of municipal authorities chose to enforce, however, it was in the courtroom that the ultimate decision to warn, punish, or pardon was made. In the final quarter of the nineteenth century, London police courtrooms became both a lynchpin of urban reform and a key locale for determining the practical boundaries of regulation in the metropolis. The daily adjudication of summonses, the form by which most of these minor offenses were prosecuted, incorporated both a legal and a moral dimension. Magistrates, defendants, and the agents who represented municipal authority sharply contested the enforcement of regulations covering almost every aspect of urban life, from health and education to public spaces and transport. Underpinning these battles was a contention over morality and the autonomy of the individual in modern society. These cases provide insight into several crucial questions about the nature of metropolitan governance and the relationship of the state to the individual. What were the limits of public authority versus individual freedom? What violations represented a genuine hazard to the public good, and how was the latter to be defined? And, finally, did the ultimate authority in court to determine the limits of reform and the moral status of its

[4] In the British metropolitan context, key works in this extensive literature include Ellen Ross, *Love and Toil: Motherhood in Outcast London, 1870–1918* (New York and Oxford: Oxford University Press, 1993); Susan D. Pennybacker, *A Vision for London, 1889–1914: Labour, Everyday Life and the LCC Experiment* (London: Routledge, 1995); Mary Poovey, *Making a Social Body: British Cultural Formation, 1830–1864* (Chicago and London: University of Chicago Press, 1995); Lynn Hollen Lees, *The Solidarities of Strangers: The English Poor Laws and the People, 1700–1948* (Cambridge: Cambridge University Press, 1998); George K. Behlmer, *Friends of the Family: The English Home and Its Guardians, 1850–1940* (Stanford: Stanford University Press, 1998); Seth Koven, *Slumming: Sexual and Social Politics in Victorian London* (Princeton: Princeton University Press, 2004); Patrick Joyce, *The Rule of Freedom: Liberalism and the Modern City* (London: Verso, 2003). Two of the most oft-cited and essential of the more established works are Asa Briggs, *Victorian Cities* (London: Odhams Press, 1964) and Gareth Stedman Jones, *Outcast London: A Study in the Relationship between Classes in Victorian Society* (Oxford: Clarendon Press, 1971).

violators lie with the municipal representatives who levied summonses or with the magistrates who adjudicated them? The picture revealed is that of a state highly fragmented over principle and execution, dependent on persuasion rather than coercion, and vulnerable to contestation and public defiance by defendants of even the most modest means and status.[5] In many ways, it was courtroom culture, the patterns of ideal and interaction that had formed a common ground of contact between the state and the local residents for more than a generation prior to the growth of the Victorian state, that helped determine the practical boundaries of the expanding regulatory state. The growing cadre of municipal agents were newcomers to this environment, and were forced to reckon with an established tradition of courtroom practice. The contrast between their understanding of the state and its role, that espoused by the magistrates, and the views of those who were the targets of these regulation shaped much of the character of municipal reform. In the process, courtroom practice and its public portrayals became a key site for expressing these tensions and for the eventual reconfiguration of the relationship between magistrates, the working class, and local state and municipal authorities.

Courtrooms played an especially important role in opening up avenues for women to engage and contest the host of new reforms aimed at working-class family life. Historians have long recognized that local courtrooms could be employed by women to negotiate marital treatment, and that this usage among upper- and middle-class women rose dramatically with the legal reforms of the nineteenth century.[6] The state's expanded role as a mediator of domestic affairs had significant consequences for working-class

[5] Martin Weiner, for example, has described the Victorian project of social moralization as a "broad and striking success." Wiener, *Reconstructing the Criminal*, 185. In contrast, scholars focusing on daily encounters in the home between parents and the state have been keen to emphasize the contestation that characterized such meetings. See Behlmer, *Friends of the Family*, ch. 2, 4, 5.

[6] A. J. Hammerton, *Cruelty and Companionship: Conflict in Nineteenth-Century Married Life* (New York: Routledge, 1992), 120–25; Shani D'Cruze, *Crimes of Outrage: Sex, Violence and Victorian Working Women* (Dekalb: University of Illinois Press, 1998), 111–49. Breach-of-promise suits were also becoming increasingly common among lower-middle-class and upper-working-class women. Ginger Frost, *Promises Broken: Courtship, Class, and Gender in Victorian England* (Charlottesville and London: University of Virginia Press, 1995), 8–9.

women as well. As the plebian home became a subject of intense state scrutiny, working-class women's roles in household management assumed a new prominence in social reform efforts. Although this transformation of "private" matters into a "public" concern made working-class mothers vulnerable to moral condemnation and legal regulation, it also brought them into local courtrooms by the thousands each year. There, they developed a host of tactics to mediate state intervention and, in the process, contributed substantively to the ongoing discourse on boundaries of government authority and the autonomy of the individual. In this, the local courtroom became an important precursor for women's subsequent involvement in formal politics, even as the opponents of their presence in legal forums argued that their behavior there only reaffirmed their inherent *unfitness* for participation in public affairs.

"The Written or Unwritten Law": Institutional Summonses in the West London Police Court

To properly understand the operation of the metropolitan police courts in this period, it is first necessary to reexamine some of the basic assumptions that have guided previous assessments of them. It is a stubbornly persistent misapprehension that cases of drunken and disorderly behavior were the most common avenue by which ordinary men and women encountered the Victorian apparatus of justice. A more accurate assertion is that, of those court proceedings tabulated in the annual judicial statistics, such cases were the largest *single category* of prosecutions brought by constables in the courts of summary jurisdiction.[7] Not only were these prosecutions dwarfed by the overall number of proceedings tabulated, but the majority of instances in which men and women engaged metropolitan courtrooms were not included in these statistics at all. If unreported occurrences of law-breaking represent the "dark figure" of crime, then these unrecorded appearances are the "dark field" of daily courtroom operation, against which formal proceedings recorded in the annual

[7] 1880 – 32,710, *Judicial Statistics, 1880, England and Wales, Pt. I, Police – Criminal Proceedings – Prisons, 1880* (PP 1881, C. 3088) [hereafter *Judicial Statistics, 1880*], 38.

criminal statistics, numerous though they may be, stand out like pinpricks of light in an otherwise stygian firmament.[8] Many of these unrecorded appearances are dealt with in succeeding chapters – applications for private summonses, for example – but the single largest discrepancy between the statistical record and what happened in courtrooms on a daily basis is that the former tabulated number of *persons proceeded against*, not the number of individual *proceedings*. Frequent adjournments, withdrawals, and dismissals due to non-appearance of the complainant or both parties meant that the latter far exceeded the former. In assembling an accurate picture of how men and women encountered courtrooms and how those courtrooms functioned on a daily basis, statistics on persons proceeded against offer only one piece of the puzzle.

The court records themselves provide a more detailed and precise, if still incomplete, picture. The oldest surviving (by nearly a decade) and most complete record is the registers of the West London Police Court. These recorded all instances of formal courtroom usage on a daily basis, including charges and summonses brought by constables, summonses brought by private individuals (henceforth referred to as "personal summonses"), and those brought by representatives of various local and municipal bodies (henceforth referred to as "institutional summonses"). Before assessing the minor summonses heard at the West London Police Court, some procedural context is necessary. Summonses were issued by magistrates when the alleged violation of the law did not merit immediate arrest and charging, either because the law itself did not allow for a charge and the heavier penalties that could accompany a conviction, because there was no constable present, or because the constable had arrived after the fact and the complainant had not requested a charge be brought. Constables themselves could serve a summons, either on their own initiative or at the request of the wronged party, at the time of the alleged violation. Compared to charges, summonses were (and still are) less punitive, cheaper to process, and did not fill the limited holding cells of police courts with hordes of minor offenders.

8 See A. D. Biderman and A. J. Reiss, "On Exploring the 'Dark Figure' of Crime," *Annals of the American Academy of Political and Social Science* 374, no. 1 (1967), 1–15.

In the West London Police Court, the majority of institutional summonses stemmed from two related developments, the expanding local and municipal government of London on the one hand and the continuing growth of Victorian social and moral reform on the other. By mid-century, roughly 250 local acts applied to the metropolis. These were administered by some 300 local bodies employing over 10,000 commissioners.[9] Such a sprawling and sometimes contradictory system of administration was ill equipped to handle the problems posed by the rapid increase of the London population in the mid-Victorian years. Consolidation of municipal authority in the Metropolitan Board of Works (MBW) in 1855 solved some of the more pressing issues of urban reform and regulation. The abolition of the Poor Law Guardians and the transfer of overall responsibility for public health and poor-law administration to the Local Government Board (LGB) in 1871 further rationalized the system.[10] This reorganization notwithstanding, a labyrinth of local acts, a lack of centralized authority and accountability, corruption, and the sheer magnitude of the issues faced continued to defy a permanent, effective solution. The MBW worked alongside the City Corporation, twenty-eight boards of guardians, forty-three vestries and district boards, and, as of 1871, the London School Board (LSB). Its limited successes aside, the MBW was plagued by scandals, culminating in an investigation by a royal commission and its subsequent dissolution in 1889.[11] It was succeeded by the London County Council (LCC), which absorbed all of the MBW's powers and some of those previously held by the guardians, vestries, and local boards. Enlivened by the spirit of Progressivism, LCC administrators and inspectors tackled urban reform with a zeal and determination unprecedented in the history of British urban governance.[12]

9 David Owen, *The Government of Victorian London: The Metropolitan Board of Works, the Vestries, and the City Corporation* (Cambridge, MA and London: Harvard University Press, 1982), 33.

10 Eric Hopkins, *A Social History of the English Working Classes, 1815–1945* (London: Edward Arnold, 1976), 110–11.

11 John Davis, *Reforming London: The London Government Problem, 1855–1900* (Oxford: Clarendon, 1988), 96–114.

12 Susan Pennybacker, *A Vision for London, 1889–1914: Labour, Everyday Life and the LCC Experiment* (Abingdon: Routledge, 1995), 2.

The LCC was animated by competing impulses of cooperative integration and coercive intervention. These shaped its engagement with the police courts and with working-class communities. On the one hand, the leadership for London's first directly elected municipal government joined Liberals in their advocacy for the constructive integration of women and working-class men into the city's administrative structure.[13] At the same time, however, the LCC presided over the most concerted campaign of social reform and urban regulation that the city had yet witnessed. Although the organization's efforts to tackle a wide range of issues, from public health and sanitation to building safety and fire prevention, ranged across the entirety of London, the successive waves of Progressivist intervention broke most heavily over working-class communities, bringing in their wake a flood of court summonses that numbered in the thousands monthly. Among the various municipal authorities, the LCC; its predecessor, the MBW; and the LSB were the most prolific employers of summonses for minor violations, though local boards of health, local guardians, and vestries (until their dissolution in the 1890s) also brought cases before the police courts. Under these authorities worked a battalion of agents who surveyed neighborhoods, recorded obedience to and violation of the applicable statutes, and, when necessary and judged advisable by their superiors, prosecuted offenders via summonses. Among the most frequent users of the courts were the LSB's divisional Superintendents of Visitors, who brought summonses against parents for their children's truancy; Medical Officers, Sanitary Inspectors, and Inspectors of Nuisances, who summonsed violators of public health statutes, especially those relating to the provision and sale of food and drink; Vaccination Officers; and Divisional Superintendents of the MBW, who prosecuted those responsible for creating fire hazards (e.g. unsafe chimneys).[14] Almost none of these shock-troops of social reform

[13] This goal would be achieved in 1894, when the Vestries were replaced with elected councils on which both women and working men could serve. Davis, *Reforming London*, 123.

[14] The division of authority, duties, and responsibilities for public health issues, even after the consolidation provided by the establishment of the Local Government Board and the passage of the Public Health Act 1875, remained especially complex. The basic organizational structure was described in Thomas Whiteside Hime, *Public Health: The Practical Guide to the Public Health Act 1875, and Correlated Acts,*

would begin their work with anything but the most basic understanding of how the police courts operated. The courtroom would be their classroom, as would it be for those whom they summonsed. The key pieces of legislation that facilitated municipal summonses were the Sanitation Act 1866, the various Vaccination Acts, the Nuisance Acts (1848, 1855, 1860, and 1863), the Public Health Act 1875, and the Elementary Education Act 1870. The rapid accumulation of summonses brought by local agents, who joined constables in seeking enforcement for lesser violations, was staggering. In 1885, the LSB alone brought nearly 15,000 summonses before the magistrates, almost matching the total of all summary proceedings (i.e. summonses and charges) heard that year in the cities of Bristol and Newcastle combined.[15] LSB members applied to the magistrates for many thousands more, but were refused. The courts issued a certain number of summonses to each municipal body, and this rationing was a constant source of complaint by agents and administrators. Just as the Metropolitan Police could arrest, but could not convict or punish, municipal and local bodies could apply for summonses, but they could not levy fines or otherwise coerce obedience. The physical service of summonses to individuals also remained in the hands of police officers detached from the regular force and assigned specifically to each court, usually in pairs.[16]

Turning to the West London Police Court itself, in the wider metropolitan landscape, the jurisdiction of the court was hardly a hotbed of social reform or rampant violation. Nor was it, as the locale might suggest to contemporary observers, an entirely salubrious

for the Use of Medical Officers of Health and Inspectors of Nuisances (London: Ballière, Tindall, and Cox, 1884), 18–24.

[15] That year, London magistrates conducted 13,990 proceedings under the Education Acts (*Judicial Statistics, 1885, England and Wales, Pt. I, Police – Criminal Proceedings – Prisons* (PP 1886, C. 4808), 28). The total number of summary proceedings in Bristol was 6,105 and in Newcastle, 8,800 (ibid., 26, 28).

[16] Hugh Gamon, *The London Police Courts To-Day and To-Morrow* (London: J. M. Dent, 1907), 66. These "warrant officers," who were also charged with pursuing those who failed to appear when summonsed (and, as their designation suggests, executing warrants for their arrest), were under the direct authority of the magistrates.

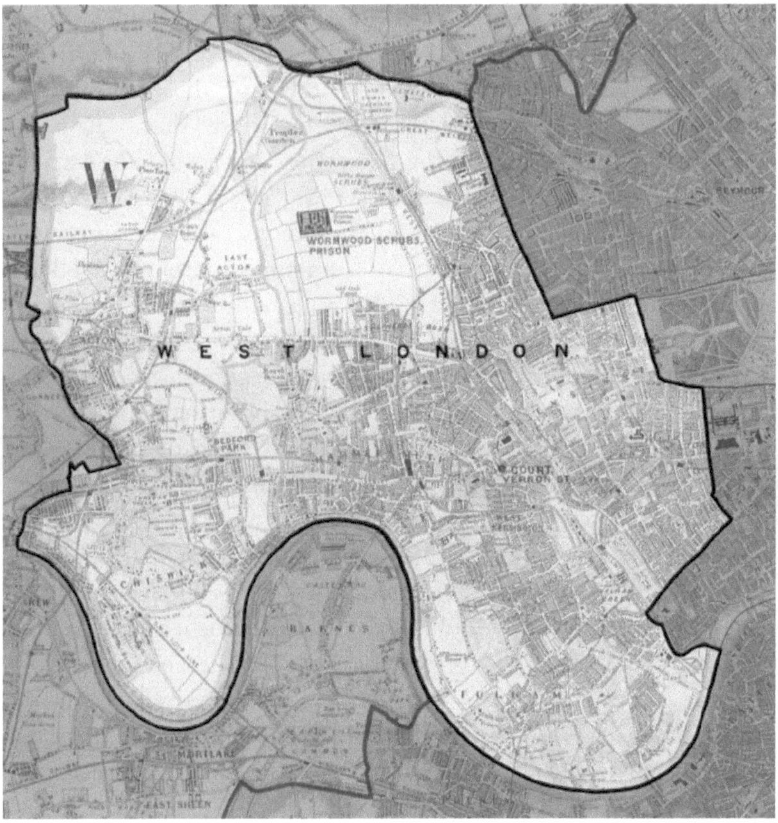

FIGURE 3.1 West London Police Court Division, 1904.

district either.[17] Like most police-court divisions, it encompassed a broad range of social and economic variation, from the wealthy environs of Hammersmith and Kensington to the solidly working-class Fulham (see Figure 3.1). The latter had become notorious for prostitution and gambling in the eighteenth century, a reputation for which the vestiges still remained in the mid-nineteenth. Though lacking the wide swaths of poverty and the notorious dens and rookeries that were the main focus of reformers and police in east and southeast London, the West London Division had its fair share of misery. The

[17] Testimony of Mr. Edmund Grant, Magistrate of the West London PC, *Minutes of Evidence, Report of the Royal Commission on Divorce and Matrimonial Causes* (PP 1912–13, Cd. 6478), May 24, 1910, 30.

direst areas were the neighborhoods immediately to the east of Wormwood Scrubs Prison, where lay the vestries of Holy Trinity, St. Mark's, and St. Clement's, all in Notting Hill. Other significant patches of poverty and want could be found in Augustine and Walham Green (today Parson's Green), which was adjacent to the Western Fever Hospital, and in the neighborhood around the Imperial Gas Works.[18] Several areas along the Thames riverside were grim, and even Chelsea, today synonymous with wealth and privilege, had many streets where the poverty was as deep as any in the metropolis was. On the whole, though, the West London Division was a highly respectable area, with a solid core of middle-class professionals, a significant number of wealthy residents, a large number of steadily employed working-class residents, and comparatively few truly impoverished ones.

The expansion of Victorian government, though not visible with the same fanfare as it was in the East End, was at the center of West London's rapidly rising caseload in the last quarter of the nineteenth century. The increasing numbers of summonses brought by various public authorities helped make the operation of local courtrooms relevant for the respectable, albeit less invasively so than it was for the residuum. In a sample of 1,000 summonses adjudicated at West London Police Court in May and the first half of July 1882, there were nearly four-dozen separate offenses, from assault to wage arrears to children caught playing games on public thoroughfares. Summonses brought by agents of various municipal and local bodies constituted the single largest category, representing nearly half (45 percent, 439 instances) of all those adjudicated. Summonses brought by private individuals were the next largest group (36 percent, 351 instances) and those brought by constables a distant third (18 percent, 177 instances).[19] A decade later, in January 1890, when 414 summonses were heard at West London, institutional summonses constituted more than half (52 percent, 211 instances), with those brought by private

[18] The latter was particularly impoverished, with several streets to the immediate south being classified by Charles Booth's surveyors as the "lowest class, vicious, semi-criminal." Booth Poverty Map, Charles Booth Online Archive, http://booth.lse.ac.uk.

[19] The cases in question are from May 1 to 31 and from July 1 to 14, found in the West London Magistrates' Court: Court Register, pt. 1, Summonses, 1882 (PS/WLN/A2/001) (LMA) [hereafter Register of Summonses, West London PC].

individuals holding steady (34 percent, 137 instances) and those brought by constables having lessened by half (10 percent, 42 instances).[20]

What brought public agents and their putative targets to the courtroom in such considerable numbers? One of the most frequent causes for institutional summonses was the collection of fees and debts owed for utilities and public services. The rapidly developing infrastructure of London required the support of rate-payers who were sometimes reluctant to contribute their share unprompted. The licensing of animals and vehicles, which were both related to public safety and health, was another common source of summonses. The extent to which these issues brought Londoners to the police courts is often not revealed in judicial statistics, but becomes immediately apparent when one looks at the court registers themselves. Fire brigade cases, in May and July 1882, represented the third-largest single category of West London summonses overall, and the second-largest in the category of institutional summonses.[21] Following the passage of the Metropolitan Fire Brigade Act 1865, local authorities could summons the occupant of any dwelling whose chimney was deemed to pose a hazard.[22] Almost all of the cases in this period were either withdrawn or adjourned, suggesting that the goal of such summonses was to goad occupants into proper cleaning and maintenance, rather than to fine them for non-compliance. The specter of city-wide conflagrations had haunted London for centuries, and rigorous enforcement of the 1865 Act was a key mechanism for conquering it.

Summonses brought by local agents for smoking chimneys, unlicensed dogs, unpaid paving fees, arrears to the gas providers, and a host of other minor offenses represented a substantial, daily legal intervention in the lives of those under the jurisdiction of the West London Police Court. Such summonses were essential to both the practical viability and moral discourse of metropolitan social reform. Whether operating in Chelsea or Clerkenwell, agents of local and municipal authorities found that, far from being an easy and straightforward procession from summons to prosecution to

[20] Register of Summonses, West London PC, 1890.
[21] 72 out of 1,000 cases. Register of Summonses, West London PC, 1882.
[22] 28 & 29 Vict. c. 90.

conviction, the way was fraught with pitfalls that could transform the most routine of institutional summonses into a matter of national debate. Much has been written about the increasing intervention of state and voluntary organizations into public spaces, homes, and businesses, but little about how these interventions were communicated and justified through public portrayals of them to local audiences.[23] These cases certainly had a practical dimension for readers of borough newspapers such as the *Islington Gazette*, who might find themselves on the sharp end of these same regulations, were they not mindful.[24] Police-court columns dealing with them also served another purpose by advertising the activities of these organizations as appropriate and ameliorative rather than intrusive and contested. In this equation, voluntary societies and municipal or local organizations of social welfare – vaccination officers, sanitary inspectors, Poor Law Guardians, and agents of the LSB – acted as both moral watchmen and legal sentinels. They possessed the personnel to investigate violators and the finances to prosecute them.[25] In 1880, one prominent municipal authority alone, the LSB, initiated 10,708 summary prosecutions.[26] Cruelty to animals, often prosecuted at the behest of the RSPCA, prompted 1,297 cases.[27] "Nuisances and offences against health," which included violations of the Public Health Act, exposing unsound food for sale, or the transgression of other sanitary offenses, were at issue in another 1,391 prosecutions.[28] Some cases in these categories received disproportionate coverage in

[23] John Davis, *Reforming London: The London Government Problem, 1855–1900* (Oxford: Clarendon, 1988); Ross, *Love and Toil*; Lees, *The Solidarities of Strangers*; Behlmer, *Friends of the Family*. See also Joyce, *The Rule of Freedom*, 125.

[24] Barry Godfrey describes the "capillary growth of regulation," in "Changing Prosecution Practices and Their Impact on Crime Figures, 1857–1940," British Journal of Criminology 48 (2008), 183. This phenomenon is also explored in Geoffrey Crossick, *The Lower Middle Class in Britain, 1870–1914* (London: Croom Helm, 1977); Clive Emsley, "'Mother, What *Did* Policemen Do When There Weren't Any Motors?': The Law, the Police and the Regulation of Motor Traffic in England," *Historical Journal* 37 (1993), 366; Gerard DeGroot, *Blighty: British Society in the Era of the Great War* (London: Longman, 1996); Andrew Kidd and David Nichols, *Gender, Civic Culture, and Consumerism: Middle Class Identity in Britain 1800–1940*; (Manchester: Manchester University Press, 1999).

[25] Kim Stevenson, "Fulfilling Their Mission: The Intervention of Voluntary Societies in Cases of Sexual Assault in the Victorian Criminal Process," *Crime, History & Societies/Crime Histoire & Sociétés* 8, no. 1 (2004), 2–3.

[26] *Judicial Statistics, 1880*, 28. [27] Ibid. [28] Ibid.

the pages of the *Gazette* and other London papers, while others, despite the frequency of their appearance in metropolitan police courts, received almost none.[29]

In their portrayal of courtrooms as locales where one could come to grief or for relief when facing the institutions of urban reform, police-court columns, now prominently in the public eye, performed a crucial ideological function. They offered a vision of a court that reinforced authority and moral legitimacy through both dread and generosity, still dispensed at the discretion of the magistrates. Increasingly, this authority operated in the name of the alleged public good, and of moral and physical health in particular, rather than providing personal redress or justice for the wronged. In this, public portrayals of the police courts were one of the most widespread and visible expressions of a general trend in Victorian criminal policy, which was to punish immorality and disruptive behavior among the working class in hopes of bringing their character more in line with middle-class standards.[30] Police intelligence columns reaffirmed the power of both state and voluntary agents as assessors of immorality and the magistrates as determinants of legal boundaries and just treatment in that context. They did so not in the looming shadow of the gibbet, as the eighteenth-century Assizes had, but in the more prosaic frame of fines, workhouses, industrial schools, and short spells of imprisonments.[31] These punishments that could, in theory, apply to almost anyone and for a wide range of activities, though the greatest weight of courtroom authority and those who wished to employ it fell on the working class.

The cultural and ideological power of public bodies, however, did not necessarily translate into courtroom successes. Although a coherent moral message about how new regulations served the public good and could only be violated at one's peril was conveyed by police-court columns, the concrete effectiveness of the interventionist state and voluntary societies in

29 The LSB prosecutions are the most prominent example of the latter.

30 Jennifer Davis, "A Poor Man's System of Justice: The London Police Courts in the Second Half of the Nineteenth Century," *The Historical Journal* 27, no. 2 (1984), 314–15; Wiener, *Reconstructing the Criminal*, 67.

31 Douglas Hay, "Property, Authority, and the Criminal Law," in Douglas Hay *et al.*, eds., *Albion's Fatal Tree: Crime and Society in Eighteenth-Century England* (London: Pantheon, 1975), 17–63.

the last quarter of the nineteenth century is another matter entirely. Its targets rapidly developed a variety of methods to mitigate or abrogate the new regulations on daily life, especially those that applied to the management of households and the raising of children.[32] Magistrates, for their part, were often unwilling to undermine their moral authority and self-constructed image as guardians of the poor by mechanically enforcing regulations of, to their mind, dubious justification and utility. The ideological operation of regulatory measures and the courtroom authority of the new municipal authorities employing them must therefore always be differentiated both from one another and from their public depictions. No process illustrated this, and how local courtrooms shaped social reform in both concept and conduct, better than the decades-long contest over Education Act summonses.

"An Extremely Delicate Jurisdiction": The Prosecution of School Board Cases in London's Courts of Summary Justice

From January to June of 1899, at the request of the London School Board, a Committee of the Home Department conducted an inquiry into the jurisdiction of the London police-court magistrates. The primary subject of this six-month investigation was the prosecution of school-attendance cases brought by the London School Board against working-class parents, which had been the courts' responsibility since the LSB's adoption of a compulsory attendance policy in 1871. The Home Department inquiry was just one skirmish in the broader contest that had been carried on between London's educational authorities and magistrates since the passage of the first Education Act nearly thirty years previously. It had been conducted through statements in the public press, articles in education periodicals, appeals to the Education Department and Home Secretary and, most frequently, vociferous debates in local courtrooms. The crux of the struggle was two interrelated issues. The first was which group, the LSB and its agents or police-court magistrates, would maintain the legal and moral authority to supervise working-class communities. The second issue

[32] Sascha Auerbach, "'The Law Has No Feeling for Poor Folks Like Us!': Everyday Responses to Legal Compulsion in England's Working-Class Communities, 1871–1904," *Journal of Social History* 45, no. 2 (Spring 2012), 686–708.

was whether magistrates could preserve their judicial autonomy in the face of the new laws on social reform and the public institutions created to administer them. Most LSB members believed that it was their prerogative alone to determine the roles that working-class children would play in London, and that parents and magistrates alike would have to accede to their views. From their perspective, the courtroom was a locale for enforcement, not discretionary adjudication. The magistrates, on the other hand, argued that every case had to be evaluated on its own merits. The courtroom, rather than the Board's committee rooms, was where decisions were to be made on guilt or innocence, and on the moral implications of either.

To properly understand the implementation of social reform through summary justice in these circumstances, we must also examine the goals and strategies of the working-class defendants in the courtroom. As was the case with the enforcement of the attendance laws outside the courts, working-class parents actively contested both School Board prosecutions and the subsequent implementation of sentences. They shared with each other the knowledge they gained through their experiences in courtrooms, rapidly learned the legal and practical obstacles faced by School Board prosecutors, determined what arguments were most effective with magistrates, and used the rules of evidence and procedure to their best advantage. These daily, public contests had profound consequences for courtroom culture as well. Across thirty years of debate over education cases, local courtrooms became crucial locales for testing the limits of Victorian social reform, determining the balance of power between different elements of the state and between the state and individual defendants, and shaping the moral significance of cases heard there.

Here, as elsewhere, courtrooms and courtroom press coverage worked in tandem to elevate the importance of these contests for the LSB, working-class parents, magistrates, and an attendant public. Throughout the 1870s, newspapers such as the *East London Observer*, the *Islington Gazette*, and the *Borough of Marylebone Mercury* regularly published School Board cases in their court columns, raising the stakes for all involved.[33] On July 27, 1872, the

[33] These typically appeared in "Local Police Intelligence" columns or, in the case of the *Mercury*, "Law and Police." For the dynamics of County Court press reportage, see Patrick Polden, "Judicial Selkirks: The County Court Judges and the Press,

East London Observer published one of its earliest, substantial accounts, describing six school-attendance cases heard before Mr. Hannay of the Worship Street Police Court. According to the report of the *Observer*, Sydney Gedge, the LSB solicitor, declared at the beginning of the proceedings that as long as the defendants expressed a willingness to obey the attendance bye-laws in the future, the Board's solicitor would not press for a fine on this, their first offense.[34] A precedent had been set, one which was in accord with police-court practice in other minor regulatory offenses. It would cause School Board officials no end of consternation in the decades to follow. In the sixth case, even though it was a first offense, the magistrate imposed a fine of five shillings, the maximum allowable in a school-attendance case.[35] The defendant's abuse of the School Board Visitor was noted, but it was his open defiance of both the law and the magistrate's authority in the courtroom itself that had prompted the harsh punishment. The contrast between the first five cases and the sixth was characteristic of how magistrates would treat such issues in the years to come – the deciding factor was often the defendant's attitude and behavior in the courtroom rather than their alleged violation of the law or their treatment of the local agent.

Magistrates' admission of the defendants' statements as evidence in court was itself a controversial policy, one that further emphasized the crucial role of the courtroom as mediator between municipal governance and the individual. The law did not allow such statements to be admitted, but courtroom practice in Education Act cases was just the opposite.[36] Magistrates permitted defendants to argue in their own defense, and the presiding justices often gave as much consideration to them as they did to the testimony of the School Board representatives. The formers' insistence that those accused of violating bye-laws had a right to make a full statement demonstrated magistrates' commitment to their own independent ideal of justice in dealing with the working class, and their long-standing belief that their courtrooms were the proper locale to

1847–1880," in Christopher Brooks and Michael Lobban, eds., *Communities and Courts in Britain, 1150–1900* (London: Bloomsbury, 1997), 245–62.

[34] *East London Observer*, July 27, 1872, 2.

[35] The limit on fines for non-attendance was set by the Education Act of 1870.

[36] *The Justice of the Peace and County, Borough, Poor Law Union and Parish Recorder* 39 (Sep. 26, 1885), 623.

determine the limits of social reform on the ground. *The Justice of the Peace*, the authoritative journal on summary court procedure, strongly advocated this practice. The argument of the editors was that, in Education Act cases, the need to protect parents from "injustice" superseded the technicalities of the law.[37]

Tracing the patterns of prosecution across the last decades of the nineteenth century, we find that the most common outcome of an LSB case was an adjournment. The purpose of such adjournments was usually to give the parent an opportunity to comply with the law. On days when their court's calendar was particularly crowded with other cases, a magistrate might adjourn all attendance summonses *en masse*, giving priority to more serious cases such as assaults and thefts. It was only in exceptional instances that the magistrates imposed a fine upon a parent in his or her first appearance before the court. In a four-month sampling of 1882 cases, the West London magistrates adjourned 60 percent of all school-attendance cases and imposed fines in only 23 percent. In slightly more than 15 percent of all cases, the summons was withdrawn by the School Board agents. In 1900, three decades after the passage of the Education Act, the distribution of decisions in the West London court remained very similar, except for a reduction in the number of withdrawals and dismissals.[38] One reason for this consistently lenient enforcement over time was that, by 1876, the "wait and see" period, in which parents were given the opportunity voluntarily to comply with the attendance bye-laws, had itself become law; a parent had to appear before the court at least twice before he or she could be fined.[39]

[37] Ibid. The editors explained, "in such a case as that before us we think the bench would do well to accept the defendant's statement if they are satisfied of its truth. By doing so they will avoid the possible injustice of convicting an innocent person in consequence of the operation of a technical rule of law."

[38] Registers of Summonses, West London PC, 1900 (Jan., Feb., Apr., Jul., Oct.) (PS/WLN/A2/50–55).

[39] When a parent now first appeared before the court for failing to send a child to school, the initial step was for the magistrate to issue an "order to attend." Only after that order had been violated could the parent be summonsed again and fined, this time for the "disobedience of the order to attend." Under this new system, the magistrate had two opportunities to issue adjournments, first in the initial summons for the issuance of the "order to attend" and then in the subsequent summons for "disobedience of the order." Elementary Education (Amendment) Act 1876 (39 & 40 Vict. c. 79 ss. 5–6).

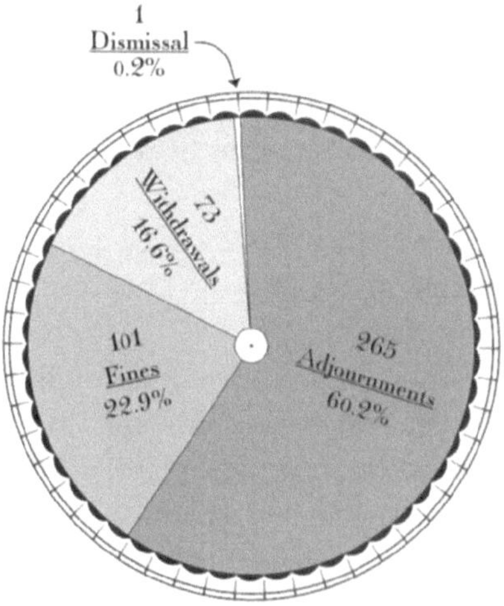

FIGURE 3.2 Outcomes of London School Board cases heard in the West London Police Court, 1882 (May, Jul., Sep., Nov.) (by Matilde Grimaldi.) Note: These percentages represent a raw calculation of all attendance case and are not corrected for parents who appeared multiple times. Tabulated from Registers of Summonses, West London PC, 1882 May, Jul., Sep., Nov. (PS. WLN/A2/1).

Magistrates' moral assessments and how they guided enforcement were a crucial factor in these summonses, but it was hardly their initiative alone that made courtrooms so vital in mitigating the impact of social reform in London communities. Especially in the initial years following the passage of the Education Act, School Board agents conducting attendance summonses confronted defendants who were much more accustomed to local courtrooms than they themselves were. Defendants' adaptability to changing legal requirements and their awareness of the practical barriers to the enforcement of minor regulations were readily apparent. The most effective response of working-class parents to prosecution was to take advantage of the limited legal liability of women in school-attendance cases. The bye-laws of the LSB held the father to be the legally responsible party in all cases, a principle that would be repeated in the Act that made compulsion national policy in 1880. This policy would continue to be a source of bitter complaint for school-attendance officers throughout the last decades of the nineteenth century. The amendment to the Elementary Education Act of 1873, in turn, allowed the summonsed parent, who was in almost all cases the father, to send a family member or friend to represent him in court.[40] This policy was adopted to avoid the ill-feeling and economic hardship that might be aroused if fathers were forced to miss work for a court date.

These two policies together proved to be a boon for working-class parents and a disaster in the eyes of London's Superintendents of Visitors. When the father appeared in person to answer the summons, the magistrate, upon conviction, could immediately collect the fine or commit the defendant to prison.[41] In the vast majority of attendance cases, however, the defendant's wife or, occasionally, another representative such as his daughter, son, or neighbor would appear in lieu of the defendant himself. According to one Superintendent, a common result in convictions was that "the wife, &c., walks out of the Court at liberty."[42] The attitudes of lawmakers and educators, which circumscribed women's legal responsibility and emphasized male domestic authority, provided an opportunity for working-class women to evade the imposition of fines or jail terms on their husbands.[43] Once convicted, if a defendant or their representative left the court unpunished, the odds that their sentence would be executed dropped dramatically. Women possessed another quality that made them preferable, from the perspective of those summonsed, as representatives of the household. As the domestic managers of their families, they were more likely than fathers (who often worked full-time) were to have detailed knowledge of their children's daytime behavior and the family's need for their labor. Both domestic expertise and legal immunity were key to their effectiveness in contesting education summonses. One magistrate

[40] Elementary Education (Amendment) Act 1873, s. 24(9), which read, "any person may appear by any member of his family, or any other person authorised by him on his behalf."

[41] The latter, it should be noted, was an *extremely* rare measure.

[42] Minutes of Evidence Taken before the Bye-Laws Committee with Reference to the Uniform Enforcement of the Bye-Laws in the Metropolis, examination of W. Hetherington, Superintendent of Visitors for Hackney, April 21, 1874, 24.

[43] It was not until 1886 that the law recognized mothers as having any guardianship or custody rights to their children. Katherine O'Donovan, "The Male Appendage – Legal Definitions of Women," in Sandra Burman, ed., *Fit Work for Women* (London: Routledge, 1979), 146.

described how this situation left him and his colleagues with no recourse but their own judgment as to the truth of women's statements in court: "We take any kind of evidence from the wife of a defendant; she says what she likes, not on oath, and we pick out the truth from it when we can, and if we can."[44]

Even as working-class defendants were developing strategies to avoid conviction and punishment in school-attendance cases, the conflict between the London School Board and the police-court magistrates continued to escalate. By the mid-1870s, members of the LSB committee responsible for overseeing enforcement (the Bye-Laws Committee, hereafter "BLC") had begun to complain vociferously to the Home Office about magistrates' conduct.[45] Their behavior, the BLC protested, was enfeebling compulsion in London. The magistrates' response drew directly on the principles of judicial autonomy, forbearance towards the contrite, and severity towards the defiant that – according to their autobiographies and their statements on the public record – had formed the core of judicial attitudes towards minor offenses for many decades.[46] In reply to the complaint, James Vaughan, the Bow Street magistrate named in one of the most extensive complaints, insisted that a more severe stance would have only aroused the resentment of working-class communities, to the detriment of the Board and its policies.[47] Rather than the mechanistic enforcement demanded by the Board, Vaughan's execution of compulsion depended upon the positive relationship between the defendants and the magistrate, the use of persuasion and, only as a last resort, the stern punishment of defiance. In his view, moreover,

44 *Report of the Departmental Committee Appointed by the Secretary of State for the Home Office Department to Inquire into the Jurisdiction of the Metropolitan Police Magistrates and County Justices Respectively in the Metropolitan Police Court District 1900* (PP 1900, Cd. 374), testimony of John Rose, Magistrate of the West London PC, June 7, 1899, 747.

45 The Home Secretary was responsible for the appointment of the metropolitan stipendiary (police court) magistrates. David Bentley, *English Criminal Justice in the Nineteenth Century* (London: Hambledon, 1998), 21.

46 Davis, "London Police Courts," 315.

47 Letter from James W. Vaughan, Magistrate of Bow Street PC, to Sir Thomas Henry, January 22, 1874, Complaint by London School Board re: Hearing of Cases under Education Acts at Metropolitan Police Courts [hereafter *Complaint*], PRO HO 45/9521/25043A/7.

the Board's complaint constituted a direct attack on the principle of judicial discretion and an attempt to subvert the rightful independence of the courtroom.[48] This perspective was shared by his fellow magistrates, who responded in like manner to similar complaints made by the LSB about their own conduct in attendance cases.[49]

Undaunted by the inaction of the Home Office on the issue of police-court prosecutions, LSB members and their agents, throughout the 1870s and 1880s, continued to protest the practice of the magistrates and to petition for more summonses and higher conviction rates. During this ongoing contest, local courtrooms became important public locales for debating personal responsibility and accountability vis-à-vis the state's regulations on child-rearing. Magistrates and School Board members in this period were particularly vociferous in their disagreements over whether working-class parents or the children themselves were to blame in school-attendance cases. In this debate, the long history of courtroom involvement in the local community was of vital significance, as it gave magistrates and LSB members very different perspectives on the issue. The magistrates, drawing on their experiences prosecuting juvenile delinquency in their courts, were more likely to see wayward children as a threat to public order; addressing that threat directly was their priority. The Board members and their agents, influenced by the new discourse on "child-saving" and deeply concerned with rehabilitating working-class parents, were more likely to see the children as the victims of bad parenting. In their eyes, punishing the children and absolving the parents publicly would only encourage the latter's irresponsibility and therefore exacerbate the problem.[50]

These differences had a political dimension, as magistrates were, by and large, not in favor of greater state interference in private life. But the integration of the local courtroom into working-class daily life played an equally important role in shaping their views. The courtroom was

48 Ibid.

49 Letter from H. L. Pasley, Superintendent of Visitors, West Lambeth Division, to the LSB, October 10, 1879, forwarded to Home Office by the LSB, *Complaint*, PRO HO 45/9521/25043A/24.

50 George Behlmer, *Child Abuse and Moral Reform in England, 1870–1908* (Stanford: Stanford University Press, 1982), 10–11. John Stack, "Reformatory and Industrial Schools and the Decline of Child Imprisonment in Mid-Victorian England and Wales," *History of Education* 23 (1994), 62–63.

magistrates' primary touchstone for their knowledge about their communities, as they had repeatedly claimed in parliamentary inquiries earlier in the century. Seeing working-class life through the context of the courtroom offered them a very detailed, but also very selective, view of family morality, parental authority, and children's autonomy in their districts. Perhaps most importantly, it meant that the principal avenue of encounter between them and local children had been via their prosecution for minor offenses such as street-games and other forms of public misbehavior defined under the Metropolitan Police Acts. Considering magistrates' central roles in the punishment of juvenile offenders, it is not surprising that they were sympathetic towards parents' frequent claims that children who had evaded compulsory education were beyond parental control.[51]

The wording of the Education Act 1876 itself, which stated that the courts could issue attendance orders only in cases where parents had "neglected" to send their children to school, further widened magistrates' discretion in how they proceeded with such cases.[52] Magistrates' desire to maintain a paternalistic relationship with the working class and their constant contact with juvenile "delinquents" encouraged them to adopt a narrow definition of neglect, one that justified their leniency towards parents who asserted that their children were incorrigible. One London magistrate, in 1882, even attempted to circumscribe *permanently* the power of the educational authorities in cases of alleged neglect. This magistrate argued that the Factory Act of 1878 invalidated the clause of the Education Act 1876 that had allowed school boards to prosecute parents for habitual neglect of a child's education. Although the Queen's Bench initially upheld the magistrate's judgment, a special court convened the same year in response to an appeal by the LSB overturned the initial decision, thereby permitting school boards to resume their prosecution of parents in cases of habitual neglect.[53] In a different case heard later that same year, however, the Queen's Bench decided that there was

[51] Peter King, "The Rise of the Juvenile Delinquency in England, 1780–1840: Changing Patterns of Perception and Prosecution," *Past and Present* 160 (Aug. 1998), 134–35. Stack, "Decline of Child Imprisonment," 62–63.

[52] Elementary Education (Amendment) Act 1876 (39 & 40 Vict. c. 79, s. 4).

[53] Gillian Sutherland, *Policy-Making in Elementary Education, 1870–1895* (Oxford: Oxford University Press, 1973), 157.

a legal limit to parental responsibility for the school attendance of refractory children. The Bench held that, in the case of *Belper Union School Attendance* v. *Bailey*, since the father had regularly sent his child off to school, the child had played truant of his own accord, and the school had not given sufficient notice to the father of the situation, the parent had a reasonable excuse for his child's absence.[54] The broader argument made by the Queen's Bench judges was that the reasonable excuses specified in the Education Act and the bye-laws – illness, no school within a two mile proximity of the home, already under efficient instruction elsewhere – were merely illustrative and that there could be other legally acceptable excuses for non-attendance.[55] This decision reinforced the pivotal role of judicial discretion in determining what constituted a reasonable excuse for a parent's failure to comply with the compulsory education bye-laws. Daily courtroom practice had contributed to the revision of national policy, rather than merely conducting its enforcement.

Shaped by a cynical view of children and a tolerant one for the limits of parental authority, both originating in their courtroom experience, magistrates were inclined towards leniency in the short run. This did not mean, however, that they opposed public education or condoned indefinite law-breaking, as the pattern of adjudication demonstrated over time. Police-court statistics confirm that the complaints made by the Board and its agents that magistrates were much more likely, upon a parent's first appearance in court, to adjourn attendance cases than they were to convict parents for disobeying attendance orders. The overall rate of eventual conviction was, nonetheless, quite high. As stated earlier, in a four-month sampling of cases from 1882, the West London magistrates adjourned 59 percent of all school-attendance cases and imposed fines in 23 percent. In 17 percent of all cases in this period, the summons was withdrawn by the School Board agents. These percentages could vary significantly from court to court in London.[56] Although these percentages seem to indicate a very low rate of conviction – in the case of the West London police court, barely

[54] Ibid. [55] Ibid., 158.

[56] Registers of Summonses, Thames PC, 1885 (PS/TH/A02/1). For February 1885, breakdown of verdicts in School Board cases was as follows: adjournments – 89; fines – 72; orders – 32; and withdrawals – 22. The Thames magistrates did not dismiss any of the School Board cases in this period.

one-third of the 65 percent conviction rate that the Metropolitan Teachers Association complained of so bitterly to the Home Office in 1883 – they are deceptive. An adjournment merely postponed the final verdict and therefore cannot be included in calculations of the overall rate of conviction. A more accurate estimation of the conviction rate is obtained by inference from the known rate of withdrawal. Since only 17 percent of all cases in the West London sample were withdrawn, allowing for a reasonable margin of error, the remaining 80 percent of all school-attendance cases heard in this period must have resulted, albeit after an indeterminate number of adjournments, in either an order to attend or a fine. This rate of conviction, assessed from the records of the courts themselves, matches the rate calculated by the LSB when it began to track police-court prosecutions in the mid-1880s.[57] Magistrates were willing to impose "orders to attend" and hand out fines to parents who disobeyed such orders, but only after such parents had been given every opportunity, and ample time, to comply with the laws.

Magistrates' lenient adjudication, combined with their rationing of attendance summonses, restricted the overall power of the London School Board to punish non-compliant parents in the courtroom. Working-class agency further limited the Board's impact in cases that were processed to conviction. Women's courtroom appearance in lieu of their husbands profoundly hampered the collection of fines and the imposition of prison terms for persistent or repeat offenders. They were merely *de facto* representatives, not *de jure* ones, and could therefore not be held legally responsible for the payment of fines or the serving of prison sentences in attendance cases. Even upon conviction, a woman could walk away without immediate penalty. The Board, if it desired to see payment of any fine inflicted, would then have to petition the court to send an officer to collect the fine, under the terms of a "distress warrant," at the cost of an additional three shillings. The

[57] This ratio, where it can be calculated, varied considerably from court to court and over time. In the sample of Tottenham School Board cases brought before the Edmonton Petty Sessions in 1890, approximately 80 percent of all cases were for "orders to attend." By contrast, at the West London PC in the same year, approximately 35 percent of all convictions were for "orders to attend," while 65 percent were fines for "disobeying an order." (PS/E/E3/15–16). Edmonton Petty Sessions Registers, 1890 (PS/WLN/A2/8–12). Registers of Summonses, West London PC, 1890. See also *Annual Reports of the School Board for London, 1887–1904*.

distress warrant empowered the officer of the court, should the defendant not have sufficient funds, to seize the property of the defendant and have it sold by a broker to recoup the cost of the fine. Because of the extra cost entailed in securing a distress warrant and the hostility that the execution of such warrants often aroused in working-class communities, the authorization to proceed with such a drastic measure was determined on a case-by-case basis by LSB members sitting in committee. In 1880, the Board issued an estimated 4,300 summonses for "disobeying an order."[58] As of November of that year, fully 1,724 of the fines imposed in such cases had yet to be collected from parents, despite the costly efforts of the Board.[59] Even assuming a best-case scenario in which the magistrates had convicted 100 percent of the attendance cases that came before them (the actual percentage of conviction was probably somewhere between 70 and 80 percent, as discussed earlier), this would still mean that, as of November, 40 percent of all the fines imposed had yet to be collected from parents.[60]

The courtroom experience ultimately prompted considerable changes in how the LSB and its agents approached the issue of summonsing and prosecution throughout London. The combination of magistrates' discretion in the courtroom and the difficulties of collecting what fines were imposed forced an abandonment of earlier attempts to broadly enforce the school attendance bye-laws. Instead, Board agents began to focus on those violators whom they thought magistrates would find worthy of punishment according to the moral standards of the courtroom, standards that had evolved over time in courtroom interactions between magistrates and working-class defendants. The high rate of *eventual* conviction (i.e. not necessarily in the first instance, but after adjournments) in the police courts suggests that, as early as 1881, the Board agents had begun to recognize the London magistrates' definitions of a "reasonable excuse" for non-attendance and were less likely to summons parents who employed such excuses. In an 1890 interview with the Board, the Superintendent

[58] Estimate of total summonses calculated from half-yearly returns for 1880, which indicated that there had been 2,168 summonses for "disobeying an order" as of midsummer. BLC, 13 Oct 1880, 244.

[59] BLC, November 10, 1880, 303.

[60] This is also assuming a further best-case scenario in which every summons issued resulted in a police-court hearing.

of Visitors for West Lambeth explained how he had adapted to the magistrates' reliance on "persuasive" rather than "coercive" measures in attendance cases where the parents expressed contrition and did not openly defy the law. The Superintendent had to tread a thin line between the demands of the Board that the law be enforced and the magistrates' unwillingness to convict without considerable circumspection.[61] LSB agents were willing, out of practicality, to defer to magistrates' approach to attendance cases and to respect the moral standards that had emerged out of their long history of daily courtroom contact with working-class men and women.

On the issue of child labor, however, the Board and its agents continued to seek sterner prosecutions and harsher penalties against parents. By the 1880s, the arguments between those on the LSB who supported the "interventionist" line and the magistrates were focusing primarily on children's waged or domestic labor. In this debate, each side interpreted the wording of the Education Act according to its own preconceptions about working-class parents, children's roles, the role of the state and the law in private life, and the moral dimensions of poverty. All of those involved in the prosecution of attendance cases – parents, Board agents, and magistrates alike – were acutely aware that the police courts were a public forum. This awareness, in conjunction with the preestablished dynamics of courtroom negotiation and magistrates' close contact with working-class defendants, shaped how parents approached these cases as well. Mothers and fathers tried to evoke the magistrates' sympathies and disarm the Board agents by exaggerating their own economic distress in courtroom dialogue and by presenting their employment of their children as justified and necessary. By this time, some magistrates were openly refusing to enforce compulsion in cases where parents claimed that the children's domestic labor or waged employment was necessary for the economic survival of the family. Outright dismissals, however, were relatively rare – in the entire period of the LSB's tenure, magistrates dismissed a mere handful of cases.[62] Such dismissals elicited howls of

[61] Report of the Special Sub-Committee of the Bye-Laws Committee on the Administration of the Bye-Laws 1891, 122–23.

[62] In 1887, for example, the LSB issued 16,000 summonses. Of those, the magistrates made "orders to attend" or imposed fines in 13,000 cases and dismissed only 31. *Annual Reports of the School Board for London, 1887–1903*.

protest from the Board and their typical court representatives, the Superintendents of Visitors. The more common protocol in cases where the magistrate did not wish to convict was for them to suggest that the Board representative withdraw the summons voluntarily, and it was only on the rare occasions that the plaintiff refused this suggestion that the magistrate would dismiss the case.[63]

As relative newcomers to local courtrooms and knowing little of their long involvement in the trials and tribulations of working-class life, the Superintendents of Visitors and the members of the LSB found the sympathy of the magistrates towards parents who used their children for domestic or waged labor inexplicable. Magistrates, in defending their practices of persuasion and adjournment, and in their decisions on individual cases, often expressed tolerance for or even commiseration with parents who claimed that their children's labor was necessary. For decades prior to the passing of the Education Act, their courtroom duties had provided abject lessons in the tenuous economic circumstances of many working-class homes, and parents did their best to solicit every possible ounce of judicial indulgence when contesting attendance summonses. Weighing the demands of the Board against parents' claims that their children's labor was necessary for the economic survival of the household, one magistrate, following his dismissal of an 1880 attendance case, summed up the arguments frequently used by his colleagues in such circumstances. "The law of necessity," he declared to the court, "is stronger than school board law."[64]

Ultimately, a working-class mother and her arguments in a higher court proved instrumental in the most significant legal alteration to educational policy since the passage of the 1870 Education Act itself. This case, decided by the Queen's Bench in 1884, made parental need for a child's earnings the legal standard for a reasonable excuse from school attendance. In this instance, moreover, legal sanction *followed* the typical outcome of negotiations between working-class mothers and magistrates in local courtrooms rather than vice-versa. The case, *London School Board* v. *Duggan*, came before the Queen's Bench on

[63] BLC, July 15, 1880, 158–59.

[64] Comment by Clerkenwell magistrate John Hosack. London School Board, School Accommodation and Attendance Committee [hereafter SAAC], March 18, 1880, 26.

appeal by the LSB. Although the child in question had proven that she could read and write, she had not passed the required standard of academic achievement for exemption from attendance. According to a summary of the case published in the *Justice of the Peace*, the mother's defense was that the child was the eldest of several children, and was employed as a nursemaid at three shillings per week and her food, and without this sum the family could not be supported, and the health of the other children would suffer if deprived of this sum. The magistrate was satisfied that the excuse was true and dismissed the summons."[65] In defending his decision, the adjudicating magistrate had cited the laws on child protection that had made it an offense "for a parent not to provide for his children adequate food, &c."[66]

Here, as on other matters related to compulsory education, the contest among magistrates, parents, and school officials was a highly visible affair. The attention that the conflict in the courts received in local and national newspapers was due in part to the controversy over compulsion itself as a political issue and in part to the public nature of the local courtroom. Although the reportage of School Board cases dropped off somewhat after an initial flurry of articles in the 1870s, cases deemed notable by newspaper editors, for one reason or another, continued to appear in courtroom columns, editorial commentary, and elsewhere throughout the last decades of the century. As the press coverage of attendance cases concentrated more and more on particularly contentious instances, the discourse surrounding the enforcing of compulsory attendance in the courts focused increasingly on the moral implications of implementing the law. The debates concerning compulsion that had preceded the passing of the Education Act of 1870 had often revolved around a moral evaluation of parents and the state's duty to intervene in private life. After the legal authority of magisterial discretion in attendance cases was established in the mid-1880s, the moral dimension of School Board cases became even more prominent in the public dialogue.

[65] *Justice of the Peace*, June 7, 1884, 356–57.

[66] 31 & 32 Vict. c. 122, s. 37. He also referred explicitly to the *Belper School Attendance Committee* v. *Bailey* case that had first established the precedent of magisterial discretion in deciding what constituted a "reasonable excuse" for a child's non-attendance. *Justice of the Peace*, November 22, 1884, 743.

In the decades after the passing of the 1870 Education Act, the result of a school-attendance case in London was often dependent on which side could most effectively solicit the agreement of the magistrates with their own moral evaluation of the case in reference to poverty and respectability. In the 1880s and 1890s, working-class parents, when brought before the magistrates, often argued that their children's wages or domestic labor were necessary for the maintenance of the home, and that they themselves were respectable and therefore deserving of mercy. School officials, for their part, used their own strategies of surveillance and investigation to try to prove that parents were making false claims about their poverty or respectability. In the courtroom, neither poverty nor respectability enjoyed a fixed definition. Both were open to courtroom manipulation and negotiation between the parties involved, transforming local courts into spaces where the meaning of the terms themselves were up for public debate.[67] The public nature of these cases only served to widen the fracture between Board agents on one hand and magistrates and parents on the other as to what role courtrooms played in assessing morality and legality. For the former, it was a topic independent of courtroom interplay, determined by parents' actions before they ever stepped foot in the courtroom. For the latter, the local courtroom was the *only* proper locale for moral and legal evaluation, a viewpoint born of the prior decades of close contact between magistrates and the working class.

In the 1890s, having failed on almost every front in their contest with magistrates, LSB officials campaigned to remove the legal enforcement of compulsion altogether from the purview of the police courts. The Board began to petition the Home Office to allow attendance cases to be heard before the unpaid county Justices of the Peace who adjudicated petty sessions throughout London.[68] In contrast to the police courts, the petty sessions were presided over by men with no formal legal training. Usually, these urban Justices were volunteers, drawn almost exclusively from the middle and

[67] On the performance of respectability, see Peter Bailey, "A Role Analysis of Working-Class Respectability," in Victor Bailey, ed., *Popular Culture and Performance in the Victorian City* (Cambridge: Cambridge University Press, 1998), 30–46.

[68] Petty sessions adjudicated cases involving lesser civic regulations such as the Weights and Measures Act, the Sale of Food and Drugs Act, and the Nuisances Removal and Sanitary Acts.

upper-middle classes in commerce, industry, and the professions, who had expressed an interest in aiding the country in the administration of minor justice in the community.[69] The efforts of the Board to shift the prosecution of attendance cases to the petty sessions reached a climax in 1899–1900, when the Home Office, at the request of the LSB, convened a departmental committee to investigate the jurisdiction of the police-court magistrates and the county Justices of the Peace. With the permission of the Home Office and the cooperation of the Justices of the Peace, the Chelsea Division of the Board had been bringing attendance cases before the Tower Hamlets Petty Sessions for nearly four years before the departmental committee convened.[70] One of the primary foci of the committee was to assess the results of this experiment and consider whether the policy should be expanded.

In the testimony of the Board officials, it became clear that their primary goal in shifting the prosecution of attendance cases was to circumvent magistrates' reliance on courtroom persuasion rather than coercion in dealing with working-class parents. In contrast, the magistrates interviewed adamantly insisted that their relationship with the working class made them the *only* appropriate mediators between the Board and parents in the enforcement of the Education Acts.[71] Board members consistently pointed to the immorality of working-class parents as the cause of truancy and claimed that the stringent application of the law was the only solution. Magistrates, in contrast, argued that only a sympathetic, paternalistic approach to defendants and their arguments would achieve any positive results. The Board's focus on punishment, they insisted, was counterproductive. In particular, magistrates emphasized the complexity of the cases and the

69 The chairman of the Poplar Petty Sessions in 1899 was a "large manufacturer," while another member was a "large timber merchant." *Jurisdiction*, testimony of Edwin Beal, Clerk of the Tower and Paddington Divisions of the County of London, January 11, 1899, 680. Their rural counterparts, which enjoyed a history dating back to the fourteenth century, had traditionally been drawn from the landed gentry. Norma Landau, *The Justices of the Peace, 1679–1760* (Berkeley: University of California Press, 1984), 6–7.

70 This practice was adopted in February 1896. SAAC, February 26, 1896, 114.

71 The chief police-court magistrate of London considered it "absolutely necessary for the poor of London" that such cases be confined to the jurisdiction of the police courts. *Jurisdiction*, testimony of Sir John Bridge, Chief Magistrate, Bow Street PC, May 15, 1899, 722.

need to take into consideration the character, circumstances, and excuses of the defendants. The approach they advocated was the same as had been taken in dealing with working-class defendants and minor offenses for many years prior to the advent of School Board summonses. Sir John Bridge, the Chief London Magistrate, describing the adjudication of attendance cases, wrote, "it wants the greatest possible knowledge of the world, and the greatest possible knowledge of the feelings of the laboring classes."[72] The magistrates, he went on to argue, were the only ones qualified to determine what constituted a "reasonable excuse," and therefore the only ones who should have jurisdiction in attendance cases.[73]

After considering the exhaustive testimony of magistrates, London School Board members, Justices of the Peace, Justices' clerks, Barristers-at-Law, and a host of others, the Undersecretary of State, in his brief introductory remarks to the committee's report, chose to address the issue of Education Act cases directly. The matter of compulsory attendance prosecutions was one with which the presiding official, Godfrey Lushington, had long been familiar, since it was to his office that the Board had been directing its complaints about magistrates in the 1880s and 1890s. In his remarks, the Undersecretary, well known for his Liberal sympathies, sided with the magistrates against the Board members and the Justices.[74] Offering a dissenting opinion from the majority of the committee, he stated, "I do not think it desirable that the School Board cases should be taken out of the hands of the Police Magistrates and given to a bench of County Justices sitting by rota."[75] Lushington felt that the original purpose of the police courts was to provide a sympathetic forum of law for the London poor. Therefore, the magistrates were the only appropriate adjudicators of laws that affected the poor so profoundly.[76] Lushington's assessment found favor in the government, and the majority of school-attendance cases remained the purview of the police-court magistrates. From 1901 to 1902, only 5,374 of the 21,640 LSB cases heard that year were adjudicated in petty sessions.[77]

72 Ibid. 73 Ibid.

74 Jill Pellew, *The Home Office 1848–1914: From Clerks to Bureaucrats* (East Brunswick: Rutgers University Press, 1982), 187.

75 *Jurisdiction*, 669. 76 Ibid.

77 SAAC, April 1902, 28. The proportion of school-attendance cases heard in the London petty sessions in the period 1901–2 (24.8%) was the same as it was in

Many of the issues raised by the prosecution of attendance cases remained unresolved when the London School Board was disbanded and its former duties taken up by the London County Council in 1904. Between the adoption of compulsory attendance bye-laws by the London School Board in 1871 and the disbanding of the LSB, the police-court magistrates and petty sessions justices had adjudicated hundreds of thousands of School Board cases. At the last meeting of the Kensington Petty Sessions before the disbanding of the LSB, the Chairman of the Justices spoke of the cases brought before the bench by the School Board. "It was," the Chairman admitted, "a very difficult piece of Magisterial work which the Bench had undertaken, and they had found it extremely difficult to try the cases with due regard to the public interest and to the interest of the parents and children."[78] Few, if any, of those who had presided over these summonses in the previous three decades would have disagreed.

This image of a rising municipal authority fractured by contestation in the courts, often at odds with the magistrates, and continually challenged by local communities mirrored the wider picture of Victorian social reform and its arbitration through local courtrooms. The nature of this contest drew on the precedents of a much older relationship between magistrates and the working class, and the integration of social life with local courtrooms. It was in the courtroom itself, and in dynamics of public speech, contestation, and moral performance that were integral to these historical precedents, that the authority of the growing regulatory state was debated and balanced against the autonomy of parents and their children's welfare. Attempts by municipal agents to label violators of new regulations as immoral regardless of what happened in the courtroom reflected their weakness and unfamiliarity in this ultimate arena of decision, rather than their strength. Such efforts were born of frustration at their failure to coerce obedience and the continued resistance of magistrates and working-class defendants alike to link respectability with respect for regulation and its myrmidons in the community and the courtroom.

1898. That year, the SAAC reported that 154 of the approximately 687 attendance cases heard each week (22.4%) were heard in petty sessions and the remaining 533 were heard in the police courts. SAAC, October 5, 1898, 170.

[78] SAAC, April 27, 1904, 13.

By the turn of the century, one of the largest and most powerful of the new institutions of social reform, the LSB, had been significantly undermined by failed courtroom confrontations. In the constant friction between more established and conservative elements of the state, the local courtroom among them, and more modern and modernizing ones such as the LSB, it was not always the latter that won out. And it was in the space of the courtroom, and through its established patterns of public contest and negotiation, that individuals, both high and low, could slow or even halt the advance of reform in daily life. Courtroom culture could thus hobble the authority of an institution and its agents just as effectively as it could amplify and legitimize it. Magistrates, Home Office officials, municipal agents, defendants, and journalists all recognized the crucial role that local courtrooms played in shaping the relationship between the new apparatus of the late Victorian state and those who were its primary targets. It was, in the words of Sir John Bridge, Chief Metropolitan Magistrate, "a very delicate jurisdiction."[79] As fraught as these adjudications were, another development in the last quarter of the nineteenth century would bring even more ferocious clashes to local courtrooms. In the decades preceding the First World War, the expansion of both private and police engagement with the local courtroom would further integrate these venues into the everyday life of metropolitan residents, making even the fiercest contest over School Board summonses seem tame by comparison.

[79] *Jurisdiction*, testimony of Sir John Bridge, May 15, 1899, 723.

4

"Two Shillings' Worth of Revenge in the Form of a Summons"

The Integration of Courtrooms and Communities in London, 1882–1902

Open any national or local newspaper in London from the 1880s or 1890s to the "Police Intelligence" page, and one is likely to find reports of drunkenness, violence, and theft among the lower orders, duly charged and punished in the police courts. In contrast, even a cursory glance at the surviving records of the London police courts, the oldest of which are brief (but comprehensive) registers of cases from the West London court in the early 1880s, reveals a very different portrait of how local men and women often found themselves in the courtroom. The earliest available full testimony of cases, which date to just after the turn of the century, further complicates this picture. To be certain, charges brought by police constables for drunken, disorderly behavior and various acts of violence and theft were ubiquitous, but they represented only the morning half of the courts' daily docket. Afternoons in police courts across the metropolis were reserved for the hearing of summonses. These, as described in Chapter 3, can be divided into two categories, those brought by individuals associated with state or voluntary organizations (which I have designated "institutional summonses") and those brought by unassociated individuals (which I have designated "personal summonses"). In the latter case, the "complainant," as the aggrieved party was designated, had to appear at the local police court in person and apply to the magistrate for the summons, paying a standard cost of two shillings.[1]

[1] In 1881, this was roughly half a day's wage for an artisan, who typically earned 25–30 shillings a week, or a day's wages for an unskilled labourer, who earned half as much.

It should be noted that magistrates did *not* formally distinguish between summonses brought by individuals representing only themselves and those brought by individuals representing municipal entities. All of the latter were included in the category of "private" summonses, the primary distinction being between these and "police" summonses (i.e. those brought by constables). However, considering the significant differences in how these summonses were sought, adjudicated, and portrayed, it is appropriate to treat them as distinct elements of courtroom activity, hence the differentiation, for the purposes of analysis, between "institutional" and "personal" summonses. The scale of the courts' activity in this domain was indeed impressive. In 1899 alone, the London police courts adjudicated nearly 94,000 "private" (i.e. non-police) summonses, which included those brought by both local men and women and by the agents of various municipal bodies.[2]

Institutional summonses, particularly those on issues relevant to local ratepayers or shop-owners and those concerning the neglect of children, were receiving a fair amount of local press and sometimes national coverage by the closing decades of the century. Personal summonses, on the other hand, despite occupying a vast amount of courtroom time and magistrates' attention, were almost never reported in either context. Excepting the occasional case of severe marital cruelty, excessive parental neglect, or an allegedly vicious assault, the lesser transgressions and punishments involved in personal summonses made for poor newspaper fare. This dearth of personal summons reporting represents another important contrast between courtroom practice and courtroom portrayals. It also complicates our picture of the historical relationship between courtrooms and their local communities, and what this relationship can tell us about the role of the individual in the modern judicial apparatus. With increasing frequency as the decades marched towards the century mark, local men and women requested the aid of constables in their interpersonal conflicts, an act which would predictably result in a summons or a formal charge and their later courtroom

A.L. Bowley and George H. Wood, "The Statistics of Wages in the United Kingdom During the Nineteenth Century (Part XIV): Engineering and Shipbuilding," *Journal of the Royal Statistical Society* 69, no. 1 (March 1906), 170.

2 The exact number of "summonses applied for by private individuals and served by the metropolitan police" was 93,535. Some 79, 599 resulted in a conviction, 13,936 in a dismissal. *Annual Report of the Commissioner of Police of the Metropolis* [hereafter RCPM], 1899 (PP 1900, Cd. 399), 42.

appearance as a complainant. Even more often, locals applied to the magistrate, paid their two shillings, and received an opportunity to publicly declare grievances, contest resources, claim entitlements, and gain redress. Just as courtroom stories had become a commodity, consumed for entertainment, personal summonses had become a commodity as well, to be sought for a variety of reasons. Increasingly, men and women in working-class communities saw summonses as a *right* to which they were entitled. This right, in their eyes, did not come with any obligation to follow approved courtroom procedure. On the contrary, often those who sought summonses did so in the firm belief that their needs and expectations for justice, however they chose to interpret it, should be paramount. The contrast between their goals, legal protocols, and magistrates' views ensured that local courtrooms were not just sites of contest between complainant and defendant, but also between both parties and the magistrate. Justices may have held the ultimate authority in these contests, but they could not prevent principals from speaking their mind in court, and they had limited control over how summonses were employed in the wider community.

This diverse and frequent use of personal summonses, along with the flexibility of courtroom usage more generally, encourages us to revise further our understanding of the relationship between the state and the individual in this period. Historians of law and social reform have generally portrayed this relationship as a top-down affair, with the state and its agents exerting their influence over an ever-wider sphere of daily activities.[3] But the increasingly common and varied employment of personal summonses by the lower orders reinforced this process from the bottom up.[4] Even as the expansion of the regulatory state brought individuals to the courtroom for wider array of daily activities, individuals were bringing a wider array of their daily activities into the courtroom. As Jennifer Davis has pointed out, the integration of daily

[3] Victor Bailey, ed., *Policing and Punishment in Nineteenth-Century Britain* (New Brunswick: Rutgers University Press, 1981); Clive Emsley, *Crime and Society in England, 1750–1900* (London and New York: Longman, 1987), esp. chs. 2 and 8; Leon Radzinowicz and Roger Hood, *A History of English Criminal Law and Its Administration from 1750*, vol. 5: *The Emergence of Penal Policy in Victorian and Edwardian England* (Oxford: Clarendon, 1990); David Taylor, *Crime, Policing and Punishment in England, 1750–1914* (New York: St. Martin's Press, 1998).

[4] For voluntary engagement with state institutions by the working-class, see Margot Finn, "Working-Class Women and the Contest for Consumer Control in the Victorian County Courts," *Past and Present* 161, no. 1 (1996), 119.

courtroom use with more informal sanctions in the conduct of neighborhood conflicts represents an important continuity between the urban police courts of the mid-nineteenth century and their amateur, rural predecessors of the eighteenth.[5] The vast increase in the scale and diversity of voluntary courtroom usage nonetheless represented a significant change in this relationship. It was only in the later nineteenth century that the bringing of personal summonses became a widespread practice among the working class, and this, along with the rise of the regulatory state, made courtrooms an integral aspect of life among the working class and lower-middle class. Integration into social life did not imply an equal distribution of authority, by any means. Police charges continued to fall heavily on the shoulders of the poor, while the most frequent summons-seekers came from the artisanal and shopkeeping classes. With these caveats in mind, the affordability and ease of access, the wide participation of the local community as both principals and witnesses, and the prevalence of women's active engagement still meant that the personal summons process was the most democratic and egalitarian aspect of metropolitan law, and of the British criminal justice system more generally.[6] The expanding use of personal summonses, like the growing array of public summonses, helped ensure that local courtrooms remained a key locale for shaping the relationship between the state and the individual in modern London. Just as public summonses set the practical limits of municipal government's authority in everyday life, private summonses helped delineate the state's role in mediating interpersonal conflict.

The widespread, voluntary usage of personal summonses not only elevated local courtrooms' importance in shaping social relations and the power of individuals vis-à-vis the state, it also amplified the significance of courtroom culture. Courtroom language and its implications became incorporated into personal contests outside the court. And just as particular phrases or concepts changed their meanings when used in a courtroom (especially when under oath), the use of courtroom language outside the courtroom had a different meaning as well. The announced intent to summons your friend,

[5] Jennifer Davis, "A Poor Man's System of Justice: The London Police Courts in the Second Half of the Nineteenth Century," *The Historical Journal* 27, no. 2 (1984), 314–15.

[6] For working-class women's management of debt and consumption in the County Courts, see Finn, "Contest for Consumer Control," 116–54.

neighbor, rival, tenant, employee, or employer could serve as a threat, a bluff, a justification for violence, a plea for better treatment, and many more purposes besides. Accordingly, the final section of this chapter will explore not just what it meant for men and women to summons one another, but what it meant to use the language of summonses in different contexts. The dynamics of announcing the intention to summons, applying for it, and having it served by an agent of the court, regardless of whether or not a court appearance was intended, all played a distinct role in social relations. With such practices, men and women brought the courtroom as an imagined space into an interpersonal contest well before they brought their contests into the courtroom itself.[7]

By the end of the nineteenth century, with knowledge of local courtrooms and summonses widely disseminated in the community, working-class and lower-middle-class men and women were able to employ both the concrete legal process and the more nebulous social leverage that it offered in a broad array of instances. The law remained, for many, a dimly realized abstraction, and the decisions and actions of individuals were guided far more by their expectations and understandings of what could happen in the summons process and, subsequently, in the courtroom. The frequent use of such measures did not imply an acceptance of law's authority, the magistrates' ideals of order and morality, or dominant visions of the social order.[8] The oscillation of conflicts between the home, hallway, street, workplace, and courtroom instead demonstrated the reciprocal influence of practices and norms in different contexts – legal, social, moral – rather than the predominance of one over all.[9] While such integration developed, the courtroom itself and the summons process continued to

[7] For how this dynamic operates in a contemporary American context, see Sally Engle Merry, *Getting Justice and Getting Even: Legal Consciousness Among Working-Class Americans* (Chicago: University of Chicago Press, 1990), 12–15.

[8] This issue is at the heart of Davis's interrogation of the police courts. Davis, "Poor Man's System," 314–15, 323–24; and "Prosecutions and Their Context: The Use of the Criminal Law in Later Nineteenth-Century London," in Douglas Hay and Francis Snyder, eds., *Policing and Prosecution in Britain, 1750–1850* (Oxford: Clarendon Press, 1989), 425.

[9] For how this process operates in the contemporary American setting, see Barbara Yngvesson, "Inventing Law in Local Settings: Rethinking Popular Legal Culture," *Yale Law Journal* 98 (1989), 1693.

evolve as social and cultural milieux, even as the distance between usage and depiction continued to widen.

"To Err Is Human ... to Take Out a Summons Feminine": Women's Use of Summonses in Neighborhood Conflicts

On February 8, 1902, Lily Wildon, a barmaid, brought a summons for assault against Kate Rowton in the Clerkenwell Police Court. Her testimony described the defendant as a veritable dervish of fury who had "abused her" and "pulled handfuls of hair out of my head, got me down on the ground and laid on me and scratched me."[10] When Wildon escaped by locking herself in her rented rooms, her assailant "broke open the door and seized me again." It was only the timely intervention of the other lodgers in the building, who seized Rowton and threw her out, that ended the assault. The catalyst for the attack, further testimony showed, was not a grievance between Wildon and Rowton, but rather a debt between Rowton and a third party, Charles Fisher. Fisher and Wildon shared the flat where the alleged attack by Rowton had taken place. Fisher, as a witness in the *Wildon* v. *Rowton* summons, testified that when, subsequent to the assault that was the subject of the summons at hand, he had gone to pay Rowton the money he owed her, he received similar treatment from her. The motivation for this second attack, he claimed, was the summons already taken out by Wildon against Rowton for the earlier assault, a circumstance for which Rowton held Fisher accountable. "She said I'd got the woman [Wildon] to summons me and I'd have to go through it [i.e. suffer an attack]," Fisher told the court. "She [Rowton] knocked me down and knelt on me."[11] Rowton, in turn, took out her own summons against Fisher for assault. The day after his visit to her to

[10] Minutes of Summonses, Clerkenwell PC, February 8, 1902 (PS/CLE/B/O3/001) (LMA). For the sake of simplicity and clarity, I have substituted the full word for the clerk's abbreviation. Common abbreviations include "sms" (summons), "sd" (said), "+" (and). When pronouns were used, or when the term "prosecutor/trix," "defendant," or "complainant" (or their abbreviations) was employed by the recording clerk, I have occasionally indicated the individual concerned in brackets for clarity. In such instances, it is unclear whether the speaker referred to the individual in question by their official designation (i.e. "the defendant"), called them by name, or simply pointed to them in court.

[11] Similar to telling someone they are "in for it" today.

pay the rent, she claimed, he "came around to my place and wanted to carry on the same game as before." When she refused, Rowton explained, "[Fisher] knocked me down giving me a black eye." Rowton further emphasized her status as victim rather than victimizer by telling the court that Fisher had frequently assaulted her in the past.

Despite the testimony and counter-testimony, and the retelling, in detail, of several distinct encounters between the three principals, this was a relatively simple and straightforward case, by police-court standards. The underlying cause of the fracas, a debt owed by Fisher to Rowton, had become ancillary to the dynamics of summons and counter-summons. The entire conflict was driven forwards by the initial assault summons of Wildon against Rowton. This summons, rather than the alleged debt, had triggered the confrontation between Rowton and Fisher. The magistrate imposed a standard penalty, binding over both Kate Rowton and Charles Fisher (the defendants in the two cross-summonses) to keep the peace for twelve months, on penalty of five pounds if they were caught violating these recognizances.

Twenty-five years later, one journalist, summing up the vast array of women's courtroom conflicts that he had witnessed, would revise an age-old old proverb. "To err is human," he wrote, "to take out a summons feminine."[12] His statement emphasized the contested place of women in local courtrooms. London magistrates' ambivalence towards them, as they had expressed in the parliamentary commissions of the 1830s, was as old as the courts themselves. Yet some of the earliest existing records of summary justice in the London area attest to the popularity of the courts as locales for the execution of interpersonal conflict between women of modest means.[13] John Wight and other early journalistic chroniclers of

[12] R. E. Corder (pseud.), *Tales Told to the Magistrate* (London: A. Melrose, 1925), 72. The identity of this author has never been established, though it seems likely he was a courtroom journalist.

[13] Most London summary court records of assaults, threats, and abusive-words summonses gave the name, gender, and address of the plaintiff and defendant, but not their occupation. Both the Clerkenwell and Thames PCs, however, were located in areas dominated by the working class and the lower middle class, and the accounts of such cases found in East End newspapers, magistrates' autobiographies, and other accounts written by court observers indicate that vast majority of those who applied for and prosecuted such summonses were drawn from these cohorts. Even within

the police courts wrote frequently about women in the courtroom, and were even less flattering in their portrayals than magistrates and police officials were during their statements to MPs. The early "Police Intelligence" columns in newspapers were likewise filled with women, as complainants and defendants, making their cases and responding vociferously to charges across the length and breadth of the metropolis. As these columns proliferated during latter half of the nineteenth century, women most commonly appeared as victims of male assault, attempted suicides, petty thieves, prostitutes, drunkards, or as termagants locked in a battle *royale* over an alleged public slight (see Figure 4.1).

Women's increasing engagement with police-court summonses, usually of their own volition, in the final decades of the nineteenth century was rarely apparent in published sources such as newspapers and memoirs. There, negative stereotypes prevailed and persisted. In 1899, one of the most prominent chroniclers of the London police courts, besides the magistrates themselves, was Thomas Holmes, a police-court missionary. A forerunner of the modern probation officer, he would later go on to publish one of the most famous accounts of the courts, as well as a series of books and pamphlets on criminology in the Positivist vein.[14] Like many magistrates, legal reformers, police officials, and fellow missionaries, Holmes was deeply concerned with the causes of crime and immorality and how they might be effectively addressed through treatment and philanthropy rather than punishment. In this endeavor, no single figure occupied his mind, and the pens of court reporters, more than Jane Cakebread did. Her sharp tongue and flamboyant manner had made her "dear to reporters, and . . . national property."[15] The "queen of this domain" had featured numerous times in the police-court columns of the *Morning Chronicle*, the *Pall Mall Gazette*, *Lloyd's*

these categories, however, there was a broad degree of variation, and whenever possible, I have looked for more specific markers of an individual's economic status through details of their testimonies (were they lodgers? did they live in an apartment block? did the reported confrontations take place in a shop belonging to the plaintiff or defendant? etc.) or through cross-referencing their addresses with Charles Booth's poverty maps.

[14] The most famous of which was Thomas Holmes, *Pictures and Problems from London Police Courts, Etc.* (London: E. Arnold, 1900).

[15] *The Contemporary Review*, May 1899, 741.

FIGURE 4.1 "Ah, you Jade, you!" Exclaimed Mrs. Foster. "If it hadn't been kind to you I was, I wouldn't think of it, but you are an ungrateful Hussey, and you shall pay for it!" (*From Humours and Oddities in the London Police Courts from the Opening of This Century to the Present Time, Illustrated and Edited by "Dogberry"* (London and New York, 1894), 41. Courtesy of the Guildhall Library.)

Weekly, and the *Illustrated Police News*, among many others.[16] At one point, it was estimated that she had appeared in excess of 200 instances

[16] Ibid.

to face drunkenness charges in the police courts.[17] Through this courtroom celebrity, she had personified the twin curses of alcoholism and the harsh punishments levied, in vain, against it. The product of this vicious cycle had been tragic, not just for Cakebread, but for a whole cohort. "A race of beings, principally women," Holmes lamented, "were called into existence whose lives alternated between the streets, the public-house, and the prison."

The missionary's rueful acknowledgment of Cakebread's national fame, and his elevation of her to the status of near-mythical prominence as a symbol of moral dissolution, was characteristic of public commentary on poor women in the late Victorian period. Late Victorian society demonstrated a deep ambivalence about working-class women's roles in the urban landscape, presenting them as hopelessly corrupt and corrupting one minute and helplessly abused the next.[18] Immoral, dissolute, degraded, or debased women received much of the blame for the social and physical maladies of the late Victorian metropolis.[19] At the same time, respectable poor women received attention as the most vulnerable victims of violence, social ills, and economic malaise.[20] In the propagation of these images of

[17] "Jane Cakebread Once Again," *Gazette*, October 13, 1890. Also noted in Paul Jennings, "Policing Drunkenness in England and Wales from the Late Eighteenth Century to the First World War," *Social History of Alcohol and Drugs* 26, no. 1 (Winter, 2012), 84.

[18] Lynda Nead, *Victorian Babylon: People, Streets and Images in Nineteenth-Century London* (New Haven and London: Yale University Press, 2000); Deborah Epstein Nord, *Walking the Victorian Streets: Women, Representation, and the City* (Ithaca and London: Cornell University Press, 1995).

[19] Judith Walkowitz, *City of Dreadful Delight: Narratives of Sexual Danger in Victorian London* (Chicago: University of Chicago Press, 1992) and Margaret L. Arnot, "Infant Death, Child Care and the State: The Baby-Farming Scandal and the First Infant Life Protection Legislation of 1872," *Continuity & Change* 9, no. 2 (1994), 271–311.

[20] Anna Clark, "Domesticity and the Problem of Wifebeating in Nineteenth-Century England: Working-Class Culture, Law and Politics," in Shani D'Cruze, ed., *Everyday Violence in Britain, 1850–1950* (Harlow: Pearson, 2000), 36. Even as reformers passed new laws on education, public health, and the treatment of children to reduce the negative influence of unfit mothers, the selfsame impetus saw the laws on marriage, assault, and divorce tightened to protect women from neglect and cruelty. Ellen Ross, *Love and Toil: Motherhood in Outcast London, 1870–1918* (New York and Oxford: Oxford University Press, 1993), 24–25; George Behlmer, *Friends of the Family: The English Home and Its Guardians, 1850–1940* (Stanford: Stanford University Press, 1998), 190–93; Shani D'Cruze, *Everyday Violence in Britain, 1850–1950: Gender and Class* (Harlow: Longman, 2000), 33–36.

women as, by turns, either victims or villains, the courtroom played a crucial role. It was the most common arena in which women from the lower social orders, like Jane Cakebread, were represented to the public on a daily basis. At first glance, it would appear that women of the working-class and lower middle-class, the most frequent cohorts to appear in police-court newspaper columns, remained targets of courtroom authority rather than wielders of it. In this, the law, Victorian discourse on gender, and portrayals of women in courtrooms were in general accord. They all drew on the assumption that women were morally weaker than men, and therefore respectable women required protection as much as disorderly women deserved disciplining.[21] Only the question of where lay the limits of men's chastisement of their wives remained. The latter was a line that, in law and courtroom practices, shifted slowly in favor of restraint as the century progressed, but which never became an absolute prohibition.[22] The best women could hope for in such circumstances was to engage the sympathy of magistrates and the courtroom audience or, in some limited and highly localized fashion, to contest negative portrayals of their actions and character.[23] Their voices were heard, it seems, but were in no way constitutive of either principles or practice.

And yet, when one probes beyond the most sensationalized and stereotyped Victorian images, or examines women and courtrooms outside the realms of marriage and domestic violence (topics for Chapter 5), a different picture begins to emerge. The common portrayals of women in courtroom environments, while shunting them into hackneyed roles as the drunken dissolute, the battered wife, or the vitriolic harpy, still offered a constant stream of women *in the courtroom*. The earliest visual depictions, from Cruikshank's illustrations of John Wight's two volumes of *Mornings at Bow Street* to *Punch* to the *London Illustrated News* portrayed them, though hardly

[21] Carolyn A. Conley, *The Unwritten Law: Criminal Justice in Victorian Kent* (Oxford: Oxford University Press, 1991), 79.

[22] Gail Savage, "'The Magistrates Are Men': Working-Class Marital Conflict and Appeals from the Magistrates' Court to the Divorce Court after 1895," in George Robb and Nancy Erber, eds., *Disorder in the Court: Trials and Sexual Conflict at the Turn of the Century* (New York: New York University Press, 1999), 245.

[23] Shani D'Cruze, *Crimes of Outrage: Sex, Violence and Victorian Working Women* (Dekalb: Northern Illinois University Press, 1998), 45.

FIGURE 4.2 "The Clerkenwell Police Office – Mr. Greenwood." (From Angus B. Reach, "The Police Offices of London," *Illustrated London News*, May 22, 1847. Courtesy of the Islington Library and Local History Archive.)

in a flattering light, as complainants, defendants, witnesses, and audience.

These women, like the ones pictured testifying in Clerkenwell in 1847 (see Figure 4.2) and in Lambeth in 1883 (see Figure 4.3), sported the typical badges of abuse, a sign of their victimization and of working-class, male violence.[24] This image of women as victims, however, contrasted with their depictions as frequent and active engagers of local courtrooms to address alleged attacks on their persons or reputations. How do we reconcile this wide spectrum of working-class and lower-middle-class women's local courtroom usage

[24] *Harper's New Monthly Magazine*, XXXIV (Dec. 1866–May 1867), 192.

FIGURE 4.3 Women applying for assault summonses at the Lambeth Police Court (From James Greenwood, *The Mysteries of Modern London* (London: Diprose and Bateman, 1883), 84.)

with the relatively narrow historical interpretations of their interactions with legal forums in this period? The explanation for the latter stems from the dominant analytical frameworks on one hand and the (unintentional) neglect of police-court records on the other. Historians examining gender and the legal structure of Victorian society have tended to focus either on the treatment of women's crime in the courts, on the laws concerning marriage and sexuality, or on violence committed against women by men.[25] To access these topics, scholars have used statistical records of charges brought against

[25] For women's crime in the courts, see Malcolm M. Feeley and Deborah L. Little, "The Vanishing Female: The Decline of Women in the Criminal Process, 1687–1912," *Law & Society Review* 25, no. 4 (1991), 719–75; Anna Clark, "Humanity or Justice? Wifebeating and the Law in the Eighteenth and Nineteenth Centuries," in C. Smart, ed., *Regulating Womanhood* (London: Routledge, 1992), 187–206. Maeve Doggett, *Marriage, Wife-Beating, and the Law in Victorian England* (Columbia: University of South Carolina Press, 1992); Shani D'Cruze, "Sex, Violence and Local Courts: Working-Class Respectability in a Mid-Nineteenth-Century Lancashire Town," *British Journal of Criminology* 39, no. 1 (1999), 39–54; Andrew Davies, "'These Viragoes Are No Less Cruel Than the Lads': Young Women, Gangs, and Violence in Late Victorian Manchester and Salford," *British Journal of Criminology* 39, no. 1 (1999), 72–89. For a discussion of the latter in the eighteenth-century context, see Margaret Hunt, "Wife Beating, Domesticity and Women's Independence in Eighteenth-Century London," *Gender & History* 4, no. 1 (1992), 10–33; and Elizabeth Foyster, *Marital Violence: An English Family History, 1660–1857* (Cambridge: Cambridge University Press, 2006).

women by constables; Old Bailey, Assize Court, County Courts, Petty Sessions, or Divorce Court cases; and newspaper portrayals. The result has been a plethora of keen insights into the myriad ways, both direct and subtle, by which a patriarchal legal system oppressed and exploited women in Victorian society while, in most cases, reaffirming male authority and shielding men from accountability for their transgressions. Even when women were successful in temporarily harnessing the courts' power in their favor, the general conclusion has been that they only did so against the grain, or because judicial or police authorities supported their efforts.[26]

For all the insights that these previous examinations have provided, crucial questions have gone unanswered, largely for two reasons. The first is that the police-court records themselves, and the registers of summonses and minutes of testimony in particular, have been ignored. In part, this has been an issue of chronology. Historical analysis of law, gender, and class has focused on the latter half of the eighteenth century through the mid-Victorian period, but the police-court registers are only available for a few courts beginning in the 1880s, and minutes of testimony only in the first years of the twentieth century. This periodization has tended to reinforce the conclusions reached by those using patriarchy as the primary analytical framework. This framework has defined women's agency in courtroom spaces, as far as it was significant in historical change, almost exclusively as resistance to male authority.[27] Ironically, efforts to understand how the overarching dynamics of patriarchy restricted women's legal agency – which they most assuredly did – have left us with an incomplete picture of what women actually said and did in London courtrooms on a daily basis. A constrained understanding of the relationship between what happened there and social relations in homes and communities has emerged as a result.[28] Nor do we have much insight into how women's daily use of police courts and its social dimensions – as distinct from the

[26] Savage, "The Magistrates Are Men," 245.

[27] Ibid.; D'Cruze, *Crimes of Outrage*, 137–43; Ginger Frost, *Promises Broken: Courtship, Class, and Gender in Victorian England* (Charlottesville and London: University of Virginia Press, 1995), 9–10.

[28] A. James Hammerton, *Cruelty and Companionship: Conflict in Nineteenth-Century Married Life* (New York and London: Routledge, 1992), 119. A significant exception to this is Finn, "Contest for Consumer Control," 116–54.

broader ideological debate carried on by social reformers, judicial professionals, Parliamentarians, newspaper editors, and others over marriage, masculinity, and gender roles in plebeian society – might have affected their status vis-à-vis the law and the state, or contributed to the evolving norms of gender in late Victorian society. The last two elements were deeply intertwined, since the expanding role of government in everyday life made interactions with the state and its representatives increasingly common for working-class and lower-middle-class women.

The key to broadening our understanding on these issues lies not just in reexamining the laws on marriage, divorce, affiliation, or domestic violence that have been the focus of previous investigations. These laws and their operation in local courts were all crucial, as will be discussed in Chapter 5. Their popular and prominent usage notwithstanding, the law that, over time, most deeply transformed working-class and lower-middle-class women's voluntary interaction with local courtrooms preceded those on marriage and affiliation by two decades. This was the Metropolitan Police Act 1839, which expanded and standardized the London police-court system and its legal authority. The 1839 Act was a watershed in the voluntary engagement of women with local courtrooms because it set the cost of a court summons at two shillings. This, along with the permitting of verbal information (as opposed to the written format) as the basis for a summons, made the police courts accessible to all but the poorest petitioners. Together, these stipulations eliminated the greatest obstacles faced by women, and working-class women in particular, who might otherwise have sought summonses – cost, literacy, and time.[29] Following their removal, the employment of urban summary justice as a milieu for social contests would begin to rise, in contrast to its rural counterpart, the Justices of the Peace, whose role in personal quarrels had been on the decline for more than a century.[30] The absence of courtroom records from the first half of the nineteenth century does not let us measure how quickly women adopted the two-shilling, verbal application for summons as a common

[29] Norma Landau has estimated that approximately 20–30% of all recognizances issued by urban justices in the eighteenth century were the consequence of disputes between female plaintiffs and defendants. Norma Landau, *The Justices of the Peace, 1679–1760* (Berkeley and Los Angeles: University of California Press, 1984), 197.

[30] Ibid., 194–5.

practice. Anecdotal evidence and newspaper police-court columns indicate that cases brought by working-class and lower-middle-class women were indeed common by mid-century. In the second half of the century, the widened access made possible by cheap summonses and verbal "informations" helped make them ubiquitous. By the early 1880s, adjudicating these cases had become one of the courts' most common daily activities. The extant court records reveal that women's summonses, in any given month, could represent nearly half of all private summonses, and upwards of 15 percent of all summonses heard by the court.[31] Contrary to the pervasive accounts of police prosecutions for female violence and drunkenness, by the closing decades of the nineteenth century, women were nearly as likely to use the courts voluntarily, through summonses, as they were to be charged in them by constables.[32]

The common perception at the time, reinforced by the general tenor of newspaper reporting, that wife-beating was the overwhelming cause of women's summonses was inaccurate as well. In any given month, in both West London and Thames Police Courts in the last quarter of the nineteenth century, only slightly more than half of all women's summonses for assault were made against men.[33] The number of

[31] Of the 324 instances of private summonses heard in the West London PC during May and the first half of July 1882, 42% (137) were women's summonses. Registers of Summonses, West London PC, 1882. In January, March, and May 1885, Thames magistrates heard 271 summonses brought by women. Registers of Summonses, Thames PC, 1885 (PS/TH/A/02/2) (LMA).

[32] In the West London PC, in January 1880, 104 women were charged with various offenses Female defendants represented roughly 15% of all those brought up on charges that month. Specifically, there were 44 charges for various drunkenness offenses (drunk and disorderly, drunk and incapable, drunk and using obscene language, etc.), 19 charges for stealing, 11 for Assault, 9 for disorderly behavior, and 7 each for begging and prostitution. In addition, there were 7 additional charges for other offenses (e.g. suspicious person, willful damage, attempting to pawn a stolen item). Registers of Charges, West London PC, 1880 (PS/WLN/A/01/006) (LMA). In the Thames PC, whose district lay in the heart of the East London docklands, women also took out summonses at a much greater rate than men did. Newspaper portrayals and court records, however, were not entirely at odds. These statistics do jibe, for example, with the common journalistic depictions of women's frequent arrests for alcohol-related offenses. In the West London cases, charges against women for various drunkenness offenses were the single largest category, constituting 40% of the total.

[33] These are the only two courts, outside of Bow Street (where the patterns of summons, as the chief police court, were different), for which full summons registers are available across this period. In January, March, and May 1885, of the 176 assault summonses made by women in the Thames PC, fully 42% (75) were made against

women's summonses for assault alone at the Thames Police Court in these three months of 1885 well exceeded the number prosecutions for theft initiated at the same court in a similar period ten years previously by petitioners of all classes (137) and was more than twice the number of theft prosecutions initiated by lower-middle-class and working-class plaintiffs of both genders then (73).[34] When compared side by side with men, it also becomes apparent that women used the courts for personal summonses far more often than men did in general. In January and May of 1890, women brought 415 instances of summonses to the Thames Police Court, whereas men brought only 286.[35] A decade later, this margin had grown, though the overall rate of summonses had gone down. In a sample of 700 summons instances across both Thames and West London Police Courts that year (1900), women's summonses were heard at nearly twice the rate of men's.[36] In sum, much of women's time in the Thames and West London courtrooms in the last decades of the nineteenth century was spent there of their own volition (at least, in the complainant's case), women's cases were among the most prevalent and frequent on the daily summons docket, and many of these cases had nothing to do with domestic violence.

So, what comprised this cavalcade of women's summonses? There was no such thing as a typical summons case between women. The circumstances were as varied and complex as their lives were.[37] Assault

other women, with summonses against males with the same last name (almost without exception, their husbands) making up 28% (50) and against other men constituting the remaining 31% (56). In the Thames PC in January, March, and May of 1900, of the 183 assault summonses brought by women, 72 were against other women, while 98 were against men. Registers of Summonses, Thames PC, 1885, 1900. In the West London PC, in May and the first half of July 1882, of the 74 assault summonses, 32 were against other women, while 41 were against men. One woman's summons was against a married couple. In 1900, 34 of the 58 assault summonses brought by women in October were against other women, while 19 were against men. Registers of Summonses, West London PC, 1882, 1900.

[34] The figures on theft cases are taken from Davis, "Prosecutions and Their Context," 406.

[35] Registers of Summonses, Thames PC, 1890.

[36] 194 vs. 112 in the West London PC during October (Registers of Summonses, West London PC, 1900). 304 vs. 138 in the Thames PC in January, March, and May (Registers of Summonses, Thames PC, 1900).

[37] Elizabeth Roberts, *A Woman's Place: An Oral History of Working-Class Women, 1890–1940* (Oxford, UK and Cambridge, MA: Blackwell, 1984), 169–201; Ellen Ross, "Survival Networks: Women's Neighborhood Sharing in London before World War I," *History Workshop Journal* 15 (Spring 1983), 4–27.

summonses, the most common circumstance that brought two women to the local courtroom, are a good point of entry. Such behavior added further fuel to popular stereotypes of working-class women as vicious and disorderly. Journalistic accounts therefore offered both a foil for "respectable" working-class readers of local papers, and confirmation of the biases common among lower-middle-class and middle-class readers. For all the conflicts recounted by women in the courts, however, women's character and conduct there did not conform to the scolding harridans or warring termagants of popular satire and newspaper columns.[38] The cases instead reveal a complex and often subtle contest for reputation, redress, control of shared resources, and economic management. They also disclose how women effectively incorporated these forums into their daily lives by employing their familiarity with both courtroom procedure and the magistrates' ideals. Finally, the testimony in these cases demonstrates how, just as women brought the community into the courtroom, they also transported the dialogue and practices of the courtroom into the community. Far from being two discrete locales, one social and governed by working-class culture (e.g. notions of respectability, gender norms) and one legal and governed by law, interpersonal conflicts flowed in and out of courtrooms, just as personal summonses and courtroom contests flowed in and out of neighborhood conflicts.

The nature of the courtroom also changed in the process. Working-class petitioners tested the boundaries of what types of actions would be recognized, through a multi-stage system of applications for summonses and the hearing of them, as being the legitimate purview of the courts. Given the flexibility of the summons process and the tolerance (or even encouragement) by magistrates that the local populace use it for a wide variety of purposes, this inevitably had an

[38] These are images that gender historians have worked hard to debunk. Melanie Tebutt, *Women's Talk?: A Social History of "Gossip" in Working-Class Neighbourhoods, 1880–1960* (Aldershot: Scolar Press, 1995), 37. Anna Clark, "Whores and Gossips: Sexual Reputation in London, 1770–1825," in Arina Angerman and Geerte Binnema, eds., *Current Issues in Women's History* (London and New York: Routledge, 1989), 234. Laura Gowing, "Language, Power, and the Law: Women's Slander Litigation in Early Modern London," in Jennifer Kermode and Garthine Walker, eds., *Women, Crime, and the Courts in Early Modern England* (Chapel Hill and London: University of North Carolina Press, 1994), 37.

effect on the operation of the courtroom as a cultural and social space – for example, as one where norms of morality and gender were defined or challenged – and its role as a legal forum. These two functions were never entirely divorced, but their relative significance in interpersonal conflict increasingly contrasted with how the courtroom operated in regulatory issues. In the latter, the courtroom exerted social and cultural influence on behavior and ideas of morality because changes in the law granted a new cohort of agents the power to force individuals to come before the magistrate. The goal there was to impose a legal penalty and through it, to change behavior – this was part and parcel of broader attempts to "civilize" the working-class in the later nineteenth century.[39] In interpersonal conflicts, by contrast, changes in the social and cultural dimensions of the courtrooms, and most specifically in how their possible influence was understood and employed by working-class petitioners, altered the idea of what law meant to them. The formal legal dimensions of the courtroom, partially understood in most instances, only had significance to them because the summons process was incorporated into social conflict and freighted with moral meaning (e.g. as a threat, a potential public embarrassment, an avenue for defending one's reputation, or a means of reprisal for a perceived slight).

This reversal of the relationship between the legal dimensions of courtrooms on one hand and their social and cultural dynamics on the other, in turn, helped shape understandings of what the state could do in the community and working-class life more broadly. It was only in the final decades of the ninteenth century that the goal articulated by the Fieldings – and reiterated by magistrates in the post-Napoleonic period – that the courtroom would be an open forum for the settling of minor personal grievances, was finally realized. But the vast scale of personal summonses, their variation, and the multitude of ways that petitioners employed them fit poorly into these earlier conceptions of a paternalistic and moralizing courtroom. As familiarity, access, and use of the courtroom all expanded in the final decades of the century, it became more and more difficult for either legislators, through law, or magistrates, through adjudication, to control the meaning of private

[39] Gareth Stedman Jones, *The Languages of Class: Studies in Working-Class History, 1832–1982* (Cambridge: Cambridge University Press, 1983), 188–89.

summonses. The courtroom's influence in interpersonal conflict was dependent on the social significance of its uses, and such significance lay in the eyes of the beholder and their community. Therefore, how working-class petitioners chose to employ summonses and the meanings they accorded to a courtroom appearance shaped the courtroom's role in their lives and communities as much, if not more so than magistrates' will or the goals of legislators did.

In assessing the concrete dimensions of these developments in the changing patterns of women's courtroom usage, the focus will be the Clerkenwell Police Court. It is the only police court for which both the full Court Minutes (testimony) and the Court Registers (short records of cases) from this period survive. The Clerkenwell court was located on King's Cross Road, Islington. According to Charles Booth's survey, the neighborhood in the immediate vicinity was predominantly working-class, most streets being designated as a mixture of those with regular earnings ("comfortable") and those who were poor or in "chronic want."[40] The rapid industrialization of the area, anchored in the expansion of King's Cross and St. Pancras rail stations and the attendant coaling depots, along with the presence of two major prisons (Pentonville and Holloway) ensured the district an ill reputation that was aptly captured in the writings of Charles Dickens (a one-time resident of Somers Town, which was on the SW edge of the court's jurisdiction), and a host of Victorian journalists and social investigators.[41] Taken as a whole, the sprawling district served by the court, which stretched from the northern boundary of the City to the south, Highgate to the north, Euston to the west, and Holloway Road to the east, was hardly the poorest in the metropolis (see Figure. 4.4). Nonetheless, its area of authority encompassed what were, at the time, some of the worst slums in London (e.g. Somers Town, Agar Town, and Pentonville), and it was confronting many of the same issues that were engines of social and economic tension and catalysts of state intervention among its more notorious neighboring districts to the east.[42] Chief among

40 *Charles Booth's Maps of London Poverty, East and West, 1889* (London: Old House, 2013 [1889]).

41 Charles Dickens, "A Suburban Connemara," *Household Words*, March 8, 1851, 562–65.

42 Steven P. Swensen, "Mapping Poverty in Agar Town: Economic Conditions Prior to the Development of St. Pancras Station in 1866," *Working Papers in the Nature of*

FIGURE 4.4 Map of Clerkenwell Police Court Division, 1904.

these issues were overcrowding, high rates of crime, and sanitation issues that posed a serious health hazard to residents in the poorer neighborhoods.[43]

It was within this mixed district, where those enjoying regular wages lived cheek-by-jowl with those in chronic want, that Beatrice Day employed her knowledge of court procedure when she brought Ellen Louie up on a summons for assault on August 15, 1900. Day, who made her case to the magistrate Cecil Chapman, was very specific in her employment of the summons, asking the magistrate that he neither imprison nor fine the defendant, but merely that he bind her over to

Evidence: How Well Do "Facts" Travel? no. 09/06 (London: Department of Economic History, London School of Economics, 2006), 1.

[43] Ibid., 3–4.

keep the peace.[44] The case had involved no actual violence, and Louie could claim some moral justification for harassing Day – the defendant's husband was living with the plaintiff, a fact which the latter openly volunteered in her testimony. Chapman, nonetheless, obliged Day's request and bound over the defendant to keep the peace for six months, on penalty of a ten-pound fine. Such requests for specific sentences were not uncommon in women's cases against one another, nor were complainants' provision of detailed arguments justifying their summonses. In these cases, the court summonses revolved around women's attempts to preserve their respectability against accusations made by other women. The defendants had publicly insulted their sexual morality within earshot of their neighbors, or so the complainants asserted, and for the cost of two shillings, the latter had harnessed the authority of the courtroom to protect their reputations from further public abuse. The magistrates' tendency to bind over both the defendant and the plaintiff did not appear to have deterred women – on the contrary, the frequent requests to have their opponent "bound over" or statements to the effect that they did *not* want them sent to jail seems to indicate that this tendency served more as an encouragement.[45] A reasonable expectation that one or both parties would be bound over made the summons an ideal pathway by which the courtroom could be employed for social purposes.

Fraught relations between neighbors were an especially fecund generator of summonses. According to the respondents in Elizabeth Roberts's oral history of working-class women's lives, the most frequent cause of conflict between neighbors was the perceived abuse of shared space, such as allowing children to play too loudly in common stairwells, corridors, or courts.[46] Scholars examining the

[44] Minutes of Summonses, Clerkenwell PC, August 15, 1900 (PS/CLE/B/03/001).

[45] Magistrates' authority to levy fines in these circumstances had been formally established with the passage of the Offences Against the Person Act 1828. Peter King, *Crime and Law in England, 1750–1840: Remaking Justice from the Margins* (Cambridge: Cambridge University Press, 2006), 28. See also Davis, "London Police Courts," 417. See e.g. Montagu Williams, *Later Leaves: The Further Reminisces of Montagu Williams, Q.C.* (London: Macmillan, 1891), 199, and Davis, "Prosecutions and Their Context," 418

[46] Roberts, *A Woman's Place*, 188.

triggers of working-class interpersonal violence in nineteenth-century Britain have lent further support to Roberts's observations.[47] The magistrate Henry Waddy similarly attested to the persistent employment of the police courts as part of such disputes well into the 1920s, arguing that the crowded, congested living spaces provoked "interminable discord" among working-class women.[48] Under such conditions, according to the magistrate, "[women] wrangle unceasingly and in the vilest language about their mats, clothes-lines, dustbins, pianos, gramaphones [*sic*], and children, about noises, stamping, smells, and above all about the common staircase."[49]

Sexual insults were another common catalyst for bringing the courtroom into a social conflict. In this, the increasing popularity of police-court summonses among plebeian women bore some resemblance to patterns of discretionary court engagement (at considerably greater time and expense) by those higher up the socioeconomic hierarchy in the first half of the century. As S. M. Waddams has shown, across England in the period 1815–55, middle-class and lower-middle-class women brought defamation suits in the ecclesiastical courts against other women, and against men, for publicly impugning their sexual reputations, the accusation of "whore" or some variation upon it being the most common form of attack.[50] The numbers of such defamation cases, however, whose cost

[47] Davis, "Prosecutions and Their Context," 417; D'Cruze, *Crimes of Outrage*, 50–62.

[48] Henry Turner Waddy, *The Police Court and Its Work* (London: Butterworth, 1925), 84.

[49] Ibid., 85. Waddy added, informatively, that the above list was "not intended to be in order of merit."

[50] S. M. Waddams, *Sexual Slander in Nineteenth-Century England: Defamation in the Ecclesiastical Courts, 1815–1855* (Toronto: University of Toronto Press, 2000), 135–39. Although slander (defamation of character by spoken words) implying unchastity was not a crime, by statute, in England until 1891 (and then for women only), Waddams has found that more than a thousand cases along these lines were brought to the Ecclesiastical Courts in 28 dioceses in England (including 103 in London) between 1815 and 1855. Roughly half of the cases in Norwich and York were brought by women, and the lower classes were well-represented in the sample, though they constituted a minority. Ibid., 126, 195–97. Laura Gowing has charted women's extensive use, in the sixteenth and seventeenth centuries, of London's ecclesiastical "church courts" to bring slander suits against one another. Laura Gowing, *Domestic Dangers: Women, Words, and Sex in Early Modern London* (Oxford: Oxford University Press, 1996), 32–38.

lay well beyond the means of working-class women to engage, paled in comparison to that of women's assault cases in the police courts of late nineteenth- and early twentieth-century London.[51] The latter, for working-class and lower-middle-class women, were an inexpensive, readily available forum for the redress of either public insults or violent attacks by other women. Although they were technically brought on different charges, women's summonses for "assault," "threats," and "abuse" freely mixed verbal and physical attacks as their justifications, and often elicited the same judicial verdicts of binding over one or both parties to keep the peace. Words had power in London's neighborhoods, and the stronger the words, the greater their influence. The "calling out of one's name" (i.e. sexual insults), particularly in a public forum, represented a significant escalation of the tenor of an interpersonal conflict in working-class and lower-middle-class communities.[52] In these summonses, women demonstrated an awareness of common courtroom practice in inflicting recognizances, which required only that the summoning party prove serious intent of violence, not its actual commission.[53] "Looks, gestures, or conduct," were sufficient, though women usually testified to concrete verbal threats.[54] Indeed, the history of bringing one's opponent to court in England for such acts was

[51] According to Peter King, in the long eighteenth century, hearings related to alleged assaults were the most common form of summary court hearings. King, *Crime and Law in England*, 27. The role of the courts in such cases, King points out, "has yet to be fully researched by historians." In the Clerkenwell PC alone, from April to July 1910, there were 54 such cases, matching the number of sexual defamation cases for the entire diocese of Exeter from 1815 to 1855. Registers of Summonses, Clerkenwell PC, April–July, 1910 (PS/CLE/A2/002, Feb., Apr., Jun.; PS/CLE/A2/003, May, Jul., Nov.; PS/CLE/A1/017, Jun., Aug., Oct.).

[52] On "gossip" as a form of community self-discipline, see Tebutt, *Women's Talk?*, 76–80.

[53] Being "bound over on own recognizance" was commonly abbreviated as "OR" in the court records. The formal legal outlines of recognizances and their use in pre-industrial England are discussed in Robert Shoemaker, *Prosecution and Punishment: Petty Crime and the Law in London and Rural Middlesex, c.1660–1725* (Cambridge: Cambridge University Press, 1991), 25–27, 95–123. The original power was granted (and employed) much earlier, with the passage of the Justices of the Peace Act 1361 (34 Edw. 3 c.1).

[54] Thomas Saunders, *The Practice of the Magistrates' Courts*, 2nd ed. (London: Law Times Office, 1858), 232.

a long one, and Justices of the Peace had been binding over defendants in such cases with regularity since the seventeenth century.[55] It is unclear whether the familiarity of working-class women in London with this process filtered down from its employment by women with more financial resources and to what extent it developed out of working-class encounters with courtrooms in other circumstances. Regardless of how such knowledge arose, seeking the courtroom to bind over a defendant only became practical for the majority of women in the Clerkenwell court's district after 1839, when the price of a summons was set at two shillings.

By the end of the nineteenth century, the sheer number of such cases, and the relatively small provocation necessary to prompt a summons, demonstrated the increasingly commonplace role that local courtrooms had come to play in women's daily social contests. Within this broad usage, it is important to pay heed to specific reasons why women might have chosen to seek a summons. Sexual reputation and insults against it could have very different meanings for women in different social and economic circumstances. Anna Clark, in her study of early nineteenth-century plebeian women, has argued that among women at the lower end of socioeconomic spectrum, resorting to part-time prostitution in order to supplement low wages was common enough to de-stigmatize such behavior in many communities.[56] For women of the artisan or shopkeeping class, on the other hand, adherence to a strict code of moral conduct became an essential marker of their higher socioeconomic status and respectability, and therefore their distinction from their poorer or less respectable neighbors. The preservation of reputation against insults, Clark argues, was particularly important in communities that encompassed both cohorts. There, lower-middle-class women were adamant to maintain their moral distance from "the most violent, criminal, and degraded population of thieves and prostitutes," who lived in close proximity to them.[57]

Clark's study focuses on a very small sample (forty cases from 1770 to 1810), and on cases in which the exact socioeconomic status of each

[55] Shoemaker, *Prosecution and Punishment*, 25–27. Landau, *Justices of the Peace*, 196–97. There were two types of recognizances, those "for good behaviour," and those "for keeping the peace." London magistrates would employ both, depending upon the violation and status of the defendant.

[56] Clark, "Whores and Gossips," 236. [57] Ibid., 240–41.

plaintiff was clear. Her cases, moreover, are drawn from a century earlier than the Clerkenwell and Thames summonses and they rarely involved violence. We should therefore be cautious about applying these keen insights unconditionally to police-court cases, especially when one takes into account the significant evolution of women's roles, the law, and class relations across the nineteenth century.

Regardless of these important differences in scope and periodization, the analysis of Clark and Waddams gives us some context for the social dynamics of plebeian women's courtroom contests over reputation, respectability, and redress in the latter decades of the nineteenth century. One would search in vain for a singular explanation for the vast array of women's police-court summonses that proliferated in this period. They could emerge from a sudden verbal conflict between relative strangers, the escalation of a private grievance into a public clash, a sharp verbal collision between family members, or a consistent pattern of disrespect that finally pushed a neighbor to seek courtroom redress. At other times, women summonsed one another for threats of harm, murder, or "mobbing" (i.e. bringing a group of other women to attack the complainant). Conflicts involving children were also a frequent cause of reported assaults and subsequent summonses. Cross-summonses were common, and the line between complainant and defendant, or between aggressor and victim, was often a very fine one. At times, courtroom usage itself could provide a reflexive context; assaults and summonses for assaults evolved out of previous uses of the law by one woman against another or against another member of her family.

A summons need not have been an escalation or the climax of a conflict. A police-court dispute could be just one part of a longer contest that had oscillated between the community and the courtroom until the issue was resolved or one party quit the field.[58] Like their catalysts, the outcome of women's summonses varied highly, depending upon the specific circumstances of the abuse or assault and its consequences. Ultimately, it remained in the magistrate's discretion to decide whether a fine, a recognizance, or a dismissal was appropriate. Sometimes, cases that involved no violence at all resulted in harsher sentences, while others where serious violence had

[58] Davis, "Poor Man's System," 323; and "Prosecutions and Their Context," 417.

allegedly occurred prompted no more than the typical binding over to keep the peace. One of the heaviest sentences handed down for a women's assault summons in the 1900 Clerkenwell Police Court, involved no substantive violence at all. On August 20, Elizabeth Christy testified that Rachel Lee had spat in her face. The magistrate, Cecil Chapman, sentenced Lee to pay twenty shillings in fines and court costs or face fourteen days in prison.[59] Five days earlier, before the same magistrate, Ellen Day testified that Elizabeth Barker had assaulted her with a hat pin, scratching her face and arm, while Barker cross-summoned Day for striking her in the mouth and stomach. Even though the latter cases involved claims of significant bodily harm, Chapman simply bound Day and Barker over to keep the peace and fined neither.[60] In this instance, the locales in which the confrontations took place might have played a part in the differential sentencing. Christy and Lee lived in a solidly middle-class neighborhood near Regent's Park, one whose residents rarely found themselves in the Clerkenwell courtroom, while Day and Barker lived in one of the poorer districts around King's Cross, fertile ground for the daily run of cases.

The impression that assault summonses were sought by women largely for social purposes rather than to see the defendant receive formal punishment via fines or jailing is strengthened by the consistently mild sentencing practices of magistrates. Absent extenuating circumstances, a complainant had little reason to expect anything stronger than a binding over for the defendant. In same-gender assault cases heard in Clerkenwell, Thames, and West London Police Courts, fines, when applied at all, tended to be light ones. Prison sentences or remands to a higher court were rare. This pattern of verdicts had characterized the treatment of assault in the eighteenth and early nineteenth century as well.[61] In the interim, magistrates had been granted increased authority and discretion in the punishment of assault by the Offences Against the Person Act 1828 and by statutes in the subsequent decades, but the available police-court records indicate that these powers went largely unused

59 Minutes of Summonses, Clerkenwell PC, August 15, 1900.
60 Ibid., August 20, 1900.
61 King, *Crime and Law in England*, 230.

in instances where the defendant was female.[62] Exceptions to this pattern, and they were rare, typically came in one of two instances: when the assault was severe and the threat (or actuality) of bodily harm high (i.e. bones had been broken or a dangerous implement employed, a hat pin apparently not qualifying) or when the assault happened in circumstances well beyond the usual context of neighborhood quarrels.[63]

If the verdicts were not assured and sentences light, what could women who brought these summonses hope to gain from the process? Summonses were not expensive, but they demanded time and effort, not only of the plaintiff, but of her family, friends, and neighbors, who were frequently called as witnesses. Complainants also ran the risk of additional costs if the summons was dismissed, or of being bound over as well as the defendant, on forfeiture of the same penalty. Sometimes women asked for, and received from the magistrate, specific verdicts that related only tangentially to the alleged attack. These could range from a demand for payment of damage to clothing to a request that the magistrate support an eviction.[64] The flexibility of sentencing in these cases may in part be what attracted women to the police-court summons in

[62] The 1828 Act grant empowered magistrates to impose fines of up to £5 and to imprison those who could not pay, though the right to decide between fine and imprisonment on the first sentence was not formalized until the early 1860s. King, *Crime and Law in England*, 243; and "Punishing Assault: The Transformation of Attitudes in the English Courts," *Journal of Interdisciplinary History* 27, no. 1 (Summer, 1996), 61. Out of 90 final verdicts in assault summonses against women in Thames PC in January, March, and May 1890, only five ended in a fine or imprisonment for the defendant. Registers of Summonses, Thames PC, January, March, and May 1890. In the same three months in 1900, only a single female defendant was imprisoned as a result of an assault summons there.

[63] The latter included lodging houses, public houses, passageways, courtyards, or the street itself. In the hundreds of assault cases between women that appeared in the Thames PC in January, March and May 1890, there were only two instances of fines 20 shillings or high being inflicted (the first was 20 shillings on March 29, before Godfrey Lushington and the second was 40 shillings on May 29, also before Lushington). In the same period in 1900, there was only one (40 shillings, May 10, before Mr. Dickinson).

[64] On January 6, 1905 and again on April 15, in the Clerkenwell court, plaintiffs brought assault summonses against their female lodgers, and in both cases, pointed out that they had given them notice to vacate the premises. The magistrates, rather than binding over the defendants or fining them, simply ordered them to acquiesce to their landlords' demands. Minutes of Summonses, Clerkenwell PC, January 6, 1905 (PS/CLE/B/03/008; April 15, 1905 (PS/CLE/B/04/008).

the first place.[65] On the other hand, by far the most typical verdict of a summons for assault or threats of violence was a recognizance, so predictability could have held equal appeal.[66] Taking out a summons was a gamble, but unless one brought a protracted (and therefore expensive) case, it was not an excessive one.

Women's particular method of employing summonses against one another at the Clerkenwell court, however, strongly suggests that seeing the defendant receive any particular sentence, or indeed any sentence at all, was often not the goal. Women frequently applied for and received summonses and subsequently failed to appear to prosecute them. In twenty-three of the seventy-five assault summonses made by women against other women in the Thames Police Court in January, March, and May of 1885, the plaintiff did not appear, neither party appeared, or the summons was withdrawn.[67] Twenty-five years later, the same pattern still held true in both the Thames and Clerkenwell courts, with roughly one-third of all women's assault summonses against other women failing to conclude with a hearing.[68] From the earliest police-court records available up until the outbreak of the First World War, women's summonses against one another continued to occupy a significant portion of the London police court dockets, and to take up a considerable amount of the courtrooms' time. Across these decades, the ease with which such summonses could be obtained, the free play given to complainant and defendant in court, and the consistent pattern of binding over rather than fines or imprisonment all encouraged women to freely employ them for social purposes. The summons process became an established and widely utilized method to seek redress or merely to continue a social contest in a more public venue. Men's summonses, on the other hand, followed quite distinct dynamics. The differing prosecution patterns of charges, discussed at length in the

[65] Robert Shoemaker has indicated that, for justices of Petty Sessions in pre-industrial London, flexibility of informal sentencing held considerable appeal. Shoemaker, *Prosecution and Punishment*, 85.

[66] In January, March, and May 1890 and 1900, in the Thames PC, about half of all assault summonses made by women against other women ended this way. Registers of Summonses, Thames PC, January, March, and May 1890 and 1900.

[67] Ibid., January, March, and May 1885 (PS/TH/A/02/2).

[68] Ibid., 1910 (PS/TH/A/02/36); and Registers of Summonses, Clerkenwell PC, 1910 (PS/CLE/A2/002, PS/CLE/A2/002, PS/CLE/A1/017). The same was true in Thames PC in 1900.

historical scholarship on crime, have revealed the considerable influence of gender on policing and punishment. The contrasts between men's and women's summonses demonstrate that such gender differences extended to voluntary engagement with local courtrooms as well.

"I Will Kill You Bloody Well Stone Dead. Order Your Funeral Coach Tonight": Men's Personal Summonses in the Clerkenwell, West London, and Thames Police Courts

Men used the courts less frequently than women did in personal disputes, the kinds of cases brought were different from those typically brought by women, the concrete stakes were higher, and the penalties inflicted upon conviction were generally more severe. Even when men employed the same kind of summons, such as the ever-popular assault summons, the circumstances prompting the case varied from those commonly found in women's summonses. Leaving aside the role of the police court in marital relations for the time being, the first major difference between men's and women's use of private summonses was simply one of frequency. Men brought fewer summonses than women did. This was true in both absolute terms and in comparison to men's presence as the target of summonses from other quarters. Men were far more likely than women were to be summonsed to a police court either by an individual or by a state agent, and also far more likely to be charged by a constable.[69] In sum, it was much more common for a man to find himself in a police court involuntarily. For them, much more so than for women, the courtroom was a place of punishment, not redress. Men's use of the police courts differed from women's in the targets of their summonses as well. Women brought summonses against one another, against male acquaintances, and against their husbands. Men, on the other hand, almost always summonsed other men, and most frequently those with whom they were in an economic relationship rather than a purely personal one.[70] The most common reasons why men applied for a private summonses were assault and for the recovery of wages or

[69] See Chapter 6.

[70] In West London PC, in May and July of 1882, there were 135 instances of summonses by men against other men, but only 15 against women. Registers of Summonses, West London PC, 1882. In Thames PC, in January, March, and May 1890 and 1900, the

recompense for damages done to goods. Such summonses often revolved around the workplace or economic arrangements such as rents owed, small debts, or payments for goods or services rendered. Public disrespect, especially towards a wife, was another common motivator for an altercation that culminated in a man summonsing another man, as were confrontations between proprietors and customers in public houses. Although the typical precedents differed, the patterns of adjudication for men's summons against other men were similar to same-gender women's assault summons. Fines were rare, heavy fines or imprisonments even rarer. Withdrawals, dismissals, or binding over to keep the peace were the most common outcomes.

The contrast between men's summonses against other men and women's summonses against other men was not a product of their status vis-à-vis the Victorian legal system. Instead, their voluntary courtroom usage reflected variations in their patterns of sociability and in their economic activity in the community. For men, the local courtroom was more often a locale by which economic disputes, rather than those over reputation and respectability, were resolved. And, unlike women's summonses against other women, men's summonses were usually the final chapter of a dispute rather than one stage in an ongoing conflict. Men, like women, could seek redress for violent attacks as well, but these summonses, too, often arose from what was originally an economic dispute. The use of summonses to elicit an economic settlement, however, was most certainly *not* the preserve of men alone. As will be discussed in Chapter 5, marital and affiliation summonses, the core of women's courtroom usage, were primarily economic in character. Women's summonses against pawnbrokers over the unlawful detaining of goods were as well.[71] On the other hand, it was unusual for economic relations to be the impetus behind working-class or lower-middle-class women's summonses against one another.

ratio was 226–55 and 105–18, respectively. Ibid., January, March, and May 1890 and 1900.

[71] See Melanie Tebbutt,*Making Ends Meet: Pawnbroking and Working-Class Credit* (Leicester: Leicester University Press, 1983). Economic issues were also significant drivers in working-class women's use of the County Courts in disputes with shopkeepers over debt and credit, see Finn, "Consumer Control in the County Courts."

Among the most frequent catalysts prompting a man to seek a summons in the late Victorian police courts was a disagreement between landlord and tenant. A disagreement over who was owed how much and for what could escalate into verbal and physical abuse, and subsequently prompt a summons for wages, detaining goods, willful damage, or assault. On January 28, 1902, almost the entire afternoon of the Clerkenwell court was taken up with two such cases, the first brought by Charles Sturman, a metal-shop owner, against William Sullivan, a bicycle repairman, for assault. In the second case, Edward Granger, who sold small "automatic machines," summonsed Richard Jones.[72] In both instances, each side accused the other of unfair business dealings and demanded recompense, the difference being in the Sturman case, the argument had devolved into violence over a small debt, while in the Granger summons, the debt owed was significantly larger, but the disagreement had remained civil (in both senses of the word). In contrast to women's summonses against one another, which remained focused on social conflict in the half-century preceding the First World War, men's courtroom usage showed an increasing propensity to focus on economic disputes as decades passed. By 1900, summonses brought under the Employee and Workman Act to recover wages in the Thames Police Court far exceeded assault summonses between men, though the former were more likely to be settled prior to a formal adjudication.[73] The increasing presence of police constables in working-class communities may also have been a factor in the changing patterns of male–male summonses. The significant level of violence that characterized the typical male–male assault summonses in the 1880s and 1890s, by the turn of the century, was increasingly likely to prompt the victim to fetch a constable, and a summons would follow only if the latter refused to press a charge.

Beyond the propensity for conflict over commercial dealings and the tendency for assaults to occur in the course of daily business, the general narratives of men's assault summonses were not remarkably

[72] Minutes of Summonses, Clerkenwell PC, January 28, 1902.

[73] In January, March, and May 1900, there were 71 wages summonses, in 23 of which the parties failed to appear in court. In comparison, there were 48 assault summonses, 11 of which did not proceed due to the absence of the complainant or both complainant and defendant. Registers of Summonses, Thames PC, 1900.

different from women's. Outside of arguments over wages, payments, and debts, male assault summonses were usually proceeded by a public exchange of insults that escalated into physical violence. The conduct and consequences of these summonses did differ in one significant way. Men's summonses were more likely to involve claims that considerable violence had been committed or grave injury inflicted by the defendant. Women most commonly summonsed each other for wounded pride and outraged reputation. Men typically summonsed each other for physical wounds and an outraged balance sheet.[74] Although assault summonses, many of them workplace disputes, remained numerous in the decades preceding the First World War, they were rarely protracted cases. Wages summonses, if not always the greater in number, almost invariably took up more time in the courtroom.[75] Such cases typically involved multiple complainants (the employees) giving evidence against the same defendant (their employer). The careful recounting of work assigned, wages promised, and the discrepancies between the two over the course of days, weeks, or even months could take multiple courtroom sessions to fully describe.[76] Brief or attenuated, such cases could prompt considerable payments, though rarely of the full amount claimed by the complainant. A typical award was one-half to two-thirds of the claim, but since workers rarely troubled themselves to bring claims for less than one pound, and often did so *en masse*, an employer could still walk out of court with his pockets significantly lightened. Such summonses were occasionally dismissed outright, but it was more common for the complainant to drop the suit (usually an indication that the disagreement had been settled out of court). These detailed cases required careful preparation on the part of the defendants, and this level of commitment was rarely apparent in men's assault summonses. Working-class men, in large part, did not seem to view the social dimension of the latter as worthy of the investment. The recovery of a debt or wages owed was another matter entirely. Whereas women frequently brought assault

[74] For an example of how a commercial dispute could escalate into serious violence, see John Rosen's summons against William Bush, Minutes of Summonses, Clerkenwell PC, July 13, 1900.

[75] The Employers and Workmen's Act 1875 had put both parties on equal footing legally.

[76] Minutes of Summonses, Clerkenwell PC, March 18, 1902.

summonses against acquaintance males, their husbands, and the putative fathers of their children, men's assault summonses against women were rare.[77] Summonses that were carried through to court were rarer still, as the complainant often failed to appear. Cases like these that resulted in a fine or imprisonment were rarest of all. In the Clerkenwell minutes from the turn of the century, in the few assault cases where a male stood as complainant and a female as defendant, it took a truly dire attack for a magistrate to inflict a serious penalty.[78] Whether because it was culturally unacceptable, socially inadvisable, legally impractical, or all three, men simply did not summons women with any frequency, with one notable exceptions. Public-house proprietors regularly summonsed women who refused to leave their premises ("refusing to quit"), or for willful damage to their property.[79]

"Strike Me Dead, I Will Pay Her if It Is a '12 Months'": Private Summonses, Courtroom Culture, and "Courtroom Consciousness"

Thus far, we have established the general pattern of summonses outside the realm of marriage and affiliation in the West London, Thames, and Clerkenwell Police Courts in the final decades of the nineteenth century and the first of the twentieth. Conflicts in the community were becoming more of an affair for the courtroom even as the local courtroom was being integrated into the social and economic operation of the local community. Although this process had been made possible by the 1839 Metropolitan Police Act, which allowed for cheap summonses on verbal information, the impetus for concrete change had been the agency of men and women in the community. By the final decade of the century, the Thames PC alone was adjudicating, on average, between 180 and 250 personal summonses a month

77 In January, March, and May of 1890 and 1900, in the Thames PC, men sought assault summonses against other men at a rate four times higher than they did against women. In those three months in 1900, there were a mere six of the latter. Of those six, two were dismissed, two failed to proceed due to the absence of principals, one was adjourned, and a single defendant was sentenced to 14 days' hard labor.

78 Minutes of Summonses, Clerkenwell PC, September 17, 1900.

79 Local constables, employing regulations passed first in the Licensing Act 1872 and later strengthened in 1902, could summon publicans for permitting excessive drunkenness on their premises (Paul Jennings, "Policing Public Houses in Victorian England," *Law, Crime and History* 1 (2013), 62).

brought by men and women in the district.[80] The West London Police Court was even more prolific, hearing as many as 300 or more monthly by 1900.[81] Each of these summonses would involve a minimum of two principals, and the presence of between one and three witnesses beyond this was common. Particularly fraught contests, such as when one complainant was allegedly "mobbed" by a group of assailants, or those involving cross-summonses, could bring upwards of eight or more individuals to the local courtroom in a welter of accusations, counter-accusations, and competing witness testimony. What can this panoply of summonses tell us about the changing character of local courtrooms and their roles in their communities? In what ways did their employment by local men and women influence their operation and the meaning of what was said and done there? Finally, how did local knowledge of courtrooms and their usages influence social relations, and the conduct of interpersonal conflict in particular, beyond the courtroom itself?[82]

First and foremost, private summonses, by the final quarter of the nineteenth century, had become the most democratic element of the police courts' daily operation. Anyone with two shillings could apply for a summons, anyone could be a complainant or defendant, and anyone could serve as a witness. There were, of course, practical limitations to this. Summonses were affordable but they were not free, except when the magistrate granted an applicant a free second summons at the conclusion of the first. The minutes of the Clerkenwell Police Court include a broad gamut of complainants, from middle-class professionals to workhouse inmates and street-peddlers. Typically, however, those summonsing and those summonsed tended to be from households in regular or semi-regular work, and who had money available to pay for the summons itself, associated costs, and fines (if necessary) rather than imprisonment.[83] The clerks' notations on the court registers indicate that, almost

80 Registers of Summonses, Thames PC, 1890, 1900.

81 Registers of Summonses, West London PC, 1900–1.

82 I focus on Clerkenwell in this analysis, as it is the one court for which all four sources of key information – court minutes, court registers, local newspaper coverage, and national newspaper coverage – are readily available.

83 This system of fine-paying suited the desire of the magistrates and the Home Office to keep the costs of the police courts' operation down.

without exception, fines and costs levied were immediately paid by one party or the other. In the Clerkenwell minutes, complainants were most commonly drawn from a cohort of men and women that included shop-owners and workers, market-stall keepers, publicans, domestic servants, tradesmen, artisans, and builders.[84]

The decision taken to seek a summons by this cohort was more based on what could be accomplished in redressing a social violation and the desire to achieve moral satisfaction than it was to secure a specific legal punishment. That is to say, bringing a summons was itself a distinct act guided by certain assumptions and expectations that were distinguished by all involved from the adjudication process that might or might not follow. Assault summonses typified this divergence. The violations involved were less physical and more social, in the sense that any of these actions by the defendant represented gross disrespect in the complainant's eyes. This is why descriptions of alleged assaults freely mixed verbal attacks with physical ones, and often included (sometimes exclusively) acts that were grossly disrespectful rather than harmful, such as spitting or dousing with water. Legally, the latter did not qualify, as an assault was defined as "an attempt or offer, with force and violence, to do a corporal hurt to another."[85] In courtroom practice, the assault was on the person as a social being, but not necessarily on the body of the defendant. Verbal threats constituted a separate offense, but summonses were only rarely sought for this.[86] The preeminence of the social and cultural dimensions of assault summonses does not indicate that the complainants were ignorant of either the general parameters of the law or the specifics of courtroom practice. Far from it – the evidence of women's courtroom employment indicates their grasp of that locale's dynamics, the limits of its purview, and even, on occasion, the specifics of the law itself. The complexity and specificity of the testimony in summons cases, which often took place weeks after the events prompting them, demonstrated the

[84] Women's socioeconomic status could often be gleaned from statements about their husbands, brothers, or fathers, who appeared as witnesses, or from other contextual elements of their testimony (e.g. their living circumstances).

[85] Thomas William Saunders, *Oke's Magisterial Synopsis: A Practical Guide to Magistrates, Their Clerks, Solicitors and Constables*, vol. 1, 13th ed. (London: Butterworths, 1882), 302.

[86] The former appeared under the category of "threats."

familiarity of local men and women with the requirements of courtroom practice in summonses and with their operation as a locale closely intertwined with the social life of the community. These were hardly simple *mano a mano* affairs. A typical summons might involve anywhere from two to eight different individuals, when one includes complainant, defendant, and witnesses. Beyond this, summonses involving multiple defendants were not infrequent, and cross-summons were common. The courtroom positions of complainant, defendant, and witness were extremely fluid, and could change from case to case and day to day.

Despite this integration between court and community, those who brought summonses understood that the local courtroom was a distinct environment, and that behavior there had distinct repercussions different from acts in the street or home. Confrontation in the courtroom, while under public scrutiny, was not the same as confrontation in the home or elsewhere in the community. In the former, days, weeks, or even months after the events that brought the parties to court, strength of emotion or moral certainty was of little consequence. There was emotion, to be certain, but its depth lay somewhere between the melodrama of police-court columns and the flat, factual enumerations of police-court minutes. The offering of a detailed account, the effective harnessing of witness testimony, careful cross-examination, and the consistency and coherency of narrative was paramount. Stating one's case in accord with the applicable laws as they were commonly applied in summonses was also crucial in the formal adjudication. This entire process, in the vast majority of summonses, was conducted solely by the complainant and defendant, with the occasional intercession by the magistrate.

Such verbal acuity is not surprising from members of a thoroughly oral community culture.[87] But the familiarity with courtroom standards of narrative and conduct, even absent respect for the rules of evidence, was apparent in more than just conduct in the courtroom itself. Further evidence of "courtroom consciousness," of a popular comprehension of potential consequences of a summons and possible courtroom appearance, lay in the frequent use of courtroom language

[87] As Ellen Ross puts it so succinctly, "the central female social activity was talk." Ross, "Survival Networks," 10; Tebutt, *Women's Talk?*, 76–80.

outside the courtroom. The threat and language of summonses was interwoven into conflicts that happened on the streets, in public houses, and on the staircases of lodging houses. The courtroom and the possibility of punishment there did not need to be further explained to those involved, it existed in the background already, and needed only a mention to be brought to the fore. When, in November 1902, James Cohen, a letting agent, learned that Annie Phillips, his lodger, had taken out a summons against his wife, his response was swift and severe. Cohen pushed her down the stairs of their lodging house, Phillips later testified, telling her "I will give you summons. You won't live to come to the m[agistrate]."[88] Cross-examined in court by James Cohen, her alleged assailant, Annie Phillips denied any knowledge that Cohen's wife, Jane, had, in turn, summonsed *her* already for assault. Much of the discussion and testimony concerned who had applied for which summons when, and whether the other parties involved had been aware of the impending court appearance. The physical confrontation between the Cohen and Phillips families was interwoven with the timing and purpose of their summonses and threats to summons. The language of the courtroom had serious implications when employed in the hallway or courtyard, serious enough to prompt violent attack – and prompt *another* summons in consequence. In other instances, parties in a summons case testified that something as specific as the length of a *potential* recognizance in a *threatened* summons was factored into the heat of a disagreement.[89]

The integration of courtroom language into daily confrontations helps explain the broader relationship between courtrooms and their local communities, and the role of private summonses in particular. Summonses and threats of summonses were only effective because all parties involved understood their implications, because they possessed a courtroom consciousness that made the language and practices of the courtroom relevant well beyond its physical confines. Even applications for summonses, as their frequent mention in police-court testimony attests, could quickly become public knowledge in the tightly knit social fabric of urban neighborhoods.[90] The courtroom

[88] Minutes of Summonses, Clerkenwell PC, November 7, 1902.
[89] Ibid., July 13, 1902.
[90] The constant presence of interested onlookers at the London courts was emphasized in every description, from press accounts to memoirs to parliamentary inquiries. See

and the personal summons process were thus more than merely extensions interpersonal conflicts. Their patterns shaped the conduct of such conflicts and helped define moral boundaries and social norms in local communities. By threatening to summons or implementing that threat, a complainant changed the tenor of a conflict, raising the concrete stakes and potential social repercussions. It could prompt a renegotiation of terms, an apology, a settlement, or redress on any number of fronts. The most common outcome for those summonses that were carried through, a binding over to keep the peace, while not financially burdensome, exerted a powerful effect on its recipients. Such was the "magical power" of these recognizances, wrote the magistrate William Saunders, that the defendants in private assault summonses not infrequently pleaded for a full trial instead, preferring the potential of a fine or imprisonment. As prolific author of magistrates' authoritative guides explained, "[seeing the defendant bound over] gives a triumph to the complainant of which he is enabled to boast, and which places the defendant in a somewhat humiliating position."[91] A summons followed through to the courtroom, however, entailed risk for the complainant as well, since it allowed defendants the opportunity to present their own version of events in a public venue to an attentive audience, and to support this with witnesses. A summons case could, in the face of an effective defense, shift moral responsibility to the complainant and see *them* bear the costs or be bound over.[92] The magistrate, while holding a monopoly on the formal verdict, was hardly the only one whose opinion mattered in such circumstances. While charges most typically pit a constable against a sole defendant, personal summonses were a thoroughly social exercise, involving the participation of the community as both witnesses and audience.

Personal summonses were also more guided by commonly held beliefs about courtroom practice than they were by knowledge of specific legal statutes, hence my earlier use of the term "courtroom

e.g. *Minutes of Evidence, Report of the Departmental Committee to Inquire into the Jurisdiction of Metropolitan Police Magistrates and County Justices* (PP 1900, Cd. 374), 13. On the tightly knit nature of urban, working-class communities in particular, see Ross, "Survival Networks," 5.

[91] Thomas Saunders, *Metropolitan Police Court Jottings* (London: Horace Cox, 1882), 68.

[92] Ibid., 38.

consciousness" as opposed to "legal consciousness."[93] As frequently as summons language appeared in social conflicts between non-intimates, explicit references to the laws that governed summonses were almost unheard of. The men and women who sought out the police courts on a daily basis understood what it meant to be summonsed or bound over. That understanding was based on past experience of courtrooms either firsthand (as participants) or secondhand (via the community or police-court columns), which shaped their own expectations of magistrates' authority. This distance between common assumptions about what could or should happen in a courtroom and what was feasible under the law was much commented on by magistrates at the time. The Chief Magistrate of London, James Vaughan, explained to a parliamentary committee in 1900 that those who sought the court's assistance believed that the magistrate was "omnipotent," and that "whatever he orders to be done must be done."[94]

Even though the magistrates themselves knew this was far from the truth, they were happy to cultivate this common misapprehension.[95] Where legal authority was lacking, a popular belief in that authority would suffice, if it increased the public faith in the magistrates and their courtrooms to address the myriad issues brought before them. Although magistrates like Vaughan expressed enthusiasm for popular misconceptions of their courtroom omnipotence, they were ambivalent about how the local population chose to engage it. Women's use of summonses in particular were vehemently and repeatedly trivialized, most famously by J. A. R. Cairns, who described them as "two shillings' worth of revenge in the form of a summons."[96]

Belittled though they may have been by magistrates, the stakes for local men and women who employed personal summonses were far from trifling. Even beyond the possible financial implications, the summons process shaped the character of interpersonal conflict in varied and significant ways. The potential alone of a courtroom appearance could have serious repercussions. The likelihood of public shaming in personal

93 For the latter, see Merry, *Getting Justice and Getting Even*, "Introduction."

94 James Vaughan, Bow Street Magistrate, *Report on the Jurisdiction of Metropolitan Police Magistrates and County Justices*, 736. William Saunders had offered a similar observation 20 years earlier (Saunders, *Jottings*, 20).

95 James Vaughan, Bow Street Magistrate, *Metropolitan Police Magistrates and County Justices*, 736.

96 J. A. R. Cairns, *The Loom of the Law* (London: Hutchinson, 1920), 227.

summons cases may have been relatively remote since, with the important exception of marital cases, press reporting of them was infrequent compared to charges or regulatory summonses. Every summons heard in court, covered in newspapers or not, was a nonetheless participatory affair for the community, be they principals, witnesses, or courtroom audience.[97] It offered an opportunity to present one's own version of right and wrong, to demand redress, to challenge a public attack on one's body or reputation, to demonstrate one's support in the community, or even to turn the tables on one's accuser and paint them as the villain.

The embedding of the courtroom and the summons process in interpersonal conflicts speaks to the ascension of popular understanding of courtrooms over popular conceptions of the law, of communities' engagement with the courtroom over collective ambivalence to the state as an institution, and of concrete, local practices over law's formal (but abstract) parameters more generally. The personal summons was most often a cultural and social act with legal implications, rather than vice-versa. This was particularly the case with women's courtroom engagement and with magistrates' pervasive employment of recognizances to keep the peace in women's assault summons in the 1880s and early 1890s. For, in that period, married women did not exist as legal entities distinct from their husbands, and therefore *could not legally enter into a recognizance at all.*[98] Women's common request for such a sentence against other women, and their common employment of personal summonses more generally, is one of several key ways in which women adapted the local courtroom to serve their own goals. That they were able to do so, and to consistently fill summons registers and the courts' afternoons with their own grievances, despite their highly constrained legal status, speaks both to their familiarity with courtroom practice and the elevation of courtroom culture over law in these circumstances. The expansion of summary justice into daily life and the affordability of personal summonses had provided avenues by which working-class and lower-middle-class women could access a public forum for articulating their visions of justice and morality. Regardless of their own liminal legal status and whether or not their grievances constituted legal violations, they could use the cultural and social power of the summons process to shape their interpersonal relations.

[97] D'Cruze, "Sex, Violence and Local Courts," 41. [98] Saunders, *Jottings*, 70.

The rising social and cultural importance of summonses increased the visibility of the local courtroom as an institution in the community, but it did not raise the moral authority of the magistrates commensurately. They determined the verdicts, but they could not prevent summonses or strictly control what was said in court. Nor could they command how the local community would view the complainant and defendant subsequently. Given the conflicting testimony frequently on offer in women's summonses of one another, often their only reasonable option was to bind over both parties. With this measure, magistrates could hope to prevent further summonses (though not necessarily further conflict), in the immediate future. Both complainant and defendant could claim victory, and the community itself would make judgments dependent on the testimony and witness accounts rather than the verdict or magistrate's pronouncements. Empty summonses posed a particular challenge to magisterial authority, since they relied *entirely* on the community's perception of such an act and the potential social impact of a courtroom appearance for effect, while granting magistrates no opportunity at all to offer their own commentary either in the courtroom or in subsequent journalistic coverage.

Seen in this context, the decision of magistrate William Saunders, author of the definitive guide to magistrates' practice, to dedicate an entire chapter of his widely-read 1882 memoir to "The Lower Classes of Women as Complainants, Defendants and Witnesses – Their Untruthfulness" looks more like a defensive reaction against women's growing courtroom prerogative rather than a dismissal of their practices from a position of authority.[99] By the end of the nineteenth century, the courtroom discretion that magistrates had so jealously guarded for more than a century was under assault from regulatory bodies and their plethora of bye-laws on one side and a cascade of women's summonses on the other. The more that summons language and the summons process became integrated into interpersonal relations, and the stronger the implications of a summons or the threat of one became, the *less* vital the courtroom appearance itself was.[100] In the private-summons process

99 Saunders, *Jottings*.

100 The evidence that magistrates regularly refused to grant summonses is ambiguous, at best, and doing so ran the risk of a much more serious confrontation occurring subsequently. Barry Godfrey, "Changing Prosecution Practices and Their Impact on Crime Figures, 1857–1940," *British Journal of Criminology* 48, no. 2 (2008), 178.

beyond the sphere of marriage and affiliation, the *idea* of the courtroom and the *anticipated consequences* of an appearance there, elements that magistrates could influence but not control, was becoming more important even as their authority in the concrete space of the courtroom was becoming less so. It would not be until the interwar period that magistrates would find a way to decisively reassert their authority over the public dimensions of the personal summons process and the moral messages of courtroom interventions into interpersonal conflicts.

The social power of the personal summons and the legal power of the magistrate were distinct, but in both cases, they attest to the growing significance of courtrooms in their local communities. The continued popularity of personal summonses across the latter decades of the nineteenth century and the early decades of the twentieth demonstrated how such courtrooms remained an important venue for individual men and women to resolve or continue interpersonal conflicts, to reinforce and define social boundaries, and to secure redress for alleged wrongs, regardless of whether or not they constituted a legal violation (or whether the putative defendant was even eligible for legal sanction). A summons, a calling to public account, could not be ignored, and these acts were taken very seriously in the community. They carried with them the potential for further humiliation, at the least, and loss of resources or even freedom at the worst. In the half-century after the passage of the 1839 Metropolitan Police Act, the introduction of cheap summonses and the broad authority of the magistrates, coupled with the initiative of local men and women, had fostered the integration of local courtrooms and their communities. Even as charges by constables dominated courtroom mornings, and regulatory cases occupied a large swath of the courtrooms' afternoon docket, personal summonses brought thousands of London's working-class and lower-middle-class men and women into the courtroom every month. There, they negotiated right and wrong, called and conducted cross-examinations of witnesses, claimed recompense, and demanded justice. Their familiarity with the courtroom, in turn, informed the confrontations that took place in the community. "I shall summons you!" was a frequent cry in the stairwell, street, stoop, and market-stall. Thus did the language of the courtroom permeate interpersonal conflicts beyond it, even as the harsh words of such contests were heard daily within it.

5

A Poor Woman's Court of Justice, 1882–1910

The case made in 1900 against Walter Skinner, a carman living on Farringdon Road, was damning indeed. In the Clerkenwell Police Court, the evidence demonstrating his unfitness as a husband and father included a detailed accounting of his poor finances, his past convictions for drunkenness, and witness testimony concerning his assaults on his wife.[1] The magistrate, convinced, granted Skinner's wife a separation order, custody, and seven shillings a week.[2] The detailed and persuasive case against Walter Skinner was made not by a solicitor, Poor Law guardian, or an agent of the rapidly multiplying social welfare edifice of the metropolis. It was put forth by Mancell Elizabeth Skinner, his wife. Her case was only one of many thousands that would be heard in police courts across London that year as working-class women sought the courtroom to ameliorate their domestic difficulties. They would employ the police courts to alleviate marital violence, to compel husbands to fulfill their financial obligations, to hold fathers accountable for their illegitimate children and, if necessary, to obtain the economic support that would allow them to leave an intolerable marriage.[3] In 1900, across England and Wales, courts of summary jurisdiction would receive 26,707

[1] Minutes of Summonses, Clerkenwell PC, June 29, 1900 (PS/CLE/B/03/001).

[2] A carman drove a horse-drawn wagon, typically used for the transportation of goods.

[3] *Judicial Statistics, 1900, England and Wales, Pt. I, Criminal Statistics* [hereafter *Judicial Statistics, 1900*] (PP 1902, Cd. 953 and 1153), 74.

applications relating to the maintenance of wives and children, for which they would grant 21,414 orders.[4]

Twelve years after Mancell Skinner summonsed her husband, when Parliament conducted an inquiry into the operation of the laws concerning marriage, separation, and maintenance in the police courts, cases similar to hers came up repeatedly. In these deliberations, the concerns of magistrates and committee members alike went well beyond the formal workings of the law and its reform. Much of their discussion focused instead on women's courtroom usage and on how courtrooms' moral atmosphere and social dimensions had changed as a result. Witness after witness, from magistrates and police-court missionaries to solicitors and representatives of voluntary organizations, attested to the close integration of marriage, marital conflict, and local courtrooms.[5] In this context, two questions came up time and again – had the easy availability of summonses for judicial separations changed working-class attitudes towards matrimony? And had the widespread newspaper reporting of such cases fostered an increase of adultery and a decline in working-class morality? The consensus, much to the chagrin of both the committee members and their witnesses, was that they had. Working-class marriage had become thoroughly entangled with courtroom culture, and the results had not been encouraging.

Chapter 3 has explored how the metropolitan police courts were integrated into the social and economic life of their communities and how the courtroom, as both a concrete and conceptual locale, could shape interpersonal relations. This chapter argues that the rapid rise of marriage, domestic relations and paternity issues in the courtroom changed its daily operation even as the rapid expansion of the law into such affairs influenced marriage and domestic relations. The courtroom was not merely a venue for the expression of law or norms of gender, class, and morality that were constituted

[4] Ibid.

[5] Testimony of Alfred Chicele Plowden, Metropolitan Police Magistrate, June 14, 1910, *Minutes of Evidence, Report of the Royal Commission on Divorce and Matrimonial Causes*, vol. 2 (PP 1912–13, Cd. 6478) [hereafter *Divorce and Matrimonial Causes 1912*, vol. 2], 277. Plowden's popular autobiography, *Grain or Chaff?*, had been produced by the noted London publishing house, T. Fisher Unwin, in 1903.

elsewhere.[6] Nor was it just space to enforce middle-class standards of sexual and marital morality, and those of patriarchy in particular.[7] Local courtrooms became significant in the negotiation and contestation of morality and gender norms in courtship, marriage and paternity. Despite the asymmetrical balance of formal legal power against them, working-class women played a decisive role in this process.[8] This alteration of the courtrooms' gender dynamics, with the rapid increase in women's usage and the elevation of their summonses to a prominent place in daily court business, changed the character of courtroom practice and dialogue as well. As local courtrooms became preoccupied with what had once been considered the private, domestic realm, they became an essential space for women's participation in wider dialogues about gender norms and the role of the state in governing marital relations and parental responsibility.

In this process, courtroom culture operated as an important avenue for lower-middle-class and working-class women's contested entry into local and metropolitan political discourse.[9] Several decades before such women could directly shape the terrain of formal politics, they were effectively navigating the terrain of local courtrooms, and influencing both their daily practices and the meanings that emerged

[6] Michael Ignatieff argued in his insightful 1983 review essay that local courtrooms were "only the official and visible end-point of a process of popular justice which began within the working-class communities." "Total Institutions and Working Classes: A Review Essay," *History Workshop Journal* 15, no. 1 (1983), 170. The work of Jennifer Davis and David Phillips guided his assessment of the relationship between police, the police court, and the working class.

[7] Gail Savage "The Magistrates Are Men," in George Robb and Nacy Erber, eds., *Disorder in the Court: Trials and Sexual Conflict at the Turn of the Century* (New York: New York University Press, 1999), 240–41.

[8] This also adds further strength to the arguments offered by gender historians that legal structures (originally developed to protect male property rights or contain women's behavior) could, to some degree, be co-opted by the latter instead. A. James Hammerton, *Cruelty and Companionship: Conflict in Nineteenth-Century Married Life* (London: Routledge, 1992); Ginger Frost, *Promises Broken: Courtship, Class and Gender in Victorian England* (Charlottesville: University Press of Virginia, 1995); George Behlmer, *Friends of the Family: The English Home and Its Guardians, 1850–1940* (Stanford: Stanford University Press, 1998), 200–201; Margot Finn, "Working-Class Women and the Contest for Consumer Control in the County Courts," *Past & Present* 161, no. 1 (1998), 188–200.

[9] Jane Lewis, *Women in England 1870–1950: Sexual Divisions and Social Change* (Bloomington: Indiana University Press, 1984), x–xi.

from them.[10] Their adaptive use of the police courts represented an astute and pragmatic employment of one of the few public forums available to them.[11] Employed this way, courtrooms became places where women could blur the line between private and public space.[12] And they did so in ways that often granted them a much greater voice on a wider range of issues than had been possible before. These usages frequently ran contrary to the aims of legislators and magistrates, who saw summary justice largely as a tool to preserve marriage, protect victimized women, or definitively resolve domestic conflict. Women, in contrast, were more likely to use the courtroom as

10 For middle-class and lower-middle-class women's roles in policy and the expanding state bureaucracy, see Jane Lewis, *Women and Social Action in Victorian and Edwardian England* (Aldershot: Edward Elgar, 1991); Seth Koven and Sonya Michel, eds., *Mothers of a New World: Maternalist Politics and the Origins of Welfare States* (New York and London: Routledge, 1993); Susan Pennybacker, *A Vision for London 1889–1914: Labour, Everyday Life, and the LCC Experiment* (New York and London: Routledge, 1995); Dina Copelman, *London's Women Teachers: Gender, Class and Feminism, 1870–1930* (New York and London: Routledge, 1996); Jane Martin and Joyce Goodman, *Women and Education, 1800–1980* (Basingstoke and New York: Palgrave Macmillan, 2004). For women and the growth of consumer culture, see Erika Rappaport, *Shopping for Pleasure: Women and the Making of London's West End* (Princeton: Princeton University Press, 2001). For women and imperialism, see Antoinette Burton, *Burdens of History: British Feminists, Indian Women, and Imperial Culture, 1865–1915* (Chapel Hill: University of North Carolina Press, 1994); Mary Procida, "Good Sports and Right Sorts: Guns, Gender, and Imperialism in British India," *Journal of British Studies* 40, no. 4 (Oct. 2001), 454–88; Elizabeth Prevost, "Married to the Mission Field: Gender, Christianity and Professionalization in Britain and Colonial Africa, 1865–1914," *Journal of British Studies* 47, no. 3 (Oct. 2008), 796–826 and *The Communion of Women: Missions and Gender in Colonial Africa and the British Metropole* (Oxford: Oxford University Press, 2010).

11 Women were given the vote (at age 30) in 1918, at which time Women's Sections of the Labour Party were also established, but the origins of working-class women's formal participation in party politics dates back to the founding of the Women's Labour League in 1906. Pat Thane, "Women in the British Labour Party and the Construction of the State Welfare, 1906–1939," in Seth Koven and Sonya Michel, eds., *Mothers of a New World: Maternalist Politics and the Origins of Welfare States* (New York and London: Routledge, 1993), 344. Rate-paying, single women had been able to vote in local elections since 1869 (Municipal Franchise Act 1869), and had paid a particularly important role in the London School Board, which was established following the passage of the Elementary Education Act 1870. Joyce Goodman, *Women, Educational Policy-Making and Administration in England: Authoritative Women Since 1800* (London: Routledge, 2000).

12 For an interpretation of how gender issues and different locales of discourse production can change the dynamics of "public" and "private," see Michael Warner, *Publics and Counterpublics* (New York: Zone Books, 2002), esp. 7–12, 65–96.

leverage in an ongoing conflict, to assert their own vision of household authority or, in the direst cases, as a mechanism for a marriage's *de facto* dissolution. In the process, the London police courts became not a "poor man's court of justice," as the London magistrate Cecil Chapman would famously assert in his interwar memoir, but a poor woman's.[13]

"Because I Had Given Him a Summons, He Struck Me Again": The Police Courts and Marital Violence

Women's initiative notwithstanding, there can be no doubt that courtrooms were part of a judicial apparatus that remained overwhelmingly patriarchal. There were no female magistrates until 1913, no female lawmakers, and not a single female solicitor prior to the interwar period.[14] The moment a woman walked through the doors of a police court, she entered a realm where, officially, men were in charge.[15] Did this always mean that they remained subject to magistrates' visions of gender norms and morality? Determining the degree to which women, through summonses and courtroom use, were able to challenge the legal, social, cultural, and economic authority of magistrates, husbands, and alleged fathers cannot be done simply or easily. It remains at the heart of this chapter's inquiry. A second crucial question involves the timing of working-class women's changing status in British society. To most gender historians, the First World War remains a watershed, albeit not one that fully transformed women's informal roles and expectations or their formal status in British society.[16] In contrast to their upper- and middle-class counterparts, whose legal and political rights advanced rapidly in the second half of

[13] Cecil Chapman, *A Poor Man's Court of Justice: Twenty-Five Years as a Metropolitan Magistrate* (London: Hodder and Stoughton, 1925).

[14] It was not until 1922, in the wake of the Sex Disqualification Act 1919, that women would first pass the examinations of the Law Society.

[15] Ginger Frost has similarly described the patriarchal environment that pervaded women's nineteenth-century breach-of-promise suits. Ginger Frost, "'I Shall Not Sit Down and Crie': Women, Class and Breach of Promise of Marriage Plaintiffs in England, 1850–1900," *Gender & History* 6, no. 2 (1994), 240.

[16] Deborah Thom, *"Nice Girls and Rude Girls": Women Workers in World War I* (London: IB Tauris, 1998); Angela Wollacott, *On Her Their Lives Depend: Munitions Workers in the Great War* (Berkeley and Los Angeles: University of California Press, 1994).

the nineteenth century, working-class women's limited financial resources and ambiguous position in the public discourse on social and moral reform put them at a severe disadvantage regardless of any official changes in their legal status. These circumstances notwithstanding, working-class women's broad and extensive employment of summonses, as explored in this chapter and the previous one, encourages us to revise the historical picture of their changing role and status vis-à-vis the state. Their frequent, public engagement with local courtrooms demonstrates both how integral working-class women were to recasting the nature of the state in this period, and also how the prewar expansion of the police and judicial apparatus represented a double-edged sword for them. Even as working-class women were becoming a focus of regulation and surveillance, they were also building on decades of past experience with the police courts and finding new ways to employ them to achieve their own ends.

Patriarchy and paternalism are crucial to consider in light of women's courtroom usage in this period, and in summonses for domestic assault, separation and maintenance, and affiliation in particular. Along with assault summonses against neighbors and other non-intimates, and summonses for detaining goods, these were the most common types of summonses brought by women.[17] The first of these, domestic assault, was the most frequent of all three types of summons. The historical scholarship on domestic violence and "wife-beating" in Victorian Britain is extensive.[18] Scholars of law, gender,

[17] Domestic assault was initially not a separate category of offense in Victorian Britain, but fell under the rubric of "common assault." As discussed below, this changed in 1853, with the introduction of aggravated assault as a distinct offense. The majority of both charges and summonses concerning violence against women, however, continued to be tried as common assault well into the early twentieth century. I use the contemporary terms "domestic assault" and "domestic violence" simply to indicate specifically that the offenses discussed here are common assault summonses where the complainant (female) and defendant (male) shared the same last name in the court registers. As indicated in the minutes of summonses, except on extremely rare occasions, this indicated that these individuals were husband and wife.

[18] Key examples include Nancy Tomes, "A 'Torrent of Abuse': Crimes of Violence between Working-Class Men and Women in London, 1840–1875," *Journal of Social History* 11, no. 3 (Spring, 1978), 328–34; Hammerton, *Cruelty and Companionship*; Maeve Doggett, *Marriage, Wife-Beating, and the Law in Victorian England* (Columbia: University of South Carolina Press, 1993); Shani D'Cruze, *Crimes of Outrage: Sex, Violence and Victorian Working Women* (Dekalb: Northern Illinois University Press, 1998) and "Sex, Violence and Local

and crime have recognized that the right to bring their husbands to court for assault was something that women, and plebeian women especially, had to establish for themselves across the late eighteenth and nineteenth century. This was achieved against considerable resistance from judicial authorities, who were reluctant to intervene in the private sphere of the household and to undermine male patriarchal authority in the process.[19] By the last quarter of the nineteenth century, however, ongoing changes in politics, class identity, and social reform had coalesced to foster a harsher view of male domestic violence. The most important of these developments were an impetus by the urban elites to "civilize" an allegedly violent and unruly urban working class, the rising importance of respectability in plebeian communities, a nascent feminist discourse that condemned male abuse, and a rising paternalistic concern among social reformers, policymakers and legal officials to protect women from those who would victimize them.[20] This halting and uneven changeover in official and popular attitudes towards male violence against women was focused on the working class. It manifested in the legal code in stages. Key legislation included the Offences Against the Person Act 1828 (9 Geo. 4 c.31), the Criminal Procedure Act 1853 (16 Vict. c. 30, introduced as "an Act for the Better Prevention and Punishment of Aggravated Assaults on Women and Children"), the amendment to the latter in 1868, and the 1882 "Wife Beaters Act," all of which widened the circumstances under which men could be prosecuted for their acts of physical aggression and raised the penalties for conviction.[21] In this process, the construction of marital abuse as being primarily a working-class problem was vital for politicians seeking to justify

Courts: Working-Class Respectability in a Mid-Nineteenth-Century Lancashire Town," *British Journal of Criminology* 39, no. 1 (1999), 39–54; Anna Clark, "Humanity or Justice? Wifebeating and the Law in the Eighteenth and Nineteenth Centuries," in Carol Smart, ed., *Regulating Womanhood: Historical Essays on Marriage and Sexuality* (London and New York: Routledge, 1992), 189–205.

19 Clark, "Humanity or Justice," 192.

20 Tomes, "Torrent of Abuse," 340–41; Martin Wiener, *Men of Blood: Violence, Manliness, and Criminal Justice in Victorian England* (Cambridge: Cambridge University Press, 2004), 37–38; Ben Griffin, *The Politics of Gender in Victorian Britain: Masculinity, Political Culture and the Struggle for Women's Rights* (Cambridge: Cambridge University Press, 2012), 5.

21 Tomes, "Torrent of Abuse," 340.

the unprecedented intervention of the Liberal state into private life and the limited curbing of male authority in the home.[22]

Considering the relatively rapid change in the laws regulating assault, and assault against women in particular, scholars' concentration on ideological clashes, legislative adaptation, and the press accounts or statistical records of the law's implementation is understandable.[23] So, too, is the focus of historical debate on the parallels and contrasts between working-class views and practices, middle-class norms of marriage and gender, and how the state – judicial authorities and police constables in particular – mediated these class and gender tensions. The raising of the maximum punishment for assault on a woman first to £20 or six month's hard labor, with the 1853 Act; later to a year, in 1868; and finally to include public flogging and pillory in 1882, drew quite the dramatic upwards trajectory of legal restrictions.[24] The creation, with the 1853 Act, of "aggravated assault," which designated violence against women and children by men as a separate subcategory of offense with correspondingly harsher punishments than "common assault" merited, and the tracking of the later laws with the increasing property and marital rights of women (discussed below) would appear to add further weight to these arguments. Even in instances where women had clearly taken the initiative, most historians have

[22] Ben Griffin, "Class, Gender, and Liberalism in Parliament, 1868–1882: The Case of the Married Women's Property Acts," *The Historical Journal* 46, no. 1 (Mar. 2003), 61.

[23] Anna Clark, *The Struggle for the Breeches: Gender and the Making of the British Working Class* (Berkeley: University of California Press, 1995), 63–87; Ellen Ross, "'Fierce Questions and Taunts': Married Life in Working-Class London, 1870–1914," *Feminist Studies* 8, no. 3 (Autumn, 1982), 578–80, 591; Tomes, "Torrent of Abuse," 339–40; Clark, "Humanity or Justice," 192–95; Wiener, *Men of Blood*, 36–39. George Behlmer has argued that the court was used to "enforce indigenous notions of right and wrong." George Behlmer, "Summary Justice and Working-Class Marriage," *Law and History Review* 12, no. 2 (Autumn, 1994), 235. In this, he is drawing on the work done by Jennifer Davis (see "Prosecutions and Their Context: The Use of the Criminal Law in Later Nineteenth-Century London," in Douglas Hay and Francis Snyder, eds., *Policing and Prosecution in Britain, 1750–1850* (Oxford: Clarendon Press, 1989), 413–14; "A Poor Man's System of Justice: The London Police Courts in the Second Half of the Nineteenth Century," *The Historical Journal* 27, no. 2 (1984), 330 31) and the assertion made by Michael Ignatieff, "Total Institutions," 90–91 (who also bases his claim on Davis's analysis).

[24] Tomes, "Torrent of Abuse," 340.

argued that the ultimate authority to enforce these new laws lay with the magistrates who, via their verdicts, had considerable discretion to condemn or excuse male violence.[25]

The records of London police-court summonses in the last quarter of the nineteenth century and the first decades of the twentieth reveal a very different picture of working-class women's entanglement with this changing legal landscape, one in which local courtrooms and marital conflicts were much more closely integrated than has been previously understood, and where women's initiative and adaptability at employing these venues played vital role.[26] Rather than a final recourse after all informal efforts had failed, a summons for marital assault could be sought by a woman at a number of different moments in the course of a relationship. The goal of these summonses could be more than to win a favorable verdict, to discipline their husbands with a magistrates' cooperation, or even to prompt a formal adjudication in the first place. Therefore, to determine the motivation and significance of such summonses, we must look beyond the realm of statistics on prosecution and punishment. A courtroom appearance offered the principals and witnesses, and other members the wider community, the opportunity to articulate their own views on gender norms, the roles of the court, and the consequences of violence.[27] Such cases were important in the wider dialogue over gender norms as well. Women's summonses against violent husbands provided grist for the mill of public commentary on marriage, violence, gender, and class at a time when popular opinion and the relevant laws were in flux. The integration of local courtrooms, as both concrete and

[25] Martin Wiener, *Reconstructing the Criminal: Culture, Law, and Policy in England, 1830–1914* (Cambridge: Cambridge University Press, 1990), 82–83; Savage, "The Magistrates Are Men," 240–41.

[26] Margot Finn has argued that working-class women's roles in contesting debt litigation in the Victorian County Courts similarly demonstrates how they were "enmeshed in legal processes, rather than positioned in clear and unequivocal opposition to them." Finn, "Contest for Consumer Control," 120.

[27] From the outset, it is important to note that assault summonses operated in a far different manner than did either police court assault charges or the more serious crimes of violence and abuse prosecuted in the Central Criminal Court. In the former, the constable had already arrested the defendant and would make the case against him in court, and in the latter, following the defendant's imprisonment, both prosecution and defense were conducted by legal professionals. Tomes, "A Torrent of Abuse," 332.

imagined spaces, into working-class marital and domestic strife had a significant effect on the courtroom and the conflicts themselves. Local courtrooms became more domestic even as working-class marriages became more civic and legalistic. And, via the discussion of intimate affairs in venues that were open to reporters and neighbors alike, they made the blurring of private and public life an everyday occurrence. These were not the intermittent scandals of the Divorce Court and breach-of-promise suits, which invited gossip and threatened humiliation for those whose social and political position made them magnets for press sensationalism.[28] Police-court cases exposed ordinary working-class homes and marriages to public commentary and official judgment on a daily basis. The stakes were more prosaic in communities where premarital intercourse, extramarital affairs, single motherhood and, in rare cases, prostitution, though condemned, were not necessarily grounds for pariah status.[29] Much of an individual's reputation depended upon the narrative of their circumstances, granting public courtroom contests a disproportionately greater significance regardless of their legal outcome.

Often brought at women's behest, these personal summonses followed a very different pattern than the top-down domestic interventions of the London School Board, Royal Society for the Prevention of Cruelty to Children, Poor Law Guardians, and other philanthropic and municipal bodies that had been exerting influence on working-class homes. Whereas the goal of an institutional summons in domestic issues was typically to prompt a formal hearing, women often initially employed the courtroom as a threat or bluff. This tactic was only useful because, as described in Chapter 4, there was a widespread understanding in working-class communities of a summons and its potential consequences. Ironically, courtroom testimony on summonses that were eventually adjudicated underscores just how common "empty summonses" were. In assault summonses that were taken to court, female complainants frequently alluded to previous

[28] Frost, *Promises Broken*, 144–45. Gail Savage, "They Would If They Could: Class, Gender, and Popular Representation of English Divorce Litigation, 1858–1908," *Journal of Family History* 36, no. 2 (2011), 174.

[29] Ginger Frost, "'The Black Lamb of the Black Sheep': Illegitimacy in the English Working Class, 1850–1939," *Journal of Social History* 37, no. 2 (Winter, 2003), 293–322.

summonses that had not been followed through. The statistical record confirms this; the single most frequent outcome (approximately 50–65 percent) of a women's assault summonses against male defendants with the same last name was that either the complainant or neither party appeared.[30] Beyond their frequency, the consequences of these empty summonses are unclear. There are indications that empty summonses only became "substantive" (i.e. either the complainant or both the complainant and defendant attended) when the threat of a court appearance alone had been insufficient to change the husband's behavior.[31] Although it was unusual for a single instance of violence to prompt an immediate summons, it was certainly not unheard of, particularly if the defendant had been grossly disrespectful or if there had been repeated aggressive acts in a short period.[32] Even an empty summons brought the courtroom, at a woman's initiative, to the very doorstep of the household. And the simple act of serving a husband with an assault summons, regardless of whether or not the wife's intention was to follow through, could have serious repercussions.[33] It, alone, was enough to prompt the husband of Elvy Davis to assault her. As she explained to Mr. D'Eyncourt, the Clerkenwell magistrate, in 1902, "because I had given him a summons, he struck me again."[34]

When an assault summons was followed through to a court appearance, it was not necessarily a last resort to an irreparable

[30] This rate was considerably higher than the rate of non-executed (i.e. "empty") summonses against other women or non-intimate males, as indicated in Chapter 4. Although a comprehensive assessment would be preferable, summonses, which numbered in the many tens of thousands for this complaint alone from 1885 to 1910, make this impractical. Instead, I have opted for "spot-check" of certain years and months to establish a common pattern. In the Thames PC, out of 50 assault summonses brought by women against men with the same last name in January, March and May 1885, 25 resulted in a withdrawal or a failure to appear by either the complainant or both parties. For January, March and May 1890 this was the case in 38 out of 72 women's assault and threats summonses. This was similarly true in 26 out of 53 women's assault summonses made in January and May 1900. In 1910, "empty summonses" were 29 out of a total 53 instances in March, May, and July. Registers of Summonses, Thames PC, 1885, 1890, 1900 and 1910. It is far higher than the rate recorded at mid-century (10%) (Tomes, "Torrent of Abuse," 333).

[31] Minutes of Summonses, Clerkenwell PC, February 2, 1902 (PS/CLE/B/4/004).

[32] Ibid., February 4, 1902.

[33] Such summonses were served by constables specifically seconded to the court for this duty.

[34] Minutes of Summonses, Clerkenwell PC, May 10, 1902.

situation. Instead, a variety of transgressions could prompt a wife to pursue her case further. The most common of these included the denial of financial support, threats of murder, attacks on their children, public disrespect, or a persistent pattern of violence (the latter as evidenced by previous summonses and sometimes previous convictions).[35] The variety of catalysts for an assault summons helps explain the great variation in sentencing and the relative rarity of heavy fines or imprisonments. The level of violence, abuse, or neglect that would prompt a wife to seek heavy punishment, or would convince a magistrate to grant it, was more likely to appear in summonses where the complainant was seeking a decisive intervention in an untenable marriage. After all, to penalize a household's primary breadwinner with fines or imprisonment could prove disastrous for all of those involved.[36] The balance of power between complainant and magistrate varied significantly between empty and substantive summonses. In contrast to an empty summons, a prosecution that went to court forced a woman to surrender much of her influence over the concrete outcome – much, but hardly *all*. In order to sustain some level of control over the consequences of a substantive summons, women often asked for very specific punishments short of punitive ones. The most commonly sought measures requested were that the husband be bound over to keep the peace or that he provide resources previously denied. Such flexibility of sentencing, and the common employment of binding over, made courtrooms a far more practical option for working-class women in difficult marriages than stern and inflexible punishments would have been.

Women's self-representation in these cases was another prominent example of how courtroom practice could deviate from the intention of the law or the desire of magistrates. Contrary to the image offered by middle-class reformers and parliamentarians, who had used women's alleged passivity as justification for the increasingly stern laws against male violence, women in court presented themselves as assertive figures

[35] Not coincidentally, these were the same circumstances that most often led women to seek judicial separations, as discussed below and in Ross, "Fierce Questions and Taunts," 593.

[36] Alfred Chicele Plowden, *Grain or Chaff? The Autobiography of a Police Magistrate* (London, Edinburgh, Dublin and New York: Thomas Nelson, 1903).

in the household, and as more than willing to stand up to disrespectful or abusive behavior.[37] When Elizabeth Penny brought her husband, George, up on an assault summons in Clerkenwell, she was candid about her refusal of his demands for a husband's privileges when, in her opinion, he had failed to fulfill a husband's duties. "Defendant came and asked for food. I said go and work for it."[38] "He said I will serve you [i.e. hit you] as Copper did his wife. I said 'oh will you.'" Although she claimed to have been struck strongly enough to send her "spinning in the corner," having had her say in court, she subsequently withdrew the summons. To take the time and trouble to state their marital grievances and expectations in a courtroom, only to withdraw the summons subsequently suggests that, in this case, the magistrates' authority and the formal verdict was less important to the complainant than the public forum offered by the courtroom itself.

With their two shillings paid, women were purchasing an opportunity to recount their husband's acts publicly, to air their grievances, to demand better treatment, and to call on the community in support of their claims. This was not, however, a woman's privilege alone. The courtroom operated in this fashion for *all* participants in summonses. Both principals and witnesses could assert their own ideas about the acceptable boundaries of marital behavior at a time when gendered violence, in its moral and legal dimensions, was under intense public discussion.[39] Friends, relatives, and neighbors could similarly testify to the specifics of the case or observe and support the complainant from the public gallery.[40] Here, the distinction between informal and formal means of conflict resolution (or continuation) in courtrooms and their communities blurred. In both, the consequences of a grievance effectively articulated and local support marshaled from friends, neighbors, and family could be social and material. In both,

[37] This self-presentation was consonant with the key roles that plebeian women played in maintaining the economic and social integrity of their homes. The image of women's alleged passivity and vulnerability in the face of male aggression, it should be noted, continued to exist alongside popular stereotypes of working-class women as being termagants and scolds who could, on occasion, provoke their husbands beyond endurance.

[38] Minutes of Summonses, Clerkenwell PC, October 12, 1910 (PS/CLE/B3/13).

[39] Wiener, *Men of Blood*, 198–200.

[40] D'Cruze, "Sex, Violence and Local Courts," 41.

the norms of morality and marital roles were fluid and contested. The courtrooms' role, in this regard, was on the rise even as the behaviors brought there were slowly beginning to wane. In the eighteenth-century legal and social landscape, marital violence was ubiquitous, while community discipline was sporadic.[41] By the end of the nineteenth century, this imbalance had lessened. Reported marital violence was on the decline, while public shaming via the courtroom was on the rise.[42] Applications for summonses, the summonses themselves, and charges for marital assault – often accompanied by the airing of grievances and harnessing of community support through witness testimony – had become everyday occurrences in the London police courts.

In this collective discussion of marriage, morality, and gendered expectations that took place in courtrooms, women's testimony rarely went uncontested. Bringing forth a summons gave husbands an opportunity to publicly chastise their wives' behavior in turn. They also brought their own summonses for assault, on occasion. Alcohol was among men's most common complaints in their courtroom appearances. Much as women did from the opposite tack, husbands often took the opportunity of a courtroom appearance to blame their wives' drinking for conflict in the home. When Catherine Petro summonsed her husband for assault in January 1902, she was able to offer little by way of evidence, since his relentless cross-examination

41 Clark in Smart, "Humanity or Justice," 196.

42 In 1880, there were 20,810 cases of assault tried by the London magistrates (17,461 being for common assault, 3,140 for assaults against peace officers (including resisting and obstructing), and 209 cases of aggravated assault against women and children (*Judicial Statistics, 1880, England and Wales, Pt. I, Police – Criminal Proceedings – Prisons* (PP 1881, C. 3088), 28). In 1890, there were 22,741 (18, 240; 4343; and 158 in each respective category) (*Judicial Statistics, 1890, England and Wales, Pt. I, Police – Criminal Proceedings – Prisons* (PP 1890–91, C. 4443), 28). By 1900, this had fallen to 19,306, and would continue to decline significantly across the decade (*Judicial Statistics, England and Wales, 1900, Pt. I, Criminal Statistics* (PP 1902, Cd. 953 and 1153), 100). The police returns for 1908 and 1910 indicated only 12,665 and 11,834 proceedings respectively for assault (*Judicial Statistics, England and Wales, 1908, Pt. I, Criminal Statistics* (PP 1910, Cd. 5096 and 5097), 108; *Judicial Statistics, England and Wales, 1910, Pt. I, Criminal Statistics* (PP 1912–13, Cd. 6071 and 6047), 104). Nancy Tomes has argued that, for various reasons, this seems to indicate a drop in the actual occurrence of violence, not just in the willingness of police and magistrates to prosecute instances of it (Tomes, "Torrent of Abuse," 330).

forced her to make statement after damning statement concerning her own behavior on the night in question. "I did have a glass of ale," she told the court, being compelled by his questions to explain her state when she returned home.[43] "I was not drunk. I wasn't singing." Despite the multiple bruises she displayed as evidence of his violence, the magistrate bound both parties over for a year. Just as women could specifically request that their husbands be bound over, the latter could do so for the former as well.[44] On rare occasions, husband and wife could even cross-summons one another for the same incident.[45] But as was generally the case with assault summonses, the numbers of men who tried to hold their wives to account in this way was extremely low. Magistrates were extremely reluctant, in these instances, to inflict anything beyond an order to keep the peace.

If men so infrequently employed summonses in domestic conflicts, where can we find their contribution to the dialogue over morality and gender roles in the courtroom? The answer lies in the testimony itself. It was a rare instance in which a man summonsed for domestic assault did not vociferously challenge the complainant's assertions. In a corollary to wives' behavior in court, husbands frequently asserted that their accusers had themselves transgressed marital and gender norms. Addressing his wife's summons for assault in October 1900, James Caffell insisted that he had been fulfilling his financial obligations, while she, in contrast, had been leading a rowdy social life. "It is my business and I go out painting," he told the Clerkenwell magistrate.[46] "I go to bed 10–11 and get up at 5. My wife and her sisters are out night after night, several hours after I am asleep."[47] In the mid-Victorian period, husbands had often claimed provocation of one sort or another as their justification for wife-beating. This was a claim that, not infrequently, found sympathy with local magistrates.[48] As with the laws themselves, however, the patterns of working-class, male

43 Minutes of Summonses, Clerkenwell PC, January 25, 1902.

44 Ibid., October 4, 1902.

45 Ibid., February 4, 1902. Cross-summonses between female complainants and defendants were more common.

46 Ibid., October 22, 1902.

47 In this instance, the magistrate, after initially deciding to bind James over, instead adjourned the case for a week. Two verdicts of binding over were crossed out by the clerk and replaced with the adjournment.

48 Tomes, "A Torrent of Abuse," 331–32.

response to assault summonses were changing in this period. Although it was not uncommon to find expressions of tolerance towards working-class marital violence among judicial officials as late as the early twentieth century, it was declining as a defense in assault trials.[49] By 1900, husbands were far less likely than they had been in previous decades to claim, at least in the courtroom, that their wife's disrespect or independent socializing alone had merited a violent response. Instead, husbands often asserted that that the wife had been the aggressor, and that they had acted in self-defense. These contested claims could be further complicated with the addition of witness testimony. Though husbands less commonly harnessed community support than their wives did, this was not always the case. Some of the most complicated and extensive domestic assault cases arose from public confrontations between husbands and wives, which afforded each the opportunity to justify their actions and could encompass a veritable squadron of witnesses on both sides. These witnesses, most typically neighbors or family members, could offer trenchant criticisms of the principals' behavior before, during, and subsequent to their altercation. This dynamic further changed the social dimensions of the courtroom. Witnesses were under oath, but risked neither reputation nor fine nor imprisonment with their participation. The magistrate could try to curb their narrative to keep it relevant, but a certain amount of leeway was necessary lest important details be elided. This relative freedom of speech, combined with the sheer number of witnesses brought to testify, could turn these cases into veritable public forums on morality, marital norms, and gender roles.

In September 1900, one case of this sort prompted a torrent of claims and counterclaims, brought witnesses for both sides of the contest, and occupied nearly the entire afternoon session of the Clerkenwell court. The principals' accounts could hardly have been more contradictory. Ellen Sessions, the complainant, told the court that her husband, Joseph, with whom she was no longer living, had viciously assaulted her and humiliated her in public, all without the

[49] As the magistrate John Rose told a parliamentary inquiry in 1910, "there is a great deal of rough usage without their being gross cruelty." John Rose (Metropolitan Police Magistrate), March 1, 1910, *Minutes of Evidence, Report of the Royal Commission on Divorce and Matrimonial Causes*, vol. 1 (PP 1912–13, Cmd. 6480) [hereafter *Divorce and Matrimonial Causes 1912*, vol. 1], 453.

slightest provocation. "My husband came up behind me, and struck me and said 'now you f[ucking] whore, have you got any money for me?' He then struck me behind the ear."[50] Worse yet, she asserted, he had kicked her companion, Elizabeth Sharp, who had been carrying a baby at the time. Sharp had only been trying to help Joseph recover his hat, which had fallen off during his initial assault. In Ellen's version of events, Joseph's sister, Hannah, had also defamed her publicly. "His sister said to me 'you dirty whore, do you make up [i.e. get dressed up] to go out whoring or to go out thieving?'" Ellen added further weight to her testimony by recalling that her husband had already received a month's hard labor for assaulting her. Her witness, Elizabeth, confirmed this version of events on almost every point, from the brutality of Joseph's unprovoked attack to the viciousness of his sister, who assailed both the witness and another woman with "a hairpin around her finger."

Joseph, in his defense, described a mobbing by the Erinyes of his wife and her companions. "My wife came behind me and struck on neck and said take that you rotten b[astard]." Ellen and Mrs. Sharp then both bit him on his hand and fingers, and he subsequently struck his wife, but only to make her release him. He then tried to protect his sister, Hannah, who was under assault from two other women. So serious were Joseph's wounds that he required treatment at the Royal Free Hospital afterward. Hannah, in turn, confirmed her brother's story, adding that their persecution had extended into the following day, when Mrs. Sharp and four other women abused her on the street. When she retreated indoors, they broke her door-knocker off with the violence of their demonstration. Even the police constable on scene had difficulty sorting out victim from assailant in this wild melee. He refused to charge Joseph Sessions, despite the demands of his wife and her allies. The magistrate's decision was to bind over both parties to keep the peace for six months, the most common verdict in such cases. Given that the overwhelming majority of substantive assault summonses ended with either a dismissal, a discharge, an adjournment *sine die* ("without a day," i.e. an indefinite adjournment), or with one or both parties bound over, there was no reason for either complainant or defendant to expect that a serious

[50] Minutes of Summonses, Clerkenwell PC, October 19, 1900.

penalty would be imposed.[51] The ambiguity of this typical verdict did not make the courtroom appearance any less significant in the ongoing contest between the two parties. Rather, the import of this case, as was true in so many other private summonses, lay in the opportunity it provided both sides to reaffirm their respectability while simultaneously maligning their opposite before a public audience.

One should not, from this incident and the thousands of others like it heard across London that year, conclude that the courtroom was merely a locale to police transgressions of moral norms and social boundaries. These boundaries were not fixed and the courtroom was hardly an end point. Instead, the content and timing of these assault summonses, interwoven as they were with the ebb and flow of marital conflict and the community's support or sanction, indicates the degree to which the courtroom operated as one of many spaces in which these boundaries were publicly contested and modified. Local courtrooms worked in tandem with the community's efforts to self-discipline and set standards for behavior, for the deeds and words of husbands and wives alike. Plebeian communities had a long history of public action in this manner.[52] By the end of the nineteenth century, courtrooms, thanks to the changing laws and easing of access, had become locales where this popular tradition of community discipline, the growing recognition of women's independent legal identity, and the newer strains of official disapproval of male violence coalesced.[53] Whatever the official verdict, summonses and courtroom appearances offered women a public forum to hold their husbands morally and socially accountable for their actions. Sometimes, the integration of the courtroom went no further than the empty summons. For substantive cases, the lesser penalties and greater flexibility of verdicts meant that a summons obtained through private application was much more fit for this purpose than fetching a constable to bring a charge was.[54] More fundamentally, a woman's full prosecution of an assault summons,

[51] In January, March, and May 1885, there were 352 assault summonses heard in the Thames PC. In these, there were 171 where a final adjudication was made. 128 of those consisted of these listed verdicts. In January and March 1900, these numbers were 242, 134, and 109, respectively. In West London during the same period, the pattern was very similar.

[52] E. P. Thompson, "Rough Music Reconsidered," *Folklore* 103, no. 1 (1992), 3–26.

[53] Clark, "Humanity or Justice," 188.

[54] The general unpopularity of the police served as further deterrent. Ibid., 199.

with witnesses in support, the magistrate involved, and an audience in attendance, was itself a reminder to all present (and the husband most especially) that the complainant *could* hold their husband publicly to account. Thus did the intertwining of domestic assault summonses and marital conflict not merely reflect the shifting balance of authority in working-class marriages and the increasing public outcry against wife-beating, but helped shape their contours as well.

"I Shall Never Live with Him Again": Determining "Neglect," "Persistent Cruelty," and the Limits of Tolerable Marriages in Local Courtrooms

In the latter decades of the nineteenth century, as assault summonses between husbands and wives became more common in London's working-class communities, changes in the laws on marriage provided a number of new ameliorative options for women.[55] Working-class women adapted to this new legal landscape and employed local courtrooms to secure release from intolerable marriages and the mitigation of difficult ones. Examining the types of cases that they brought and how they articulated marital issues demonstrates the substantial expansion of the courtroom's role in working-class domestic life across the final decades of the century. It also provides another useful perspective on working-class women's changing role vis-à-vis the state, and on the uneven pace of their progress towards legal emancipation. During this period, although the Matrimonial Causes Act 1857 had made divorce a civil action and therefore the responsibility of the secular courts rather than the church, the expense involved kept this recourse out of reach for most working-class women.[56] It was, in any

[55] The only way to accurately determine the number of private summonses is to go to the police-court registers, and there, the pattern is clear. In West London, the number of female private summonses rose nearly 40% between 1880 and 1900 alone (Registers of Summonses, West London PC, 1882, 1890, and 1900).

[56] At the turn of the century, an "undefended" (i.e. uncontested) suit in the Divorce Court without still cost over £35, and a contested one over £75 (Plowden, *Grain or Chaff?*, 284). As both Gail Savage and A. J. Hammerton have indicated, some working-class petitioners, thanks to the occasional provision of free legal services, were able to bring suit in the Divorce Court, though the overall numbers were extremely low (e.g. 16 in 1882). Hammerton, *Cruelty and Companionship*, 103–4. Savage, "English Divorce Litigation," 184.

case, a measure designed largely to facilitate divorce at the behest of middle- and upper-class men, most commonly on the grounds of their wives' adultery.[57] In contrast, the Matrimonial Causes Act 1878, whereby a local magistrate could grant a legal order of non-cohabitation if the husband was convicted of aggravated assault, made temporary marital separations more accessible, in principle.[58] These could be obtained for the price of a single summons (two shillings) and without the aid of legal counsel, avoiding the time and expense of the Court for Divorce and Matrimonial Causes (est. 1857). For working-class wives, nonetheless, such "judicial separations" remained largely impractical unless accompanied by financial support. The latter was granted only in cases where the magistrate believed that the wife was in dire peril of serious (and potentially fatal) violence. Such a high bar was difficult to achieve, given magistrates' respect for patriarchal domestic authority and tolerant attitude towards husbands' disciplining of their wives, especially in working-class homes.[59] Even when maintenance was granted, it could not be given directly to aggrieved wives, but was instead distributed via the parish authorities.

Evolution of the laws on marital issues was guided by two mutually reinforcing principles. The first was a desire, common among ratepayers and government authorities alike, to keep women off of the poor rolls.[60] The second was a longstanding legal doctrine stipulating that the economic maintenance of a wife and household, barring the rarity of an official divorce, remained a husband's insoluble duty.[61] A third impetus had been further encouraging reform. A concerted campaign by those who sought legal independence for middle-class women was slowly chipping away at the principle of

[57] Prior to the 1857 Act and the creation of the Court for Divorce and Matrimonial Causes, divorce was a cumbersome procedure that required the aggrieved husband to bring charges of "criminal conversation" against another man, a move necessitated by a patriarchal legal system that denied women an independent legal identity.

[58] The latter category of offense, it should be noted, was itself a relatively new introduction to law and judicial practice.

[59] Behlmer, *Friends of the Family*, 193; Griffin, "Class, Gender, and Liberalism in Parliament," 65; Savage, "Magistrates Are Men."

[60] Mary Lyndon Shanley, *Feminism, Marriage, and the Law in Victorian England, 1850–1895* (Princeton: Princeton University Press, 1989), 150.

[61] O. R. McGregor, Louis Blom-Cooper, and Colin Gibson, *Separated Spouses*, Legal Research Unit, Department of Sociology, Bedford College, University of London (London: Gerald Duckworth & Co. Ltd., 1970), 6.

couverture, which subsumed a married woman's legal rights (including property) to those of her husband.[62] The main goal was hardly liberation for women, and certainly not for working-class women, but rather a desire to give middle-class women relief from abusive marriages and to protect their familial property in cases of divorce. Granting working-class women an independent voice in the courtroom was not the intention of the vast majority of those involved in such reform or its advocacy. Nonetheless, the consequences of these legal changes for a cohort that was increasingly familiar with local courtrooms – thanks to their involvement in Education Act cases, assault summonses, and a myriad of other charges and summonses (e.g. detaining goods, threats) in the final decades of the nineteenth century – would be significant.

Three pieces of legislation subsequent to the 1878 Act finally made judicial separations a more viable and palatable option for working-class women. The Married Women (Maintenance in Case of Desertion) Act 1886 allowed magistrates, in cases of wrongful desertion, to make an order for maintenance directly payable to the aggrieved wife rather than through the local Poor Law Guardians.[63] It also abrogated the necessity of women first going to the workhouse (a dreaded option) to qualify for such support.[64] The Summary Jurisdiction (Married Women) Act 1895 authorized judicial separations on the grounds of "persistent cruelty" or "wilful neglect to provide reasonable maintenance."[65] And, lastly, the Licensing Act 1902 added habitual drunkenness to the circumstances under which magistrates could grant a judicial separation to either spouse.[66] The passage of the 1895 Act was followed by a rapid acceleration of applications for judicial separations made to the magistrates' courts. These nearly doubled between 1895 and 1900 alone, growing from 5,000 to 9,553.[67] Two key factors in this increase were the radical reduction in the time frame of judicial separation summonses and the substantial broadening of the qualifications for seeking maintenance. By the terms of the 1857 Matrimonial Causes Act, the legal justification for a divorce or

[62] See Shanley, *Feminism, Marriage, and the Law*, ch. 4. For a detailed discussion of couverture, see Margot Finn, "Women, Consumption and Couverture in England, c.1760–1860," *The Historical Journal* 29, no. 3 (1996), 703–22.

[63] 49 & 50 Vict. c. 52. [64] Shanley, *Feminism, Marriage, and the Law*, 150.

[65] 58 & 59 Vict. c. 39. [66] 2 Edw. 7 c. 28. [67] Savage, "Magistrates Are Men," 233.

judicial separation was a desertion of two years' duration.[68] The 1886 Act similarly retained a husband's desertion as the key qualification. The 1895 legislation did away with the two-year time limit and allowed for maintenance to be sought in cases of desertion *or* neglect.

In theory, the 1895 measure gave women the right to seek separation and maintenance in a much wider scope of circumstances. In practice, stipulating that a woman *had* to leave her home before she could apply for a summons on the grounds of persistent cruelty or willful neglect lowered the legal bar without removing the practical obstacles. This was particularly true for poor women, and for those with children most especially.[69] It required them to secure lodging and some means of support, and offered a resolution (i.e. a maintenance order) that was neither expeditious nor guaranteed.[70] The London magistrate Alfred Chicele Plowden speculated, in his 1903 memoirs, that the aim of legislators was to prevent frivolous or precipitous separations, but he was acutely aware of the difficulties this posed for the women involved.[71] The alacrity with which Poor Law Guardians sought to secure maintenance from husbands whose desertion had thrown their wives and children onto the rates or into the workhouse attested to the unreliability of this system. This stipulation of non-cohabitation prior to seeking a summons for separation, maintenance, or custody was later dropped. By the interwar period, the general practice of paying maintenance to the court rather than forcing a woman to demand it directly from her husband had made the transaction less fractious as well.[72] While remaining an option of ultimate resort, the rise in the

68 Sydney Davey, *Maintenance and Desertion under the Poor Law and Summary Jurisdiction (Married Women) Act 1895* (London: Poor Law Officer's Journal, 1904), 81.

69 Plowden, *Grain or Chaff?*, 282. Shanley, *Feminism, Marriage, and the Law*, 176.

70 As George Behlmer has pointed out, this hardly constituted a "poor woman's charter of freedom." Behlmer, *Friends of the Family*, 194. However, although a separation order was almost invariably accompanied by a maintenance order, by the interwar period, a magistrate could also order maintenance alone. The London magistrate Henry Waddy explained how crucial this was, since "the granting of a separation order may be actually to the prejudice of a woman" (Henry Turner Waddy, *The Police Court and Its Work* (London: Butterworth, 1925), 101). This was because if a woman sought a dissolution of marriage on the basis of her husband's misbehavior *subsequent* to a separation order, the latter stood as a bar to a decree of a dissolution of the marriage.

71 Plowden, *Grain or Chaff?*, 282. 72 Waddy, *Police Court*, 100–101.

numbers of women seeking separation with maintenance after 1895 were readily apparent.[73] By 1905, magistrates' orders granted across England (6,585) under the 1895 and 1902 Acts had well exceeded the number *applied for* just ten years previously, with nearly a quarter of them (1,534) emerging from the London courts alone.[74] Between 1905 and 1909, the average number of applications for such orders each year was just over 11,000.[75] As Gail Savage has argued, by the conclusion of the nineteenth century, England was effectively operating "a two-tiered judicial system, roughly bifurcated by social class, providing divorce for the middle-class and well-to-do and separation and maintenance for abused and deserted working-class wives."[76] The former came via the Divorce Court, and the latter via the magistrates' courts. Accompanying the segregation of classes in legal venues was a divergence in judicial attitudes towards marital conflicts in local courtrooms. While police-court magistrates could, at times, demonstrate sympathy for working-class wives suffering from abuse or neglect, there was little inclination on their part to follow the example of their colleagues in the higher courts by recognizing the common plight of wives with neglectful or abusive husbands.[77] As often as not, working-class women would have to achieve their goals with the summons process despite magistrates' reluctance rather than with their cooperation.

The Clerkenwell court records confirm the prevalence of working-class women as the most common complainants under the Married

[73] Municipal authorities, too, took a strong hand in the regulation of marital affairs. Since the Poor Law Amendment 1834, Poor Law authorities could prosecute husbands for deserting or neglecting to support their wives and children (Nick Wikeley, *Child Support: Law and Policy* (London: Bloomsbury, 2006), 54–55). In London there were 1,318 such prosecutions in 1890 and the number rose steadily across the final decade of the nineteenth century *Judicial Statistics, 1890*, 28). Exact numbers are hard to determine after 1895, when judicial statistics ceased to tabulate these separately from other "Poor Law Offences," such as the very commonly-prosecuted instances of disorderly workhouse conduct.

[74] *Judicial Statistics, England and Wales, 1905, Pt. II: Civil Courts* (PP 1907, Cmd. 3477), 172.

[75] Gibson, *Separated Spouses*, 33. [76] Savage, "Magistrates Are Men," 233.

[77] A. J. Hammerton has argued that, after the reforms of 1857, the cases heard by the Divorce Court forced higher judges to confront the prevalence of "unreasonable" behavior by husbands across the class spectrum. This encouraged them to look more sympathetically on wives' pleas, and to support a more "companionate model which demanded restraint and forbearance from husbands." Hammerton, *Cruelty and Companionship*, 119.

Women's Acts in the first decade of the twentieth century. The vast majority of cases brought before the magistrates were from the wives of laborers, artisans, and shopkeepers earning 15–35 shillings a week. The typical award of weekly maintenance was a third of this, 5–12 shillings weekly. Occasionally, lower-middle-class women (e.g. clerk's wives) would seek amelioration via the magistrates' courts, but this was relatively rare, and rarer still among those of middle-class status or above. The latter could afford the Divorce Court, and the former far preferred the County Courts to the moral "Gehenna" of the police courts.[78] The true "residuum" of those in the deepest poverty were likewise scarce users of local courtrooms to seek separation and maintenance. Their cases were more frequently pursued by the Poor Law Guardians. The latter's goal was to secure a husband's contribution so that his wife and children could be removed from the poor-relief rolls. Courtroom usage in marital conflict was segregated by class and characterized by "enduring local and occupational patterns," not unlike much of the late Victorian social structure.[79]

Consigned to the second tier of marital adjudication, over which magistrates held sway, a working-class woman's ability to operate effectively in the local courtroom became pivotal if she wished to ameliorate a bad marriage. In that milieu, short of a conviction for aggravated assault, the granting of separation orders and the specific amount of maintenance were at the magistrates' discretion. A woman's employment of assault summonses, empty or substantive, was particularly crucial, since these measures could serve as effective precursors for a judicial separation on the grounds of persistent cruelty. The succession of summonses for threats or assault would be heard in the same court and often by the same magistrate. These could be part of a longer trajectory that culminated in a request for the magistrates' decisive intercession. A woman's demands for judicial intervention could escalate over the course of months or years, or it could take place in a single day. Formal judicial separations, however, were only one small part of a much larger picture. To accurately assess

[78] Evidence of John Rose, Magistrate of the Tower Bridge PC, March 1, 1910, *Divorce and Matrimonial Causes 1912*, vol. 1, 95. Since the Married Women's Act 1882 covered property issues, suits brought under it could be heard in the County Courts.

[79] Olive Anderson, "State, Civil Society and Separation in Victorian Marriage," *Past and Present* 163 (1999), 165.

the prevalence of marital cases, it is vital to distinguish between the formal granting of judicial separations, which remained relatively few in number, and the employment of the courtroom in marital issues, which was becoming increasingly common. The 9,553 judicial separations granted across England and Wales in 1900 may seem like a significant number, but compared to a married population of over 11,000,000 in 1901, it was paltry indeed.[80] The apparently miniscule numbers of those who sought divorce or judicial separation was a perennial point of emphasis in the annual judicial statistics published by Parliament. They were held up as proof of the general stability of marriage as a social institution and evidence of a popular aversion to its abrogation.

The court records themselves provide a very different picture, revealing how marital and domestic issues appeared on a daily basis in local courtrooms throughout the metropolis. In May 1910 alone, for example, the Clerkenwell Police Court heard some forty cases concerning marital issues. These included summonses for neglect to maintain children (thirteen, brought by public and private parties), attempts by wives to recover maintenance arrears (seven), requests to vary maintenance orders already made by the magistrates (two), and requests for maintenance orders on the grounds of desertion (ten) or persistent cruelty (eight).[81] In comparison, that same month, the Clerkenwell magistrates granted only seven judicial separations. July saw a further thirty summonses in these former categories.[82] The tallies, it should be noted, exclude both the most common instances in which women employed courtroom summonses to address marital issues – assault cases brought by wives against their husbands – and the most protracted domestic cases, which were those concerning affiliation. There were fourteen of the latter in May and sixteen in July.[83] Also excluded from this count are cases brought by men against their wives, and the marital cases that were prosecuted via charges rather than summonses, both of which represented a small but visible segment

[80] *Divorce and Matrimonial Causes 1912*, final report, Table V, 29. See also Anderson, "Separation in Victorian Marriage," 167–70.
[81] Registers of Summonses, Clerkenwell PC, May 1910 (PS/CLE/A/02/03). [82] Ibid.
[83] In July, there were 16 cases of "same-name" assault summonses by women (i.e. the defendant had the same name as the complainant, most typically, these were wife-vs.-husband summonses).

of the record. In the Thames Police Court during the same period, although the overall volume of summonses was lower, those concerning marital and domestic affairs (including assault and affiliation) constituted roughly the same proportion of women's summonses (i.e. half).[84]

The summons registers of the Thames Police Court, which cover the final two decades of the nineteenth century, reveal the speed at which women adapted to the new laws on maintenance and separation. In January, March, and May of 1885, one year prior to the passage of the 1886 law that made maintenance orders directly payable to the wife, the number of "married women's" cases was negligible (eight).[85] Five years later, there were more than four times as many (thirty-seven) in the same period. By 1900, in the same three months, the number had doubled again to nearly ten times the 1885 count (seventy-seven).[86] By the first decade of the twentieth century, it was clear to outside commentators and magistrates alike that summonses concerning marital issues had become a common occurrence in the London police courts. Magistrates' conservative views on the issue, however, worked as a counterbalance to women's courtroom initiative. By encouraging informal settlements, employing ancillary court personnel as mediators, and outright refusal of summons applications, they were able to keep the number of separation and maintenance orders granted to a moderate level despite the overall growth in domestic summonses. One London magistrate, speaking to a parliamentary commission in 1910, reported that between 1903 and 1909, the thirteen London police courts awarded women 4,874

[84] In May, women brought a total of 76 summonses, of which 9 were directly related to marital affairs, 11 were for affiliation (seeking either an order for support or recovery of arrears), and 15 were same-name assault summonses. July was even busier, with 18 marital summonses, 18 affiliation cases, and 20 same-name assault summonses, representing more than a half of women's overall summonses that month. Registers of Summonses, Thames PC, May and July, 1910 (PS/TH/A/02/36).

[85] i.e. the Married Women (Maintenance in Case of Desertion) Act 1886. Registers of Summonses, Thames PC, January, March, and May 1885 (PS/TH/A/02/2), 1890 (PS/TH/A/02/12), and 1900 (PS/TH/A/02/35).

[86] It is worth noting that affiliation cases moved in the opposite direction, from a high point of 37 in January, March, and May 1890 to 18 in the same span in 1900. This was despite changes to the law in 1872 that had allowed Poor Law Guardians to sue for affiliation on behalf of any woman who was chargeable to the union. This made them, technically, public suits, albeit ones conducted on behalf of individual women. My thanks to Ginger Frost for this key observation.

separation orders with maintenance.[87] They granted a further 448 to husbands on the grounds of their wives' habitual drunkenness.[88] Clerkenwell had the most (685/58), followed by Lambeth (656/49), South Western (542/34), and West London (511/62). Bow Street (32/3), Marlborough Street (42/17), and Woolwich (91/20) had the fewest. These numbers excluded those summonses applied for but denied, applied for and granted but not adjudicated (i.e. empty summonses), and dismissals and adjournments *sine die*. As such, they belie just how frequently women employed this measure.[89]

Numbers alone do not demonstrate the full significance of these summonses in both the courtroom and working-class marriage. Adjudication of marriage-related cases often required women to give substantial testimony about their circumstances and their husbands' behavior. This presented yet another opportunity for them to publicly articulate their own definitions of morality, gender norms, and justice in the context of marriage and sexual relations. It also offered the chance to negotiate the legal definitions of "neglect" and "persistent cruelty," both of which were far from precise. Given the complex usage of summonses already revealed in Chapter 4 and the discussion of assault cases above, the rising importance of local courtrooms and their public portrayals in the changing legal purview of marriage comes into sharper focus. The established patterns of courtroom negotiation and contest would influence both the public perception and concrete consequences of these new laws. They would also play a role in the ongoing relocation of contests over moral norms from a religious context to a civil one. This development had been underway among the middle class since mid-century. It accelerated rapidly in working-class communities with the passage of new laws on separation and maintenance and with the increase of marital summonses prompted by women's initiative.[90] With the bench joining the pulpit as

87 Testimony of Robert Henry Bullock Marsham, London Magistrate, *Divorce and Matrimonial Causes 1912*, vol. 1, February 28, 88. Tower Bridge was excluded from the magistrates' assessment, as they kept no return on these cases.

88 Ibid.

89 This underestimation is further attested to by the discrepancy between the Thames summons count from the registers in 1900 and the magistrates' report that the court had granted women only 399 separations with maintenance from 1903 to 1909. Ibid.

90 For the changing nature of middle-class marriage with the advent of the Divorce Courts, see Hammerton, *Cruelty and Companionship*, 118–25.

an authority on acceptable behavior in working-class marriages, magistrates demonstrated a clear bias for paternalism and a strong desire to preserve marital bonds rather than dissolve them, barring severe and persistent neglect or abuse. The latter circumstances, however, were often defined in the context of the courtroom itself, allowing women considerable influence in setting the terms on which the state could govern marital affairs and assess marital morality.

The flexible nature of summary procedure and magistrates' willingness to follow the established tradition of relatively free dialogue in the courtroom were key factors in how these cases played out. Absent the formality and expense of the Divorce Court or the intervention of solicitors, courtroom contests opened up space for working-class men and women to offer competing moral narratives and to assert their own definitions of acceptable behavior. Some married women's cases, if uncontested by the husband, could be resolved in a single, brief hearing. The potential for such swift resolution, communicated through the dense social networks of working-class communities or in the local newspaper's police-court columns, could further encourage others to pursue similar measures, and this might help explain the rapid rise in applications in the years following the passage of the 1895 Act.[91] Other married women's summonses, in contrast, could produce some of the longest, most complex, and most fiercely contested of all privately initiated cases heard in the magistrates' courts. Husbands' testimony in desertion summonses stood as one prominent example of how the flexibility of police-court procedure facilitated a more open dialogue on marital norms than was possible in other legal venues. The typical response in such testimony was not denial. Quite to the contrary, husbands were generally forthright about their reasons for leaving the marital home, justifying their departure with claims of their wife's abuse, violence, drunkenness, or other improper behavior. A husband's right to cross-examine his wife and to call evidence (typically in the form of witnesses) was another element of marital summonses that had been

[91] As discussed below, magistrates were all but certain that, by this time, working-class communities were keenly aware of how these cases were playing out in the local police courts.

established over time through courtroom custom, rather than explicitly in the law itself. Its practice dated back to the original Matrimonial Causes Act 1857 and had been subsequently legitimized by judicial verdicts and commentary.[92] By the time that the 1895 law was passed, husbands had, for some decades, been narrating their own versions of events, condemning their wives' alleged transgressions and calling witnesses to attest that, following the language of the 1857 Act, their desertion had not been "without reasonable excuse."[93]

The flexibility of summary procedure and the wide degree of latitude that magistrates, in the tradition of the police courts, allowed for testimony offered openings to wives and husbands alike. In these very public courtroom dialogues on the norms and limits of wedlock and child-rearing, and their relation to the new laws on these subjects, a husband's successful defense was the exception, not the rule. In the majority of substantive married women's summonses, Clerkenwell magistrates decided for the wives and outright dismissals were exceedingly rare.[94] A wife's victory could be pyrrhic, however, as magistrates retained the option of less severe verdicts such as binding the defendant over to keep the peace. Women's ability to successfully portray their husbands as transgressors of moral and legal boundaries, while offering evidence that they themselves had behaved properly (or at least not as badly), was particularly key after 1895 because of the crucial role played by a husband's accusations of adultery. This, if proven in the courtroom, had long been the most effective disqualifier of a wife's claim on maintenance.[95] Such proof could be hard to come by. Short of a confession by the wife, or testimony from her alleged paramour, it was almost impossible to establish adultery with any degree of certainty. A husband's breaking of marital oaths, in contrast, was hardly worth raising in most courtroom contests. Neither a long absence, nor adultery, nor even his cohabitation with

[92] S. G. Lushington and Guy Lushington, *The Summary Jurisdiction (Married Women) Act 1895 as Extended by the Licensing Act 1902, with Introduction, Notes, and Index*, 2nd ed. (London: Butterworth, 1904), 37–38.

[93] Ibid., 37.

[94] According to Gibson's analysis of judicial statistics, in this period, nationwide, the success rate of Matrimonial Orders was 69%. Gibson, *Separated Spouses*, 33.

[95] Danaya Wright, "Untying the Knot: An Analysis of the English Divorce and Matrimonial Causes Court Records," *University of Richmond Law Review* 903 (2004), 909.

another woman alone constituted neglect or persistent cruelty; absent financial neglect or other extenuating circumstances, none were grounds for a separation with maintenance.[96] The 1904 magistrates' guide to practice emphasized how much the burden of proof in maintenance summonses lay heavily on the wife, regardless of the widened justifications made possible by the 1895 Act.[97]

Such constraints notwithstanding, by expanding the legal grounds for granting maintenance, the 1895 Act ensured that, more than ever before, the ubiquitous married women's summonses would become forums for defining the limits of tolerable treatment in working-class marriages. In many of the cases that followed, neither complainant nor defendant had a clear monopoly on legal or moral justifications. Their contingent nature was accentuated by the 1902 Licensing Act, which made a wife's habitual drunkenness grounds for denying maintenance, just as a husband's was grounds for separation. By this time, in addition to the above, the specific grounds justifying a wife's application for a judicial separation with maintenance included the following: a husband's conviction for aggravated assault, his conviction for common assault with a punishment of no less than a five-pound fine or two months' imprisonment, desertion, persistent cruelty, willful neglect to provide maintenance, or cruelty or neglect causing the wife to leave.[98] With the exception of the assault convictions, all of these circumstances were open to interpretation in the courtroom. Even desertion, as mentioned earlier, could be forgiven if the husband could prove that his wife's actions had made living with her unbearable. And as one of the two magistrates' guides published in 1904 explained, a wife was only justified in seeking separation and maintenance on the grounds of cruelty or neglect when they were "carried to the point of aggravation."[99] As to what constituted these circumstances, the guide's author openly

[96] Sydney Davey, *Maintenance and Desertion under the Poor Law and Summary Jurisdiction (Married Women) Act 1895* (London: Poor Law Officer's Journal, 1904), 77.

[97] This volume used, as its precedents, two cases that dated back 30 years prior to the liberalization of the law, *Ward* v. *Ward* (1858) 1 Sw. and Tr. 85, and *Williams* v. *Williams* (1864) 3 Sw. and Tr. It cited extensively from the judge's observations in the latter (Lushington and Lushington, *Summary Justice (Married Women) Act 1895*), 11.

[98] Lushington and Lushington, *Summary Justice (Married Women) Act 1895*, 2.

[99] Davey, *Maintenance and Desertion*, 27.

admitted that "there is no authority on the matter."[100] The information offered in the guide was more detailed about what did *not* qualify as cruelty or neglect than what did. In addition to adultery and cohabitation, neither a husband's verbal demand that his wife leave the home nor a "mere quarrel" were sufficient.[101] A husband could even insist that his wife depart, but unless his conduct *compelled* her to leave, she was not entitled to maintenance.[102]

In bearing the burden of proof, wives tried to demonstrate that their claims were drawn on common standards rather than their own personal views by marshalling witnesses to corroborate their accounts, much as they had in assault cases in the years prior to the 1895 Act. Wives who summonsed their husbands also adapted another courtroom practice from the assault and threats summonses they had brought so frequently in the preceding years. In these latter summonses, women employed very specific terms to justify having their attacker bound over. In maintenance cases, they similarly tailored their courtroom language to justify their departure and refusal to return to the home, explicitly referring to their husband's "cruelty" or even "persistent cruelty" in their testimony.[103] Even when such claims were supported with detailed descriptions of repeated violence, abuse and intimidation, magistrates could sometimes prove reluctant to grant separation and maintenance. This was especially true when faced with a remorseful husband who expressed willingness to take his wife back and support her. As acts themselves, desertion or neglect by the husband, regardless of whether the magistrate decided they merited a granting of separation and maintenance, were relatively straightforward to prove in the courtroom. They included a physical departure or withdrawal of financial support (or both). Most husbands, faced with such assertions, chose the path of justification on the grounds of their wife's actions rather than outright denial. Cruelty so great that it had compelled a wife to leave the home indefinitely, in contrast, was a more ambiguous matter. It had to be effectively argued by the complainant in the courtroom, preferably

100 Ibid. 101 Ibid., 74. 102 Ibid.

103 A practice remarked upon by magistrates as well. See testimony of John Rose, Police Court Magistrate, March 1, 1910, *Divorce and Matrimonial Causes 1912*, vol. 1, 90.

with witness corroboration, physical evidence or, most convincing of all, a history of past assault summonses as support.[104]

In parsing the integration of local courtrooms into working-class marital conflict, another noticeable pattern was that husbands, once brought to court on separation summonses, often indicated their consent, but they did so at a lesser weekly maintenance than that requested by their wives. This raises several possibilities. Were women attempting to hold their husbands to their promises through a magistrate's official order? Were they unsatisfied with the initial offer and seeking a higher amount? Or did the husbands not finally consent to provide maintenance until their wives took the case to court? Given the information available, it is hard to determine, except by inference from courtroom testimony, the precise relationship between informal agreements reached by husbands and wives and the formal decisions in separation and maintenance cases.[105] As with other types of courtroom use, it is important not to assume that these summonses were brought merely for instrumental purposes. The enforcement of maintenance orders was a wholly separate matter from the decision to award maintenance in a courtroom. As will be discussed below, there is strong evidence that many maintenance orders were honored more in the breach than in the observance. And yet, despite the difficulties involved, women continued to bring such summonses in considerable numbers. This distance between what happened in the courtroom and what happened beyond it encourages us to recognize the social and cultural function of separation and maintenance summonses, and to assess these in conjunction with their more concrete economic dimensions.[106]

Whatever obstacles there were to realizing the benefits of a successful summons beyond the courtroom, it is hard to deny working-class women's acumen within it. Their detailed and evocative narratives of the husband's violent behavior over time, their careful use of language (e.g. "cruelty" and "persistent cruelty") in their testimony, the employment of

104 Davey, *Maintenance and Desertion*, 74.

105 What is clear from police-court testimony, on the other hand, is that both parties recognized that there was a profound difference between the two, and that what one said and agreed to in the courtroom had consequences that words and deeds beyond it did not.

106 See Ginger Frost, "Claiming Justice: Paternity Affiliation in South Wales, 1870–1900," Rural History 24, no. 2 (Oct. 2013).

past summonses as evidence of violent behavior, their recruitment of friends and neighbors as corroborating witnesses, and the long trajectory of involving the court in their marital conflicts all attest to this. As the pace of domestic law reform accelerated at the end of the nineteenth century, the speed of women's adaptation rose in tandem. The increasingly frequent employment of drunkenness as a justification for separation demonstrated just how rapidly they could respond to changes in the legal landscape, especially when such changes conformed to predating moral norms. In the Clerkenwell married women's summonses from 1900, a husband's drinking habits appeared in wives' testimony regularly, but most typically as an explanation for his violent behavior, the latter being employed as the primary qualifier of "persistent cruelty." The Licensing Act 1902 made habitual drunkenness alone grounds for separation. Announced in February, the bill, as it had serious implications for public houses, the Temperance campaign, and marital law, as well as being a controversial issue in Parliament, was widely publicized in local and national newspapers.[107] The very same year, Clerkenwell women, for the first time, began seeking separations based solely on their husband's drunkenness. A husband's drinking habits also became a much greater focuses of women's narratives about "persistent cruelty." In the absence of physical evidence, previous summonses, or witnesses to a consistent pattern of violence, after 1902, habitual drunkenness was a reliable foundation for a wife's separation and maintenance case. On occasions where the supporting evidence for violence was available, convincing the court that a husband was also a habitual drunkard only strengthened the case. Men, as defendants, adapted too. In courtroom testimony from the year the Licensing Act was passed, habitual drunkenness became a sword that cut both ways. If a husband could prove that his wife was a habitual drunkard, this stood as legal justification for a separation *without* maintenance. These circumstances could also reduce or absolve a husband's obligations if he had been the one to leave. With alcohol being a common aspect of socialization among working-class husbands and wives alike, the line between acceptable and unacceptable levels of inebriation in the context of marriage was a matter of courtroom debate. In this way, much as with the "reasonable excuse" clause of desertion

[107] *The Times*, for example, printed nearly 100 commentaries on the issue between January and December 1902 alone.

summonses, the Licensing Act 1902 added another facet to courtroom discussions about the norms and tolerable limits of working-class marriages.

In addition to seeking separation and maintenance solely on the grounds of their spouse's drunkenness, by the first decade of the twentieth century, working-class men and women had introduced another novel tactic to the conduct of marital summonses, one in which the cumulative effect of the "domestication" of local courtrooms was clear. Borrowing from a courtroom practice much employed by Poor Law Guardians in the previous decade, they began to bring their children as witnesses.[108] In some instances, children as young as fourteen were brought in to testify on the violent, abusive, or drunken behavior of one parent or the other.[109] Here, the intersection of working-class adaptation to new laws, the indeterminacy of grounds for separation and maintenance, and the courtroom discussion of marital norms and boundaries could sometimes allow even the generally voiceless members of the community to contribute, albeit in modest ways, to these public contests. Children's testimony represented a novel entanglement of local courtrooms and the working-class household, but such entanglement more generally was becoming increasingly common in *fin de siècle* London. Far from a drastic or unexpected sortie, a separation summons could be just one aspect of an ongoing contest between husband and wife about the terms of their marriage. Even as the various magistrates' guides on how to handle the ubiquitous married women's cases were running to over a hundred pages to accommodate the many permutations of judicial separations and maintenance, the possible informal outcomes of these summonses exceeded these by far. They could be employed to elicit more financial support from a husband, as an opportunity to coerce a wife's return to the home, or even as leverage for the dismissal of an unwelcome in-law from the marital household.[110]

[108] See Minutes of Summonses, Clerkenwell PC, August 14, 1902 and September 30, 1902 (case of Sarah Ann Freer). Children's evidence was not given under oath, and required either personal or circumstantial corroboration. Hugh Gamon, *The London Police Courts To-Day and To-Morrow* (London: J. M. Dent, 1907), 138.

[109] Minutes of Summonses, Clerkenwell PC, April 5, 1902.

[110] Frederick Twine, summonsed by his wife for a separation order on the grounds of persistent cruelty, told the magistrate that "I want her to live with me on the condition that her mother stays away." Ibid., April 8, 1902.

These cases moved the courtroom further away from its ostensible purpose of adjudicating law and closer to its role as a social space for negotiating the terms of working-class marriages. Any magistrate's hope that, after a long and acrimonious summons case with multiple witnesses and contested claims, his final decision would be the end of the matter might well have been hoping in vain. A decisive verdict for separation and maintenance often did not signal the end of the court's involvement in any given marriage. Just as such summonses were often preceded by empty or substantive assault summonses, which could then be redeployed in their testimony for separation and maintenance, the latter could, in turn, be followed by subsequent summonses to collect maintenance arrears. Arrears summonses represented a significant escalation from maintenance orders. Unlike the latter, arrears summonses were enforceable through warrants for arrest, and a failure to comply could result in hefty fines or even imprisonment for the obstinate.[111] Husbands were not without recourse either. They could appeal to the local magistrate to "vary" their original maintenance order, should their economic situation take a downturn, or should their wives take up permanent residence with (and, by implication, receive maintenance from) another man. Both types of cases could occupy considerable amounts of the court's time, since they often required a detailed recounting of how each parties' circumstances had changed since the initial decision. Even the specific terms under which a husband and wife had already consented to separate could become an issue of vociferous debate in a subsequent court summons. Although far fewer in number than maintenance summonses themselves, arrears and "vary" summonses attested to the attenuated involvement of the courtroom in working-class marriages and its significance as a forum in which the limits of tolerable treatment were negotiated and contested.[112] This involvement could begin with an assault summons, empty or substantive, when the ink on their marriage certificate was still

[111] G. Glover Alexander, *The Administration of Justice in Criminal Matters, England and Wales* (Cambridge: Cambridge University Press, 1915), 61. From 1905 to 1909, across England and Wales, an average of more than 2,100 men were imprisoned each year as a result of failure to abide by maintenance orders. Gibson, *Separated Spouses*, 33.

[112] There were, for example, 18 such cases heard in the Thames court in January, March, and May 1900. Registers of Summonses, Thames PC, 1900.

wet, continue throughout their cohabitation with further summonses for assault or threats, reach an apex with a separation and maintenance summons, and persist for months or even years post-separation as one side or the other sought to modify their obligations.[113]

Just as local courtrooms served as forums to define and contest gender norms and expectations in working-class marriages, they also served as conduits to broadcast local courtrooms' involvement into the wider cultural discourses on these topics. The reporting of marital summonses in the local and national press disseminated courtroom dialogue into the ongoing public debate over marriage, morality, and the balance of authority between husband and wife.[114] By the turn of the century, the parade of drunken, dissolute, and violent women that appeared in the police-court columns had been joined by a small but growing number of aggrieved wives taking their husbands to task. They have not received the attention, from either readers then or historians now, that the much higher-profile Divorce Court cases, with their scandal and acrimony, have.[115] Absent the sensation of the latter, they did portray, time and again, women as active, adaptive employers of the courtroom, and as a cohort who could secure their entitlements by law and publicly lambast the transgressions of their neglectful or abusive husbands. They also further cemented public perception of local courtrooms as a crucial venue for the mediation of working-class marriage and parental responsibility. Although the majority of these cases were quotidian, Marie Rose provided readers of the *Islington Gazette* some of their sought-after courtroom drama when she brought her husband, Samuel, to the North London Police

[113] Although this is nearly impossible to prove from the extant record, in theory, it is possible (even likely) that the court's involvement could *precede* the marriage, should a woman have summonsed her future husband before they were wed.

[114] A. J. Hammerton has made a parallel claim about the press reporting of mid-century Divorce Court cases which, though lengthier and more prominent, were far smaller in number. Hammerton, *Cruelty or Companionship*, 102–3. Margot Finn, similarly, has argued that debt and credit cases involving working-class women in the County Courts were ensured a "broad public audience" in the 1880s by their reporting in local newspapers, as well as in the commercial and legal press. Finn, "Contest for Consumer Control," 144.

[115] Three days prior to the Rose case, described below, the Divorce Court case brought by James Robert Perfect against his wife on the grounds of adultery received a full column and a half of coverage in the *Islington Gazette*. *Islington Gazette*, May 4, 1900.

Court for non-payment of maintenance arrears in May 1900.[116] When the latter, a house-painter, claimed indebtedness and promised, now that he was back in work, to make amends, she was intractable. The true cause of Samuel's poverty, Marie insisted, was his adultery. The proof, she further proclaimed, was there for all to see in "that woman in the green cape standing at the back of the Court." As the magistrate, Robert Marsham, ordered Samuel to pay £12 in maintenance arrears or face a month in prison, one could only wonder if other Islington men reading the story might think twice about how they managed their affairs both inside and outside the courtroom.

A key question to pose at this point is whether or not the contributions of local courtroom contests to the dynamics of working-class marital affairs represented change or continuity in marriage's trajectory as a social institution. At first glance, like the police-court columns describing battered wives and their abusive or neglectful husbands, the courtroom's role in separation and maintenance cases appears to have been a conservative one. Many of the standards of behavior described in courtroom testimony accorded well with popular gender and marital norms. Husbands were expected to provide financial support for their households, to refrain from excessive or repeated violence, and to forbear from public disrespect or accusations of infidelity. By the same token, men's most typical complaints – wives' drunkenness, neglect of their children, disregard for household duties or questionable socialization with other men – were widely seen as transgressive among the cohort of artisans, laborers, and small shopkeepers that most frequently appeared in Clerkenwell marital summonses.[117] The addition of habitual drunkenness to the grounds for separation was hardly revolutionary either. Working-class alcohol use had been a focus of policing and public moral discourse for decades by the time the Licensing Act 1902 was passed.[118] Though one indicator of change in these standards was the decreasing tolerance for marital violence, since extreme or frequent attacks, along with neglect and

[116] Ibid., May 7, 1900. [117] Tomes, "Torrent of Abuse," 330–31.

[118] This also begs the question of whether legislation followed common practice or vice-versa. Since the minutes of summonses prior to 1902 are largely unavailable, this is difficult to determine for the metropolitan police courts. But the answers may be found in the surviving records of other summary justice venues, and further information (with caveats) can be cleaned from newspaper coverage.

desertion, were women's most common grounds for requesting a separation with maintenance.[119]

Despite their general accordance with the moral discourse on working-class drinking, however, women's employment of marital summons challenged these norms in a number of ways. First, the cases brought by wives against their husbands did, on occasion, stray well outside the bounds of common marital practice. Women demanded that the court support their legal entitlements even when their behavior represented a clear transgression of moral standards, or at least of those articulated by magistrates, newspapers, legislators, and other public commentators on marriage and morality. When Margaret Sewell summonsed her husband, Anthony, for separation and maintenance on the grounds of persistent cruelty, she freely admitted that she had been the mistress of another man when they married, that they had both lived off of his patronage for two years, and that she had supplemented this income with prostitution.[120] Margaret claimed that her husband had not just colluded in this, but had been responsible for her turn to solicitation, telling the court that "[he] introduced me to this life." Margaret was not, however, setting herself up as the victim of her husband's corruption and appealing for the court's paternalistic intervention; she was not seeking separation and maintenance on these grounds. Instead, she sought merely to prove that her actions as a mistress and prostitute were conducted "with his knowledge." Under the 1895 Act, adultery committed by the wife with the husband's knowledge or collusion did not abrogate the latter's responsibility for maintenance.[121] It is highly unlikely that legislators were thinking of jilted prostitutes when they included these stipulations, especially since it had long been a serious crime for a man to live off the earnings of

119 Peter King has traced a broader change in judicial attitudes towards assault (of all types) to an even earlier period, 1750–1820. And he, too, looks to courtroom practice as the defining mechanism, with legislation following afterwards. Peter King, "Punishing Assault: The Transformation of Attitudes in the English Courts," *Journal of Interdisciplinary History* 27, no. 1 (Summer, 1996), 72.

120 Minutes of Summonses, Clerkenwell PC, October 29, 1900.

121 This clause was intended to deter a husband from luring his wife into adultery and subsequently using that as grounds for denying maintenance (Davey, *Maintenance and Desertion*, 75). A husband's forgiveness of the adultery, followed by cohabitation, was also a disqualifier for subsequent denial of maintenance on those grounds. The relevant case precedents were *Keats* v. *Keats* (1858) 1 Sw. and Tr. 334, and *Glennie* v. *Glennie* (1862) 32 L.J., P. and M. 17.

a prostitute.[122] Margaret herself could hardly have been unaware of the moral judgments that the courtroom audience and the community beyond might pass on her, if it had not already, due to her prior activities. Such moral judgments notwithstanding, once it had been established, by his own admission, that Anthony was aware of her activities, Margaret could proceed unhindered with her request for separation and maintenance on the grounds that he had repeatedly beaten her and, just two weeks ago, had "put his knee on my back and fought me like he would a man" (i.e. aggravated assault tantamount to persistent cruelty). Such was the disjuncture between the law's intended moral purpose and the range of courtroom usages that even an admitted prostitute could demand the court's support in securing her marital entitlements, and do so in full public (and press) view.[123]

Although summonses that departed as radically from moral norms as Margaret Sewell's did were rare, women who brought marital cases were generally a poor fit for the molds of battered wives or savage scolds offered by newspapers, lampooning cartoons, and popular literature. Such stereotyped depictions belied the moral ambiguities and social complexities of what happened in the courts themselves. The dissonance between how women employed courtrooms and how they were portrayed in public emphasizes the incomplete expression of patriarchal authority there, be it that of husbands or magistrates. Neither martyrs nor termagants, women's courtroom narratives covered a wide moral spectrum, from piteous tales of savage brutality to prostitution and drunkenness to a business-like agreement of a marriage's end. Even if the majority of the cases were hardly radical in their engagement with gender expectations, each one saw wives taking courtroom initiative and demanding their rights in the only public forum available to the vast majority of

[122] By the terms of the Poor Law Amendment Act 1834. This was commonly referred to as "living off immoral earnings."

[123] Margaret Sewell's original economic status is unclear, the only clue lying in her report of a brother who was a soldier in Colchester. Her husband was slightly better off than the typical defendants in Clerkenwell marital cases were. Anthony claimed to have recently been earning £2 weekly as a "traveller in tea trade." But Margaret reported his earnings as being only 40 shillings weekly, and he told the court he was unemployed at the time of the summons. Minutes of Summonses, Clerkenwell PC, October 29, 1900.

working-class women at the time. Their willing engagement was responsible for the rapid rise of marital summonses – be they for assault, aggravated assault, or separation and maintenance – in the final decades of the nineteenth century and the first decade of the twentieth. The acts passed in the 1880s and 1890s, and the Married Women's Act 1895 and Licensing Act 1902 in particular, made the close involvement of local courtrooms and working-class marriages a possibility. Women's agency transformed this into a social reality.

By the early twentieth century, affiliation cases had joined assault summonses and marital summonses as common avenues for women's voluntary engagement with the London police courts.[124] In these cases, women sought to hold putative fathers to account for support of their children out of wedlock. The economic and social costs at stake were considerable. A successful suit entitled them to financial support for a child (or children) until they reached their majority. Failure, in contrast, could leave the complainant with a publicly tarnished reputation and the considerable economic and social burden of single motherhood.[125] For the men involved, the potential damage to sexual reputation was, in most cases, less severe, though the financial risk was great. The results of these fraught circumstances were some of the longest and most complex of all cases triggered by personal summonses. Although far fewer in number than assault cases, a typical affiliation case occupied considerably more time. Two of them, or even a single case could consume the entirety of a court's

[124] In February, April, May, June, July, September, and November of 1910, for example, women brought 70 bastardy cases before the Clerkenwell magistrates. In the same period, women also brought 31 cases demanding arrears for unpaid orders made under previous bastardy convictions. Unlike assault summonses, moreover, the incidence of empty summonses in bastardy cases was remarkably low – in only 4 of these 101 cases did women fail to appear in order to prosecute the summons. In the Thames PC, during January, March, and May of 1885, women brought 23 bastardy cases and 20 bastardy arrears cases. In March, May, and July of 1910 they brought 17 of the former and 18 of the latter. Registers of Summonses, Thames PC, 1885 (PS/TH/A/02/2) and 1910 (PS/TH/A/02/36).

[125] Although single motherhood is a more complicated state to determine, and unmarried parents could register themselves as married to avoid the branding of their children at birth, current estimates put illegitimacy in England and Wales at 7% of all births in 1850, dropping to 4% by 1902, and rising again to 9% during the First World War. Pat Thane and Tanya Evans, *Sinners? Scroungers? Saints?: Unmarried Motherhood in Twentieth-Century England* (Oxford: Oxford University Press, 2012), 6–7.

morning or afternoon session.[126] The comparatively small statistical footprint has disguised the vast amount of courtroom time these summonses consumed, but their significance was not lost on contemporary commentators, particularly those who opposed such measures.[127]

Courtroom conflicts over affiliation, not merely through their verdicts but through their conduct, became vehicles for working-class women to make public claims about male sexual mores and paternal obligation, to assert their own rights of cross-gender sociability, and to vociferously defend their own standards of respectability.[128] These efforts changed courtrooms as well, as their constant and widespread use further raised their visibility as venues to arbitrate and define gender norms. In this process, women's employment of the courts served both their own needs and the goals of magistrates, who fervently wished to see their courts exert a greater moral influence on working-class households. Magistrates writing earlier in the century had insisted that their own personal influence would be the keystone of this process and that middle-class norms would be the guidelines for reforming less-privileged households. Working-class women's initiative and adaptability, however, often fostered a compromise between their aims and the magistrates' visions of orderly, patriarchal households.

As with marital summonses, although women's engagement drove the practical application of the law, the avenue was opened by an expansion of the summary courts' authority. The laws governing the support of illegitimate children in England had undergone a series of reforms in the later nineteenth century, reflecting Victorian society's concern with child welfare. In response to the Poor Law Report of 1833, the framers of the bastardy clause of the 1834 New Poor Law

[126] Such was the case, for example, in the December 19, 1900 Clerkenwell bastardy cases brought by Janet Newton, who worked as an assistant to Walter John Harris, an engineer, and in the December 21 case brought by Blanche Blunden against Jack Hardwick, a printer. Minutes of Summonses, Clerkenwell PC, 1900 (PS/CLE/B4/1).

[127] Ginger Frost as similarly emphasized that maintenance was often not necessarily the goal of women bringing affiliation suits in the Welsh courts during this period. Frost, "Claiming Justice," 177–98

[128] For a discussion of the social and cultural dynamics of illegitimacy in late eighteenth- and early nineteenth-century plebian Glasgow and London, see Clark, *Struggle for the Breeches*, 42–49.

had placed the burden of care for illegitimate children solely on the mother. Under the previous law, once the mother had identified the father, the parish authorities could – in theory though rarely in practice – sue him for support or coerce him into marriage.[129] This measure, it was hoped at the time, would reduce promiscuity and encourage poor mothers to adhere more closely to middle-class standards of sexual morality.[130] An 1844 amendment to the bastardy clause gave mothers some legal recourse, but required a corroborative witness to attest to paternity.[131] This hobbled the effectiveness of the measure. In the following decades, the growing child-welfare movement, combined with popular concern over "baby-farming" (poor mothers giving their infants over to foster-carers who would discretely dispose of them) and infanticide, prompted substantial reform.[132] In 1872, Parliament passed the Bastardy Laws Amendment Act, which gave mothers the right to sue alleged fathers in court for support of their offspring, raised the maximum level of provision from two shillings and sixpence to five shillings a week, and extended the father's liability until the child's sixteenth year.[133]

This boon to working-class mothers met with a harsh reception in certain quarters. Women's enhanced legal authority to sue fathers in court, combined with magistrates' broader flexibility in determining fathers' specific obligation prompted strong concerns among leading figures in Parliament and the British legal community. The prominent barrister and positivist Henry Crompton, on the eve of the bill's passage, expressed his anxiety over the shifting balance of power between magistrates, women, and working men in a lengthy letter to *The Times*. In affiliation cases, Crompton asserted that "false accusations, causing lifelong misery, are only too frequent, so easily is the law now made a weapon of attack," and used this claim as his

[129] Susan Zlotnick, "'The Law's a Bachelor': *Oliver Twist*, Bastardy, and the New Poor Law," *Victorian Literature and Culture* 34 (2006), 131.

[130] Ivy Pinchbeck and Margaret Hewitt, *Children in English Society, vol. II: From the Eighteenth Century to the Children Act 1848* (London and Toronto: Routledge and University of Toronto Press, 1973), 588.

[131] Ibid., 591–93.

[132] George Behlmer, *Child Abuse and Moral Reform in England, 1870–1908* (Berkeley: University of California Press, 1982), 19–40.

[133] The Bastardy Laws Amendment Act 1872 (35 & 36 Vic. c. 65); Behlmer, *Child Abuse and Moral Reform*, 40; *The Times*, January 18, 1872, 8.

introduction to a much more substantial assault on the growth of summary jurisdiction more generally.[134] Giving local magistrates authority over affiliation, a reform that could greatly ease the path of poor mothers seeking to prove paternity and receive child support, was one thing. Convincing London magistrates themselves to employ this authority while under sharp public scrutiny, particularly in the face of the concerns raised by Crompton and others, was another matter entirely. In affiliation cases, the onus of proof, even after the 1872 reform, still lay with the mother. And there was a considerable degree of continuity between the older, more stringent requirements for proving paternity and the newer, more elastic ones. A mother's testimony alone remained insufficient grounds for the granting of support. The Act was quite specific in its insistence that maintenance was only to be ordered from the father "if the evidence of the mother be corroborated in some material particular by other evidence to the satisfaction of the said justices."[135] London magistrates' views on the issue were anything but straightforward. At one level, many adhered to a middle-class perspective on family relations, gender roles, and the aversion to swelling the poor rolls (and thus the local tax burden) with impoverished mothers and their illegitimate children – all predilections that encouraged them to hold defendants responsible for the children that they had fathered. Magistrates of this hue found powerful allies in the Poor Law Guardians, whom the 1872 Act authorized to sue for affiliation on behalf of any woman who was chargeable to the union, until such time as she left the workhouse.[136] For another cohort of magistrates, the pervasive mistrust of women's testimony and suspicion towards their means and motivations in other summonses could be extended to affiliation cases. Epitomizing the ambivalence with which his colleagues could approach these cases, the magistrate

[134] Crompton wrote that, in light of these unwelcome increases in the reach of summary jurisdiction, he was preparing to recommend to the Nottingham Trades Union Congress that they advocate the full repeal of the Criminal Law Amendment Act. *The Times*, January 16, 1872, 4.

[135] The Bastardy Laws Amendment Act 1872 (35 & 36 Vic. c. 65 s. 3).

[136] The usefulness of the measure did not end at her exit, since it could be used as a precedent if the women later sued on her on behalf. My thanks to Ginger Frost for providing this information. See also Frost, "Claiming Justice," 177–98.

Henry Turner Waddy expressed strong skepticism towards female witnesses in general, while also asserting that male defendants were invariably "wicked" men who were willing to commit the "grossest perjury" in order to avoid the rightful obligations of fatherhood.[137]

Class differences added a further level of tension and complexity to these cases. The majority of marital summonses in the London magistrates' courts, whether for domestic assault or separation and maintenance, were between men and women of the working class.[138] Affiliation summonses, in contrast, pitted working-class women against a broader class spectrum of male defendants. Although putative fathers were most frequently working-class as well, women also sought such summonses against men from the lower-middle class or middle class. This contrast between the class dynamics of affiliation and marital summonses reflected the relative infrequency of inter-class marriage in London, as opposed to the more common practice of inter-class sexuality. This was especially the case across the rather indefinite line between laborers and shopkeepers or between artisans and clerks (or others at the lower end of the white-collar spectrum).[139] When present, such class contrasts between complainant and defendant only increased the obstacles – legal, social, and cultural – that working-class women faced in the courtroom. They had to pit their word against that of a man, and sometimes against a man of a higher class; they had to publicly and explicitly discuss sex, considered a most private affair in Victorian Britain, especially among the middle class; and they had to acknowledge sexual activity that was often illicit and invariably extramarital, while simultaneously presenting themselves as the moral and monogamous partner of the alleged father.[140] The public

[137] Waddy, *Police Court*, 192, 61.

[138] As with marital summonses, Lower-middle-class (e.g. clerks) and middle-class (e.g. professionals) appeared as well, but the generally disrespectable atmosphere and unwonted potential publicity of the magistrates' courts deterred them. The middle-class, especially, could also afford to hire solicitors and bring their cases before the Divorce Courts (though publicity was a deterrent there as well).

[139] See Geoffrey Crossick, ed., *The Lower Middle Class in Britain 1870–1914* (London: Croom Helm, 1973); A. James Hammerton, "Pooterism or Partnership? Marriage and Masculine Identity in the Lower Middle Class, 1870–1920," *Journal of British Studies* 38, no. 3 (Jul. 1999), 291–321.

[140] Married couples in working-class communities tended to be more frank and open in discussions of sexuality and reproduction, but mothers worked hard to keep their daughters ignorant and, by extension, "respectable" on such matters. Ellen Ross,

nature of these cases only raised the stakes further. Even though they were not extensively reported in the newspapers, they were conducted in front of a courtroom audience, and the negative repercussions of revelations there were very much on the minds of at least some complainants.[141] In such challenging circumstances, women's ability to successfully maneuver within the moral expectations of magistrates and the culture of the courtroom was essential. As they did in marital summonses, working-class women proved adept at securing witnesses and constructing convincing narratives of their morality and entitlements. Women in these cases often claimed – or brought witnesses to testify to the effect – that they had lived with the defendant "as man and wife" for lengthy periods, though this was of secondary consideration to the admission of paternity before a witness. A public acknowledgment of paternity alone was generally all that was required to secure a court order for child support. A defendant's only recourse was to plead that he was fulfilling his familial duty in another capacity, such as by supporting an ailing parent, though this strategy was largely ineffective in prewar Clerkenwell.[142]

The situation became more complex when the defendant denied paternity and there were no witnesses to corroborate the complainant's claim. In these cases, women had to provide far more detailed and convincing narratives to establish their status as deserving mothers and to verify the defendant's responsibility for the child. The sexual conduct of the complainant was a critical issue, since the only way to prove paternity was for her to convince the court of her monogamy. Contested affiliation cases could involve multiple, opposing witnesses and a series of testimonies and cross-examinations conducted by both complainant and defendant on the issue of the former's sexual activity. In Maud Brown's 1904 suit against Joseph Hilliard, the absence of witnesses, the defendant's effective cross-examination, and the complainant's own admission to sex with multiple partners a full two years before she had

Love and Toil: Motherhood in Outcast London, 1870–1918 (New York and Oxford: Oxford University Press, 1993), 98–100. As with illegitimacy itself, extramarital intercourse, though hardly embraced among the working class, was less ruthlessly stigmatized than it was among the middle class (though not necessarily more frequently practiced). Frost, *Promises Broken*, 46–47.

141 See e.g. the case reported in *The Times*, January 6, 1893.

142 In none of the cases from 1910 where putative fathers used this defense did magistrates rule in their favor.

met the defendant were enough to derail her case.[143] Even though the question of her sexual intimacy with other men in close proximity to her pregnancy remained a matter of debate, in the absence of corroborating witnesses for her account and in light of her own admission to sexual relations with other men in the previous years, enough doubt had been thrown upon Brown's sexual propriety to prompt the magistrate's dismissal of her suit.

The significance of reputation in these cases provides some insight into why single working-class and lower-middle-class women took public aspersions against their sexual behavior so seriously in other contexts, and why they were so keen to seek redress for them in local courtrooms through summonses for assault or threats. The risk of loss of reputation was greater for them, in some ways, than it was for married women. Here, the social component of courtroom testimony took precedence. Much of the evidence in contested affiliation cases emerged from hearsay, rumor, and presupposition. A complainant's reputation in the community could be of paramount importance in this. When even the suggestion that a woman had been seen "going about" with other men could be used by a defendant to disavow paternity in court and consequently deny a single mother support payments, the threat posed by accusations of prostitution or promiscuity becomes clear. The frequent use of witnesses in such cases also turned these events from personal contests into communal ones, since other members of the community – friends, neighbors, family members, co-workers – could be asked to lend their voice to one side or the other.[144] In affiliation summonses, sexual reputation was actively constructed and contested by plaintiffs, defendants, and the broader community, and the consequences of an effective argument were of great significance to all involved. A woman's success could secure her financial support for her child until such age as they could earn their own living, while failure freed the putative father from all further financial obligation. The defendant's sexual behavior, on the other hand, was rarely discussed in affiliation cases, and its omission reflected the inherent double standard of Victorian sexual morality.[145]

143 Minutes of Summonses, Clerkenwell PC, April 26, 1904 (PS/CLE/B/03/009).

144 The same was often true in sexual assault cases. D'Cruze, *Crimes of Outrage*, 61, 169.

145 Frost, *Promises Broken*, 44.

Local courtrooms also offered a forum to redress the balance of class authority in Victorian gender relations, presenting working-class women with one of their few opportunities to hold men of the middle-class or upper-class accountable for using their social advantage to gain sexual access.[146] The master–servant relationship, in particular, was one that put women in a position of acute vulnerability, since it brought men and women of contrasting class positions into close daily contact with one another in the relative privacy of the home.[147] If the sexual liaisons that sometimes resulted could be legitimized, a working-class woman could hope to raise her economic and social status considerably, even if such matches were often looked at askance by those in the husband's social circle. The affiliation summonses that arose from master–servant liaisons that were not followed by marriage, however, could be extremely complex and highly contested. The stakes for both sides in such cases were very high, especially for the women involved. Failure to prove the legitimacy of the union would leave her bereft not only of her reputation and of financial support but also of the likelihood of future employment, at least locally. What household would knowingly hire a female servant with a history of having "connections" with her previous employer?

In Ada Mary Bose's April 1905 suit against John Bernard Olde, the complainant described, in careful detail, how her relationship with the defendant had changed from that of servant to that of mistress, with a consequent alteration in her status and treatment within the household. "Up to the time I was seduced I wore cap and aprons," Bose told the magistrate, Mr. Bros, in the Clerkenwell court.[148] "After that, I was treated as one of the family, had my meals with the family, left off my cap and aprons. Became housekeeper and associated with my master's friends." She also emphasized Olde's immorality, portraying him as a seducer and a corrupter who had abused his

[146] There is a rich and growing literature on the social history of domestic service in the eighteenth, nineteenth, and early twentieth century. Recent works include Carolyn Steedman, *Master and Servant: Lobe and Labour in the English Industrial Age* (Oxford: Oxford University Press, 2007) and *Labour Lost: Domestic Service and the Making of Modern England* (Oxford: Oxford University Press, 2009); Lucy Delap, *Knowing Their Place: Domestic Service in Twentieth Century Britain* (Oxford: Oxford University Press, 2011).

[147] Frost, *Promises Broken*, 59; D'Cruze, *Crimes of Outrage*, 89.

[148] Minutes of Summonses, Clerkenwell PC, April 18, 1905 (PS/CLE/B/03/009).

position of power when it suited him. Bose testified that Olde had given her whiskey, lent her a book of pornography, encouraged her to abort her child upon learning of her pregnancy and, when angry at her, had sent her back the kitchen "to know my position." Although Bose's role in the household seemed to have oscillated between that of a mistress and that of an employee, the complainant claimed that she had effectively occupied the role of both wife and mother after the death of Olde's first wife. Bose also refuted the defendant's attempts to paint her as a prostitute. She denied his assertion that she had asked Olde to send money when she left him, insisting that the only funds she had ever received were her housekeeper's wages. Lastly, Bose explained that she had been driven from the household by Olde's repeated disrespect and abuse. When angry, he had reasserted his position as her employer and treated her like a servant. She brought a witness to testify to her own willingness to make the union an honest and permanent one, and to affirm the defendant's continued lack of decency. "[Olde] said will you come back," Bose's witness told the court, "[Bose] said not on the old conditions. [Olde] said not on those conditions and he sneered." The court ordered Olde to pay not only the maximum maintenance of five shillings a week, but an additional five pounds to cover support since the birth of the child and the typical eight shillings costs for the suit itself.

No systematic study has been made previously of women's affiliation summonses in the police courts. Thanks to Ginger Frost, however, there is a thorough examination of more formal breach-of-promise suits, in which women sought damages for broken engagements, available for comparison. The two types of cases shared several key aspects. In both, moral character was a key issue for the plaintiff and the defendant; the double-standard of Victorian sexual morality held men responsible for promises made to women but tolerated their promiscuity while condemning women for the same behavior; and the interplay between the narrative of the case as constructed by the plaintiff and the moral standards of those in the position of judgment were essential considerations.[149] The differences between police-court affiliation cases and breach-of-promise cases, however, outweighed the similarities. Breach cases were expensive,

[149] Frost, *Promises Broken*, 30–39.

relatively rare, and both sides almost invariably engaged solicitors. By end of the nineteenth century, affiliation summonses, on the other hand, were a daily presence in the police courts. The two-shilling cost for an application made them accessible to all but the poorest women. Although both complainants and defendants in police-court affiliation cases occasionally hired solicitors, in sharp contrast to breach-of-promise suits, where only written evidence was permitted, affiliation cases were conducted solely on the basis of oral evidence – another aspect that made them accessible to working-class complainants. Lastly, breach-of-promise cases were tried before a jury, while affiliation cases were tried summarily before a magistrate. The success or failure of police-court affiliation cases often rested solely on the ability of the complainant to provide a convincing narrative of events, to support this narrative with witness testimony, and to respond effectively against any attacks that the defendant made upon her sexual reputation. This reliance on oral evidence could work to the advantage of working-class and lower-middle-class women, since oral communication and contestation were essential elements of their broader social culture.[150]

In the wider legal and cultural context, affiliation summonses did share two other important features with breach-of-promise suits. Although legal reforms across the latter half of the century increased women's ability to call men to account for both their promises and their deeds, the reaction against such reforms revealed a deep ambivalence among those with judicial or political authority towards women's use of the courts, and considerable suspicion of their honesty and integrity more generally. Political opponents of the Evidence Amendment Act 1851, much like Henry Crompton two decades later, expressed concerns that women would misuse the courts by bringing false accusations against innocent men.[151] The Evidence Amendment Bill 1869, in order to address these concerns, included a provision aimed specifically at preventing women from using perjury to obtain awards in breach-of-promise suits.[152] The same skepticism this measure indicated towards women's character and goals in affiliation cases was pervasive among the London police-court magistrates, who could express sympathy for abandoned mothers at one moment and

[150] Tebutt, *Women's Talk?*, 40–43. [151] Frost, *Promises Broken*, 20. [152] Ibid., 21.

contempt towards those whom they thought were bringing false accusations the next. It was up to the women in question to convince the magistrate in the courtroom that they were the former and not the latter.

Both breach and affiliation cases gave working-class women the opportunity to publicly contest the morality and social protocol of courtship and betrothal, as the promise or expectation of marriage was a common element in women's testimony. By describing how the putative father of her child had pledged to marry her, given gifts or even posted banns (i.e. official marriage announcements), a complainant could mitigate the public stigma of premarital intercourse and an illegitimate child.[153] Affiliation cases brought another key element of social life into the realm of courtroom culture by allowing men and women to publicly discuss what constituted paternal behavior. Delineating how fathers were expected to treat their young children and proving that the defendant had conducted himself commensurately could be the key to a successful affiliation summons. The close integration of local courtrooms with contests over paternity was often clear from principals' recounting of their discussions previous to a mother's summons application. It was not unusual for complainants to threaten a court case, and the accompanying embarrassment for both parties, prior to taking further steps. Likewise, putative fathers, if they offered support upon learning of a pregnancy, invariably pledged amounts within the range typical of weekly maintenance awards (i.e. 2–5 shillings weekly). Men accused of paternity could themselves challenge a woman's resolution, all but daring them to apply for a summons.[154] In other instances, the summons itself merely added official sanction to a more informal agreement already reached between the parties.[155] Although magistrates were increasingly willing to grant orders for support, such orders were notoriously difficult to execute.[156] They were not initially enforceable through a warrant, and only became so after another court appearance by the complainant a month later, at which

[153] In this period, premarital sex as part of an established courtship was not considered particularly abnormal or immoral. D'Cruze, *Crimes of Outrage*, 127.
[154] Minutes of Summonses, Clerkenwell PC, May 6, 1902. [155] Ibid., June 7, 1902.
[156] To address this, the Affiliation Orders Act 1914 (4&5 Geo. 5 c. 6) stipulated the appointment of a "collection officer" to every magistrates' bench.

time she had to attest, under oath, that the sum stipulated in the order had not been paid.[157] These summonses also required the complainant to broadcast events that, by most measures of respectability, could be damning indeed.[158] Despite the obstacles to fulfilling maintenance orders once they were made, and the social risks that complainants were taking with such summonses, the integration of courtrooms into public contests over courtship, paternity, and sexual morality helps explain why women spent so much time and effort applying for summonses, corralling witnesses, and bringing these cases to court, all of which would only expose them further to shame and calumny.[159] For an unwed mother, an affiliation summons was more than just an instrumentalist avenue to secure financial support. It represented an opportunity to assert that she was not immoral, that she was not sexually profligate, and that her sexual behavior had been in the context of premarital courtship.

The cultural and social aspect of the courtroom was also important in men's decisions to publicly contest such claims, rather than settling them discreetly. They provided a public forum for those under scrutiny to vociferously deny paternity, most commonly by undermining a woman's case with the assertion that she had "connections" with other men. Both aspects of affiliation cases, the attention they drew and the hazards for those accused, were recognized at the highest levels of government, and particularly by officials at the Home Office, which appointed and supervised the London magistrates. The potential damage to a man's reputation posed by these very public cases was strong enough to merit detailed discussion by members of a 1909 parliamentary committee, the latest in a long series of such bodies that had investigated the workings of the magistrates' courts and made recommendations on policy changes. This committee, convened to examine reforms to the law on affiliation, while agreeing that justices should have the authority to bar press and public alike from the

157 Alexander, *Administration of Justice*, 61.

158 Magistrates viewed these cases and the frank discussions of premarital sex they involved as mortifying for the complainants. Alfred Chicele Plowden, June 14, 1910, *Divorce and Matrimonial Causes*, vol. 2, 273.

159 As does the involvement of the Poor Law Guardians, who could bring cases on behalf of pauper mothers. See Ginger Frost, *Illegitimacy in English Law and Society, 1860–1930* (Manchester: Manchester University Press, 2016), 109–45.

courtroom, specified that this could only apply if both parties consented. This ensured that putative fathers had the opportunity to challenge paternity claims publicly and, in doing so, to counter the gossip and hearsay that inevitably surrounded such cases. As Ernley Blackwell, then the Assistant Under-Secretary of State for the Home Office, observed, "people know of the accusation and that he has been had up [i.e. held accountable] as the father of the child ... he has a right to have his story heard in public and to cross-examine the applicant."[160] Blackwell, a prominent barrister, would soon become the chief legal adviser to the British Cabinet, whose powerful membership, hand-picked from the House of Commons and the House of Lords by the Prime Minister, constituted the primary decision-making body of the government. Blackwell understood that these cases were not solely about money, but spoke instead to sexual reputation, respectability, and family honor. The courtroom could serve as a public arena for challenging or restoring all of these.

Considering the obstacles to enforcing support orders, for many women, some public recognition of their respectability and the promise of granting legitimacy to the child's conception was all they could hope for in any case. These alone had great value in working-class communities where the label of illegitimacy, like that of prostitution, carried a special stigma.[161] The opportunity to shape reputation and respectability notwithstanding, one certainly cannot discount women's desire – out of fairness, economic necessity, or both – to obtain financial support for their children born out of wedlock. This was particularly true for women whose pregnancy and responsibilities of child-rearing (both of which could interfere severely with employment) or abandonment by their child's father had landed them in the workhouse.[162] Economic need was a more obvious impetus behind the "Bastardy Arrears" cases that appeared in the police-court record almost as frequently as affiliation cases themselves did. Women sought

160 Testimony of Ernley Blackwell, July 1, 1909, *Report from the Select Committee on Bastardy Orders, 1909* (PP 1909) (London: Wyman and Sons, 1909), 22.

161 Testimony of Alfred Chicele Plowden, June 14, 1910, *Divorce and Matrimonial Causes*, vol. 2, 274. See also Thane and Evans, *Unmarried Motherhood*, 6; Frost, "Illegitimacy in the English Working Class," 293–322.

162 In which case, as explained earlier, the Poor Law Guardians could sue on her behalf, and she could also due so subsequent to her release with their cases as supporting evidence.

these subsequent to winning an affiliation case, in instances where the father had refused to provide the weekly payment awarded. Tracking down recalcitrant fathers in these circumstances, as in affiliation summonses, could prove problematic.[163] In contrast to affiliation orders, however, an arrears judgment *could* be enforced with a demand for immediate payment, confiscation of goods in lieu of payment, imprisonment if neither payment nor goods were forthcoming or, at the very least, a warrant for arrest on non-appearance. Even such drastic measures did not guarantee that a woman who was successful in an affiliation case would receive the support she had been awarded. Courtrooms were not always effective, but they remained available as a recourse as long as a woman was willing to pursue her case, for months and even years after the birth of a child. The attenuation of these campaigns was so common that, by the turn of the century, police-court clerks had begun to segregate cases into bastardy summonses "prior to 12 months" after the birth of a child and those sought beyond this period.

The multiplication of affiliation cases was significant enough for the state to take a keen interest, and reforms to the law in the prewar years were discussed by the nation's foremost legal experts. Though the primary concern here was as much financial as it was moral, justices, reformers, and municipal authorities (e.g. Poor Law Guardians and their successors) alike were eager to keep poor women and their illegitimate children off of the rates.[164] Of all the different types of summonses, affiliation cases were among the most significant culturally, since they involved long public discussions about issues of sexual morality, courtship and child-rearing, and parental responsibility. They could make or mar an individual's reputation in the community, preserving or abrogating their aspirations to respectability, employment, or a future union.[165] And they were among the most significant financially. Even given the difficulties of

163 Hence the occasional mention, in affiliation summons testimony, of previous orders that had not been paid, or of the mother's difficulty in tracking down the father to hold him accountable.

164 Testimony of George Craighill, Justice of the Peace for the County of Durham and member of the Executive Council of the Association of Poor Law Unions in England and Wales, June 25, 1909, *Report from the Select Committee on Bastardy Orders*, 11.

165 Waddy, *Police Court*, 192–93.

enforcement, the consequences could be most severe, making a father accountable for support until the child reached its majority or leaving a new mother deprived and vulnerable to that most dreaded of fates, consignment to the workhouse.

"A Charitable Work More than a Legal One": Magistrates, Working-Class Marriage, and Courtroom Culture

By the early twentieth century, courtroom culture could intersect and shape intimate relationships at several points, from the negotiations of courtship and extramarital child-rearing to the struggle for authority and fair treatment in the household to the dissolution of a marriage. Considering the length and complexity of many such cases, it is worth asking what the larger implications were. By the same token, our reliance on the statistical record and the evolution of legal statutes (rather than courtroom interactions) to understand the relationship between working-class women and the state merits close examination.[166] Historians and legal scholars have interpreted the rising numbers of marital and affiliation cases as the result of broader changes in the law, gender relations, social dynamics, political discourse, and women's legal status. Given the long history of women's courtroom usage in interpersonal conflicts and the frequency with which they were bringing summonses and seeking the courts' intervention in the final decades of the nineteenth century, however, courtroom practice was at least as much the wind as it was the weathervane. Legally, marriage became a civil affair in 1858. But in working-class communities, it was not defined and treated as such before the 1890s and early 1900s, when working-class women, in ever-greater numbers, sought summonses for domestic assault, "married women's" cases and affiliation. By 1913, across England and Wales, there would be 11,369 applications for maintenance orders and arrears and 8,582 applications for affiliation orders and arrears made in courts of summary justice.[167] Changes in the

166 Chapman estimated that Tower Bridge Police Court received three times as many applications for separation orders each year as were granted, a ratio he said was typical for a London police court. Testimony of Cecil Chapman, Police Court Magistrate, May 25, 1910, *Divorce and Matrimonial Causes 1912*, vol. 2, 48.

167 Table XIV, *Judicial Statistics, England and Wales, 1913, Pt. I, Criminal Statistics* (PP 1914–16, Cd. 7767, 7807), 62.

law made the integration of marital conflict and local courtrooms possible, but women's initiative in seeking summonses made it prevalent.

The courtroom itself changed in the process, becoming a prominent forum for contesting and defining norms within working-class marriage. The most powerful impact of courtroom culture on relations between working-class husbands and wives in London was reflected in an even more fundamental change: the transition of marriage itself from an institution whose concrete boundaries and perceived social dimensions (especially in times of conflict and dissolution) were defined largely in the religious context to one understood by men and women alike to be civic and legal. Such, at least, was the conclusion reached by the most prominent parliamentary investigation into the relationship between the state and working-class marriages conducted in the early twentieth century – the 1910 Royal Commission on Divorce and Matrimonial Causes. The Commission was chaired by Lord Gorell (née John Gorell Barnes), who had recently stepped down as President of the Probate, Divorce and Admiralty Division of the High Court of Justice. When discussing the need for reform of the marriage laws and their potential impact, witnesses and commission-members alike returned again and again to the profound changes that the integration of courtrooms and marriage had wrought in the preceding decades. There was a near-universal consensus that the working-class now viewed civic institutions, rather than religious ones, as the final arbiters on marriage and sexuality.[168]

In this new configuration, the state, most often in the form of the magistrate, wielded not only the legal wherewithal but also the cultural and social authority to bind working-class men to their vows. "Taking up the civil contract before a tribunal like the registrar or a judge or a magistrate," the Magistrate Cecil Chapman asserted in 1910, "a man would have a greater sense of obligation to fulfill his duty as a citizen than he would when he goes with a girl in an inconsiderate way before a clergyman and does something in the nature of a religious act he does

[168] As the magistrate Cecil Chapman told the committee in May 1910, "I think it is important, that marriage should be looked upon as it really is to everybody, as a social contract, and it should not be looked upon as a sacramental contract except by those people who really feel it to be so." Testimony of Cecil Chapman, Police Court Magistrate, May 25, 1910, *Divorce and Matrimonial Causes 1912*, vol. 2, 50.

not understand, and an obligation he does not appreciate."[169] This understanding of "civil obligation" as a "real thing," and religious obligation as, by comparison, "a mysterious thing they do not appreciate," had been largely the result of negotiations and contractual relations becoming predominant in the sphere of labor, the slow decline of the church's influence, and the increasing integration of the courts, morality, and working-class life.[170] The result, Chapman explained, was that working-class men "make a sort of distinction between sin and crime; sin they look upon as something they are frail enough to commit, and a crime as something they are going to be punished for."[171] John Rose, another magistrate at Tower Bridge Police Court, told the commission that recourse to the court had become so common and procedure there so familiar that husbands and wives regularly colluded to achieve a mutually agreeable separation order.[172] As Rose, Chapman, and their fellow magistrates explained, a summons – be it for separation, maintenance, or maintenance arrears – was rarely a definitive end point or a last resort. Rather, in this chapter, they described how, in working-class communities across the metropolis, such summonses and courtroom appearances were integrated into ongoing negotiations between husbands and wives over the conditions of their marriage or the husband's post-separation responsibilities.

Despite their emphasis on the integration of summonses and courtroom negotiations into working-class marital conflicts, the magistrates did not argue that local communities now viewed marital and child-rearing affairs primarily through the lens of law. Instead, they described how men and women alike saw the concrete locale of the *courtroom* and the person of the magistrate as the means through which conflicts over them could be addressed. As Alfred Chicele

169 Ibid., 52.

170 Testimony of Cecil Chapman, Police Court Magistrate, May 25, 1910, ibid., 55.

171 In Chapman's words, "they will recognize a contract. It does not matter what the contract is." Ibid., 55.

172 Testimony of John Rose, Police Court Magistrate, March 1, 1910, *Divorce and Matrimonial Causes 1912*, vol. 1, 94, 90. Rose also shed light on the purpose of women's summonses for arrears on maintenance payments. Sometimes, they could serve as a goad to payment, but in many cases, the arrears accumulated to several pounds, and the men, unable to pay, were sent to jail (ibid.).

Plowden, a magistrate of twenty years' experience, asserted "I do not think they know any law outside a police court."[173] Because of the long history of contact between the courts and their communities, contact which had brought the former "in closest possible touch with the poorer classes," the local courtroom had become the most "suitable tribunal to deal with these matrimonial quarrels."[174] For this highly functional relationship to be maintained, Plowden and his colleagues argued that the laws on marriage, separation, and divorce must be altered to accord with the general trends of courtroom usage, the specific needs of working-class men and women, and the moral good of working-class communities. This advocacy demonstrated how much of a powerful, if largely indirect, influence women's initiative had exerted on the larger legal discourse concerning working-class marriages and the courtroom's integration with them.

Beyond this assertion that the law should be reformed to match needs and current practice, however, the magistrates' views on marriage and morality tended to be at odds with working-class courtroom use in marital affairs. Plowden, Chapman, and Rose were all in agreement that the laws on divorce currently made the measure inaccessible to the poor, largely because of the expense involved. They also acknowledged that working-class men and women were employing separation and maintenance orders to arrange what was, in practice, a permanent dissolution of marriage, a type of *de facto* divorce. But they deplored the cynical use of marital summonses and were ambivalent to the proposal that their courts might be empowered to grant divorces. Except in cases where the husband was demonstrably abusive, a drunkard, or failed to provide for the household, moreover, they saw their role as one of mediating conflict and reconciling marital difficulties rather than facilitating separations. Their patriarchal leanings, while moderated, were hardly in abeyance. Cecil Chapman argued that the primary purpose of making divorce available was not to ease the dissolving of matrimony, but to elevate and strengthen it. It was, he told the Commission, "the only way by which we shall get a better ideal of married life. There is nothing else which will bring

[173] Testimony of Alfred Chicele Plowden, June 14, 1910, *Divorce and Matrimonial Causes 1912*, vol. 2, 277.

[174] Ibid.

home to the senses of a man that he ought to behave himself with a sense of morality in married life."[175] Albeit unwittingly, Chapman was advocating that the threat of divorce be employed in the same manner that working-class women, for nearly two decades prior, had often sought summonses for assault and separation – as leverage to secure better treatment from their husbands and as an opportunity to publicly negotiate marital obligations.

This convergence of method between Chapman's proposed reform and women's daily practice, however, was equaled by a divergence in magistrates' vision of their own morality and authority in relation to their courtroom clientele. The magistrates consistently designated themselves as the moral authority in their communities. They alone could employ the courtroom and its powers to the benefit of all, whether this meant protecting women from the violence of brutish husbands, freeing tormented husbands from the clutches of drunken, conniving wives, or preventing precipitous flights from matrimony. Working-class men and women, by the magistrates' descriptions, were creatures of whim; they were prone to immorality, poor judgment, and disregard for the institution of marriage; and women's use of the courts in marital affairs was generally either rash or devious. These sentiments were clear in the magistrate Edmund Garratt's declaration that the common knowledge of judicial separations had wrought havoc on the general grain of working-class respect for wedlock.[176] Summing up the abuse of working-class women's separation summonses, among the most egregious being complainants who made multiple applications and obtained multiple separations on different occasions, the magistrate concluded that "it is a very great evil" and one that served to "further embitter the relations of domestic life."[177]

Garratt's fellow magistrates, although less vociferous than he was, were in general agreement that the summons process was often misused and manipulated by working-class women. His colleagues were more willing, in contrast, to point out the benefits of the Married Women's

175 Testimony of Cecil Chapman, London Police Court Magistrate, May 25, 1910, ibid., 49.

176 Testimony of Edmund William Garratt, Police Court Magistrate, May 29, 1910, ibid., 31.

177 Ibid., 31.

Act 1895 (and the Licensing Act 1902's provisions on separation merited by drunkenness) when used in what they saw as its original intents. These were to offer a salutary check on a husband's misbehavior, to provide victimized women with a viable exit from a marriage where abuse was persistent or drunkenness habitual, and to ensure that separated women and their children were supported by the husband to some degree afterwards.[178] Most magistrates also recognized the social power of such summonses to deter abuse by inflicting shame upon the accused.[179] Whatever their merits for abused wives, magistrates' perspectives on the separation and affiliation laws for women remained firmly embedded in a patriarchal context. The key to their effective operation was not women's initiative, but magistrates' discretion, they insisted. In their own view, they were the only ones in a position to segregate the valid claims from the many invalid or frivolous ones.[180] In this equation, working-class women who sought separation orders could only be victims deserving of protection, feckless and jealous harpies, or unscrupulous manipulators. The first group merited the magistrates' full support and whatever aid the law could grant. The latter deserved sound advice or stern rebuke, respectively.

Magistrates' reliance on their moral assessments as well as their legal judgment, and their faith that the courts' proper role in working-class marriages was patriarchal mediation, was evident throughout their testimony. In line with these claims, they repeatedly asserted that local courtrooms had become not merely the legal arbiters of disputes, but the moral and social touchstones of contestations over marriage and affiliation in general. This role was absolutely vital, the magistrate Alfred Plowden insisted, because of the profound social and cultural importance of marriage as an institution. "It concerns the masses," he declared in a parliamentary commission, "it is not a private arrangement between people here and there; it concerns the whole community."[181] This tendency to both emphasize the public import of these issues and to draw a stark moral picture of working-

178 Testimony of Alfred Chicele Plowden, ibid., June 14, 1910, 273.

179 Testimony of Cecil Chapman, May 25, 1910, ibid., 47.

180 Testimony of Robert Henry Bullock Marsham, London Police Court Magistrate, February 28, 1910, ibid., vol. 1, 85.

181 Testimony of Alfred Chicele Plowden, June 14, 1910, ibid., vol. 2, 275.

class marital life and courtroom behavior was equally apparent in one of the magistrates' core arguments for reform of the laws on separation and divorce. Such arguments revolved around the dire cultural and social impact of women's widespread (mis)use of separation agreements. In a testament to the effect of these cases on moral norms, witnesses bemoaned the pernicious influence that such separations had on working-class communities by creating an environment that was permissive towards reckless marriages, rash separations, and subsequent adulterous relationships with new partners.[182] Magistrates argued that this widespread misapplication of marital summonses, more so than any other practice, justified the reform of the divorce laws so that final dissolutions could replace the *de facto* ones provided by separation orders.[183]

Support for reform, regardless of the many objections to the system, was hardly enthusiastic or unqualified. Magistrates' negative evaluations of working-class morality and their conviction that working-class women used the laws on separation immoderately, when combined with their paternalistic concern, left them in an awkward position. On the one hand, they expressed keen enthusiasm to reduce the rampant misuse of separation orders and the resulting prevalence of adultery by making divorce a more feasible option. They saw themselves and their courts, on the other hand, as dedicated to the preservation of marriage in both practice and principle in working-class communities, and had little desire for their venues to become the equivalent of Divorce Courts for the poor.[184] They were also acutely aware of the press sensationalism that had accrued around the latter, much to the detriment of the general moral atmosphere among an avid readership.[185] So damaging were such reports that the magistrate John

[182] Edmund Garratt painted a canvas of rampant debauchery, asserting that the vast majority of separated men lived immorally with other women, often supporting "a large family of bastard children, and all the evils resulting from it." Testimony of Edmund William Garratt, Police Court Magistrate, May 29, 1910, ibid., 31. John Rose declared, more simply, that "immorality [i.e. adultery] almost invariably follows on the part of the man, and not infrequently on the part of the woman." Testimony of John Rose, Police Court Magistrate, March 1, 1910, ibid., vol. 1, 90.

[183] Alexander, *Administration of Justice*, 64, 63.

[184] Ibid., 64; Testimony of John Rose, Police Court Magistrate, March 1, 1910, *Divorce and Matrimonial Causes 1912*, vol. 1, 97.

[185] According to Cecil Chapman, the publication of such material had led to "disastrous talk and conduct" among young people. Testimony of Cecil Chapman, London

Rose labeled them "indecent publications," and advocated their strict censorship and harsh punishments for editors who published them.[186] A similar demoralizing of working-class communities would follow, he predicted, if marital affairs in the police courts were to receive equally broad press dissemination.[187] Given such fraught circumstances, magistrates were often ambivalent as to whether not their courtrooms were the proper locale to adjudicate working-class divorces, should subsequent reforms make them more accessible. Some, such as Robert Marsham, feared that making divorce a summary procedure would allow it to devolve upon county and borough justices, who lacked both the experience and qualifications for so serious a matter.[188] John Rose, with some prodding from the parliamentary committee, concluded that the magistrates' close relationship with the poor left them more qualified than any other justices were to deal with such delicate issues.[189] Variations of opinion on this and the other topics discussed meant that the parliamentary commissioners were unable to compose a unanimous recommendation for reform, and they ultimately produced both a majority and minority report. The former advocated the transfer of matrimonial cases to the County Court justices, largely on the grounds that they would be best dealt with by the experienced solicitors who staffed these benches, though Rose was not alone in his assertion that practical experience mattered more than legal expertise in such matters.[190] Three years after the submission of the committee's reports, the issue remained unresolved.

Regardless of their views on the police court's suitability as venues for working-class divorce, should reform have made it possible, magistrates were in agreement that they were the only ones suitable to judge not just the legal validity, but the moral suitability of marital and affiliation summonses. In this, they set themselves up as the arbiters of the court's

Police Court Magistrate, May 25, 1910, *Divorce and Matrimonial Causes 1912*, vol. 2, 49.

186 Testimony of John Rose, Police Court Magistrate, March 1, 1910, ibid., vol. 1, 90, 99.

187 Ibid., 93.

188 Testimony of Robert Henry Bullock Marsham, London Police Court Magistrate, February 28, 1910, ibid., 85.

189 Testimony of John Rose, Police Court Magistrate, March 1, 1910, ibid., 97.

190 Alexander, *Administration of Justice*, 64.

social and cultural operation as well as its legal dimensions, and elevated their courtrooms as the paramount venue for assessing the expectations of marriage, the norms of behavior within it, and the grounds for its abrogation. In this final space of judgment – legal, moral, and social – the magistrate was to hold sway. While reaffirming their own discretion in these matters, however, magistrates also credited women, the primary employers of summonses, with integrating courtrooms and working-class marriages. Magistrates' views on this integration depended on *how* women used summonses. Women who sought the courts intervention in humility, asking for protection from abuse or relief from an intolerable marriage, they portrayed sympathetically. Those who used summonses as a tool for negotiation, to castigate or shame their husbands, or in a rash manner, magistrates labeled as immoral manipulators of the system. Magistrates' resolute condemnation of these social uses of summonses, when viewed in light of their inability to prevent them, emphasized the degree to which working-class women's daily use of the summonses and the courtroom environment often ran counter to magistrates' ideals. Irrespective of the latter's authority, women were not effectively co-opted into the magistrates' vision of morality, marriage, and the courtroom's roles in both. The integration of working-class marriages and the courtroom was not a top-down affair, but one driven considerably by women's goals and agency. Neither was it a process spurred only by legal reforms nor solely reflective of broader changes in public discourse on marriage, gender relations, and the state's role in working-class communities. This integration was shaped by the social and cultural dimensions of summonses and courtroom practice, and it was in these latter facets that women's initiative was most influential. After all, the magistrates' urging of divorce reform in 1910 was itself leant impetus by the 13,193 applications for maintenance orders made in England and Wales the previous year, the vast majority by women.[191] The rising tide of affiliation summonses, of which there were 8,517 in 1908, similarly prompted a parliamentary inquiry all its own in 1909.[192]

[191] Of these applications, 9,835 resulted in orders being made. Table XIV, Courts of Summary Jurisdiction – Proceedings in Non-Criminal Matters, *Return of Judicial Statistics, England and Wales, 1909, Pt. I, Criminal Statistics* (PP 1911, Cd. 5473, 5501), 70.

[192] Of these applications, across England and Wales, 6,819 resulted in orders. Ibid., 72.

Viewing marital and affiliation summonses through the lens of courtroom culture sheds considerable light on this integration of marriage, affiliation, and courtrooms. What was at issue between magistrates and working-class women was not just the latter's access to the courtroom nor their right to employ summonses as they saw fit in marriage and affiliation issues. This was also a contest over the moral meaning and social impact of summonses and courtroom usage. Although magistrates could filter out "frivolous" cases, they could not simply deny women access to the summons process, nor could they control how women used summonses, their motivations, or what they said in the courtroom. The combination of law and courtroom protocol (which was in part governed by expectation and tradition) limited magistrates in this regard even more so than it did working-class woman. After all, a woman who bent the rules – for example, with an empty summons – was nowhere near as publicly accountable as a magistrate who did was, nor did women necessarily view the law itself as an *a priori* good. And although magistrates had considerable discretion in the final verdict, they exercised limited influence over the initial stages (e.g. applications for summonses). With these verdicts, their public pronouncements in courtrooms and to the press, and their testimony in official inquiries, magistrates were attempting to control the moral implications of courtroom usage and the broader public dialogues about working-class marriages and child-rearing. By the same token, whether magistrates were willing to recognize it or not, working-class women were doing much the same on a daily basis. Women's use of summonses and local courtrooms allowed them to participate substantively in the ongoing public discussion of these key issues and to influence the concrete expressions of the laws on matrimony, separation, maintenance, and affiliation. In this process, the courtroom itself became a space that contributed significantly to the debates over what was considered moral and just in working-class domestic matters.

6

"The Very Centre of Observation and Information"

Constables, Magistrates, and Changing Patterns of Prosecution and Punishment, 1880–1913

In 1906, the Toynbee Trust commissioned a study of the London police courts as part of their mission to investigate and disseminate the "true principles of political and social economy."[1] Their conclusion was that these venues had become an important reference point in the lives of the metropolitan populace. The introduction to the Trust's published volume, *The London Police Courts To-Day and To-Morrow*, was written Samuel Barnett, the co-founder and warden of Britain's first University Settlement House, Toynbee Hall (Whitechapel).[2] As a leading figure in social reform and one deeply involved in the daily tribulations of East End life, Barnett's assessment carried considerable authority, and he was unequivocal in his description of the police courts' significance:

> To the majority of citizens, the police-court is the very centre of observation and information. Its reports are read, when nothing else is read except football news. It has close dealings with the readers or with neighbors, who in trouble or sorrow have made acquaintance with its methods. It gives dramatic form to familiar experiences of poverty, oppression, suffering and crime. It is the exponent of law, the visible representative of the "justice" of which they hear in speeches and in sermons.[3]

1 Samuel Barnett, "Introduction," in Hugh Gamon, *The London Police Court To-day and To-morrow* (London: J. M. Dent, 1907), viii.

2 Emily K. Abel, "Toynbee Hall, 1884–1914," *Social Service Review* 54, no. 1 (Dec. 1979), 606. See also Seth Koven, *Slumming: Sexual and Social Politics in Victorian London* (Princeton: Princeton University Press, 2004), 230–57.

3 Barnett in Gamon, *London Police Court*, vii–viii. Fifty years later, Richard Hoggart would echo this observation, explaining how, among the British working class, "the

The summonses, both personal and institutional, were one way in which "the majority" were experiencing the courts by the turn of the century. The other was in charges brought by constables. Through the conduct of these charges, local courtrooms mediated many of the most common interactions between the police and the populace. To understand how courtroom culture shaped this relationship, we must address several key questions. How did the authority of police and magistrates operate in these cases? What was the relationship between charge cases, definitions of crime, and moral norms in this period? And what vision of "justice" was offered by the conduct and portrayal of charges? Every charge began with an arrest, and each one concluded with either the defendant's release or the imposition of a penalty. In between the two existed a process that was fraught with contest, subject to public scrutiny, and rife with opportunities for negotiation. If the workhouse, the gaol, and the police station were the three great "moral teachers" of the poor, then the courtroom was the doorway to their schoolrooms.[4]

The study of crime and policing has produced a vast array of scholarship ranging from histories of the police and penal reform, studies of late Victorian law and legal institutions, urban social history, and the history of modern governance.[5] The local courtroom itself, in

popular Sunday newspapers are read as much for their full sports reports as for their accounts of the week's crimes." Richard Hoggart, *The Uses of Literacy: Aspects of Working-Class Life with Special Reference to Publications and Entertainment* (London: Penguin, 1957), 91.

[4] D. J. V. Jones, "The New Police, Crime and People in England and Wales, 1829–1888," *Transactions of the Royal Historical Society* 33 (1983), 160.

[5] The most oft-cited volumes include David Philips, *Crime and Authority in Victorian England: the Black Country 1835–1860* (London: Croom Helm, 1977); V. A. C. Gatrell, Peter Lenman, and Geoffrey Parker, eds., *Crime and the Law: The Social History of Crime in Western Europe since 1500* (London: Europa Publications, 1980); Victor Bailey, ed., *Policing and Punishment in Nineteenth-Century Britain* (Rutgers: Rutgers University Press, 1981); David Jones, *Crime, Protest, Community and Police in Nineteenth-Century Britain* (London and New York: Routledge, 1982); Carolyn Steedman, *Policing the Victorian Community: The Formation of English Provincial Police Forces, 1856–80* (London: Routledge, 1984); Clive Emsley, *Crime and Society in England, 1750–1900* (London and New York: Longman, 1987); David Taylor, *Crime, Policing and Punishment in England 1750–1914* (New York: St. Martin's, 1998); Barry Godfrey and Paul Lawrence, *Crime and Justice 1750–1950* (Cullompton, Devon: Willan, 2005); Peter King, *Crime and Law in England, 1750–1840: Remakiing Justice from the Margins* (Cambridge: Cambridge University Press, 2006).

contrast, has received very limited attention, and the police-court records have remained largely *terra incognita*.[6] Accordingly, this chapter addresses three questions that are crucial to interpreting the relationship between local courtrooms and their communities within the analytical framework of courtroom culture. First, what did the daily prosecution of crime look like in the courts, with a focus on Clerkenwell? Secondly, what was the contrast between the treatment of crime by constables on the street (i.e. the apprehension and charging stage) and its adjudication in courtrooms? Thirdly, how did both change in the decades preceding the First World War? And, lastly, what can these changes tell us about the evolving relationship between the legal, social, and cultural aspects of courtrooms' daily operation and public portrayals? By addressing these questions, this chapter will demonstrate how courtrooms served as a crucial fulcrum in determining the authority of police constables and the balance of power between the individual and the state in the processes of arrest and prosecution. It will also explore how the expanding role of police constables in the courtroom altered urban policing and criminal prosecution across the course of the nineteenth century.

The conclusions of recent histories of crime, whether or not they view policing as a positive move towards urban order or a more coercive project of social control (largely the latter), emphasize the increasing authority of police and criminal policy in the wake of reforms in the 1830s and 1840s.[7] Though historians have been keen

[6] Jennifer Davis has offered an insightful but brief study of Victorian theft prosecutions in the Middlesex Sessions in "Prosecutions and Their Context: the Use of Criminal Law in Later Nineteenth-Century London," in Douglas Hay and Francis Snyder, eds., *Policing and Prosecution in Britain 1750–1850* (Oxford: Clarendon, 1989), 397–426.

[7] The contrast between older histories charting the development of public order and more revisionist histories that focus on social control is summed up in Martin Wiener, *Reconstructing the Criminal: Culture, Law, and Policy in England, 1830–1914* (Cambridge: Cambridge University Press, 1990), 261–62. The complexities of unpacking "crime as a social phenomenon," are deftly handled by V. A. C. Gatrell in "The Decline of Theft and Violence in Victorian and Edwardian England," in V. A. C. Gatrell, Bruce Lenman, and Geoffrey Parker, eds., *Crime and the Law: The Social History of Crime in Western Europe since 1500* (London: Europa Publications, 1980), 238–43.

to point out the resilience of working-class culture, the persistence of informal methods of conflict resolution, and the continued antipathy towards unwonted police interference in community affairs, this recognition of the reach and power of policing largely mirrored the sanguine claims made by policymakers in the late Victorian period.[8] Chief among these were that violent crime was on the wane and that, in the eyes of officials and the urban middle-class alike, by the end of the nineteenth century, crime no longer posed a serious threat to the social order. The immorality of the urban poor and working class, reformers asserted, had been largely contained through the police, prisons, and workhouses.[9] These attempts to understand policing and police prosecutions through broader analytical frames of social control, crime, and class, and through a reliance on the statistical records of policing and prosecution, have been enlightening. The dynamics of courtrooms themselves, in contrast, have often been eclipsed. It was left to the London magistrate Horace Smith to point out that the picture painted by the official statistics – which have been so central to contemporary histories of crime and policing – did not necessarily match the daily experience of those tasked with adjudicating the law.[10] Any attempt to draw a decisive conclusion about the overall

[8] Stephen Inwood, "Policing London's Morals: The Metropolitan Police and Popular Culture, 1829–1850," *The London Journal: A Review of Metropolitan Society Past and Present* 15, no. 2 (1990), 129; Davis, "Prosecutions and Their Context," 413; V.A.C. Gatrell, "Crime, Authority, and the Policeman-State," in F. M. L. Thompson, ed., *The Cambridge Social History of Britain 1750–1950, vol. 3: Social Agencies and Institutions* (Cambridge: Cambridge University Press, 1990), 284–86.

[9] D. J. V. Jones, "The New Police," 160. It should be noted that Carolyn Steedman points to a very different picture in rural England, where the small numbers of police highly constrained their authority and influence, if not their historical significance. Steedman, *Policing the Victorian Community*. For rural policing, see also B. J. Davey, *Lawless and Immoral: Policing a Country Town, 1838–1857* (New York: St. Martin's Press, 1983).

[10] Smith was hardly alone in his skepticism. The unreliability of the statistics supplied by police had been apparent to Edward Troup, the Undersecretary of State for the Home Office, who was largely responsible for overhauling the organization of the annually published *Judicial Statistics* in the early 1890s. Leon Radzinowicz and Roger Hood, *A History of English Criminal Law and Its Administration from 1750, vol. 5: The Emergence of Penal Policy in Victorian and Edwardian England* (Oxford: Clarendon, 1990), 106.

incidence of serious crime in the metropolis from these numbers would be highly problematic in any case, not least because the category itself was fluid.[11] The rapid upswing in the police courts' activity, on the other hand, was clear and considerable. As fast as the London population was increasing, the police courts' daily work was rising at an even faster rate. The London population more than doubled from the 1860s to the eve of the First World War, growing from over 3 million to over 7 million.[12] In that same period, although the number of police apprehensions rose at roughly the same rate, the number of convictions by metropolitan magistrates more than tripled, from 31,698 in 1867 to 101,121 by 1913.[13] The increase in police summonses, which, as opposed to charges, did not merit an apprehension, was even more dramatic. These rose nearly sixfold across a similar time frame, from under 6,000 in 1860 to 35,318 in 1913.[14]

Since the number of courts and magistrates increased only marginally across these decades, this rapid upward trajectory of police charges and summonses, when combined with summonses by private individuals and municipal authorities, translated into an enormous upsurge in daily courtroom business. Given the complexity of the relationship between the commission of crimes, the statistics on arrests and prosecution, and the classification and reporting of criminal behavior, an examination of

[11] See Gatrell, "Decline of Theft and Violence," 242–43. The full list of these crimes as tabulated in the *RCPM* consisted of the following: murder; attempts to commit murder, wounding, etc.; manslaughter; unnatural offenses; attempts to commit unnatural offenses: rape, defilement of girls, attempts to commit rape, etc.; child stealing; abduction; procuring or attempting to procure abortion; assaults to rob; and demanding money with menaces. Between 1867 and 1905, the rate of all of these combined per 100,000 population in the metropolis varied from a high of 9.036 in 1867 to a low of 5.572 in 1889. In 1900, it was at 7.237 (*RCPM 1905* (PP 1906, Cd. 3180), 67). Adjusted for the growth of the metropolitan population, the reported occurrence of certain serious crimes in London had dropped since the 1860s, while that of other offenses had remained stable. Manslaughter and rape were in the former category, while murder, attempted murder, wounding, and robbery with violence were in the latter.

[12] The Register-General's returns placed the London population in 1865 at 3,341,082. *RCPM 1900* (PP 1902, Cd. 881), 77. In 1913, it was estimated to be 7,467,307 (*RCPM 1925* (PP 1926, Cmd. 2660), 30).

[13] *RCPM 1875* (PP 1876, C. 1594), 20; *RCPM 1913* (PP 1914, Cd. 7671), 30.

[14] *RCPM 1869* (PP 1870, C. 150), 2; *RCPM 1913*, 32.

how crime was treated in the courtroom cannot demonstrate if the crime rate, however it was defined, was increasing or decreasing. It can, on the other hand, add to our understanding of the balance between interventionist policing and that sought by the community, and therefore provide a clearer picture of the social dimensions of London's growing apparatus of criminal justice. Since the prosecution of *all* crime in the metropolis, even that too serious to fall under the ultimate remit of the police courts, had to commence with a hearing before the magistrates, police-court records can provide insight into the ground-level interaction between police and the people to a degree that those of no other judicial venue can match. Specifically, courtroom records reveal a wealth of detail on a topic that has long preoccupied historians of crime, policing, and society – namely, how working-class men and women combined informal conflict resolution with the more formal legal recourse of the courts.[15] The cultural aspects of charges, how they were portrayed, and how they generated meanings about crime and morality in wider public discourse were also highly significant. Assessing police activity, courtroom dynamics, and public portrayals in conjunction is particularly useful to understand the changing relationship between crime and morality in the decades prior to the First World War. Martin Wiener has argued that the expansion of criminal justice into late Victorian social life was driving a "depreciation" of the criminal law's "moral currency" and a consequent reduction of the stigma attached to offenders.[16] The changing social and cultural dynamics of charges demonstrate that their adjudication still retained important moral dimensions in the early twentieth century, and not just for the accused. The relationship between policing, adjudication, and punishment was far from straightforward in this period; it was continually being redefined not only for those who were its targets, but for its wielders as well.

[15] Looking at courtroom prosecutions by constables also adds to our understanding of how nineteenth- and early twentieth-century policing operated in the context of urban surveillance and the creation of the self-policing Liberal individual. See Patrick Joyce, *Rule of Freedom: Liberalism and the Modern City* (London and New York: Verso, 2003), 2–4. Michel Foucault's concept of "governmentality" has been key here, elucidated in "Governmentality," in Graham Burchell, Colin Gordon and Peter Miller (eds.), *The Foucault Effect: Studies in Governmentality* (Chicago: University of Chicago Press, 1991), 87–104.

[16] Wiener, *Reconstructing the Criminal*, 363.

"No Crime Is Committed When a Policeman Is in Sight": Police and Private Initiative in Bringing Charges to the Courts

Although still small in comparison to the population of London, by the end of the nineteenth century, the Metropolitan Police had expanded considerably from their modest origins. Their numbers grew from 5500 in 1851 to more than 9000 in 1871.[17] This increasingly professionalized and centralized force swelled further to 17,000 by 1905 and to over 21,000 by the eve of the First World War.[18] The most thorough and detailed documentation of their activity both within the courtroom and beyond was not to be found in the annual *Judicial Statistics* published by the Home Department each year, but rather in the annual *Report of the Commissioner of Police of the Metropolis* (*RCPM*). The latter, first introduced mid-century, was a comprehensive, annual accounting of the activities and personnel status of the Metropolitan Police. It covered a wide gamut of topics, from how many constables had been absent on sick days to a minute record of what charges had prompted apprehensions, the exact numbers of cases tried, convictions and discharges in the magistrates' courts, and details on pay and injuries to police personnel. In 1905, the *RCPM* indicated that 127,317 men and women had been apprehended by the police, and that 103,362 of these had been summarily convicted by magistrates.[19] The same year, police served 67,266 court summonses at the behest of private individuals.[20] The police themselves also applied for and received 32,205 summonses.[21] Charges of drunkenness and drunkenness "with aggravations" (e.g. obscene language, disorderly behavior) alone accounted for more than half of both apprehensions and convictions (59,189 and 53,905, respectively), and the overwhelming majority (97 percent) of the latter resulted in a fine.[22]

[17] Taylor, *Crime, Policing and Punishment in England 1750–1914*, 88.

[18] The total authorized strength on December 31, 1905 was 17,210. On the same date in 1913, it was 21,020, consisting of 33 superintendents, 619 inspectors, 2810 sergeants, and 17,558 constables. *RCPM 1913*, 21.

[19] *RCPM 1905*, 41. [20] Ibid., 43. [21] Ibid., 45.

[22] Ibid., 61. 9,757 men and 5,228 women were convicted of simple drunkenness. A much larger number – 27, 307 men and 11, 613 women – were convicted of "drunkenness with aggravations." The latter alone could prompt imprisonment, and only in exceedingly rare instances. That year, there were 629 sentences of imprisonment for 14 days and under, and 936 for between 14 days and one month. Ibid., 75.

After these offenses, the next most common cause of apprehensions was violations of the Metropolitan Police Acts (MPA), which prompted 16,964 arrests in 1905.[23] The 1839 Metropolitan Police Act and subsequent amendments covered a wide range of offenses, all concerned with behavior in public spaces. The most frequent violations of the MPA were enumerated in section 54 of the 1839 Act, which empowered police to arrest those responsible for "nuisances by persons in thoroughfares," such as reckless driving of a cart, van or horse ("furious driving") and disorderly behavior that disturbed the peace ("disorderly conduct").[24] Other violations that typically prompted arrest were running and knocking over pedestrians on public walkways, and "insulting behaviour." This last was often the charge leveled at an alleged prostitute the first time she was identified as such by a constable. It could also be prompted by a public argument in which the offender used obscene language and refused to desist when approached by a policeman.[25] The MPA, in addition, authorized constables to arrest those they had "good cause to suspect of having committed or being about to commit any felony, misdemeanour, or breach of the peace," ("suspicious persons," in the court records).[26] Lastly, the Act encompassed a broad array of common street pastimes in working-class neighborhoods (playing games, throwing stones, rolling hoops, etc.); activities defined as a public annoyance, usually with some level of assumed immorality (e.g. loitering or soliciting as a prostitute, selling or displaying profane or pornographic literature); and sanitary measures (e.g. depositing refuse on the street, keeping pigs near a public thoroughfare).[27] After drunkenness and MPA violations, the most common specific causes of arrest in 1905 were simple larceny (7,790), begging (5,866) and other violations of the Vagrancy Acts (e.g. sleeping out-of-doors), and common assault (4,582).[28]

The decade leading up to the First World War represented a high-water mark of police activity in both the streets and the courtroom. After remaining relatively steady across the 1880s, both began to rise rapidly beginning in 1895, for reasons described in more detail below. That year,

[23] Ibid., 62. [24] Metropolitan Police Act 1839, c. 47, 2 & 3 Vict. s. 62.
[25] Henry Turner Waddy, *The Police Court and Its Work* (London: Butterworth, 1925), 185.
[26] Metropolitan Police Act 1839, c. 47, 2 & 3 Vict. s. 62.
[27] Inwood, "Policing London's Morals," 41. [28] *RCPM 1905*, 63, 59, 58.

the police effected 85,763 apprehensions, and secured 58,222 convictions from magistrates.[29] By 1905, the metropolitan population had increased by only 15 percent (from 6.1 million to 7.08 million), while apprehensions had shot up to 127,317 and summary convictions to 103,362. The primary driver was a rise in the number of arrests and convictions for MPA violations and for drunkenness and drunk and disorderly behavior.[30] At first glance, these figures convey the impression that the police were operating as an interventionist force in the metropolis, and that they spent the majority of their time clearing the streets of inebriates and beggars, preventing reckless vehicle operation, breaking up public altercations, pursuing thieves, and addressing public safety issues. This picture of a vigilant constabulary that operated largely on commendable initiative to preserve public order, protect property and persons, and mind the common weal was reinforced by *RCPM*, the most important official document by which Metropolitan Police administrators communicated police activity to the Home Office and Parliament every year. These annual tabulations highlighted how frequently constables had dealt with unmuzzled, ferocious, or wandering dogs under the Rabies Orders 1895 and 1897 (38,191 in 1905), how many missing persons they had located and restored to friends and family (13,814), the value of stolen property that they had recovered (£52,915), and the number of "doors or windows found open or insecurely fastened" (26,618) – this last offering an undesirable enticement to would-be pilferers.

These statistics, illuminating as they are on police activity in the streets, reveal almost nothing about how constables spent their time in court. Although their days and nights were indeed occupied collaring drunkards, accosting wayward canines and apprehending those caught begging in public, in the courtroom, such issues were dealt with in the briefest manner possible. The impression given by the close correlation between arrests and convictions was also misleading. The high rate of conviction was only partly the result of police effort. The records of the Clerkenwell Police Court in the decade prior to the First World War reveal two other crucial patterns that are nowhere to be found in either the *RCPM* or the

[29] *RCPM 1895*, 50.

[30] In 1895, London constables made 9,374 arrests for the former and 39,427 for the latter, securing 5,040 and 29,808 convictions, respectively. *RCPM 1895*, 41–42. By 1905, those numbers stood at 16,964 and 59,184 for arrests and 13,323 and 53,905 for convictions (*RCPM 1905*, 61–62).

Judicial Statistics for those years. The first is the frequency with which local residents voluntarily sought the intervention of police to bring charges against one another for assault, much as they sought the intervention of the courts, *sans* police, through summonses. The second is how commonly those arrested by the police on various charges besides assault pled guilty, foregoing the need for anything more than a cursory courtroom appearance by the arresting constable. Although constables' efforts shaped the courtroom's treatment of offenders, these practices did as well, and in ways that threw the distinction between police activity and courtroom dynamics, and the moral character and consequences of criminal prosecutions, into sharp relief. The rising number of criminal prosecutions prompted significant changes in both how constables approached prosecutions in the Clerkenwell courtroom and how defendants responded to charges. These changes were largely invisible in local newspaper accounts as well, which conveyed a very different image of crime and its adjudication. This distance between practice and portrayal was similarly present in the conduct of summonses. But the focus of newspapers on police charges made the gap between courtroom dynamics and their depictions even more significant, since the inaccurate image was replicated far more frequently and the content, given the popular concern with crime, was more compelling to a reading audience.

Although the choice of Clerkenwell is dictated largely by the availability of detailed court records there, it represents a useful microcosm for any examination of police activity vis-à-vis crime and the courtroom in this period. Sitting astride the boundary area between the sprawling and largely working-class East End and the wealthier neighborhoods of central London and the West End, the district covered by the court encompassed a broad social cross-section of metropolitan residents. This diversity was not, however, reflected in the defendants against police charges. The overwhelming majority of those who appeared in the Clerkenwell court to face charges were male and from the working class.[31] Although they could hardly match the

[31] In a sample of 3,341 cases across May, July, September, and October 1910, among male defendants (2,534) 2,392 were drawn from various types of laboring or artisanal trades, while 273 were from the lower-middle-class of shopkeepers, clerks, and a smattering of lesser white-collar employments (e.g. journalists, commission agents,

many obstacles that working-class men faced when confronted by the apparatus of criminal justice, the circumstances encountered by police themselves in the courtroom and the community remained highly contested across this period. The records of the Clerkenwell court reveal both the rising authority of constables and the significant limitations on that authority in courtroom encounters. They also undercut the claims made by Met and Home Office administrators that police activity had been largely responsible for the decline of assault in working-class communities.[32] In Clerkenwell, the rise in MPA charges in the decades preceding the First World War does suggest that the policing of working-class communities was becoming more intrusive and coercive. The dynamics of assault prosecutions, on the other hand, suggest increasing integration between policing, courts, and the community, rather than merely a top-down process. It was, in large part, a voluntary engagement with policing that drove the prosecution of assault forwards, and this impetus was built on the foundation of voluntary engagement with local courtrooms. There can be little doubt, after decades of increasing familiarity, that local residents were aware of the process by which summonses and charges were followed invariably by adjudications, and that the latter was a far cry from a certain conviction. For the local populace, law was

butlers, opticians, photographers). In the same period, 778 women were brought up on charges. Their class status is harder to determine, since the single largest category (312) was simply "married." Of those occupations that were listed, however, the majority were laborers of one sort or another. Charwomen (97) were the most common, but the range of employments was diverse and included machinists, florists, milliners, shopkeepers, and prostitutes. Registers of Charges, Clerkenwell PC, 1910. See Gatrell, "Crime, Authority, and the Policeman-State," 282–83; Davis, "Prosecutions and their Context," 401–2.

32 The decline in assault apprehensions and subsequent convictions is discussed in more detail below. In 1890, with the London population at 5.8 million, the Metropolitan Police made 7,338 apprehensions for common and indecent assault and 2,882 for assault on police, securing 4,511 (61%) and 2,843 (98%) summary convictions subsequently (*RCPM 1890* (PP 1890–91, C. 6472), 28). By 1900, the population stood at 6.6m, while the number of apprehensions for common assaults had dropped to 6,303 (+268 aggravated) and those on constables had risen slightly to 3,022 (*RCPM 1900*, 56). The conviction rate in the former had also dropped slightly to 55% (3,515) in the former, while remaining very high in the latter (2,807, 93%). By 1910, with a metropolitan population of 7.25 million, apprehensions for common assault had dropped to a mere 3,336 (*RCPM 1910*, 42). Assaults on constables, while not witnessing the same dramatic decline, had also decreased to 2,584.

not the constable, the charge, the summons, the magistrate, or the courtroom in isolation, but all of them in conjunction, and each with its own patterns of use and consequence.

Like so much other court business, many assault charges arrived before the bench as a result of private initiative rather than police intervention. The catalyst for a typical assault charge in the Clerkenwell court followed much the same pattern as assault summonses did – a verbal confrontation that escalated into violence. The primary determinant between whether an assault was tried as a charge or a summons was not police initiative. More often, it was the decision of the alleged victim to involve either the courtroom alone (i.e. through a summons) or to seek out a constable and have the defendant arrested on the spot (i.e. a charge). Less frequently, constables leveled assault charges after being drawn to the scene of conflict by a crowd, by the sounds of violence, or by cries for help. Rarer still was constables' own witnessing of interpersonal violence in action.[33] In 1905, Islington constables were three times more likely to become involved at the direct request of an alleged victim than they were to do so after witnessing violence or an attendant disturbance.[34] The records of the Clerkenwell Court, at least, do not support the claim made by previous historians that the overwhelming majority of assault charges heard by London magistrates in this period were initiated by the police.[35] In particular, this was very rarely the case when women brought assault charges against men. Most typically, the putative prosecutor or a witness to the attack sought police aid after the fact. This involved fetching the constable from his beat, which was well-known in the community, or visiting the police station to make a complaint. Men, in contrast, were more reluctant to seek out a constable, with two exceptions. Publicans were not hesitant to call

33 In the Clerkenwell 1905 charges, which include several hundred assault cases, there are only a few instances (typically 2–3 each month) where the constable was an eyewitness to the alleged attack.

34 Of the approximately 133 assault charges (excluding those against constables) heard in the Clerkenwell from July to December, where the catalyst was clear, only 30 were the result of constables' initiative following their observation of a disturbance (e.g. cries for help, sounds of conflict, breaking glass, or a crowd gathered to watch a fight). In only a handful of these 30 cases did constables observe a violent act in person. Minutes of Charges, Clerkenwell PC, July–December 1905.

35 Davis, "London Police Courts," 320.

a policeman to deal with customers who became violent and unruly, and landlords were willing to do the same when they were assaulted by their tenants.[36] In 1910 Clerkenwell, the charges of assault against men outnumbered those against women by a ratio of three to one, though whether this was because men were more commonly involved in violent conflict, because those altercations were more likely to attract police attention, or because constables were more willing to level assault charges at men cannot be determined from the records.[37] Local residents could employ assault charges with some degree of flexibility, much as they did summonses in other circumstances.[38] In at least thirty assault trials in the second half of 1905, Clerkenwell magistrates discharged prisoners because the prosecutor failed to appear in court in order to substantiate the charge.[39] Those who had brought charges could also recant the accusation, refuse to press the case, or request a lesser punishment (e.g. that their assailant be bound over).

The voluntary engagement of constables by the community should not be equated with wholesale submission to the growing apparatus of criminal justice in London. As with summonses, the willingness of Islington residents to seek a constable's intervention did not necessarily indicate their acceptance of police authority as legitimate, nor did it imply a consensual view of what role the police and the courts should play in everyday affairs.[40] Residents, and working-class residents in particular, were not eager to have the police intrude in their affairs absent invitation. Integration did not imply full acceptance

[36] The greater willingness to seek constables in such instances might have reflected the differences between interclass and intraclass violent conflict, especially in the case of landlords.

[37] Registers of Charges, Clerkenwell PC, 1910.

[38] For the translation of social problems into legal ones by litigants in contemporary courtroom practice, see Barbara Yngvesson, *Getting Justice and Getting Even: Legal Consciousness among Working-Class Americans* (Chicago and London: University of Chicago Press, 1990), 37–63; Sally Engle Merry, *Virtuous Citizens, Disruptive Subjects: Order and Complaint in a New England Court* (New York and London: Routledge, 1993), 6–8.

[39] The brevity of the record (generally just an indication of discharge, the name of the defendant, and the gender of the prosecutor) makes it unclear how the charge came about initially. Minutes of Charges, Clerkenwell PC, July–December 1905.

[40] Jennifer Davis, "Prosecutions and Their Context: The Use of Criminal Law in Later Nineteenth-Century London," in Douglas Hay and Francis Snyder, eds., *Policing and Prosecution in Britain 1750–1850* (Oxford: Clarendon, 1989), 419.

from the other direction either, and the police maintained their own distinct identity and culture, "always among the people, but not of the people."[41] Accounts of life in working-class communities also indicate that there were innumerable acts of violence of which the police were unaware and in which their involvement was not desired by the participants.[42] One clear sign of ongoing tension between communities and constables was the frequency of assaults on the latter. In the decades preceding the First World War, these continued at what was, to police administrators, an alarming rate.[43]

When constables did level assault charges, it was most commonly because one party or another had sought them out, rather than the result of police initiative alone. As was the case with assault summonses, this voluntary engagement with legal authority was more frequent among women than it was among men. And for good reason, since such charges were deeply entangled with marital conflict as it played out in local courtrooms. Assault charges against an abusive husband could serve as a justification for a judicial separation, and magistrates could incorporate the latter process into the conduct of an assault trial at the prosecutor's request.[44]

Courtroom records emphasize how much, by the end of the century, the local constable was integral to social landscape of conflict in the community. As court testimony in assault cases reveals, he was often the subject of personal appeals for aid that were, if not ubiquitous, then at least common.[45] The familiarity of local residents with the constables' authority and its uses was further apparent in the detailed legal language with which those seeking police intervention could frame their demands and by the broad social cohort that conveyed them.[46] Police aid could even be requested, on occasion, by those who

41 Gamon, *London Police Court*, 15.

42 Robert D. Storch, "The Policeman as Domestic Missionary: Urban Discipline and Popular Culture in Northern England, 1850–1880," *Journal of Social History* 9, no. 4 (1976), 494.

43 In 1900, there were 2,807 summary convictions for assaults on constables, at a time when there were 13,268 working in the metropolis. *RCPM 1900*, 79, 28.

44 For example, in lieu of a fine or imprisonment, magistrates could bind over the defendant to keep the peace, pending the granting of a judicial separation. Minutes of Charges, Clerkenwell PC, August 21, 1905.

45 Gatrell, "Decline of Theft and Violence," 276.

46 David Phillips, *Crime and Authority in Victorian England: The Black Country 1835–1860* (London: Rowman and Littlefield, 1977), 121–22.

were more accustomed to being the on the sharp end of their intervention. Constable Horace Resh was no doubt startled when, on an early morning in November 1905, he witnessed Samuel O'Neill climbing out of a flat window on Little Sutton Street. The occupant of the flat, a "known prostitute" named Jane Bancroft, was quick to clarify her expectations of the constable. She demanded that O'Neill be jailed for assaulting her and for, in her words, "living on my immoral earnings."[47] She was one of two women who leveled this specific charge that day in court.

Although private initiative was, in most cases, what prompted constables' involvement in assault charges in 1905 Islington, the decision by the prosecutor to level a charge as opposed to seeking a summons decreased their control over the case in court. Technically, the alleged victim was the prosecutor in each case. This practice – which was diminishing in higher courts, but remained prevalent in summary assault charges – sustained the principle of private prosecution that had long pervaded English justice.[48] While the prosecutor's presence was necessary, the value of their testimony and their autonomy in the courtroom decreased once the police were involved. The magistrate Thomas Saunders had asserted that police testimony was so essential that more than half of all charges "would fall through and be utterly without proof," without it.[49] With a constable present, the relative authority of parties' subsequent testimony in the courtroom shifted in the police's favor. As opposed to a summons, which pitted the statements of a complainant and their witnesses against the defendant and theirs, charge cases brought in a third party (i.e. the constable) whose evidence was, quite literally, the final word. In summons cases, the complainant gave their account, which was then supported by whatever witnesses, if any, they had brought. The defendant then rebutted their testimony, also with witness corroboration when possible.

47 Minutes of Charges, Clerkenwell PC, November 6, 1905.

48 For the diminishing role of private prosecutors in larceny cases, see Bruce Smith, "The Myth of Private Prosecution in England, 1750–1850," in Markus D. Dubber and Lindsay Farmer, eds., *Modern Histories of Crime and Punishment* (Stanford: Stanford University Press, 2007), 151–53.

49 A Magistrate (Thomas William Saunders), *Metropolitan Police Court Jottings* (London: Horace Cox, 1882), 51.

In charges, by contrast, the role of witness testimony was considerably smaller. In assault charges where the victim had sought a constable, witness testimony for the prosecution was common, but limited. For the defense, in many of the most common types of charges (e.g. MPA, assault, larceny), witness support was negligible. This dynamic served to reinforce the authority of constables' courtroom testimony; they were often the only people to give evidence besides the prosecutor (in the case of solicited charges) and the defendant themselves. The order in which testimony was given, with the constables almost invariably last, emphasized their authority further. This, together with the relatively dry and unadorned character of their contributions, gave their words the air of a summation, rather than being one of several accounts in competition. Speaking after the principals and witnesses, they testified with full knowledge of both the prosecutor's case and the defendant's. They could specifically confirm or contradict any of the testimony given prior to their own.[50] It was also not infrequent, particularly in cases involving violence, for more than one constable to give evidence, adding further weight to accounts that invariably confirmed one another. Beyond this practical advantage offered by the timing of testimony, constables brought both experience and expertise. By the early twentieth century, London policemen were being provided with special training in how to give evidence in court.[51] In addition, newcomers to the force were sent to the police courts to observe and learn from the proceedings. Constables were trained to be as concise as possible without excluding any information material to their cases, though not all hewed to this instruction.[52] Their testimony could range from a brief statement to a detailed recounting of events, though

[50] Hugh Gamon, in his 1905 chronicle of the London police courts, wrote that one of the key rights of defendants, one which they rarely exercised and of which they were typically unaware, was to demand that the witnesses for the prosecution be excluded from the court until their evidence was required. Gamon, *The London Police Court*, 91. It is unlikely, however, this would have applied to the constables themselves, given the special status they occupied in the courts.

[51] Waddy, *The Police Court*, 53.

[52] Pendleton Howard, "The Rise of Summary Jurisdiction in English Criminal Law Administration," *California Law Review* 19, no. 5 (1931), 489. According to the magistrate Henry Turner Waddy, some were "addicted to grandiloquence." Waddy, *Police Court*, 53.

the former was not necessarily less effective than the latter. Constables also shaped the character and outcome of a case by recounting how the defendant had behaved towards the constable himself, both prior to and after their apprehension. The officer's testimony could be either damning or exonerating, and it was theirs alone to offer or withhold.[53]

Given the weight and precision of their testimony, a constables' presence could not help but dramatically change the dynamics of courtroom interactions even when, as was commonly the case in summonses and sometimes the case in charges, they had not personally witnessed the alleged crime. Assault summonses were typically a contest between complainant and defendant on relatively equal footing in the courtroom, with both sides offering competing narratives and calling witnesses that would often give contrasting accounts. In charges, by contrast, the defendant faced a professional policeman whose testimony benefitted from his official status, his specialized training in courtroom procedure, and his experience of hundreds, if not thousands, of other cases beforehand. The advantages these brought were apparent in the stark contrast between the brevity and exactitude of police testimony in charges and the attenuated narrative more common in private summonses. As the sheer numbers of charges and summonses began to rise in the decades preceding the First World War, the inability of private applicants to state their complaints concisely could be a source of exasperation for London magistrates.[54] Constables, by comparison, tended to confine their testimony to the minimum necessary detail. In the busy, crowded courtrooms of prewar London, prolixity and vagueness were hardly advantages. Such details as constables did offer were consistently effective in justifying the defendant's arrest and neatly framing the substance of their offense. In this, they also had the advantage of their own written records, as it was common practice to

[53] When George Rose charged Mary Fisher with assault on July 10, 1905, the constable who had taken the latter into custody testified to the defendant's admission of guilt at the time. "She said he shouldn't have insulted me," he told the court, concluding the testimony, "he has got what he deserved." Minutes of Charges, Clerkenwell PC, July 10, 1905.

[54] One solution to this, Hugh Gamon wrote, was to have a court officer introduce the morning's applicants for summons with a translation of their complaint into a specific offense (e.g. "summons for assault, your worship"), and a brief summary of the relevant details. Gamon, *London Police Court*, 77.

take brief notes of the particulars in incidents and arrests.[55] Two observations that frequently appeared in constables' testimony were the sobriety level of those involved and the use of obscene language on the part of defendants. A prosecutor's reported inebriation undermined their case, while a defendant's could strengthen it. Obscene language, like public drunkenness, was itself a chargeable offense, but was more frequently employed in constables' testimony as either a justification for arrest in conjunction with the defendant's disorderly conduct or as further indication of the latter's defiance of constables' orders to desist. Both alcohol and the oft-mentioned "bad language," no matter what the charge at hand was, also cast the prosecutor or defendant in a negative light morally. Experience, training, precise and concise testimony, written records, and undermining a defendant's moral status through assertions of insobriety or defiance all worked to lend constables a distinct advantage in local courtrooms. For all their effectiveness as witnesses, constables' charges could still be sharply contested. Although declining in comparison to convictions across the decades preceding the First World War, discharges and dismissals remained a common outcome in local police courts.[56] Even if a defense against a charge, supported by witnesses, did not abrogate a conviction, it could still mitigate the punishment, especially when the offense was not a serious one to begin with.

The cultural dimensions of courtrooms could also constrain police authority. The harsh glare of public scrutiny presented one such limitation, further motivating constables to ensure that their courtroom testimony was concise, accurate, and effective. Since police-court reporters tended to focus their attention on charges (typically heard in the morning) rather than on summonses (typically heard in the afternoon), the relationship of the courtroom to the press could play an even more crucial role in the former than it did in the latter. Cases that came into the spotlight through the ubiquitous courtroom columns in local and national newspapers raised the stakes for all involved. The longest Clerkenwell Police Court case heard in 1905 was the result of

[55] Ibid., p. 8.

[56] In 1910, London magistrates convicted in 83,362 and discharged in 26,657. The most common offenses ending in discharges that year were MPA violations (2,121 out of 9,936 apprehensions) and common assault (1,290 out of 3,336). *RCPM 1910*, 44, 42. These are discussed in more detail below.

a spirited defense against a charge that, in the vast majority of circumstances, would have been a nearly automatic conviction.[57] When PC Alex Clark brought Lilian Gray up on charges of prostitution, the resulting contest took the better part of a month to resolve, encompassed five separate courtroom sessions, and involved nearly two-dozen witnesses in a fierce exchange of examination, cross-examination, and reexamination by both the defendant's solicitors (a relative rarity in summary cases) and the police prosecutor. The public scandal played out simultaneously in the Clerkenwell Police Court and in the pages of *The Times*. And it aptly demonstrated the immense pressure that the public forum of the courtroom could place on police constables, the keen attention with which reporters and the readership alike seized onto any hint of scandal, and the powerful effect that such public scrutiny could exert. It was not only the defendant's reputation that was at stake in the Gray case, but that of the arresting officer, the colleagues who corroborated his account, his superiors on the force, and, by extension, the Metropolitan Police as a whole.

The Gray case first appeared in the Clerkenwell court on August 24, and its beginning was simple enough. PC Clark testified that, on the previous evening, having seen the defendant accost a man in Woburn Place, he had delivered a caution (a common practice in such cases). Witnessing Gray repeat the act in Bernard Street an hour later, he apprehended her. "She is a prostitute," he told the court.[58] "Known her as such for 6 months." Gray, in response, denied both incidents and refuted Clark's accusation. The case was adjourned until September for the calling of witnesses. In the complex interplay of witness testimony and press coverage that followed, the constraints on constables in the courtroom and the high price to be paid for error in cases that had drawn public attention were thrown into stark relief. Gray's attorneys subjected PC Clark to a probing cross-examination on September 7. They interrogated every aspect of his account, from the timing of when he encountered Gray and how long he had observed her to the circumstances of her arrest and the constable's actions subsequently.

[57] In 1905, of the 4,970 prostitutes apprehended in London, a mere 252 were discharged. Of the remainder, 3,772 were convicted of "Annoying Male Passengers for the Purpose of Prostitution and as Disorderly Prostitutes," and the balance were convicted on other charges (e.g. disorderly conduct). *RCPM 1905*, 83.

[58] Minutes of Charges, Clerkenwell PC, August 24, 1905.

Under fierce questioning, the constable recounted how Gray had become hysterical upon her arrest, shouting for help from bystanders on the way to the police station.[59]

Most damning of all was what appeared to be witness-tampering by Clark the day after Gray's arrest. Newspaper reports from the initial police evidence given in the first hearing of the case on September 1 had thrown doubt on the constable's version of events. There, the possibility that the constable might be perjuring himself had been raised (it is not clear by whom).[60] Following the publication of these initial reports, according to the subsequent testimony of two key witnesses, Clark had attempted to shore up his case, now apparently in jeopardy, by badgering one eyewitness to the initial arrest. The particular point of contention was whether or not, as the constable had testified, Gray had accosted a second man in the area around Marchmont Street and Bernard Street, thus precipitating her arrest. This detail quickly became a secondary consideration. Gray's counsel focused relentlessly on Clark's alleged attempts, prompted by fear of a potential perjury charge, to intimidate a key witness. In cross-examination, the constable denied these allegations emphatically.

The Gray case, due to the controversy swirling around it, had attracted journalistic scrutiny from the very beginning, and in the witness testimony delivered on September 13, the cumulative effect of this media attention, much on the mind of the principals themselves, became dramatically clear. William Gaston, a crane driver at the Bernard Street Underground Station, gave credence to the most damning accusations made against the arresting constable. Gaston testified that, in the week following Gray's arrest, Clark had indeed encouraged him to perjure himself in court in order to protect the constable from a similar charge. "He asked me if I had seen him lock a woman up on the Wednesday night, I said yes," Gaston told the court.[61] "He asked if I would swear false that there was another man

[59] Minutes of Charges, Clerkenwell PC, September 7, 1905.

[60] The first hearing was referred to by the magistrate, James Bros, in his final summation of the case prior to his adjudication (*The Times*, September 23, 1905, 4). However, as an initial inquiry, the details were not recorded in the police-court minutes. All that appears there is a notation of the further adjournment until September 7. Minutes of Charges, Clerkenwell PC, September 1, 1905.

[61] Minutes of Charges, Clerkenwell PC, September 13, 1905.

coming up Marchmont St. I said no, I have sisters of my own. He said what the b[loody] hell did you want to see it for, haven't you read the papers. I said yes. He said can't you see they are having me for perjury?" As he was leaving, Gaston testified, Clark had told him to deny that they had met, a statement that added willful deception to the constable's alleged perjury and efforts at witness-tampering. In any case, the constable's intimidation had backfired. Instead, when Gray herself came by the tube station to make inquiries a few days after her arrest, Gaston told her he would come and testify *against* Clark in court.[62]

The combination of Clark's action, Gaston's testimony, and the wide press coverage they received definitively altered the dynamics of the Gray case. In this compelling and controversial incident that concerned, as *The Times* dubbed their articles on the trial, "The Police and the Public," it was hardly just the guilt or innocence of the defendant that was at stake. Rather, as the case developed in both the court and the press, the focus shifted to constables' authority and their moral fitness to wield that authority wisely on the one hand, and to the influence of newspapers on both the behavior of constables and the public's assessment of them on the other. As the adjudicating magistrate, James Bros, asserted in his closing statements, the relevant evidence all indicated Gray's guilt. She was a "night-walker," and PC Clark had been justified in arresting her. None of this, the magistrate concluded, had been contradicted by the arguments and witnesses for the defense.[63] Clark had acted in a commendable and appropriate manner in making the arrest. The newspaper coverage and the constable's impetuous response to it, however, had forced the magistrate to reckon with the wider repercussions of a case that was now being closely observed by press and public. Bros decried the "stigmas" and "mischief" prompted by press reports, railing against their pernicious influence on the behavior of the witnesses and the principals.[64] The "unfortunate publication" of the initial details of the case in early September had prompted Clark's unwise decision to

[62] After the preliminary hearing in the police court on September 1, in which the evidence was surveyed, Gaston went to the defendant's solicitors and made a statement. This volunteering of evidence had culminated in Gaston's appearance on the witness stand to give some damning evidence against Clark on September 13.

[63] *The Times*, September 23, 1905, 4. [64] Ibid.

approach Gaston, and had, in turn, prejudiced Gaston against the constable. The witness was predisposed against the practice of apprehending women in the streets, hence his reference to his own sisters when the constable encouraged him to give false testimony.[65] In the magistrate's view, the entire affair was apt proof of how important it was that the press withhold from commenting on cases in process. Following this tirade, few readers would have taken, at face value, Bros's insistence that his decision to give Gray "the benefit of the doubt" was based merely on "some contradictory evidence." The defendant, for her part, was clearly unsatisfied as well. Despite being discharged, Gray left the courtroom "declaiming that four of her witnesses had not been heard."[66]

Who was Lilian Gray? Was she, as Bros had termed her, a "night-walker," a known prostitute who had been arrested only after long, careful observation and repeated warnings to desist? Or was she, as the defense portrayed her, a "respectable" but "delicate" woman, unjustly persecuted by an unscrupulous constable?[67] Whatever one chose to believe, the implications of her behavior, the morality of the constable who arrested her, and the justice of her treatment subsequently were something decided in both the courtroom and the public reports of what had transpired there. In the Gray case, the press had played a crucial role, not just as the arbiters of justice and the limits of police authority, but as a forum where, unlike the courtroom itself, allegations could be made unconstrained by oaths or other formal protocols. Newspaper reports had prompted Clark to badger his key witness, catalyzing a series of responses that, in the end, had undercut the prosecution's case. The scandal generated by these reports and Gray's assertive defense had leant the trial a notoriety that all involved, the adjudicating magistrate included, had been forced to take into account in their courtroom speech and action. The attention

[65] It is worth noting that Bros did not mention, in this instance, the even more definitive statement made by Gaston's co-worker. William Fielding, who testified immediately after Gaston and corroborated his account in almost every detail. He described how Clark had approached him at his place of work in an "excited" fashion, how he had overheard the word "perjury," and how the constable had shouted at the crane-driver "mind I haven't seen you" to cover his tracks. Minutes of Charges, Clerkenwell PC, September 13, 1905.

[66] *The Times*, September 23, 1905, 4.

[67] Minutes of Charges, Clerkenwell PC, September 13, 1905.

paid to police-court newspaper columns by constables, witnesses, magistrates, and defendants was a testament to the potent, reciprocal relationship between courtrooms and the press. The Gray trial and Bros's commentary demonstrated the persistence of this connection, which had been a key concern of police-court magistrates since the John and Henry Fielding had begun making accommodations for press representatives back in the eighteenth century.

Constables like PC Clark were easy targets for public criticism, and never more so than in the courtroom itself. More than half a century after the establishment of the Metropolitan Police, suspicion of constables' honesty was widespread, both within the courtrooms and beyond it. Hugh Gamon, the long-time court missionary and chronicler, was especially acerbic, asserting that "the motives for lying on the part of a P.C. may be exceedingly strong, and there is no corresponding curb."[68] The power of the courtroom oath, which could sometimes cow other witnesses, had been thoroughly diluted by endless repetition. "For him," the missionary insisted, "it is meaningless, just part of the formalities which must be observed." This poor reputation was a taint that followed policemen from the street to the courtroom, since the moral authority of a constables' charge and a magistrates' judgment were also influenced by the moral stature of their conveyers. Metropolitan constables were drawn largely from outside the capital, and typically from the ranks of laborers and tradesmen.[69] Although they were, officially, supposed to uphold very high standards of public discipline, and were forbidden to consume alcohol or gamble in public, their predilection for welcoming a free drink was widely known, and of perennial concern to those who commanded the force.[70] Constables' reputations for excessive familiarity with separated women and with prostitutes who wished to ply their trade without police interference further tarnished their standing.[71] To defendants, magistrates, and courtroom reporters, constables could hardly rely on an unassailable moral authority to

[68] Gamon, *London Police Court*, 129.
[69] Ibid., 11; Taylor, *Crime, Policing and Punishment*, 90–91.
[70] Taylor, *Crime, Policing and Punishment*, 95.
[71] Ibid. In the words of Hugh Gamon, a force composed primarily of unmarried men was "prone to the vice of 'single men in the barracks.'" Gamon, *London Police Court*, 28.

give weight to their courtroom testimony. As the Gray trial demonstrated, the stakes for them testifying in court could be extremely high, and the consequences of misbehavior, should they come to the attention of an astute defendant or their counsel, could be dramatic. By the turn of the century, the Metropolitan Police had to number themselves among the observed as well as the observers. The proliferation of court coverage, rising literacy rates, and the growing popularity of newspaper readership among the class most likely to face charges in a local courtroom all ensured this.

Even more so than constables, the magistrates were under constant observation by the press. Ever since the advent of independent police-court columns in the early nineteenth century, reporters had been quick to lampoon justices who were too vitriolic or overbearing. By the end of the nineteenth century, with the police courts busier and receiving more press coverage than ever before, the management of the courts' public image had become an even more crucial aspect of the magistrates' work. In the 1830s, magistrates could discuss "the public" as a relative abstraction. They were a cohort that, when compared to their Home Office superiors, magistrates could claim to serve, but need not fear. With the expansion of the franchise in the last quarter of the century, the rise of literacy, and with the latter, newspaper readership, this was no longer the case.[72] The public, manifested concretely in courtroom reporters, was a powerful presence in the courtroom. The keen eye of the "penny-a-liners" for dramatic copy was supported by their editors, who were also quick to criticize magistrates' conduct.[73] Adding further complications were the diversity of press representation, the capacity of reporters to sell their stories to multiple papers, and the tendency of different newspapers to borrow stories from one another.[74] The heightened press attention

[72] The rise of popular literacy, which was nearly universal by the eve of the First World War, has been charted in a number of studies. See Robert K. Webb, "Working-Class Readers in Early Victorian England," *The English Historical Review* 65, no. 256 (Jul. 1950), 333–51; Lawrence Stone, "Literacy and Education in England 1640–1900," *Past & Present* 42 (Feb. 1969), 69–139; David F. Mitch, *The Rise of Popular Literacy in Victorian England: the Influence of Private Choice and Public Policy* (Philadelphia: University of Pennsylvania Press, 1992); David Vincent, *Literacy and Popular Culture: England 1750–1914* (Cambridge: Cambridge University Press, 1993).

[73] Marjorie Rose, *Justice and Journalism* (London: Barry Rose, 1974), 41.

[74] Chief among the organizations of news dissemination were the Press Association (est. 1868), the Central News Agency (est. 1870), and the Exchange Telegraph Company (est. 1872). Ibid., 54.

brought readers into the courtroom vicariously, allowing them to make their own assessments of a defendant's guilt or innocence, whether or not they deserved to be treated as they were – the law notwithstanding – and what, in the end, constituted "justice." In his investigation of the London police courts, Hugh Gamon was unequivocal about the potent influence of the reporter and his sway over the public. "He is the public spy, the public itself articulate. It is of him that the magistrate has to be afraid."[75]

In the harsh light of the public eye, magistrates' reconciliation of working-class hostility towards the police who intervened in their affairs without invitation (i.e. constables not "fetched" for private summonses or charges) with their desire to avoid castigation in the press and for their courtrooms to maintain the appearance (if not necessarily the reality) as a forum for "poor man's justice" was no easy task. Balancing enforcement with public image became more problematic as the century waned, with the rapid multiplication of statutes and the expansion of the police in personnel and authority. Both trends brought growing numbers of defendants to court on relatively minor infractions such as Metropolitan Police Act violations. This, coupled with the continued attention paid by newspapers to police court events, heightened the pressure on magistrates to address crime in a way that satisfied the law and their own sense of order without running afoul of public opinion. One common tactic of magistrates was the public expression of sympathy for offenders, even as they were trying ever-greater numbers of cases and convicting ever-higher percentages of defendants. As Douglas Hay has pointed out, mercy, selectively deployed, could be a very effective tool for securing social order and promoting the impression of a just legal system.[76] This option was far less likely to provoke defiance than the hectoring tone adopted by magistrates such as Laing – and so effectively satirized by Dickens – earlier in the century. Although defendants in the police courts were not, in most instances, facing the looming shadow of the gallows, the potential for several month's

[75] Gamon, *London Police Court*, 111.

[76] Douglas Hay, "Property, Authority, and the Criminal Law," in Douglas Hay *et al.*, eds., *Albion's Fatal Tree: Crime and Society in Eighteenth-Century England* (London: Pantheon, 1975), 40–41. This is also discussed in Jennifer Davis, "A Poor Man's System of Justice: The London Police Courts in the Second Half of the Nineteenth Century," *The Historical Journal* 27, no. 2 (1984), 314–15.

imprisonment with hard labor was intimidating nonetheless. One can only imagine the relief of first-time offenders who were released with a lesser term of imprisonment, a small fine, or a recognizance instead. Magistrates' willingness to press constables and challenge their assertions was yet another way to demonstrate at least the appearance of sympathy. Though the degree to which they substantively intervened for defendants in police prosecutions was a matter of some debate among observers.[77] Magistrates, in theory, were supposed to guard the welfare of defendants facing charges and ensure that their lack of knowledge about the legal system did not unfairly prejudice their defense. Hugh Gamon observed that the accused in charge cases made assertions and commented on the evidence against them, but rarely cross-examined the witnesses for the prosecution, and were generally unaware that such witnesses could be excluded from the courtroom until their evidence was required.[78] George Ingersoll, writing for the *Yale Law Journal* in 1892, described how magistrates' compensated for this with their close scrutiny of police testimony.[79]

Clerkenwell Police Court minutes support their observations, to a degree. One can find, accompanying a probing question to the prosecution's witnesses, the clerk's notation of "by mage" (i.e. by the magistrates). But these were not frequent, and magistrates' intervention in charge cases was highly selective. Even serious charges where those convicted faced months of hard labor were often concluded after only a few brief lines of evidence from the arresting constable, especially if defendants had been caught in the act of committing a property offense. Police-court registers also suggest that Ingersoll's generous assessment of the time devoted to even the most routine charge case and the extent to which magistrates questioned constables might have been exaggerated.[80] By the first decade of the twentieth century, in the morning hours devoted to hearing charges, the Clerkenwell court typically processed around

[77] George P. Ingersoll, "The London Police Courts," *Yale Law Journal* 54, no. 2 (Oct. 1892–Jun. 1893), 56; Thomas Leaming, *A Philadelphia Lawyer in the London Courts*, 2nd ed. (New York: Henry Holt, 1912), 46–47; Pendleton, "Summary Justice," 490; Saunders, *Metropolitan Police Court Jottings*, 51.

[78] Gamon, *London Police Court*, 90. [79] Ingersoll, "Police Courts," 56.

[80] He asserted that even the most routine cases, which would have taken an American police court five minutes to resolve, occupied half an hour in the London courts. Ibid., 56.

two-dozen cases, which was about average for a London police court.[81] On a busy day, this could climb to three or even four dozen. It is also worth noting that Ingersoll penned his description in the early 1890s, when police constables apprehended, on average, less than 85,000 suspects a year.[82] By 1905, that number had risen to over 127,000, with no significant increase in judicial personnel to handle the excess.[83] It would not have been feasible, given such packed dockets, for magistrates in each and every single case to cross-examine the arresting constable and carefully coach the defendant on his or her rights in the courtroom.[84] The Clerkenwell court minutes, accordingly, reveal a wide variance in the duration of different charge cases. The majority were resolved after only the briefest of testimonies, while others took up considerably more time. The length of the case bore little correlation to the seriousness of the charge – longer cases typically resulted from solicitors' involvement and instances where the evidence was largely circumstantial.[85]

Whether in a short case or an extended one, by the end of the nineteenth century, public scrutiny of magistrates, constables, witnesses, prosecutors, and defendants was a natural accompaniment – though hardly a guaranteed one in every instance – to the courtroom experience of charges. Given such heightened levels of observation by press and public, the growing political importance of the working class, the expansion of the Metropolitan Police, and the array of statutes bringing greater numbers of petty offenders to court, one might expect that the discharge rate in police prosecutions would have risen. Court records reveal that the opposite was true. Even as the numbers of apprehensions and charges were swelling in relation to

[81] Bow Street, West London, and Thames PCs, as their registers reveal, all carried a roughly similar caseloads on a daily basis.

[82] In 1889, London constables apprehended 78,795 suspects and in 1890, 83,414. *RCPM 1890*, 37.

[83] In 1905, the number was 127,317. *RCPM 1905*, 41.

[84] A keen understanding of the courtroom on the part of defendants, far from aiding them, could be a distinct disadvantage, for the only way to acquire this knowledge would be from prior experience, and to demonstrate it was a sure sign of one's past transgressions. Gamon, *London Police Court*, 90.

[85] Charges of managing a brothel or of allowing one's place of business to be used for illegal betting were the most common of this former type. These involved considerable periods of observation, the defendants were often represented by a solicitor, and the fines upon conviction were considerable, all of which tended to prolong the deliberations.

the metropolitan population and the range of offenses was expanding considerably, the most startling statistical trend was the dramatic *decline* in the ratio of discharges to arrests. Whereas, in the 1860s, London magistrates had discharged nearly half of all those apprehended, by the decade preceding the First World War, they were discharging, on average, fewer than one in every five defendants.[86] How could the courts maintain any legitimacy for local communities, or magistrates make any claim that their venues were a "poor man's court of justice," in such circumstances? One answer is that summonses continued to rise in tandem with charges, and that local residents were using the courts and soliciting constables' intervention with greater frequency. As already discussed, magistrates' demeanor and willingness to challenge police constables was also important. A further key to reconciling rising charge convictions and the image of public justice is to take into account the types of charges that were being brought before the courts, the manner in which they appeared, and the character of punishment. Even though courtrooms were busier than they ever had been before, and police were arresting more and more suspects, the vast majority were being charged with very minor offenses that carried correspondingly light punishments. By the decade before the First World War, convictions for public drunkenness (e.g. drunk and disorderly, drunk and incapable, drunk and obscene language) and violations of the Metropolitan Police Acts were collectively constituting between 60 and 70 percent of the annual total. Although outright discharges were not common, in almost all of these cases, conviction brought only a fine. Imprisonment was rare, and it was generally inflicted only on those who were repeat offenders or who had attacked or abused constables in the course of their apprehension.[87] The harshest punishments were used in only a very small majority of cases; in 1910, magistrates

[86] *RCPM 1913*, 30.

[87] Overall, in 1910, of the 83,200 convictions handed down by London magistrates, the punishment was fines in 65,198 instances (78%). *RCPM 1910*, 56. This had been the trend across the late nineteenth century, but it accelerated as the war approached. In 1895, by comparison, 71% of all convictions had been for fines (*RCPM 1895* (PP 1897, C. 8352), 61).

inflicted imprisonments of over three months' duration in less than 1 per cent of all instances.[88]

Even as the arrests for minor violations were rising, the number of charges for certain serious offenses of violence and theft, when adjusted for the growth of the metropolitan population, was declining considerably across the last quarter of the nineteenth century and the first decade of the twentieth.[89] Arrests for minor offenses were going in the opposite direction. In 1869, constables made 9,538 arrests for drunkenness and another 10,853 for drunk and disorderly behavior in a London population that numbered roughly 3.8 million.[90] By 1899 the number of arrests had nearly trebled to 56,066 for drunkenness and drunkenness "with aggravations" in a population that had grown by roughly two-thirds to 6.4 million.[91] The trajectory of arrests for violations of the Metropolitan Police Acts rocketed upwards in an even more impressive arc. In 1869, they stood at a mere 1,030.[92] By 1913, they had increased to more than 12,000.[93] The picture of crimes' alleged decline in London, however, was more complex than first appeared. It was defined and contested in public discourse between policymakers, police administrators, and magistrates, regardless of what the statistics collected by different parties might say. The steady drop of assault charges across England and Wales, for example, was much ballyhooed by the government administrators who oversaw policing.[94] The statistical records of the

88 675 in total.

89 In 1869, the Metropolitan Police apprehended 7,110 suspects on charges of common assault, of whom 3,155 were discharged by magistrates (*RCPM 1869*, 18). By 1896, those numbers were 6,269 and 3,139, respectively (*RCPM 1895*, 38). The percentage of discharges to apprehensions had risen slightly, but the numbers of those arrested, when adjusted for a population that had grown nearly threefold, had declined dramatically. This trend was even more evident by 1913, when police apprehended a mere 3,481 suspects for common assault (*RCPM 1913*, 42).

90 *RCPM 1869*, 18. The 1871 census recorded a London population of 3,840,595.

91 *RCPM 1913*, 38. In 1899, the population of London was 6,620,434 (based on the Registrar-General's returns, *RCPM 1900*, 77). In 1913, constables made 70,122 arrests in a population numbering just under 7.5 million, which translated into 9.4 arrests per 1,000 residents (*RCPM 1913*, 38).

92 *RCPM 1869*, 18. 93 That year, 12,458 arrests were made. *RCPM 1913*, 44.

94 Sir John Macdonell, one of the premier law reformers and legal experts of the time, was especially sanguine. In his introduction to the annual *Criminal Statistics* from 1899, he declared, "on the whole, the above facts seem to indicate a great change in manners: the substitution of words without blows for blows with or without words; an approximation

police offered one picture, but the London court records offered quite another. Although assault charges, both in the capital and across Britain, were decreasing rapidly over time, assault cases still remained one of the most common types brought before the London magistrates.[95] This was not due to aggressive policing, but rather to the frequency with which private individuals summonsed one another for the offense. In the busy Thames Police Court, assault summonses continued to represent roughly one out of every five summonses overall in the final decades of the nineteenth century.[96] By 1900, the courts were hearing the roughly same number of assault summonses (10,025) as they had in 1880, while charges had decreased by half (3,515).[97] Court records also reveal how often such charges were the result of a private individual fetching a police constable, rather than a consequence of a constable's intrusion, absent invitation, into a conflict. The continued prevalence of assault summonses in the face of declining assault charges helps reconcile the message promoted by the Home Office and the Commissioner of Police for the Metropolis in the early twentieth century, that crime was on the decrease, with the magistrate Horace Smith's insistence that this was not the case. The statistics collated annually by the former relied on apprehensions and charge convictions to measure crime, while largely ignoring summonses. Magistrates, on the other hand, could hardly overlook the constant parade of alleged victims that crowded the

in the manners of different classes; a decline in the spirit of lawlessness." *Judicial Statistics, England and Wales, 1899, Pt. I, Criminal Statistics* (PP 1901, Cd. 659, 705), 37.

95 For a more detailed discussion of these statistics and their implications, see Gatrell, "Decline of Theft and Violence," 284–93.

96 Registers of Summonses Thames PC, 1885–1900. In 1880, the police brought 7,129 charges for assault, while assault summonses numbered 10,332 (*RCPM 1880* (PP 1881, C. 2969), 14; *Judicial Statistics, England and Wales, 1880, Pt. I, Police – Criminal Proceedings – Prisons* (PP 1881, C. 3088), 28). The number of assault summonses is calculated by subtracting the number of police charges (tabulated in the *RCPM*) from the overall number of assault cases tried summarily in London that year (tabulated in the *Judicial Statistics*).

97 *RCPM 1900*, 70; *Judicial Statistics, England and Wales, 1900, Pt. I, Criminal Statistics* (PP 1902; Cd. 953, 1115), 68. After that, there was a steady decline in both summonses and charges, but the former continued to well exceed the latter every year. In 1910, when police brought only 3,336 charges of common assault, the courts adjudicated 4,370 assault summonses (*RCPM 1910* (PP 1911, Cd. 5959), 42; *Judicial Statistics, England and Wales, 1910, Pt. I, Criminal Statistics* (PP 1912–13, Cd. 6071 and 6047), 62).

courts every morning to apply for summonses and every afternoon to conduct them.

Avoiding "Trial by Newspaper": Guilty Pleas and the Defendant's Option of Summary Trial

The statistics on rising police intervention in daily life, when combined with information on how the courts operated in the late Victorian period, reveal an ambiguous picture of the policeman's role in the courtroom and the community. They belie just how common it was for those arrested on minor offenses to walk out of court with minimal concrete consequences – though one should not discount the social stigma of an arrest and brief courtroom appearance, especially for respectable defendants. Far from being dramatic or overly coercive, in the years leading up to the First World War, the majority of constables' charges were tried through a routine and often uncontested process. The likelihood of conviction rose as the years progressed, but the seriousness of the charges and the chances of harsh penalty declined. Assault summonses were most likely to end in a recognizance, and if not that, then a small fine. Similarly, the myriad apprehensions for drunkenness and violations of the Metropolitan Police Acts only rarely elicited harsh penalties. The ubiquitous charges of drunkenness and MPA violations were similarly offered only token resistance, the defendant's testimony typically being so brief that it was not even recorded by the court clerks in the minutes. In a very high percentage of cases, the defendant simply pled guilty.

Local courtrooms mitigated the coercive aspects of police intervention and authority in other ways as well. As with minor offenses, the high conviction rate for charges of certain more serious offenses was, at least in part, the result of negotiations both tacit and explicit between the defendant, the police, and the magistrate. In these circumstances, defendants themselves could have considerable influence on how their own trials were conducted. This was provided that, though the charge might be serious, the act itself was not severe and the accused did not have a record of prior offenses.[98] In those indictable cases (i.e. those that required, on conviction, imprisonment without option of

[98] Howard, "The Rise of Summary Jurisdiction," 502.

a fine in lieu) that could be tried either by jury or summarily, the defendants had some say in which course was pursued. Particularly if the case against them was a strong one, with the magistrate's assent, defendants could choose to have an indictable crime tried summarily. This was to their advantage, since a summary trial was conducted with much greater expediency than a jury trial was and held, upon conviction, the potential of a much shorter term of incarceration (the maximum allowable being six months with hard labor).

By the interwar period, the desire of defendants to "have it done" was evident even to outside observers.[99] As Pendleton Howard, writing for the *California Law Review*, explained, in cases where the weight of evidence for the prosecution was strong, a tacit agreement could be reached between a defendant and the police. If the case was tried summarily, the former would save all of those involved time, effort, and expense by pleading guilty.[100] This practice, Howard observed, was favored by the police as well, since "they are more interested in conviction than in punishment."[101] Such pretrial accommodation between defendant and constable represented a continuity of practice from the mid-Victorian period. According to Thomas Holmes, a one-time police-court social worker who later became the secretary of the Howard Association for Penal Reform, negotiations between prisoner and constable to secure the former a better account from the latter in court had been a quite common practice in the 1880s. This discussion would be conducted while both were in the court waiting-room prior to the trial. After sentencing, the prisoner would fund the constable's visit to the pub.[102]

Some of these strategies and dynamics may seem familiar, since they are integral to contemporary legal procedure. But the entry of a guilty plea and the pretrial negotiation of it (i.e. "plea bargaining") had, as general practices, followed an uneven trajectory in early-modern and modern Britain. Common in the early seventeenth century, they had

99 Ibid.

100 Ibid. Howard, a Professor of Law at the University of Idaho, published a book-length study titled *Criminal Justice in England* (New York: Macmillan, 1931) the same year.

101 Howard, "The Rise of Summary Jurisdiction," 501.

102 "Hundreds of times," Holmes wrote, "I have heard prisoners ask the prosecuting policeman to 'make it light for me,' and many times I have heard the required promise given and an arrangement made." Thomas Holmes, *Known to the Police* (London: Edward Arnold, 1908), 4.

gone out of favor by the late eighteenth, only to become a widespread practice in summary justice again by the later nineteenth century.[103] Although the defendant had, in theory, retained the right to plead guilty, eighteenth-century judges actively discouraged it.[104] Given the speed with which criminal trials were conducted in that period, such pleas offered little advantage to either the defendant or the judge. The advent of the adversarial criminal trial, with attendant time and expense, made it appealing from the procedural perspective. The expansion of summary justice in the late nineteenth century made it a sensible option from a defendant's perspective. A guilty plea for an indictable offense in a late eighteenth-century assize trial might earn the sympathy of the presiding judges, but the option of sternness or mercy lay, ultimately, with them.[105] A summary trial, on the other hand, left the magistrate, no matter what his inclination, with no greater recourse at hand beyond the maximum allowable penalty of six months' imprisonment. And this most puissant of police-court punishments was inflicted only in extraordinary circumstances. In some felony cases, defendants may have been advised of this option by solicitors; in many instances, the decision would have been based on their own knowledge or on preliminary discussions with court personnel.[106]

The cultural aspects of local courtrooms could play a key role in this decision. A defendant's choice of summary justice was sometimes prompted by their fear of newspaper coverage. Individual jury trials, being both far fewer and for more serious crimes than summary trials were, attracted commensurately greater press attention. Such publicity, in

[103] Peter King, *Crime, Justice, and Discretion in England, 1740–1820* (Cambridge: Cambridge University Press, 2000), 231. It was all but unknown prior to the mid-eighteenth century, according to John Langbein. He sees its origins in the rise of the adversarial criminal trial, the advent of counsels for defense, and the attendant attenuation of the trial process. Prior to that, the "non-adversarial" jury trial was expeditious enough to satisfy those involved. John Langbein, "Understanding the Short History of Plea Bargaining," *Faculty Scholarship Series, Yale Law School*, Paper 544 (Jan. 1979), 292–94 (http://digitalcommons.law.yale.edu/cgi/viewcontent.cgi?article=1545&context=fss_papers).

[104] Ibid. [105] Hay, "Property, Authority, and the Criminal Law," 48.

[106] Howard, "The Rise of Summary Jurisdiction," 497. It is important to remember here that the preliminary hearings for criminal trials had to begin in the magistrates' court, the route to the Central Criminal Court and an attendant jury trial being via a remand.

an era where the restrictions on press reportage of ongoing cases were limited, could adversely affect a jury. On the other hand, by choosing a brief and speedy case in a police court, with only a magistrate to decide the verdict and punishment, a defendant might hope to avoid "trial by newspaper."[107] This was a particularly attractive option for defendants in instances where the alleged crime had garnered the opprobrium of the community.[108] The decision to opt for a summary trial, while preventing the prejudicing of a jury through unfavorable newspaper reports, did little to allay the public embarrassment that could accompany the trial itself.[109] A police-court defendant might not be "tried" by the newspaper, but he or she could still be condemned by the newspaper reporter.[110] In England, from 1911 to 1913, 80 percent of all indictable offenses were tried summarily, though this course was considerably more prevalent with non-violent property crimes than it was with violent crimes or crimes against the person.[111] In the Clerkenwell court minutes from the decade prior to the First World War, the practice was ubiquitous. Hardly a week could go by without half a dozen instances where the charge and the clerk's notation of "C" or "by consent" indicated that a defendant had opted for summary justice over a jury trial. Larceny was the most frequent offense where this course was followed. Defendants could also employ the option in a broad spectrum of other instances, such as charges for the management of a brothel, cruelty to against children, violations of parole (under the Prevention of Crimes Act 1871), or running an unlawful gaming house.

Even more common than defendants choosing summary trial for an indictable offense were guilty pleas for non-indictable crimes. Defendants most commonly chose this option when charged with either illegal betting or with gaming. The dynamics of the two charges offer a study in contrasts, demonstrating the wide appeal of this alternative across the gamut of defendants. Illegal street-betting on races was a common pastime among Victorian working-class men and, to a lesser degree, among women as well. It was conducted through bookmakers who were well-known in the community to patrons and

[107] Ibid., 502. [108] Ibid. [109] Gamon, *London Police Court*, 48. [110] Ibid., 114.

[111] 89% of all indictable offenses against property without violence were tried summarily in this period, as opposed to only 27% of offenses against the person and 26% of offenses against property with violence. Gatrell, "Decline of Theft and Violence," 274.

police alike.[112] With nearly mechanical regularity in the prewar decades, defendants pled guilty to betting charges. Clerkenwell magistrates commonly imposed the maximum fine of £5, which was promptly paid by the defendant out of the pocket of those who funded and ran the business behind the scenes. Between 1895 and 1915, London magistrates tried a few hundred betting cases each year.[113] Considering the vast profits that were made, these fines served as poor deterrence.[114] Gaming charges were of a very different character. These were regulated under the Vagrancy Amendment Acts 1873 and 1876, and were aimed largely at curbing the practice, common among juveniles, of playing street-games such as pitch-and-toss. Spurred by middle-class fears of "hooliganism" and the alleged threat of juvenile immorality to the social order, police waged a long-running campaign against the practice that continued, unabated, well into the interwar years.[115] Whereas betting laws were directed at bookmakers and their employers, the players themselves were the targets in gaming prosecutions. By 1900, London courts were trying over 2,600 gaming charges yearly, with all but a small fraction of such charges concluding in a conviction.[116] A typical penalty on conviction began at two shillings and sixpence for a first offense and went up on successive charges before reaching a maximum of seven shillings or a week's imprisonment. Convictions were commonplace, but the mediation of arrests by courtroom decisions were as well. Clerkenwell magistrates varied the fines according to the age of the defendant within any particular group, such arrests usually being made in bunches. This was particularly evident when those apprehended consisted of both juveniles and those past the age of minority.[117] Magistrates typically

112 Charles Booth, *Life and Labour of the People of London. Final Volume: Notes on Social Influences and Conclusion* (New York: Macmillan, 1903), 53.

113 In 1895, they tried only 181. *RCPM 1895*, 60.

114 Booth, *Life and Labour. Final Volume*, 57.

115 Clapson, *Popular Gambling*, 81. For a more general history, see Geoffrey Pearson, *Hooligan: A History of Respectable Fears* (Basingstoke: Palgrave Macmillan, 1983). For the rising prosecution of juvenile offenses in the first half of the century, see Peter King, "The Rise of Juvenile Delinquency in England 1780–1840: Changing Patterns of Perception and Prosecution," *Past and Present* 160 (Aug. 1998), 116–66.

116 In 1900, of 2,666 apprehensions, 2,416 ended in a conviction. *RCPM 1900*, 59.

117 Presumably this was because they assigned responsibility for the crime to the eldest, though it may also have been that the elder boys were more likely to have been charged previously in court.

discharged children aged twelve or younger and rarely fined those under fifteen more than three shillings. Gaming and betting cases forced magistrates to confront the problematic issue of how to punish practices that, although illegal, were widespread and morally acceptable in working-class communities.[118] Both betting and gambling cases demonstrated the limits of police authority beyond the arrest phase, and how even concerted police campaigns against certain crimes, supported by the moral outrage of public opinion, could make little difference beyond the threshold of the courtroom door. In betting cases, the profits of an illegal industry abrogated the deterrent of fines, while in gaming cases, the magistrates convicted almost every offender over a certain age, but used their discretion to shield the youngest violators from punishment.

The treatment of women arrested as prostitutes was another key instance in which police vigilance of common activities in the community was mediated by courtroom practice. I use the term "as prostitutes" rather than "for prostitution" intentionally. The likelihood of a constable apprehending a woman *in flagrante* was exceedingly small, though it did happen.[119] More typically, constables arrested women whom they had witnessed accosting men in the street and whom they suspected, due to their current or past behavior, of practicing prostitution. These charges, like assault charges, could also emerge from private initiative when a man so accosted tracked down the local constable to make a complaint. The women apprehended were sometimes charged with offenses under the MPA that were specific to the practice of prostitution (e.g. "soliciting for the purposes of prostitution," or "disorderly prostitute") and sometimes with other offenses, disorderly conduct being the most common. The authority to define women *as* prostitutes lay partly in the hands of constables themselves. Constables' power of identification was made formal in the *Annual Reports of the Commissioner for the*

[118] For police interference in common practices as a motivator for working-class hostility, see Barbara Weinberger, "The Police and the Public," in Victor Bailey, ed., *Policing and Punishment in Nineteenth-Century Britain* (New Brunswick: Rutgers University Press, 1981), 74. Taylor, *Crime, Policing and Punishment*, 109.

[119] On such occasions, they could be charged with indecent exposure as well. Public intercourse was a separate offense under the London County Council bye-laws, and was typically leveled at such acts that did *not* involve prostitution.

Police of the Metropolis, which recorded not only the numbers arrested for "Prostitution" (1,804 in 1900), but the much larger number of "Prostitutes Apprehended" (3,862 in 1900).[120] The latter was a designation that emerged from police witnesses identifying them as prostitutes *in court*, regardless of whether or not they were convicted or discharged and, if the former, specifically of a prostitution-specific offense. After reaching a peak of 6,214 in 1886, this number declined until the early 1890s, when it stabilized between 3,500 and 4,500 up until the outbreak of the First World War.[121] The statistics of the *RCPM* depicted a very stern treatment of women arrested on these grounds. In 1900, only 262 of those charged with soliciting or as disorderly prostitutes were discharged, the remaining 1,542 being convicted or held to bail.[122] Throughout the two decades prior to the war, this high ratio of conviction and low number of discharges was characteristic.

The court records, in contrast, reveal a wide variation in punishment. To begin with, the majority of those arrested *as* prostitutes were not charged *with* prostitution, but rather with other MPA violations such as disorderly conduct, drunkenness, or drunkenness "with aggravations" (e.g. and obscene language, drunk and disorderly). The punishment could vary depending both on the charge and on the adjudicating magistrate. Those women arrested who insulted or abused the constable, who were reported to have been drunk or, most serious of all, who assaulted the arresting officer, could face weeks – in some cases, months – of imprisonment with hard labor. On the other hand, the charge of "common prostitution" rarely met with more than a fine, usually between seven and forty shillings.[123] Although outright discharges were rare, being bound over to keep the peace on forfeit of a surety was typical. The constables retained the authority to classify women as prostitutes, and to charge them on any number of grounds. It lay in the hands of the magistrate to decide which defendants and which acts under which circumstances should be punished harshly. This decision could be strongly influenced both by the defendant's behavior as reported by the constable and by the latter's testimony as to whether or not the defendant was a "known prostitute."[124]

120 *RCPM 1900*, 58, 79. 121 Ibid., 79; *RCPM 1913*, 69. 122 *RCPM 1900*, 58.

123 This had been the maximum under MPA violations since the passage of the law in 1839.

124 Minutes of Charges, Clerkenwell PC, October 7, 1905.

Despite their visible, and sometimes violent, contests in the streets and the thousands of prostitution-related arrests made each year in London, prostitutes and police were not unvaryingly at odds in the courtroom. A long tradition of tacit accommodations between the two groups in the community saw increasingly explicit expression in the prosecutions brought against men for their mistreatment of women who supported them financially. Prostitutes cooperated with constables in bringing charges of "living off prostitution" (aka "living off of immoral earnings"), which was criminalized under the first Vagrancy Act 1824, against these men.[125] Although far fewer in number than prosecutions against prostitutes were, these charges secured convictions on a more regular basis, and the penalties were considerably heavier.[126] The contrasting circumstances that could bring an alleged prostitute to court as a defendant against a charge of soliciting one week and as a prosecutor against a man who had abused or exploited her the next aptly demonstrated the moral and legal fluidity of local courtrooms. It also revealed the ambivalent position of the local constable, who could find himself charging a woman in the former and testifying on her behalf in the latter.

Another common type of case, larceny, demonstrated both the power of magistrates' discretion and how courtroom practice could mitigate the implications of a constables' arrest and charge. Although declining in proportion to the population, larceny remained among the most common crimes to come before London magistrates in the decades preceding the First World War. Following the general pattern in magistrates' courts, defendants were less and less likely to be discharged as the years passed.[127] The prevalence of larceny charges

[125] 5 Geo. 4 c. 83.

[126] Of the 253 men charged with this offense in 1913, more than half (163) received sentences of over three months' imprisonment. *RCPM 1913*, 56. In comparison, of the 2,359 convictions handed down for assaults on constables, only 44 defendants received such heavy sentences. *Per capita*, this made the former offense, along with aggravated assault, the most harshly punished of all those tried summarily in London that year (*RCPM 1913*, 55–56).

[127] In 1880, they heard 8,290 charges for simple larceny; 1,852 for larceny by servants; and 1,852 for larceny from the person. Of these, 2,720 were discharged for simple larceny (including attempted larceny) and 516 and 976 from larceny by servants and larceny from the person (including attempted), respectively (*RCPM 1880*, 14). In 1900, simple larceny (and attempted) accounted for 6,918 charges (5,808 men and 1,110 women), of which 1,667 (1,362 men and 305 women) were discharged. Larceny by servants came

and the seriousness with which magistrates approached them was apparent across the entirety of the London police-court system, as the surviving court registers from the period – which include those from the Clerkenwell, Thames, West London, and Bow Street Courts – reveal. In these charges, as in assaults, the trial was greatly strengthened by the presence of the prosecutor, who retained some influence over how the case proceeded. Especially when the amounts concerned were small, the alleged victim sometimes did not attend court, making a discharge a perennial possibility.[128]

In 1900, London police courts convicted 3,715 men and 689 women of simple larceny, with 654 defendants (15 percent) receiving a term of imprisonment that exceeded two months.[129] A further 398 were whipped, while merely 562 were allowed to leave court carrying only a fine as punishment. By comparison, only one of the 3,515 defendants convicted of common assault was imprisoned for over two months, and 1,921 (just under 55 percent) were punished with a fine. Even those convicted of the more serious offense of assault on a constable received such long prison terms at less than half the rate that simple larceny defendants did (201 out of 2,807, or a little over 7 percent). The punishments for larceny against the person were even more severe. The sharp contrast between how crimes of violence and crimes of property were treated in London police courts was also apparent in the numbers of discharges. In 2,782 instances, defendants were discharged in common assault charges, a number only 20 percent less than the total for convictions.[130] By comparison, in simple larceny

before the magistrates on 1,267 occasions (with 265 discharges), and larceny from the person was tried 1,450 times, resulting in 549 discharges (*RCPM 1900*, 54). By 1913, the charges of simple larceny against male defendants still remained at 1900 levels (6,002) but the number of discharges had dropped by nearly 50%, to a mere 726 (*RCPM 1913*, 41). "Simple Larceny" referred to larceny without "aggravations" (i.e. without violence or other actions that deepened the seriousness of the offense). The category had been created when the distinction between "Petty Larceny" and "Grand Larceny" was abolished in 1827. Old Bailey Online, https://www.oldbaileyonline.org/static/Crimes.jsp#simplelarceny.

128 The same day that the above defendants were tried, another was discharged when the prosecutor failed to appear to press the charge of stealing an umbrella, value one shilling and sixpence.

129 The category listed in the *RCPM* was "simple larceny and offences punishable as simple larceny," the latter consisting primarily of attempted larceny charges. *RCPM 1900*, 70.

130 Among men, there were 2,950 convictions and 2,356 discharges. Among women, it was 565 convictions and 428, respectively. Ibid.

cases, convictions outnumbered discharges by a ratio of more than five to one (4,404 to 832).

At first glance, it seems that the dynamics of larceny charges favored constables' authority and testimony in the courtroom. This was because the range of charges that covered theft of property was much wider and the material evidence was more telling. Also, unlike assault, police action against theft could restore the stolen property to its original owners and erase the concrete damage of the crime, if not the social harm.[131] In addition to the various types of larceny (simple, servant, from person), suspects could be charged with attempted larceny, unlawful possession, and intent to steal. In these charges, magistrates could proceed with a conviction, even *sans* the victim's active cooperation, if a constable had witnessed the crime himself or had caught the offender with the stolen property in their possession. None of these latter offenses ever approached the arrest and prosecution levels of simple larceny cases, though their consequences could be equally dire for the accused. A conviction for attempted larceny could carry just as stiff a penalty as a larceny conviction could, and since the alleged victim's presence was not essential, the defendant's slim chance of a discharge in the latter dropped to almost none in the former. In determining a penalty upon conviction, as in other types of charges, the defendant's record was a key factor. First offenders were most apt to receive leniency, while repeat violators were vulnerable to the strongest penalties of the law. Not only could the punishment for the same crime vary widely depending on the circumstances and status of the offender, but such variation was possible even among multiple defendants tried together and convicted for the same single act.[132] This was determined only at the sentencing

[131] In 1905, the *RCPM* tabulated that, of £181,018 worth of property reported stolen, £52,915 was recovered, for a net loss of £128,103. *RCPM 1905*, 42. Charges in property offenses were often supported with further evidence of the offender's possession of stolen goods or of their attempts to fence or pawn it (Gatrell, "Decline of Theft and Violence," 294).

[132] When Robert Humphries, Bert Barnes, and Alfred Woodcock were all convicted in July 1910, under the Vagrancy Act, of being in an enclosed premises with intent to steal, the first two defendants, both of whom had previous convictions, received one month and three months imprisonment with hard labor, respectively. Woodcock, in contrast, was determined to be of "good character," and was released on a recognizance for causing willful damage. Minutes of Charges, Clerkenwell PC, July 22, 1905.

stage, since magistrates took careful steps to ensure that prior offenses did not prejudice the adjudication process. Prisoners' criminal records were not kept by the court, and past convictions were not brought to light until after their guilt or innocence had been decided.[133]

The treatment of property crimes by the criminal justice system has received considerable attention from historians. The sustained focus of policing and punishment, to the first generation of historians studying the social history of law and society, reinforced the impression of a system that largely served the interests of property-holders over the poor.[134] This has been taken as evidence of a persistent concern with property crimes from the eighteenth century into the nineteenth and even the twentieth, though more recent works have emphasized how frequently the working-class made use of the police courts to bring theft prosecutions in the nineteenth century.[135] The focus of later nineteenth-century policing and criminal justice administration on property offenses rather than on violence also reflected an understanding of the former as being a more serious, persistent, and endemic threat to public order and personal security, and the latter as more likely to be sporadic, spontaneous, and committed by offenders not otherwise inclined to crime.[136] Although no longer a capital offense after the reforms of the late eighteenth century (i.e. the abrogation of the "Bloody Code"), the prevalence of charges and harsh treatment of property offenses – which were far more likely to be a cross-class affair than violent offenses were – in London police courts seems to support this view.

For all the apparent severity of punishment, however, the summary adjudication of larceny cases still represented a compromise between defendants and magistrates rather than merely demonstrating the authority of the latter and their support of vigilant policing. Unlike most of the charges that came through the police courts on

[133] Ingersoll, "The London Police Courts," 57; Gamon, *London Police Court*, 91. It is unclear at what point, if ever, a prisoner's records were expunged by the court, though the official memory seems to have been indeed a long one. In one 1905 Clerkenwell assault charge, the clerk's notation made reference to an assault conviction from 22 years previously (*Minutes of Charges, Clerkenwell PC*, September 27, 1905).

[134] See Hay *et al.*, eds., *Albion's Fatal Tree*; E. P. Thompson, *Whigs and Hunters: The Origins of the Black Act* (New York: Pantheon, 1975).

[135] Davis, "Prosecutions and Their Context," 413.

[136] Gatrell, "Decline of Theft and Violence," 300.

a typical day, larceny was an indictable offense. Prior to 1855, London cases had to be tried in the Central Criminal Court. This left the defendant, upon conviction, liable to face long terms of imprisonment, well exceeding those possible in a summary trial, with no option of paying a fine in lieu. This equation changed with the Criminal Justice Act 1855, which authorized police courts to try such cases involving thefts of less than £5 value, providing that both the magistrate deemed it appropriate and the defendant was willing. By consenting to be tried summarily, the accused might eventually face several months of incarceration, but would be spared the possibility of years in prison. As a result of this procedure, the felony charges made by police were, most often, only punished with the force of a summary conviction, albeit sometimes with its full potency.[137]

This disjuncture between the circumstances of arrest and the process of adjudication, although apparent in many of the charges brought by constables in the decades preceding the First World War, was not universal. In one of the most serious charges, magistrates and constables were very much in accord in their commitment to both policing and punishment. Even as an rising percentage of overall assault cases arrived in the courts as summonses rather than as charges, a growing proportion of the latter was represented by assaults against the police themselves. In 1880, common assault charges outnumbered charges of assault on a constable by nearly three to one (7,129 vs. 2,571).[138] By 1905, that gap had closed to less than two to one (4,582 vs. 2,443).[139] By the eve of the First World War, the relationship between the two types of assault charges had been completely reversed. In 1913, 2,359 charges of assault on a constable were heard before the London magistrates, as opposed to 1,849 charges of common assault.[140] Across this period, magistrates demonstrated little patience for those who inflicted violence on policemen. The rate of discharge for this offense was among the lowest of all summary cases, and the penalties on conviction were consistently stern, absent extenuating circumstances.[141] In 1880, less than 3 percent of all those

[137] In 1910, only 1,193 of the 8,006 defendants charged with simple larceny were remanded to the higher court, where 1,000 were convicted. *RCPM 1910*, 41.

[138] *RCPM 1880*, 14. [139] *RCPM 1905*, 59. [140] *RCPM 1913*, 54.

[141] In 1905 Clerkenwell, it was rare for those convicted to receive less than three weeks' hard labor for the offense.

apprehended were discharged by the magistrates, and this rate, while rising in successive decades, remained low across the period prior to the First World War.[142] The increasing police entanglement with everyday affairs in working-class communities, both solicited (e.g. by the fetching of constables) and unsolicited, was accompanied by a decreasing judicial tolerance towards attacks against constables. Defendants might feel free to contest a policeman's assertions in the courtroom, but they would likely think twice about raising a hand to them in the street, given the near certainty of arrest and punishment to follow.

Despite the rapid and dramatic changes in the character of charges and the conduct of their adjudication, the press reportage of police courts remained remarkably stable in the decades preceding the First World War. Newspaper coverage across this period, as had long been the case, offered a very different picture of policing and punishment than that apparent from the court records themselves. Private initiative in the fetching of constables was omitted entirely from court reports, as was the voice of constables, in most cases. These stories related the alleged criminal acts themselves, a brief summary of the courtroom exchange, the magistrates' comments, and the sentence. When constables' statements in court were included in any given article, they were offered as part of the description of the actions of the defendant and the surrounding circumstances, rather than as dialogue. At times, even the indication that the constables were participating at all in the case was absent, their information being designated instead as merely "evidence" (i.e. indicated with statements such as "the evidence showed"). As individuals, constables disappeared almost entirely from portrayals of adjudication. The result was that their testimony became the core of what courtroom columns offered as the objective narrative of events. In this way, newspaper portrayals granted police testimony even more authority than the courtroom itself did. In the courtroom, defendants could, and frequently did, contest constables' accounts of the incident, while in the former (i.e. newspapers), the information offered was abstracted from the individual offering it, making it largely immune

142 67 out of 2,571. *RCPM 1880*, 14. In 1910, magistrates convicted 2,090 defendants and discharged 430 (*RCPM 1910*, 64).

to challenge or alternative interpretation. Their statements became, and were sometimes explicitly designated as, the facts of the case.

As had been the case since mid-century, the magistrates' moral commentary on cases often received pride of place in newspaper accounts. The most commonly prosecuted cases, MPA violations, received minimal coverage – small wonder given their lack of drama, their banal nature, and the unwillingness of magistrates to publicly condemn violators. Following a well-established pattern, tales of violence and theft, suicide, and outrageous or scandalous attacks on women remained popular. Since charges of assault that involved serious violence tended to be the ones that resulted in the harshest sentences, the common reporting of such cases also meant that most uncommon punishments, imprisonments of a month or more, were represented in the press out of all proportion to their actual occurrence. Cases that highlighted the alleged brutality of working-class men against women, assaults on police, high-value thefts, and charges against adolescent boys or girls (typically also thefts) formed the bulk of daily reporting on charges. The initiative of private individuals in such cases, when offered at all, only served to highlight the magistrates' authority. Whether it was defendants' claims of justification or the occasional requests of the alleged victims that the charges be dropped (a not uncommon occurrence when the defendant was the husband), newspaper accounts put the power to forgive or condemn solely in the hands of the adjudicating magistrate. The portrayal of magistrates' monopoly on courtroom judgments in charges extended to their moral evaluation as well. Their designation of defendants as brutal, conniving, mean, inhumanly cruel, or even "blackguards" was often the final passage of any given press account.[143] In this, the *fin de siècle* reporting of police-court charge cases in the *Gazette* and in other London papers looked very much as it had in the 1870s and 1880s.

The clearest change in police-court reporting at the turn of the century was one that reflected the local courtrooms' key role in

[143] The latter was reported as the North London magistrate Edward Fordham's succinct judgment on two "well-dressed young men" arrested on disorderly conduct charges. After hearing the constable narrate how the defendants had harassed passers-by and forced their affections on young girls returning from church, Fordham's reported response was "two blackguards. Each pay 40s. or go to prison for a month." *Islington Gazette*, May 15, 1900.

determining the boundaries of public duty and nationalist fervor during wartime. During the Second Anglo-Boer War (1899–1902), the Clerkenwell Police Court, the North London Police Court, and other magistrates' courts around London became the primary venues for processing deserters seized by constables. The reporting of such prosecutions was every bit as brief as their processing in court was–merely a matter of verifying the charge and remanding them to the local military authorities. Such cases were rarely given anything more than the baldest label of "Deserters." The courts' role became more complex, and the press coverage more extensive, however, when the excesses of popular nationalism prompted a police entanglement. Here, magistrates took the opportunity to draw a very public line between what was acceptable enthusiasm and what constituted vandalism or a public danger. London police courts dealt with a slew of drunk and disorderly charges in the wake of popular celebrations following the May 1900 relief of the British garrison at Mafeking, which had received a surfeit of press coverage during its 217-day siege by Boer forces. The North London magistrate Edward Fordham was tolerant towards one celebrant who became so insensate with drink and excessive merry-making that he required the services of a doctor after his arrest, at the cost of three shillings and sixpence.[144] Later that day, in contrast, the same magistrate sharply castigated two men who had attacked a hairdresser's shop after the proprietor hung what appeared to be a Boer flag outside his business. Fordham inflicted heavy fines and a stern warning to others who might be tempted to defy the laws on riotous assembly and stone-throwing.[145] The magistrate's statements in court, regardless of the punishment inflicted, reflected some respect for the anger that the provocative actions of the hairdresser, whom Fordham referred to simply as "a German," had provoked among his neighbors. While emphasizing the sanctity of property, Fordham chided the shop-owner for behaving in so foolish a manner, and implied that, while the attack itself was unjustified, he had played no small part in catalyzing it. In the early years of the twentieth century, the reporting of desertion cases and Boer War exuberances added another element to the catalogue of issues in which local courtrooms could shape, for a public audience, the moral

[144] Ibid., May 22, 1900. [145] Ibid.

implications of an individual's actions. The courtroom's engagement with issues of nationalism, ethnic identity, and masculine duty during this period foreshadowed the much more prominent role they would occupy during the First World War, when dealing with conscription-resistors, deserters, and the excesses of an increasingly xenophobic population would become a daily affair.[146]

Press reporting of prosecutions for desertion and nationalistic demonstrations, even as they widened the public sense of what activities were fit subjects for the court, remained profoundly conservative in their portrayal of constables' roles in the courtroom. The naturalization of constables' testimony as narrative fact and the continued fore-fronting of magistrates' moral commentary highlighted the paradox of police-court activity in the decades preceding the First World War. Even as working-class men and women were helping set the standards, through their own initiative, of what was or was not a proper affair for the courtroom – be it through marital summonses, the fetching of constables or any number of voluntary engagements with the judicial apparatus – police-court columnists and newspaper editors were continuing to foster a very different impression. In the latter, the courtroom, in charges as in other instances, was first and foremost the realm where the moral consequences of one's actions, and even the basic narrative of any given incident, were entirely the purview of the state. Local engagement with the police or the courtrooms, however, did not necessitate an adoption of the accompanying ideology with regards to law, crime, morality, or authority. The process by which an action in the community became a charge in the courtroom offered defendants a number of opportunities to shape the encounter according to their own priorities or to mitigate the impact of a charge. Their influence on this process has been obscured by the statistical records, newspaper accounts, and high-court trials that have formed the bedrock of previous understandings of criminal justice in prewar London.

The divergence between arrest and adjudication, and between courtroom charges and their public portrayals, has significant implications for our historical understanding of the role of the police

[146] See Sascha Auerbach, "'You Have Lost All That Is German of You in the Dock': Citizens, Aliens and the Wartime State in London's Local Courtrooms, 1914–1918," *Twentieth Century British History*, forthcoming.

in the court and the community, and the relationship between the daily execution of criminal policy and the construction and expression of morality in London. Previous studies have argued, on the one hand, that the police were increasingly an intrusive presence in working-class communities and on the other, that the lessening of the moral implications of criminal violations was the result of changing attitudes among policymakers and the perceived success of Victorian criminal policy at reducing serious crime.[147] The journey from apprehension to trial to resolution in the courtroom complicates this picture. The process of "demoralization" did not end with the transfer of many violations to the lesser venues of summary jurisdiction, especially since offenses tried there were hardly without moral implications. On the contrary, morality was at the center of these locales where, as Hugh Gamon observed, the police court was "a meeting ground for a great diversity of moral standards and social grades." The morality of the "police news" column in local and national newspapers, however, was often at odds with the morality of the courtroom itself. In the latter, the recasting of certain offenses as routine and of certain offenders as unworthy of moral condemnation emerged in part from courtroom practice rather than solely from police initiative, the reform of criminal policy, and the ongoing dialogue between policymakers, legal experts, and police administrators.

The contrasting dynamics of arrests and adjudication in the decades prior to the First World War reveals how the intrusive power of policing could be mitigated. Local courtrooms, even in the case of charges, could be integrated into working-class life as more than merely a procedural addendum to coercive policing. The details of these processes remind us that the law did not proceed in a simple trajectory from apprehension to punishment, that its enforcers were subject to public scrutiny and moral assessment, and that a constable's stern hand could be allayed by a magistrate's lighter

[147] V. A. C. Gatrell, examining the growth of policing and the legal bureaucracy at the end of the nineteenth century, has argued that the Edwardian working classes were more closely regulated than either their mid-Victorian antecedents or their descendants in the mid-twentieth century (Gatrell, "Crime, Authority, and the Policeman-State," 280–82). See also Barry Godfrey, "Changing Prosecution Practices and their Impact on Crime Figures, 1857–1940," *British Journal of Criminology* 48 (2008), 171–89). For "demoralization," see Wiener, *Reconstructing the Criminal*, 262–64.

touch. Conversely, a relatively minor charge could result in a severe punishment, though this was rarer. As the conduct of charges in Clerkenwell and other London courts reveals, constables' intervention was frequently sought voluntarily by alleged victims. And it was often at the latter's initiative that moral wrongs were translated into legal violations, even if the police themselves were more frequently assuming the prosecutorial role once held overwhelmingly by private individuals.

The apparent increase in authority granted to police and magistrates by a widened array of legal powers must also be seen in the light of increased scrutiny by the public. With the courtroom facing close observation from reporters, editors, and their readers, magistrates and police alike were under pressure to take heed of public opinion in their actions or, as was the case in PC Clark's behavior across the course of the Lilian Gray case, their overreactions. In local courtrooms, agents of the state were both knowing and known, both observers and the observed. Even what would seem to be the most clear-cut demonstration of sterner legal regulation, high conviction rates, did not invariably indicate relentless legal coercion. Negotiated guilty pleas, trying indictable crimes summarily, small fines, recognizances, and magistrates' discretion could all mitigate the impact of police campaigns against activities that were demonized in public discourse but nonetheless remained common and accepted in working-class neighborhoods. Viewed through the lens of courtroom culture, constables' authority to define the moral implications and concrete consequences of crime remained contested well into the early twentieth century. It was in the courtroom, as well as in the public discourse of reformers and policymakers, that the dynamic relationship between the consequences of offense and apprehension, between prosecution and punishment, and between law and morality was shaped in the decades preceding the First World War.

"The Authoritative Teacher of the Unwritten Law of Morality": Magistrates, the Courtrooms, and Their Communities in Prewar London

As much as the courtroom helped shape the relationship between constables and the communities they policed, policemen still spent much of their time beyond its confines. In contrast, magistrates' understanding of their communities was based primarily on the view from the courtroom itself. Their authority in this milieu rested not just on their official powers, but also on their claims to intimate knowledge of their districts and on their constant references to their storied judicial predecessors. Magistrates' formal standing gave them the power to adjudicate, but their self-proclaimed cultural authority granted them the right to *judge*. By the turn of the century, police-court magistrates could look back on more than a hundred years of prominence in the legal and cultural landscape of the metropolis. Their pronouncements were endlessly reproduced in press reports, their counsel was eagerly sought in parliamentary committees on the reform of law and social services, and their decisions or commentary were looked to as guidelines for summary practice throughout the nation.[148] This strengthened magistrates' resolve to confirm, beyond all contradiction, their image as men in full command of their venues and the moral norms propagated through them.

A primary vehicle in this process was first introduced in 1890. With his widely read two-volume series, *Leaves of a Life* (1890) and *Later Leaves* (1891), the magistrate Montagu Williams inaugurated a new medium by which the "view from the bench" would be heard, the magistrates' memoir. In the first decades of the twentieth century, Williams would be joined by a host of colleagues whose names would become indelibly associated by contemporaries – and remain broadly cited by historians of metropolitan law and society to this day – with everyday justice in London. This cohort included Alfred Chicele Plowden, J. A. R. (John Arthur Robert) Cairns, Cecil Chapman, Henry Turner Waddy, H. L. Cancellor, and the prolific Claud Mullins. Each of their volumes provided a wealth of insights into how these men viewed their courts' public roles and their relationship to the individuals and communities over which they wielded authority. Prior to this period, it is very difficult to access magistrates' personal perspectives. They appear in brief glimpses in parliamentary inquiries and commissions in the 1820s, 1830s, and 1840s, and were quoted succinctly, if ubiquitously, in

148 The most common point of access being either the guide to magistrates' practice (e.g. Lushington) or the pages of the official publication that concerned itself with summary justice, the *Justice of the Peace*.

newspaper courtroom columns. But aside from some very basic information about their social backgrounds and the story of one or two noteworthy individuals (e.g. the infamous Allen S. Laing of *Oliver Twist* fame), they remain obscured in the historical record.

The dearth of material on the "view from the bench" for most of the nineteenth century is compensated for by the rich detail available from the 1890s onwards. The series of memoirs, autobiographies, and commentaries produced in the early decades of the twentieth century revealed how magistrates saw themselves and how they understood their role, and that of their courtrooms, in their communities. At the core of this identity was their claim to deep expertise on the social and cultural dynamics of their environment, and their assertion that this expertise guided their decisions as much, if not more so, than the law itself did. Magistrates, in their memoirs and elsewhere, would frequently refer to their keen understanding of "humanity" and "human nature" as their primary qualification for dealing with the broad spectrum of courtroom affairs that encompassed both legal and moral wrongs. This expertise, they claimed, was particularly essential for dealing with the tribulations of working-class women and domestic affairs, which had been a rapidly expanding aspect of their duties since the marital reforms of the 1880s and 1890s. The magistrates' knowledge of human nature, they asserted, served to mediate the social distance between them and their charges. Assuming the mantle of this authority had been a common tactic since mid-century, when it was first articulated by Victorian, middle-class men and women whose professional or philanthropic activities brought them into close contact with the poor.[149]

Magistrates' claims of deep insight into human nature notwithstanding one glance was all that was necessary to reveal the gulf in social status, education, and wealth that separated one side of the police court bar from the other.[150] As a group, the magistrates were qualified in matters of the law and well-paid for their services. Eligibility required seven years of experience as a barrister, and the appointment carried an annual salary of £1,400.[151] By the latter half

149 George Behlmer, *Friends of the Family: The Working-Class Home and Its Guardians, 1850–1940* (Stanford: Stanford University Press, 1998), 33–37.

150 Ibid., 189.

151 Davis, "Poor Man's System," 311. An 1839 Act of Parliament stipulated that magistrates had to be drawn from the ranks of practicing barristers. Solicitors

of the nineteenth century, the men who took up these positions, according to Jennifer Davis, "were, for the most part, either socially or professionally prominent, occasionally both."[152] The magistrate Alfred Chicele Plowden, for example, could trace his lineage back to a crusader who rode with Richard the Lionheart at the siege of Acre. He was proud to say in his autobiography that his family was among a select group in England that could claim to have passed down the same family lands from father to son from the twelfth century to the present.[153] The more recent history of his family was hardly less distinguished than his distant ancestry was, though their fortune and fame had been made farther east than that of their crusading ancestor. Plowden's great-uncle served as a Director of the East India Company and, according to his grand-nephew, "was one of the very few men then living who had personally conversed with Napoleon Bonaparte, at St. Helena, in 1816."[154] His father had served as a distinguished member of the Bengal Civil Service and his mother was the daughter of a Danish nobleman who had been killed in a slave uprising at his estates in Manila.[155] Plowden's own upbringing was commensurate with his family's status. He attended preparatory school at Westminster, went up to Brasenose College, Oxford, and then began a career as a barrister after serving briefly as private secretary to his uncle, a Colonial Service official working in Jamaica. Other London police-court magistrates could make claims to backgrounds equally distinguished, though not necessarily as cosmopolitan as Plowden's was.[156]

By the early twentieth century, the architectural arrangement of the courtrooms – several of which were renovated, relocated, or rebuilt entirely in the decades preceding the First World War – only

would not become eligible as candidates until more than a century later. J. R. Spencer, ed. *Jackson's Machinery of Justice*, 6th ed. (Cambridge, UK, 1972), 232.

152 Sir James Taylor Ingham, who would serve as the Chief Metropolitan Magistrate in the last decade of the nineteenth century, "was a scion of the English gentry and a graduate of Trinity College, Cambridge." Davis, "Poor Man's System," 311.

153 Alfred Chicele Plowden, *Grain or Chaff? The Autobiography of a Police Court Magistrate, Alfred Chicele Plowden* (London: T. Fisher Unwin, 1903), 2–3.

154 Ibid., 17. 155 Ibid., 18–19.

156 The police magistrate George Denman, for example, was the grandson of the Lord Chief Justice of the Common Pleas Court at Westminster. Behlmer, *Friends of the Family*, 169.

emphasized the social distance between the justices and the judged. The Tower Bridge Police Court, although built later than most of the other London police courts were, was identified by one informed commentator as "the culmination of police-court building ideals."[157] The general design isolated the defendant or petitioner from the staff of the court and, in particular, from the magistrate himself. In this milieu, the magistrate's chair "stood at the far end of the room on a carpeted dais and beneath a canopy, a stately figure of oak and red leather, flanked with curtains. To the left and right are solemn cupboards, devoted to the repose of heavy legal tomes."[158] As if the elevation and distinction of the "judgment seat" itself were not enough, another obvious physical barrier divided the magistrate from the rest of the court. "Along the front of the dais and across the room runs a paling of finished woodwork, cutting his worship off from all contact with the common herd. He has, in effect, a small apartment to himself, from which he looks out commandingly upon the rest of the court."[159] Whereas the magistrate's physical elevation reaffirmed his authority, the defendant's position implied a quarantined vulnerability. "In the middle of the clear space left between the settle and the solicitor's pen, fixed on a raised wooden platform with a couple of steps leading up into it, is the narrow iron dock, capable of holding four or five persons at one time in a single line. It looks out over the heads of the solicitors towards the magistrate's chair, and its elevation and isolation make its occupants the most conspicuous people in the court."[160] (See Figure 6.1.) This conspicuous isolation was further emphasized by the requirement that defendants, alone among participants in a trial, had to remain standing for the duration. The precise physical orchestration and general social contrasts of the police courtroom were depicted on the cover of the 1911 edition of police-court missionary Thomas Holmes's memoir, *Pictures and Problems from the London Police Courts*. (See Figure 6.2.[161]) It showed the magistrate and clerks seated, consulting documents or keeping a record, respectively. A bewigged barrister intensely regarded the defendant, while the latter, dressed in a workingman's garb answered with cap in hand.

[157] Gamon, *London Police Court*, 57. [158] Ibid., 60. [159] Ibid. [160] Ibid., 62.

[161] Holmes worked primarily in the North London PC, but since no images of that venue have survived, it is unclear whether the artist was specifically depicting that court or employing another London police court as the model.

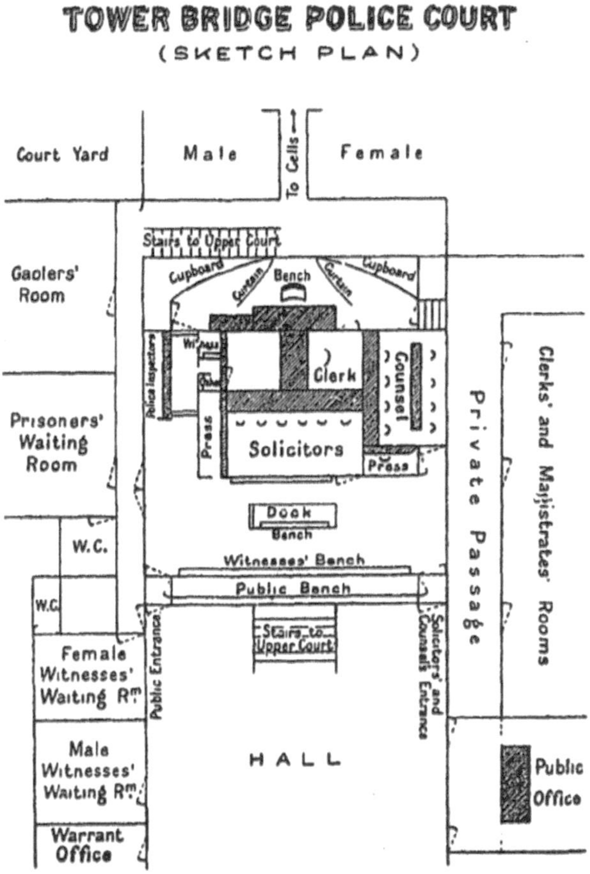

FIGURE 6.1 Ground plan of the Tower Bridge Police Court (From Hugh Gamon, *The London Police-Court To-day and To-morrow* (London: J. M. Dent, 1907), 1.)

While assuming the position of legal arbiters over an ever-greater number of matters, however, magistrates remained keen to emphasize their affinity with the working class and the confidence that the latter put in their judgments. Time and again, they declared that this rapport was what distinguished law from courtroom practice and, in doing so, allowed them to exert a moral influence over their communities that their legal powers alone could never grant.[162] A bond born out of long,

[162] Plowden, *Grain or Chaff?*, 294.

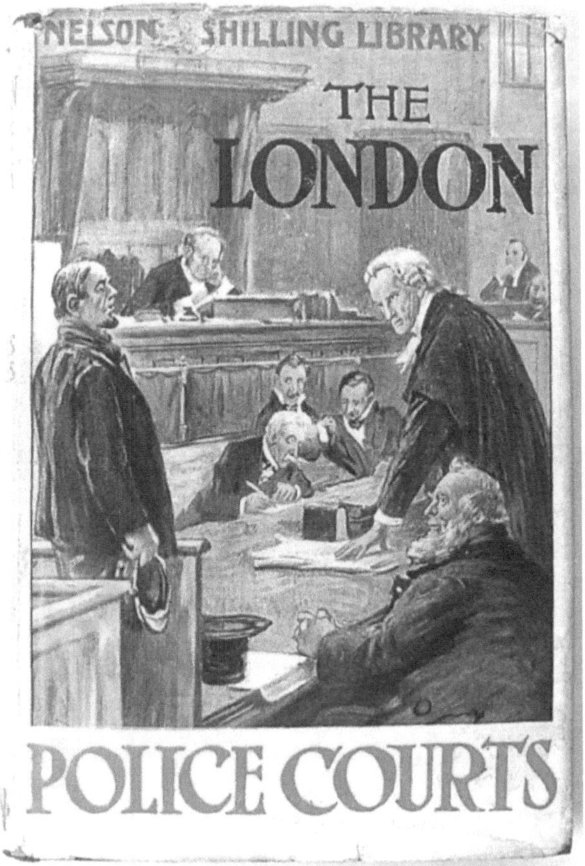

FIGURE 6.2 Cover illustration from Nelson Shilling Library edition of Thomas Holmes, *Pictures and Problems from the London Police Courts* (1900; reprinted London: Thomas Nelson & Sons, 1911).

intimate association with their affairs was at the heart of their claimed expertise. Magistrates were nonetheless adamant in their insistence that this familiarity with their clientele did not equate with indulgence when it came to matters of morality. In their informal dealings with the poor, they drew on the same qualification as others in the middle-class who were involved in private charity or state-supported social service: a moral authority based on their class position. Considering that the magistrates, much like London School Board members or philanthropic reformers, were members of the professional elite that formed the backbone of charity and social reform in the metropolis, this shared sense of moral superiority is hardly surprising.[163] The increasing legal regulation of non-criminal activity and minor crimes in the second half of the nineteenth century had augmented the magistrates' sense of themselves as the watchdogs of working-class morality, though they sometimes disagreed with other agents of the state over what particular norms of behavior merited legal coercion.[164] As one chronicler wrote, "he is the authoritative teacher of the unwritten law of morality."[165]

The practical qualification that anchored magistrates' claims to moral authority, for both their official duties and informal roles, was an intimate personal knowledge of the character of their districts and their residents.[166] As with their reconciliation of moral superiority over the working-class on one hand and social rapport with them on the other, this claim, too, was shot through with contradictions. Magistrates were under considerable public pressure *not* to allow their personal knowledge to interfere with their judgments in criminal cases.[167] To entertain the pretense of an intimate acquaintanceship with one's district was no modest claim, in any case, considering that even the smaller police-court districts often encompassed tens of thousands of inhabitants.[168] A closer

163 Gareth Stedman Jones, *Outcast London: A Study in the Relationship between Classes in Victorian Society* (Oxford: Clarendon Press, 1971), 239–40. See n. 5 above. For the social composition of the Scottish police court magistracy in the early nineteenth century, see David Barrie, "Public Men, Private Interests: The Origins, Structure and Practice of Police Courts in Scotland, *c.*1800–1833," *Continuity and Change* 27, no. 1 (May 2012), 83–123.

164 Davis, "Poor Man's System," 331. 165 Gamon, *London Police Court*, 102.

166 As Behlmer has written, "magistrates in the late nineteenth and early twentieth centuries were typically products of the upper middle class – anything but 'born' experts on proletarian life. Yet because they constituted the base of England's judicial pyramid, they tended to couch their claims to social recognition in terms of an acquired knowledge about the habits of the poor." Behlmer, *Friends of the Family*, 189.

167 John Crump and Bertram Crump, *The Magistrate's Pocket Manual* (London, 1904), 45. John Crump was a solicitor and Bertram Crump was an exhibitioner of Exeter College, Oxford.

168 The smallest of the police-court districts was that administered by the Westminster PC. The largest, geographically, were the South Western and Greenwich PC districts. Among the most densely populated police-court districts were those of the Thames PC and the Tower Bridge PC. London Police Court Maps, London Metropolitan Archives.

examination of police-court practice reveals that, contrary to magistrates' assertions of local expertise, their firsthand knowledge of their districts was often sparse. Most of the magistrates' experience was acquired in the courtroom itself. Since the courts so often dealt with violence, theft, and other forms of misbehavior, magistrates' experiences there were more likely to reinforce their prejudices than to provide them with a balanced and comprehensive view of life in their districts. Another factor limiting magistrates' familiarity with their clientele was the frequency with which justices were reassigned to different courts within the metropolis. During the period 1890–1901, only four of the twenty-five sitting magistrates remained in the same court, and by the latter date, nearly half of those serving were new to the position.[169] No magistrate stayed in the same court for his entire career, and fewer than a third served in the same jurisdiction for more than a decade in the period 1890–1911. Cecil Chapman, during his twenty-five years as a magistrate, was assigned successively to six different police courts (Clerkenwell, Southwark, Lambeth, Greenwich and Woolwich, Tower Bridge, and finally Westminster).[170] In addition, the overall turnover rate among stipendiary magistrates, primarily due to retirement or death, was quite high. New magistrates were constantly being appointed from the ranks of practicing barristers to fill vacancies left by the departure of veterans.[171] Fluctuation and mobility of personnel, rather than stability, was the typical situation. Nearly half the magistrates who were serving in 1891 had died or retired by 1901, and by 1911, more than a third of those working in 1901 had been similarly replaced.[172] Mobility also typified the day-to-day conduct of a magistrate's duties. Even though they were generally resident at only one or two courts, the small size of the cohort and the unceasing demand for their services often required magistrates to sit at several different venues for brief periods of time.[173]

[169] Information concerning jurisdictions of individual magistrates taken from the *London Directories*, 1890, 1891, 1901, 1911. London Metropolitan Archives, mf146.

[170] It should be noted that the Tower Bridge PC was the successor to the Southwark PC and administered the same district.

[171] Plowden, *Grain or Chaff?*, 201.

[172] Tabulated from the *London Directories*, 1890, 1891, 1901, 1911.

[173] Williams, *Later Leaves*, 181.

Such was the peripatetic schedule of magistrates that even maintaining continuity of adjudication within a single case could pose a serious challenge. Magistrates made every effort to either conclude cases in a single sitting or, barring that, to coordinate adjourned hearings with their own schedules. But this was not always possible, and they could find themselves either handing cases over to their colleagues for conclusion on a later date or, alternatively, having to pick up the reins of a case whose initial stages and testimony had already been conducted by another magistrate. Small wonder that they were so reliant on the court clerks and the minutes of testimony they kept; this documentation and personal recall could form the only link between the disparate hearings of more attenuated cases. Professional migration casts one doubt on magistrates' claims to intimate familiarity with their districts. Remoteness of residence and limited exposure to the local environs presents another. Only a tiny minority lived where they worked, and their time *in situ* was typically confined to the court and its immediate surroundings.[174] In 1890, only four out of twenty-three police-court magistrates had residences within the districts where they worked.[175] None of the magistrates assigned to the busy courts that served east and south London, both the source of much professional commentary on working-class life, lived there. The preference, almost without exception, was to reside in the more salubrious West End.[176]

The most serious obstacle to a magistrate's accurate assessment of life in his district, however, was neither professional migration nor a lengthy commute. It was how the magistrates typically acquired knowledge about affairs beyond the courtroom. Aside from that provided by the court clientele themselves, most of their knowledge came from a diverse conglomeration of formal and informal agents.

[174] Gamon, *London Police Court*, 104.

[175] The court districts which had a serving magistrate who resided in the same area were Bow Street, Marlborough Street, Marylebone, and Westminster – all in the West End. *London Directories*, 1890.

[176] Two notable exceptions were Thomas Saunders, who lived in Herne Hill, and Frederic Mead, who resided in Dulwich. Neither of the magistrates, moreover, worked at the police court which had jurisdiction over the district encompassing Dulwich and Herne Hill (Lambeth Police Court). Saunders and Mead worked at the Thames and Wandsworth PCs, respectively.

Chief among these were the police-court missionaries, the court clerks, and the police constables assigned to the court. They advised the magistrate about specific cases and their actors or more generally about the workings of their districts. Montagu Williams described the typical magistrate as a man who rested at the center of a broad information network: "he is surrounded by officers who, in the discharge of their duties – the serving of School Board summonses, the execution of warrants, etc., acquire an intimate knowledge of the poor in the division."[177] The intelligence born from this network was a far cry from the intimate familiarity to which magistrates laid claim. It was both indirect and colored by the prejudices of men whose most frequent contacts were with those accused of violating the law and, as often as not, moral norms.

Magistrates were both uniquely independent in their authority and uniquely constrained in their understanding of those over whom they wielded it. Their insight was broadly recognized by court clientele, newspaper reporters, and state agents alike, while the limitations of their expertise were acknowledged by only their most ardent critics and the occasional defiant defendant. Magistrates' repeated assertions that their strongest qualification was their intimate knowledge of the poor in their districts, and a profound comprehension of human nature beyond that, went largely unchallenged. This contrast between the claims of expertise made by magistrates and the practical constraints imposed by their lifestyle and professional practice explains why they often relied on either archetypes or generalizations in their descriptions of their courtrooms, their districts' residents, and the relationship between the two. Their autobiographies were rife with references to "the poor," "the people," "human nature," and "humanity." Such general designations were granted more specificity through the employment of anecdotes, usually delivered as moral parables that demonstrated the unvarying patience and wisdom of the magistrates in dealing with the trials and tribulations that beset the residents of their districts. When necessary or expedient, magistrates defended their decisions against criticism by deferring to the law. More frequently in their memoirs and other writings, they described themselves as

[177] Williams, *Later Leaves*, 155.

sympathetic judges of morality, character, and the many flaws that afflicted human nature. The law could not be altered to accommodate these assessments, but their discretion, from the position of one qualified to make moral evaluations, allowed them to "temper justice with mercy."[178] And it was in such discretion, rather than within the law itself, that justice was made manifest in the courtroom. This tradition of paternalism, of being, in the words of the magistrate J. A. R. Cairns, "the 'father' of his people," was central to magistrates' identity and their professed vision of their courtrooms' purpose.[179]

Magistrates' memoirs and autobiographies written in the early twentieth century demonstrated this principle with their ubiquitous references to storied colleagues of the past, and to the Fieldings in particular. A common opening gambit was for the author to begin with a brief history of the courts, constructing a distinct trajectory of evolution between their hallowed predecessors and their contemporaries. This relationship was also employed to elevate the social purpose and moral character of their courts. It served as a defense against those who criticized these venues for being seedy and immoral, both in appearance and, more importantly, by their association with the criminal element, the residuum, and the debauched sluices of the city. The physical environment of the police courts, Plowden wrote, might carry the "taint of the prison," but the hard work over many decades had helped build "a confidence in the justice and impartiality of the magistrates . . . which is the proudest and most satisfying boast of every Englishmen."[180] In this formulation, the wise judgment and moral influence of magistrates, and the respect and appreciation afforded to them by their charges, represented even more than the best that English justice could offer. It was the essence of what it meant to *be* English. This sentiment was the unifying theme that ran through the gamut of police-court descriptions by magistrates and foreign admirers alike from the early nineteenth century to the prewar years. In magistrates' memoirs, the provision of justice to the

178 H. L. Cancellor, *The Life of a London Beak* (London: Hurst & Blackett, 1930), 37. For a discussion of how mercy, strategically deployed through judicial discretion, could serve to reinforce the social order in an earlier period, see Hay, "Property, Authority, and the Criminal Law," 31–35.

179 J. A. R. Cairns, *The Sidelights of London* (London: Hutchinson, 1923), 113.

180 Plowden, *Grain or Chaff?*, 345, 242–43.

poor was the fulfillment of the promise first made by the Fieldings and later expanded on by Colquhoun and Peel. The ideals of these hallowed antecedents were finally brought to fullest fruition in the courtrooms of Williams, Plowden, Cairns, Chapman, Waddy, and their colleagues who filled the benches of the London police-court system in the final decade of the nineteenth century and the opening ones of the twentieth.

The idea that magistrates occupied a position of wisdom and benevolent paternalism over the poor, however, had itself been generated in the realm of courtroom culture. The magistrates' expertise was a construction, and one with an entirely circular justification. Their knowledge of working-class communities and social relations allegedly arose out of their experience with the working class in local courtrooms, which in turn granted them the wisdom to deal with the problems of interpersonal relations that were brought to their courts. Most magistrates, however, had little foundation of direct experience *beyond* the courtroom, and even that courtroom experience had only a tenuous connection to the community, given the peripatetic nature of magistrates' work and the intervening levels of process and personnel (e.g. applications for summonses taken by constables, legal expertise provided by clerks, summations of cases provided by officers of the court). The moral authority, paternalistic sympathy, and profound expertise magistrates laid claim to was a lofty ideal, inherited from their revered predecessors and carefully maintained over the decades even as growing regulatory caseloads, the changing character of summonses, and expedited, bureaucratic police court processes pushed it ever further away from daily experience.

Conclusion

The Historical and Cultural Legacies of the London Magistrates' Courts

The previous chapters have examined the historical evolution of the police courts' roles in metropolitan law, society, and culture. The focus has been on the courts' evolving relationships with working-class communities, broader structures of the state, the concept of justice, and morality in public discourse. In all of these milieu, local courtrooms' influence was inextricably entangled not only with the formal structures of law but also with the more informal dynamics of customary practice, popular expectation, and public portrayals. This book has also explored the reciprocal influence between the police courts and social identity, most especially in regards to class and gender norms. Throughout the nineteenth century, these judicial venues allowed their various participants and portrayers to modify cultural meanings and social practice. Operating in tandem with broader structures such as law and class relations, local courtrooms generated their own distinct dynamics and customs that facilitated their engagement by a broad variety of historical actors. The police courts remained a vital part of London's cultural and social terrain because they combined formal authority and informal influence with accessibility and adaptability. They also attracted wide public attention because of their reputation for melodrama, comedy, scandal, and tragedy. The distinctive practices that emerged from this potent mix, from empty summonses to the patterns of police-court journalism, along with the meanings generated by the experience of local courtrooms both in person and vicariously, constituted courtroom culture. Three wider frames of analysis, all engaged in the introduction and throughout the volume, merit some closing considerations that will pave the way for further exploration of courtroom culture in other contexts. The first of these frames is the legal and administrative development of London and how its intertwining with the magistrates' courts might help us reconsider metropolitan history. Secondly, the prominence of police courts in popular journalism and the contrast between these portrayals and daily practice have important implications for how we understand culture, both in the metropolitan context and in relation to governance. A final topic worthy of further attention is how the relationship between the modern state, Liberalism, and the individual was changing over time, and the role that police courts and their depictions played in these changes.

Beginning with London, what stands out most about the police courts as an element of metropolitan history is their institutional persistence. Following the major expansion and reforms of the 1830s, the courts remained in a roughly similar configuration of number and personnel well into the interwar period. There were some amalgamations and relocations, and the prewar decades witnessed a wave of rebuilding or the construction of new, purpose-built courts, but these were adaptations to the growing authority and caseload of the courts rather than revolutionary transformations. This relative stability stood in contrast to the rapid and drastic changes that other elements of metropolitan governance underwent in the second half of the nineteenth century. Crucial to these changes was the tension between the perceived need, on the part of policymakers, for centralized institutions and the common desire of ratepayers for administration that was sensitive and responsive to local needs and popular demands. These contrasting impulses constituted what John Davis has called "the metropolitan problem."[1]

Police courts stood at the crossroads of this debate between the merits of centralized authority and the efficacy of responsive local administration. As they were not officially part of metropolitan governance, but were rather under the auspices of the Home Office,

[1] John Davis, *Reforming London: The London Government Problem, 1855–1900* (Oxford: Oxford University Press, 1988), 2–3.

the courts constituted a coherent, city-wide system of legal authority that helped knit London together administratively and linked it to the national legal apparatus. The laws that applied in one court applied in them all, while at an informal level, customary court practice in charges, summonses, *ad hoc* charity, conflict resolution, press access, and a host of other elements was shared across London and in other cities with magistrates' courts.[2] The coherency of the courts' legal remit was particularly important in this regard as all of the other entities in metropolitan governance could only enforce their regulations *via* local magistrates and their courtrooms. Since magistrates across the metropolis looked to Bow Street and the senior justices there for guidance, they tended to take relatively similar approaches to these cases. The London School Board's repeated grievances to the Home Office, for example, singled out specific magistrates as being particularly reluctant to enforce their attendance bye-laws, but emphasized that they were meeting resistance from the entire professional cohort. One of the keys to the police courts' longevity as an institution was their ability to achieve this balance of centralized, institutional cohesion on the one hand and responsiveness to local concerns on the other. They successfully addressed "the metropolitan problem" to a degree that several other experiments in administrative reform (e.g. the Metropolitan Board of Works and the London School Board) notably failed to achieve. And they did so cheaply and consistently for more than a century, with an economy of provision that seemed to satisfy budget-wary policymakers, tax-sensitive ratepayers, and cost-conscious court clientele alike.

The importance of these courts and their personnel to daily governance was hardly confined to London. Magistrates' courts or their corollaries played key roles in other cities across Britain.[3] How

[2] For Victorian Manchester magistrates' use of their courtrooms as platforms to disseminate their views of gender and morality, see Andrew Davies, "'These Viragoes Are No Less Cruel than the Lads': Young Women, Gangs and Violence in Late Victorian Manchester and Salford," *British Journal of Criminology* 39, no. 1 (Jan. 1999), 72–89; for working-class use of local courtrooms for interpersonal conflict in mid-Victorian Lancashire, see Shani D'Cruze, "Sex, Violence and Local Courts: Working-Class Respectability in a Mid-Nineteenth Century Lancashire Town," *British Journal of Criminology* 39, no. 1 (Jan. 1999), 39–41.

[3] Barry Godfrey, "Changing Prosecution Practices and Their Impact on Crime Figures, 1857–1940," *British Journal of Criminology* 48, no. 2 (Mar. 2008), 171–89.

courtroom culture operated there in comparison to how it did in London is worth further examination, as is the influence of London magistrates and courtroom portrayals beyond the metropolis. The police-court accounts authored by foreign observers and the reporting of London courts in non-metropolitan and foreign newspapers offer one starting point.[4] Exploring the ways in which courts of summary justice interwove the social, cultural, and legal fabric of North American cities such as New York, Chicago, and Toronto offers another.[5] Magistrates were also important figures in the British Empire, where a peripatetic judicial cohort, most of whom received their legal training in London, were essential in anchoring colonial authority and bringing British justice to regions from British Guiana to Australia.[6] In the plantation societies of the Empire's tropical colonies, much as they did in London, magistrates' courtrooms served as both forums for the grievances of the laboring

[4] Emily Murphy, the first female magistrate in Canada, made careful consideration of how London magistrates had approached narcotics and interracial sexuality when she composed her own approach. Emily Murphy, *The Black Candle* (Toronto: Thomas Allen, 1922), 200–204. See also Thomas Leaming, *A Philadelphia Lawyer in the London Courts*, 2nd ed. (New York: Henry Holt, 1912), 126–30. In addition to coverage across national newspapers (e.g. *The Times*, the *Morning Chronicle*, *Reynolds's Weekly*, the *Morning Post*, the *Freeman's Journal*), the London courts were also covered in major metropolitan papers such as the *Liverpool Mercury*, the *Newcastle Currant*, and the *Nottinghamshire Guardian*. In the latter cases, the primary focus of reporting was on local courts.

[5] New York City's police courts may well prove an especially fruitful comparison, as they mirrored their London counterparts in a myriad of ways, from their moral and social influence to their theatrical character and entertainment value. Mary Roberts Smith, "The Social Aspects of New York Police Courts," *American Journal of Sociology* 5, no. 2 (Sep. 1899), 145–54. For Toronto, see Paul Craven, "Law and Ideology: The Toronto Police Court, 1850–80," in David H. Flatery, ed., *Essays in the History of Canadian Law, vol. II* (Toronto: Published for the Osgoode Society by the University of Toronto Press, 1983), 248–307. Tellingly, a review of this piece refers to the "human menagerie called the police court," and observes that "the ambience of that court has changed very little in the intervening century" (Graham Parker, "Review of *Essays in the History of Canadian Law, v. II*, ed. David H. Flaherty," *Archivaria: the Journal of the Association of Canadian Archivists* 18 (Summer 1984), 278). For Chicago, see Michael Willich, *City of Courts: Socializing Justice in Progressive Era Chicago* (Cambridge: Cambridge University Press, 2003).

[6] Clifton Crais, "Chiefs and Bureaucrats in the Making of Empire: A Drama from the Transkei, South Africa, October 1880," *American Historical Review* 108, no. 4 (Oct. 2003), 1034–56; Douglas Hay and Paul Craven, eds., *Masters, Servants, and Magistrates in Britain and the Empire, 1562–1955* (Chapel Hill and London: University of North Carolina Press, 2004).

population and as stern instruments of public order and morality.[7] Establishing to what extent London and the Empire shared a common courtroom culture as well as a common legal structure, and whether this culture was constructed reciprocally over time, would address an understudied dimension of historical connections across metropolitan–imperial and transcolonial axes.[8]

Along with longevity and relative stability, another primary characteristic of the police courts was their broad impact in shaping the meaning of personal interactions with institutions of law. The reach and commonality of the police-court experience, whether in person or vicariously, along with the courts' role in normalizing the state as part of common experience in the metropolis influenced not just the legal and social landscape of London, but its cultural terrain as well. From modest petitioners and courtroom audiences to constables and regulatory agents, the courtroom offered a platform for the expression and public dissemination of views on a broad spectrum of topics. Individual courtroom experiences helped determine how petitioners understood law and the state, but in the wider realm of public portrayals, courtrooms were even more important in constructing images of how different *groups* related to the state. One could see this, for example, in the popular stereotypes of the working-class woman who took out frivolous summonses, the patient and

[7] Colonial magistrates tended to reinforce the authority of planters and other employers through rigorous application of labor, contract, and vagrancy laws. But by the end of the nineteenth century, a few magistrates had employed their expertise and experience to mount fierce critiques of the plantation labor system, which was dependent in many areas on indentured labor from India and China. John Edward Jenkins, *The Coolie: His Rights and His Wrongs* (New York: Routledge, 1871), 100–113; Joseph Beaumont, *The New Slavery: An Account of the Indian and Chinese Immigration in British Guiana* (London: Ridgeway, 1871).

[8] The legal history of the British Empire is a burgeoning field, but the magistrates have received little notice, and the courtroom environment almost none. The comparative history of legal institutions is especially sparse, though interest in the topic is growing, most demonstrably with Craven and Hay, eds., *Masters, Servants, and Magistrates*; Richard Price, "One Big Thing: Britain, Its Empire, and Their Imperial Culture," *Journal of British Studies* 45, no. 2 (Jul. 2006), 622; Lauren Benton, *Law and Colonial Cultures: Legal Regimes in World History, 1400–1900* (Cambridge: Cambridge University Press, 2002); Laura Benton and Lisa Ford, eds., *Rage for Order: The British Empire and the Origins of International Law, 1800–1950* (Cambridge, MA: Harvard University Press, 2016). See also Mitra Sharafi, "South Asian Legal History," *Annual Review of Law and Social Science* 11 (2015), 309–36.

paternalistic magistrate, the abusive husband, or the unrepentant petty criminal. With the widening of courtroom access over time, moreover, came a diminution of the significance of any given individual's contribution to the practices in which they were embedded. This was visible in the mass verdicts passed by magistrates in regulatory summonses, where dozens or even scores of cases could be decided according to a standard protocol in a matter of minutes. It was also apparent in the standardization of verdicts for certain charges and summonses, such as the regularity with which complainant and defendant alike were bound over to keep the peace in personal summonses for threats or assault. Such personal summonses, by the end of the nineteenth century, had become little more than a commodity to be purchased at will and often on a whim. As the magistrate Henry Turner Waddy wrote in his memoir, by the interwar period, the women in his district sought summonses with the same casualness that they might "walk into a grocer's and buy a pound of tea."[9]

For the general run of courtroom participants, the commodification of summonses, the standardization of charges, and the dissemination of courtroom archetypes counterbalanced the spectrum of agency made possible by local courtrooms' widened usages and increased publicity. As the individual's range of agency in the courtroom narrowed over time, the social and cultural consequences of those actions rose. Increased visibility meant increased moral accountability for courtroom participants as the impact of their speech and action could reverberate, via a nationwide network of courtroom columns, from the local pub to Parliament. Magistrates felt this contrast keenly, and they struggled throughout the second half of the nineteenth century to preserve their autonomy and discretion against the demands of regulatory agencies and policymakers on one hand and the expectations of the local community on the other. They were acutely conscious of their prominent place in the public limelight, hence their reliance, beginning in the late nineteenth century, on memoirs to disseminate their personal views on justice and morality. Through such writings, magistrates could continue to present themselves as paradigms of paternalistic justice and thus as lineal

[9] Henry Turner Waddy, *The London Police Court and Its Work* (London: Butterworth, 1925), 9.

descendants of the Fieldings and Colquhoun, regardless of their ambiguous position in labor disputes and often hostile representation in working-men's newspapers. In these memoirs, which ranged from the flowery stylings of J. A. R. Cairns to the earthy pragmatism of Alfred Chicele Plowden and Cecil Chapman, magistrates depicted themselves and their courtrooms as the primary mediators between the state and the community, while offering strong justifications for their judicial independence and the maintenance of the distinct traditions of their venues.

With these developments, courtroom portrayals diverged significantly from the visible demonstrations of justice and punishment that had characterized judicial spectacles in the eighteenth century. In the latter, when the discontent of the lower orders was a serious threat to political stability, spectacular justice had been staged to impress onlookers with the power of the state and, in doing so, to dramatically deter would-be lawbreakers.[10] In contrast, the nineteenth-century police court, rather than epitomizing stern and exemplary punishment, was a locale where ordinary men and women appeared every day for a variety of reasons. The public depictions that emerged were not so much deterrent as they were morally didactic, informing an attentive reading audience that once-common practices were no longer permissible, and that tighter legal restrictions on both private and public behavior were necessary for the common weal.[11] The conflation, in such accounts, between moral wrongs and even minor regulatory violations helped reinforce this message. Readers were being made aware of problems in their community, and defendants were publicly shamed in a way that leant more weight to convictions whose tangible consequences were relatively mild. Here, the fate confronted by lawbreakers whether they were penitent or defiant was not the scaffold, but the stern reprimand of the magistrate, a fine and, in only the most serious cases, a short term of imprisonment.

As the nineteenth century wore on, the individualized and animated exchanges that had characterized early police-court coverage were replaced by a more formulaic pattern of reporting police charges.

10 Douglas Hay, "Property, Authority, and the Criminal Law," in Douglas Hay *et al.*, *Albion's Fatal Tree: Crime and Society in Eighteenth-Century England* (London: Allen Lane, 1975), 27.

11 Martin Wiener, *Reconstructing the Criminal: Culture, Law and Policy in England, 1830–1914* (Cambridge: Cambridge University Press, 1990), 65.

These reduced or eliminated the voice of the defendant and elided the energetic exchanges that remained common in personal summonses. In such portrayals, individual action, whether that of a complainant, witness, defendant, constable, agent, or magistrate became subsumed to more prosaic arrangements of minor crime and lesser punishment with their attendant moral messages. The figures of the exemplary complainant or defendant, whose compassion or villainy could serve as a warning to others, were replaced by the prosaic lawbreaker receiving their unvarying and inevitable penalty. The local courtroom, for the common run of complainants and defendants, appeared to be operating less like a stage and more like an assembly line. And whereas newspaper accounts in the 1830s and 1840s might have included detailed dialogue from all sides, by the end of the century, the voice of the defendant was often absent entirely or, barring that, was confined to a single, defiant exit line. As often as not, the magistrate in such accounts served as the disembodied voice of a diffuse justice, passing sentence and offering moral assessments with the predictability of a metronome. Drama could be manufactured by journalists who sought out particularly heinous or scandalous cases, but such sensationalized stories bore little resemblance to the daily dockets of London's local courtrooms, which were occupied largely by domestic spats, smoking chimneys, and furious drivers. These courtroom dramas, alongside the comedies, melodramas, and tragedies pioneered by John Wight and his immediate successors, contributed to popular understandings of these genres. The courtroom as an imagined locale became a central setting in popular journalism and popular fiction as a place where one's fate could be decided, while the local courtroom in its daily operation became more and more *un*dramatic.

Just as courtroom accounts shaped the public image of justice and morality, they also contributed to the cultural identity of the city, fostering a distinct image of London while simultaneously depicting the unique identity of districts and neighborhoods. In courtroom newspaper stories, magistrates' memoirs, and popular fiction, the police court appeared prominently, operating as a lens through which metropolitan life, and life among the working-class in particular, could be viewed. Police-court stories, such as those of John Wight, offered some of the earliest and most detailed characterizations (and caricatures) of London's working-class residents. They inspired a host of writers to follow suit, from Charles Dickens (who began his career as a court reporter) to Thomas Burke. The courts tied together the legal and literary life of London along a multitude of axes, as one would expect from an institution whose early founder, Henry Fielding, was himself one of England's foremost novelists. This tradition would continue through the late nineteenth and twentieth century with magistrate-authors such as Montagu Williams, J. A. R. Cairns and, in the interwar period, the prolific Claud Mullins, all of whom presented the life of the city through the window of their courtroom experiences.[12]

As these portrayals helped knit together an image of London life in general, over time, the depictions of individual courtrooms helped construct distinct images of specific districts and their inhabitants as well. The magistrates' courts, by the later nineteenth century, were preoccupied by regulatory offenses, and though violent crime and theft were certainly more common in some districts than they were in others, courtrooms across London all heard their fair share of charges and summonses for assaults and larceny. Courtroom journalism and fictional portrayals hewed to the tastes of readers rather than to an accurate geography of crime and prosecution. These fostered the reputation of some local courts and the communities they adjudicated as having a near-monopoly on violence and theft, and others as being riven by frequent scandal and sensation. The vehicles of courtroom journalism and popular fiction thus elided both the broad variation of poverty and wealth within districts and the predominance of regulatory prosecutions across them. Thomas Burke, in his best-selling wartime fiction anthology, *Limehouse Nights*, reflected this dichotomy. The East End, in his writing, was a den of iniquity, and proof positive of this was the pervasive awareness among its residents

[12] On the power of middle-class Victorian authors to reconfigure the discourse on poverty in London, see Judith Walkowitz, *City of Dreadful Delight: Narratives of Sexual Danger in Late-Victorian London* (Chicago: University of Chicago Press, 1992), 30; Montagu Williams, *Leaves of a Life*, 2 vols. (London and New York: Macmillan, 1890), *Later Leaves* (London and New York: Macmillan, 1891), and *Round London: Down East and Up West* (London and New York: Macmillan, 1892); J. A. R. Cairns, *The Sidelights of London* (London: Hutchinson, 1923); Claud Mullins, *In Quest of Justice* (London: Murray, 1931) and *Wife v. Husband in the Courts* (London: Allen & Unwin, 1935).

that they were "never far" from the Thames Police Court and its threat of swift justice.[13] In similar fashion, Marlborough Street Magistrates' Court in Soho was identified early on by courtroom journalists as a rich vein of material for stories about the peccadilloes of the wealthy and the scandals that emerged from the London theater and later Bohemian scene. This overrepresentation of crime and decadence in some districts was also the result of reporters' tendency to cluster at certain courtrooms while paying scant attention to others. The trends of reporting and the representation of London life through the courtroom fed directly into the perceived division of the metropolis into the middle-class and wealthy West End and the working-class East End. Such a stark separation belied both the economic and social diversity within districts and the highly localized nature of violent crime and deep poverty across the metropolis.[14]

If London's various districts and their character served as the backdrop for courtroom practices and their portrayals, close encounters between individuals and the state occupied the foreground.[15] Here, again, the longevity of the magistrates' courts and their role in local communities are both key to understanding their historical significance. These courts originated in the period of personalized, *ad hoc* justice in the eighteenth century, were central in the administrative rationalization of policing and prosecution during the early Victorian period, and helped introduce the modern, bureaucratic, regulatory state of the late Victorian and Edwardian eras. The same time span witnessed the transformation of Britain, politically, from a nation governed by a relatively small, wealthy elite

[13] The main character of *Limehouse Nights*, Hunk Bottles, not only reads the police columns regularly, but is described as someone for whom the Thames Police Court was never far from his mind (Thomas Burke, *Limehouse Nights* (New York: McBride, 1917), 262, 264). Marlborough Street, which hosted Oscar Wilde's criminal libel charge against the Marquess of Queensbury in 1895, maintained its reputation for sensationalism well into the later twentieth century, when it conducted the trials of Mick Jagger (1969), Keith Richards (1973), and Johnny Rotten (1977), all for drug possession, and John Lennon (1970) for exhibition of sexually explicit pictures in the London Art Gallery.

[14] For the contribution of crime literature more generally to this paradigm, see Simon Joyce, *Capital Offenses: Geographies of Class and Crime in Victorian London* (Charlottesville: University of Virginia Press, 2003).

[15] My thanks to Marjorie Levine-Clark for coining this term and granting permission to use it here.

elected through a narrow franchise to one of increasingly broad electoral participation; the ascendancy of the middle-class to positions of influence; the burgeoning power of enfranchised, working-class men; and, finally, working-class women's struggles for marital emancipation and property rights. Local courtrooms remained throughout this time the place of ultimate accounting for alleged transgression against the law and, to a certain degree, the norms of their society. They did so throughout considerable change in the governing statutes, the political status of those they governed, and official and popular views on what the state *could* and *should* do with regards to behavior both private and public. In the process, the local courtroom became a key locale for determining the practical boundary of the state's authority vis-à-vis the individual.

Magistrates' courtrooms enhanced the power of the state in some regards and constrained it in others. London's relatively small police force, which limited the state's ability to compel obedience to a widening array of statutes, was supplemented by the growing cohort of regulatory agents serving London's various municipal bodies (e.g. the London School Board, the London County Council). The latter's summonses represented the fastest-growing element on court dockets until the decade prior to the First World War, when the police themselves began to use summonses with greater frequency. By the eve of that conflict, London had become a city that was at least as much regulated as it was policed, if not more so. The local courtroom was the keystone in this process. Magistrates could restrict the authority of constables and regulatory agents in a number of ways. They could ration summonses, demand the adherence to certain protocols, refuse to impose anything but the minimum allowable penalty upon conviction, allow a defendant to plead guilty in first instance and therefore receive a lesser punishment than a jury trial could have inflicted, or simply adjourn a case multiple times or *sine die* ("without a day," i.e. permanently). In contrast, magistrates could also amplify the power of the state. Even absent a conviction, the hearing of a case could legitimize the state's right to intervene in the matter. By the same measure, magistrates could openly oppose such intervention, at once reducing the power of the prosecuting agent while confirming their own position as the arbiters of government authority over individual behavior. They could also inflict harsh penalties for relatively minor infractions, explicitly link legal violations with moral turpitude, grant state agents excessive leeway in providing evidence or testimony and, almost universally, accord constables' accounts more respect than they granted those of defendants and their witnesses.

As Patrick Joyce has emphasized, the intersection of Liberalism, governance, and the agency of the individual in the Victorian city is a complicated affair, particularly as "freedom became the principle of state rule" in the mid-nineteenth century.[16] For ordinary men and women, it is easy to see how the expansion of the police-court system and the laws governing everyday behavior restricted their freedom in myriad ways. Local courtrooms did, nonetheless, open new pathways for individual agency through their increased accessibility, their operation as public platforms for individual speech, and their mediation of state intervention into private life. Working-class and lower-middle-class women, who had used local courtrooms to a limited extent before the early nineteenth century, made best use of their rapid expansion. They employed these venues in their interpersonal conflicts, as arbitration sites for marital and affiliation contests, and to challenge domestic reform measures. Women of modest means also harnessed the court as a platform from which to publicly articulate their views on morality and gender norms. The latter was only possible, however, because both law and public discourse held such women increasingly accountable for child-rearing and household affairs, making them prime targets for the widening swath of new regulations and amplifying negative stereotypes of working-class women as contentious and frivolously litigious.

Ultimately, when judging the balance of power between the state and the people, the most significant change brought about by the expansion of the police-court system and its portrayals in nineteenth century London was simply to make the relationship between the judicial system and ordinary men and women itself a more central aspect of everyday life. Increased access, for even the most modest petitioners or those with ambiguous legal status, made local courtrooms the most egalitarian of Britain's legal venues. With two shillings in hand, anyone could apply for a summons. At the same time,

[16] Patrick Joyce, *The Rule of Freedom: Liberalism and the Modern City* (London and New York: Verso, 2003), 15.

the expansion of regulatory statutes and the legitimation of state intervention in everyday life meant that almost anyone could be *compelled* to appear in a local courtroom. Whether or not one "internalized" these aspects of governance, one could hardly escape the practical impact of being governed via the local courtroom, even if only for leaving one's dog unmuzzled or failing to clean one's chimney properly.[17] As Charles Dickens Jr. put it so aptly in 1890, by the end of the nineteenth century, a day in the police court had become "the common lot" for metropolitan residents.[18]

Two final thoughts are worth considering as we assess the significance of the police courts and courtroom culture to our historical understanding of modern Britain. The first is Clifford Geertz's assertion that "'law' here, there, or anywhere is part of a distinctive manner of imagining the real."[19] The second, a corollary to this, is James Scott's argument that the primary function of the modern state was to simplify and categorize social activity along the lines of official interest. This process, "when allied with state power ... enable[d] much of the reality [that elements of the state] depicted to be remade."[20] The London police courts were both distinctive places for reimaging the social order and for transforming that vision into a practical reality. They combined the legal authority to regulate behavior with the cultural authority to define the moral meaning of that behavior and to legitimize the state's right to intervene. But the personal nature of cases, their public view, the wide host of participants, and the adaptability of local men and women with their own visions of courtrooms' roles in their lives continually subverted

[17] For the importance of Foucault's concept of "internalising" government authority in the modern era, see Graham Burchell, Colin Gordon, and Peter Miller, eds., *The Foucault Effect: Studies in Governmentality* (Hemel Hempstead: Harvester Wheatsheaf, 1991).

[18] Charles Dickens Jr., "A London Police-Court," *All the Year Round: A Weekly Journal* 4 (3rd series) (Jan.–Jun. 1899).

[19] Clifford Geertz, *Local Knowledge: Further Essays in Interpretive Anthropology* (New York: Basic Books, 1983), 184.

[20] James C. Scott, *Seeing Like a State: How Certain Schemes to Improve the Human Condition Have Failed* (New Haven: Yale University Press, 1999), 3. "Legal discourse is a creative speech which brings into existence that which it utters. It is the limit aimed at by all performative utterances." Pierre Bourdieu, *Language and Symbolic Power*, trans. Gino Raymond and Matthew Adamson (Cambridge, MA: Harvard University Press, 1993), 42.

this authority. London's police courts facilitated the contested integration of the state into everyday life in practical ways, by mediating the growing legion of regulatory measures and the power of the agents who enforced them, and in more ideological ways, by providing a platform to broadcast individuals' views of governance, morality, and justice. Local courtrooms were thus sites both for the performance of state authority and for the performance of resistance against it.

Did this performance have any significance beyond providing a safety valve for popular grievances? Did magistrates succeed, as Jennifer Davis has suggested, in co-opting the working class in order to maintain the social status quo?[21] And were the courts, as in V. A. C. Gatrell's formulation, simply part of a "policeman-state" whose ultimate goal was social control?[22] These were certainly aspects of the local courtroom's function, but the police courts were far more than merely a tool to convince or coerce the lower orders into obedience. The number of uses to which they were put, the variety of actors who employed them, and the dynamics of their operations – legal, social, cultural, and political – made them institutions often characterized as much by the fracture of authority as by its cohesion. The courts occupied an important role in metropolitan culture and governance from the eighteenth century to the twentieth. They rose to prominence in a time when direct participation in state processes was highly constrained for the majority of the population, to a period when "close encounters" between state institutions and ordinary men and women had become commonplace and could range from life-changing to banal. In the intervening time span, local courtrooms became part and parcel of defining, in daily experience, both what the state was and what the individual's relationship was to it.

Operating across the long nineteenth century and into the period of more modern, bureaucratic, and democratic governance in the interwar years, police courts and their portrayals played a particularly important

[21] Jennifer Davis, "A Poor Man's System of Justice: The London Police Courts in the Second Half of the Nineteenth Century," *The Historical Journal* 27 (1984), 333.

[22] V. A. C. Gatrell, "Crime, Authority and the Policeman-State," in F. M. L. Thompson, ed., *The Cambridge Social History of Britain, vol. 3: Social Agencies and Institutions* (Cambridge: Cambridge University Press, 1990), 244.

role in introducing ordinary men and women to legal processes and in sustaining popular images of law and justice. Although they were among the most accessible of Victorian legal institutions, to what extent they ever became, as the magistrate Cecil Chapman called them, "the poor man's court of justice" remains a matter of debate.[23] The police courts offered a convenient local venue that functioned according to customary practices and gave principals a wide latitude of speech and action. The growing range of statutes, however, made comprehension of the system's formal rules increasingly *inaccessible* to court clientele, preserving the authority of judicial and police officials with their experience and specialized knowledge. The law, in this environment, governed formal operations, but its niceties often remained opaque to courtroom clientele. Their relationship was forged with the courtroom's customary practices, the person of the magistrate, and the overarching concept of justice. The latter loomed ever large in public perception. According to George Ingersoll, the distinguished observer from the *Yale Law Journal*, the police courts were "Temples of Justice" in late Victorian London. Ten years later, the magistrate Alfred Plowden scoffed at such an idea, instead declaring that "anything less like a Temple of Justice can hardly be imagined."[24] Then, as now, justice remained a matter of perspective, and for many Victorian Londoners, vicariously or in person, their gaze was invariably drawn to the magistrate's courtroom. These courts remained prominent due to their wide remit in everyday life and the proliferation of portrayals that made them, in the public mind, "the true home of drama."[25] In contrast to the higher courts such as the Old Bailey, the police courts were close to the warp and weft of daily travail in London's teeming districts. The stories and figures that emerged from them were both relatable and compelling for the general public and their operation was, at least on the surface, comprehensible to the majority. They hid the power of the state in plain sight, elevating the informal freedom of the individual in the

[23] Cecil Chapman, *The Poor Man's Court of Justice: Twenty-Five Years as a Metropolitan Magistrate* (London: Hodder and Staughton, 1925).

[24] Alfred Chicele Plowden, *Grain or Chaff? The Autobiography of a Police Magistrate* (London: T. Fisher Unwin, 1903), 175.

[25] J. A. R. Cairns, *The Loom of the Law* (London: Hutchinson, 1920), 42.

public courtroom even as they formally constrained it through the enforcement of new statutes.

The power of nineteenth-century courtrooms, from the Old Bailey to the London magistrates' courts, to shape popular understandings of law and justice has proven remarkably resilient.[26] Images of courtrooms, which were intrinsic to the development of popular newspapers, continue to surround us today, from newspaper "crime" stories to popular fiction to television and movie dramas where the ultimate confrontation between protagonist and antagonist is often a trial scene. Equally common are depictions of courtrooms as melodramatic or farcical, a place where the foibles and petty conflicts of rivals, neighbors, and spouses are on display for public amusement.[27] Because of these portrayals, it is common to imagine courtrooms as places of sharp contest, where the lines between both right and wrong and legal and illegal are clearly drawn.[28] In practice, modern courtrooms are highly procedural, bureaucratic, and often unintelligible to those without the necessary background. They are the realms of legal expertise, not common knowledge.[29] It may be that the origin of the courtroom's image as a site of drama, comedy, or tragedy lies, at least in part, with the London police courts and their

[26] In the twentieth century, the magistrates' courts would also be the subject for three of the popular Penguin editions, two authored by F. T. Giles (Chief Clerk of the Clerkenwell Magistrates' Court), *The Magistrates' Courts* (London: Penguin 1949) and *The Criminal Law* (London: Penguin, 1954), and one by the prominent barrister Henry Loveridge Hodgkinson, *English Justice* (London: Penguin, 1932).

[27] When describing this project to those unfamiliar with nineteenth-century British history, I often told them that I was writing about the Victorian version of *Judge Judy* or *The People's Court*.

[28] Stewart Macaulay, "Images of Law in Everyday Life: the Lessons of School, Entertainment, and Spectator Sports," *Law & Society Review* 21, no. 2 (1987), 185–218.

[29] On the importance of such expertise in the growth of modern governance, particularly in terms of quantification, see Nikola Rose, "Governing by Numbers: Figuring Out Democracy," *Accounting, Organizations and Society* 16, no. 7 (1991), 673–75. On the more common use of specialized knowledge in governing, and the ways in which it distances governed subjects from power and political processes in Liberal societies, see Joyce, *Rule of Freedom*, 24–25. For the importance of legal expertise in the Victorian state, see Gavin Drewry, "Lawyers and Statutory Reform in Victorian Government," 27–40 and Jill Pellew, "Law and Order: Expertise and the Victorian Home Office," 59–72, both in Roy McLeod, ed., *Government and Expertise: Specialists, Administrator and Professionals, 1860–1919* (Cambridge: Cambridge University Press, 1988).

many portrayals. It would be problematic to trace a direct lineage, but given their social impact and cultural footprint, it is certainly plausible. From Dickens's "Mr. Fang" to the contemporary taste for courtroom dramas, the legacy of courtroom culture may yet endure, even if many of the courts where it originated have adjourned *sine die*.

Bibliography

PRIMARY SOURCES

MANUSCRIPT SOURCES

London Metropolitan Archives, Clerkenwell

Local Courts

Bow Street Police Court. Registers of Charges. 1900.

Bow Street Police Court. Registers of Summonses. 1901.

Clerkenwell Police Court. Minutes of Charges. 1905–1915.

Clerkenwell Police Court. Minutes of Summonses. 1900–1915.

Edmonton Petty Sessions. Minutes of Summary Proceedings. 1837–1838.

Edmonton Petty Sessions. Registers. 1890.

Hammersmith Police Court. Registers of Charges. 1880

Thames Police Court. Registers of Summonses. 1885–1910.

West London Police Court. Registers of Charges. 1880–1915.

West London Police Court. Registers of Summonses. 1882–1915.

Metropolitan Government

Annual Reports of the School Board for London. 1887–1903.

London School Board. Minutes of the School Accommodation and Attendance Committee. 1880.

London School Board. Report of the Special Sub-Committee of the Bye-Laws Committee on the Administration of the Bye-Laws. 1891.

The National Archives, Kew

Home Office Papers

Complaint by London School Board re: Hearing of Cases under Education Acts at Metropolitan Police Courts. PRO HO 45/9521/25043A. 1873–1884.

PUBLIC DOCUMENTS

Great Britain, Parliament, House of Commons.

1832. 13 Parl. Deb. H.C. (3d ser.).

Parliamentary Papers (pp).

House of Commons

1828 (533). "Report from the Select Committee on the Police in the Metropolis."

1833 (675). "Report from Select Committee on Metropolitan Police."

1834 (600). "Select Committee on the Police of the Metropolis with Minutes of Evidence, Appendix and Index."

1837 (451). "Report from the Select Committee on Metropolis Police Offices with the Minutes of Evidence, Appendix and Index."

1837–8 (578). "Report from the Select Committee on Metropolis Police Offices with the Minutes of Evidence, Appendix and Index."

1860 (2692). "Judicial Statistics, 1859, England and Wales, Pt. I, Police – Criminal Proceedings – Prisons."

1861 (2860). "Judicial Statistics, 1860, England and Wales, Pt. I, Police – Criminal Proceedings – Prisons."

1866 (3726). "Judicial Statistics, 1865, England and Wales, Pt. I, Police – Criminal Proceedings – Prisons."

1871 (442). "Judicial Statistics, 1870, England and Wales, Pt. I, Police – Criminal Proceedings – Prisons."

1876 (1595). "Judicial Statistics, 1875, England and Wales, Pt. I, Police – Criminal Proceedings – Prisons."

1881 (3088). "Judicial Statistics, 1880, England and Wales, Pt. I, Police – Criminal Proceedings – Prisons."

1886 (4808). "Judicial Statistics, 1885, England and Wales, Pt. I, Police – Criminal Proceedings – Prisons."

1890–1 (6443). "Judicial Statistics, 1890, England and Wales, Pt. I, Police – Criminal Proceedings – Prisons."

1900 (374). "Report of the Departmental Committee Appointed by the Secretary of State for the Home Office Department to Inquire into the Jurisdiction of the Metropolitan Police Magistrates and County Justices Respectively in the Metropolitan Police Court District 1900."

1900 (399). "Annual Report of the Commissioner of Police of the Metropolis, 1899."
1901 (659, 705). "Judicial Statistics, England and Wales, 1899, Pt. I, Criminal Statistics."
1902 (953). "Judicial Statistics, 1900 England and Wales, Pt. I, Police – Criminal Proceedings – Prisons."
1907 (3477). "Judicial Statistics, England and Wales, 1905, Pt. II, Civil Courts."
1909 (236) "Report from the Select Committee on Bastardy Orders, 1909."
1910 (5096 and 5097). "Judicial Statistics, England and Wales, 1908, Pt. I, Criminal Statistics."
1912–13 (6478) "Report of the Royal Commission on Divorce and Matrimonial Causes."
1912–13 (6479). "Royal Commission on Divorce and Matrimonial Causes. Minutes of Evidence Taken Before the Royal Commission. Vol. 1."
1912–13 (6480). "Royal Commission on Divorce and Matrimonial Causes. Minutes of Evidence Taken Before the Royal Commission. Vol. 2."
1912–13 (6481). "Royal Commission on Divorce and Matrimonial Causes. Minutes of Evidence Taken Before the Royal Commission. Vol. 3."
1912–13 (6482) "Appendices to the Minutes of Evidence and Report of the Royal Commission on Divorce and Matrimonial Causes."
1912–13 (6071 and 6047). "Judicial Statistics, England and Wales, 1910, Pt. I, Criminal Statistics."
1914–16 (7767, 7807). "Judicial Statistics, England and Wales, 1913, Pt. I, Criminal Statistics."

Acts of Parliament

Act for Further Improving the Police in and Near the Metropolis 1839, 2 & 3 Vict. c. 41.
Affiliation Orders Act 1914, 4 & 5 Geo. 5 c. 6.
Bastardy Laws Amendment Act 1872, 35 & 36 Vict. c. 65.
Criminal Justice Act 1855, 18 &19 Vict. c. 126.
Criminal Statutes Repeal Act 1827, 7 & 8 Geo. 4 c. 27.
Elementary Education (Amendment) Act 1873, 36 & 37 Vict. c. 86.
Employers and Workmen's Act 1875, 38 & 39 Vict. c. 90.
Elementary Education (Amendment) Act, 1876 39 & 40 Vict. c. 79.
Justices of the Peace Act 1361, 34 Edw. 3 c.1.
Juvenile Offenders Act 1847, 10 & 11 Vict. c. 82
Juvenile Offenders Act 1850, 10 & 11 Vict. c. 82.
Larceny Act 1827, 7 & 8 Geo. 4. c. 29.
Larceny Act 1850, 13 &14 Vict. c. 37.
Licensing Act 1902, 2 Edw. 7 c. 28.
Malicious Damages Act 1861, 24 & 25 Vict. c. 97.

Malicious Injuries to Property Act 1827, 7 & 8 Geo. 4 c. 29.
Married Women Act 1886, 49 & 50 Vict. c. 52.
Matrimonial Causes Act 1857, 20 & 21 Vict. c. 85
Metropolitan Fire Brigade Act 1865, 28 & 29 Vict. c. 90.
Offences Against the Person Act 1828, 9 Geo. 4 c. 31.
Offences Against the Person Act 1861, 24 & 25 Vict. c.100.
Poor Law Amendment Act 1834, 4 & 5 Will. 4 c. 76.
Poor Law Amendment Act 1868, 31 & 32 Vict. c. 122.
Summary Jurisdiction Act 1848, 11 &12 Vict. c. 43.
Summary Jurisdiction Act 1895, 58 & 59 Vict. c. 39.
Vagrancy Act 1824, 5 Geo. 4 c. 83.

Legal Cases in the High Courts

Glennie v. Glennie (1862) 32 L.J., P. and M. 17.
Keats v. Keats (1858) 1 Sw. and Tr. 334.
London School Board v. Duggan (1884) 8 QBD 176.
School Attendance Committee of Belper Union v. Bailey (1882) 9 QBD 259.
Ward v. Ward (1858) 1 Sw. and Tr. 85.
Williams v. Williams (1864) 3 Sw. and Tr.

NEWSPAPERS AND PERIODICALS

Bee-Hive
Cleave's Weekly Police Gazette
The Contemporary Review
East London Observer
Illustrated London News
Islington Gazette
The Justice of the Peace and County, Borough, Poor Law Union and Parish Recorder
Leeds Mercury
Lloyds's Weekly Newspaper
Morning Post
New York Times
Pall Mall Gazette
Reynolds's News
The Times of London

PRINTED PRIMARY SOURCES

Barnett, Samuel. "Introduction." In T*he London Police Court To-day and To-morrow*, by Hugh Gamon. London: J. M. Dent, 1907.

Beaumont, Joseph. *The New Slavery: An Account of the Indian and Chinese Immigration in British Guiana*. London: Ridgeway, 1871.

Booth, Charles. *Life and Labour of the People of London. Final Volume: Notes on Social Influences and Conclusion*. New York: Macmillan, 1903.

Booth Poverty Map, Charles Booth Online Archive. http://booth.lse.ac.uk.

Burke, Thomas. *Limehouse Nights*. New York: McBride, 1917.

Byrne, William Pitt. *Undercurrents Overlooked*. London: Richard Bentley, 1860.

Cairns, J. A. R. *The Loom of the Law*. London: Hutchinson, 1920.

Cairns, J. A. R. *The Sidelights of London*. London: Hutchinson, 1923.

Cancellor, H. L. *The Life of a London Beak*. London: Hurst & Blackett, 1930.

Census Returns of England and Wales, 1861. Kew, Surrey, England: The National Archives of the UK (TNA): Public Record Office (PRO), 1861.

Census Returns of England and Wales, 1871. Kew, Surrey, England: The National Archives of the UK (TNA): Public Record Office (PRO), 1871.

Census Returns of England and Wales, 1881. Kew, Surrey, England: The National Archives of the UK (TNA): Public Record Office (PRO), 1881.

Chapman, Cecil. *A Poor Man's Court of Justice: Twenty-Five Years as a Metropolitan Magistrate*. London: Hodder and Stoughton, 1925.

Colquhoun, Patrick. *A Treaty on the Police of the Metropolis, 6th ed*. London: H. Baldwin, 1800.

Cruikshank, George. "Commentary upon the late 'New Police Act.'" *George Cruikshank Collected Plates*. Vol. II of *Collection of Prints from Drawings by George Cruikshank c.1841–1843*, Nos. 2130–2239. *George Cruikshank's Omnibus* (1842).

Crump, John, and Bertram Crump. *The Magistrate's Pocket Manual*. London, 1904.

Davey, Sydney. *Maintenance and Desertion under the Poor Law and Summary Jurisdiction (Married Women) Act 1895*. London: Poor Law Officer's Journal, 1904.

Dickens, Charles, Jr. "A London Police-Court." In *All the Year Round: A Weekly Journal* 4 (3rd series) (Jan.–Jun. 1899).

Dickens, Charles. "A Suburban Connemara." *Household Words*, March 8, 1851.

Dogberry [pseud.] ed. *Humours and Oddities in the London Police Courts from the Opening of This Century to the Present Time*. London and New York: Leadenhall Press, 1894.

Fielding, Henry. *An Enquiry into the Causes of the Late Increase in Robbers, 2nd ed*. London: A. Millar, 1751.

Fielding, John. *A Plan for Preventing Robberies within Twenty Miles of London*. London: A. Millar, 1755.

Fielding, John. Fielding, John. *Account of the Origin and Effects of a Police Set on Foot by His Grace the Duke of Newcastle in the Year 1753, upon a Plan presented to his Grace by the late Henry Fielding*. London: A. Millar, 1758.

Fletcher, Joseph. "Statistical Account of the Constitution and Operation of the Criminal Courts of the Metropolis." *Journal of the Statistical Society of London* 9, no. 4 (Dec. 1846).
Gamon, Hugh. *The London Police Courts To-Day and To-Morrow*. London: J. M. Dent, 1907.
Giles, F. T. *The Criminal Law*. Harmondsworth: Penguin, 1954.
Giles, F. T. *The Magistrates' Courts*. London: Penguin Books, 1949.
Grant, James. *Sketches in London*. London: W.S. Orr, 1838.
Greenwood, James. *Mysteries of Modern London, by One of the Crowd*. London: Diprose & Bateman,1883.
Hime, Thomas Whiteside. *Public Health: The Practical Guide to the Public Health Act 1875, and Correlated Acts, for the Use of Medical Officers of Health and Inspectors of Nuisances*. London: Ballière, Tindall, and Cox, 1884.
Hodgkinson, Henry Loveridge. "Solicitor." In *English Justice*. London: Penguin Books,1932.
Holmes, Thomas. *Known to the Police*. London: Edward Arnold, 1908.
Holmes, Thomas. *Pictures and Problems from London Police Courts, Etc.* London: Edward Arnold, 1900.
Ingersoll, George P. "The London Police Courts." *Yale Law Journal* 54, no. 2 (Oct. 1892–Jun. 1893).
Jenkins, John Edward. *The Coolie: His Rights and His Wrongs*. New York: Routledge, 1871.
Leaming, Thomas. *A Philadelphia Lawyer in the London Courts*. 2nd ed. New York: Henry Holt, 1912.
Lushington, S. G., and Guy Lushington. *The Summary Jurisdiction (Married Women) Act 1895 as Extended by the Licensing Act 1902, with Introduction, Notes, and Index*. 2nd ed. London: Butterworth, 1904.
Mullins, Claud. *In Quest of Justice*. London: Murray, 1931.
Mullins, Claud. *Wife v. Husband in the Courts*. London: Allen & Unwin, 1935.
Murphy, Emily. *The Black Candle*. Toronto: Thomas Allen, 1922.
Passmore, J. *Lives of the Illustrious*. In *the Biographical Magazine, vol. 3*. London: Partridge, 1856.
Plowden, Alfred Chicele. Grain or Chaff? *The Autobiography of a Police Magistrate*. London, Edinburgh, Dublin and New York: Thomas Nelson, 1903.
R. E. Corder [pseud.]. *Tales Told to the Magistrate*. London: A. Melrose, 1925.
Reid, Thomas Wemyss, and William Henry Cooke. *Two Idle Apprentices, Briefs and Papers: Sketches of the Bar and The Press*. London: Henry King, 1872.
Returns from the Commissioners of Metropolitan Police. Excerpted in *The Journal of the Statistical Society of London, vol. 1*. London: Charles Knight, 1839.
Richie, James Ewing. *The Night Side of London*. 2nd ed. London: William Tweedie, 1858.
Saunders, Thomas William. *The Practice of the Magistrates' Courts*. 2nd ed. London: The Law Times Office, 1858.

Saunders, Thomas. *Metropolitan Police Court Jottings*. London: Horace Cox, 1882.

Saunders, Thomas William. *Oke's Magisterial Synopsis: A Practical Guide to Magistrates, Their Clerks, Solicitors and Constables. Vol. 1.* 13th ed. London: Butterworths, 1882.

Statistical Abstract for London. Vol. IV. 1901.

Waddy, Henry Turner. *The Police Court and Its Work*. London: Butterworth, 1925.

Watts, W. H. *London Life at the Police Courts*. London: Ward and Lock, 1864.

Watts, W. H. "Records of an Old Police Court." *St. James Magazine*, Nov. 1864.

Wight, John. *Mornings at Bow Street: A Selection of the Most Humourous and Entertaining Reports Which Have Appeared in the Morning Herald*. London: Charles Baldwyn, 1824.

Williams, Montagu. *Later Leaves: The Further Reminisces of Montagu Williams, Q.C.* London: Macmillan, 1891.

Williams, Montagu. *Leaves of a Life*. 2 vols. London and New York: Macmillan, 1890.

Williams, Montagu. *Round London: Down East and Up West*. London and New York: Macmillan, 1893.

SECONDARY SOURCES

Books and Articles

Abel, Emily K. "Toynbee Hall, 1884–1914." *Social Service Review* 54, no. 1 (Dec. 1979): 606–632.

Alexander, G. Glover. *The Administration of Justice in Criminal Matters, England and* Wales. Cambridge: Cambridge University Press, 1915.

Anderson, Olive. "State, Civil Society and Separation in Victorian Marriage." *Past and Present* 163 (1999): 161–201.

Anderson, Olive. *Suicide in Victorian and Edwardian England*. Oxford: Clarendon, 1987.

Andrew, Donna T., and Randall McGowan. *The Perreaus and Mrs. Rudd: Forgery and Betrayal in Eighteenth-Century London*. Berkeley and Los Angeles: University of California Press, 2001.

Arnot, Margaret L. "Infant Death, Child Care and the State: The Baby-Farming Scandal and the First Infant Life Protection Legislation of 1872." *Continuity & Change* 9, no. 2 (1994): 271–311.

Asquith, Ivor. "The Structure, Ownership and Control of the Press, 1780–1855." In *Newspaper History from the Seventeenth Century to the Present Day*, edited by George Boyce, James Curran, and Pauline Wingate. London: Constable, 1978

Auerbach, Sascha. "Beyond the Pale of Mercy, Victorian Penal Culture, Police Court Missionaries, and the Origins of Probation in England." *Law and History Review* 33, no. 3 (Aug. 2015): 621–23.

Auerbach, Sascha. "'Some Punishment Should Be Devised': Parents, Children, and the State in Victorian London." *The Historian* 71, no. 4 (Winter 2009): 757–79.

Auerbach, Sascha. "'The Law Has No Feeling for Poor Folks Like Us!': Everyday Responses to Legal Compulsion in England's Working-Class Communities, 1871–1904." *Journal of Social History* 45, no.2 (Spring 2012): 686–708.

Auerbach, Sascha. "'You Have Lost All That Is German of You in the Dock': Citizens, Aliens and the Wartime State in London's Local Courtrooms, 1914–1918." *Twentieth Century British History* (forthcoming).

Babbington, Anthony. *A House in Bow Street.* London: Macdonald, 1969.

Baggs, A. P., Diane K. Bolton, and Patricia E. C. Croot. "Islington and Stoke Newington Parishes." In *History of Middlesex*, ed. T. F. T. Baker and C. R. Elrington. Vol. 8. London: Victoria County History, 1985.

Bailey, Peter. *Popular Culture and Performance in the Victorian City.* Cambridge: Cambridge University Press, 1998.

Bailey, Victor, ed. *Policing and Punishment in Nineteenth-Century Britain.* New Brunswick: Rutgers University Press, 1981.

Barrie, David. "Public Men, Private Interests: The Origins, Structure and Practice of Police Courts in Scotland, c.1800–1833." *Continuity and Change* 27, no. 1 (May 2012): 83–123.

Barthes, Roland. "Dominici, or the Triumph of Literature." In *Mythologies.* Les Lettres Nouvelles, 1957.

Beattie, J. M. *Crime and the Courts in England, 1660–1800.* Oxford: Oxford University Press, 1986.

Beattie, J.M. "Sir John Fielding and Public Justice: The Bow Street Magistrates' Court, 1754–1780." *Law and History Review* 25, no. 1 (Apr. 2007): 61–100.

Beattie, J.M. *The First English Detectives: The Bow Street Runners and the Policing of London, 1750–1840.* Oxford: Oxford University Press, 2012.

Beattie, John. *Policing and Punishment in London, 1660–1750.* Oxford: Oxford University Press, 2001.

Behlmer, George. *Child Abuse and Moral Reform in England, 1870–1908.* Stanford: Stanford University Press, 1982.

Behlmer, George. *Friends of the Family: The English Home and Its Guardians, 1850–1940.* Stanford: Stanford University Press, 1998

Behlmer, George. "Summary Justice and Working-Class Marriage in England, 1870–1940." *Law and History Review* 12, no. 2 (Fall, 1994): 229–76.

Bentley, David. *English Criminal Justice in the Nineteenth Century.* London: Hambledon, 1998.

Benton, Laura, and Lisa Ford, eds. *Rage for Order: The British Empire and the Origins of International Law, 1800–1950*. Cambridge, MA: Harvard University Press, 2016.

Benton, Lauren. "Beyond Legal Pluralism: Towards a New Approach to Law in the Informal Sector." *Social & Legal Studies* 3 (Jun. 1994): 223–42.

Benton, Lauren. *Law and Colonial Cultures: Legal Regimes in World History, 1400–1900*. Cambridge: Cambridge University Press, 2002.

Bertelsen, Lance. "Committed by Justice Fielding: Judicial and Journalistic Representation in the Bow Street Magistrates' Office, January 3–November 24, 1752." *Eighteenth-Century Studies* 40, no. 4 (1997): 337–363.

Biderman, A. D., and A. J. Reiss. "On Exploring the 'Dark Figure' of Crime." *Annals of the American Academy of Political and Social Science* 374, no.1 (1967): 1–15.

Bierbrauer, Giinter. "Toward an Understanding of Legal Culture: Variations in Individualism and Collectivism between Kurds, Lebanese, and Germans." *Law & Society Review* 28, no. 2 (1994):243–45.

Blankenburg, Erhard. "Civil Litigation Rates as Indicators for Legal Cultures." In *Comparing Legal Cultures*, edited by David Nelken, 41. Aldershot: Routledge, 1997.

Bonnell, Victoria E., and Lynn Hunt, eds. *Beyond the Cultural Turn: New Directions in the Study of Society and Culture*. Berkeley and Los Angeles: University of California Press, 1999.

Bourdieu, Pierre. *Language and Symbolic Power*. Translated by Gino Raymond and Matthew Adamso. Cambridge, MA: Harvard University Press, 1993.

Bourdieu, Pierre. "The Force of Law: Toward a Sociology of the Juridical Field." *Hastings Law Journal* 38 (1987): 805–853.

Boyce, George, James Curran, and Paul Wingate, eds. *Newspaper History from the Seventeenth Century to the Present Day*. London: Constable, 1978.

Brewer, John, and John Styles, eds. *An Ungovernable People: The English and Their Law in the Seventeenth and Eighteenth Centuries*. New Brunswick: Rutgers University Press, 1980.

Brewer, John, and John Styles. "Popular Attitudes to the Law in the Eighteenth Century." In *Crime and Society: Readings in History and Theory*, edited by Mike Fitzgerald, Gregor McLennan, and Jennie Pawson, 32–35. London: Routledge, 1981.

Briggs, Asa. *Victorian Cities*. London: Odhams Press, 1964.

Brooks, Christopher, and Michael Lobban, eds. *Communities and: Courts in Britain*, 1150–1900. London: Bloomsbury, 1997.

Burchell, Graham, Colin Gordon, and Peter Miller, eds. *The Foucault Effect: Studies in Governmentality*. Hemel Hempstead: Harvester Wheatsheaf, 1991.

Burns, W. L. *The Age of Equipoise: A Study of the Mid-Victorian Generation*. London: George Allen & Unwin, 1964.

Burton, Antoinette. *Burdens of History: British Feminists, Indian Women, and Imperial Culture, 1865–1915*. Chapel Hill: University of North Carolina Press, 1994.

Carlen, Pat. "The Staging of Magistrates' Justice." *British Journal of Criminology* 16, no. 1 (Jan. 1976): 48–55.

Casey, Christopher A. "Common Misperceptions: The Press and Victorian Views of Crime." *Journal of Interdisciplinary History* 41, no.3 (Winter 2011): 376–378.

Charles Booth's Maps of London Poverty, East and West, 1889. London: Old House, 2013.

Clapson, Mark. *A Bit of a Flutter: Popular Gambling and English Society, c. 1923–1961*. Manchester: Manchester University Press, 1992.

Clark, Anna. "Domesticity and the Problem of Wifebeating in Nineteenth-Century England: Working-Class Culture, Law and Politics." In *Everyday Violence in Britain, 1850–1950*, edited by Shani D'Cruze. Harlow: Pearson, 2000.

Clark, Anna. "Humanity or Justice? Wifebeating and the Law in the Eighteenth and Nineteenth Centuries." In *Regulating Womanhood: Historical Essays on Marriage, Motherhood and Sexuality*, edited by C. Smart. London: Routledge, 1992.

Clark, Anna. *The Struggle for the Breeches: Gender and the Making of the British Working Class*. Berkeley: University of California Press, 1995.

Clark, Anna. "Whores and Gossips: Sexual Reputation in London, 1770–1825." In *Current Issues in Women's History*, edited by Arina Angerman and Geerte Binnema. London and New York: Routledge, 1989.

Clark, J. C. D. "Secularization and Modernization: The Failure of a 'Grand Narrative.'" *The Historical Journal* 55, no. 1 (Mar. 2012): 161–94.

Conboy, Martin. *The Language of Newspapers: Socio-Historical Perspectives*. London: Continuum, 2010.

Conley, Carolyn. *The Unwritten Law: Criminal Justice in Victorian Kent*. New York and Oxford: Oxford University Press, 1991.

Copelman, Dina. *London's Women Teachers: Gender, Class and Feminism, 1870–1930*. London: Routledge, 1996.

Cosh, Mary. *A History of Islington*. London: Historical Publications, 2005.

Crais, Clifton. "Chiefs and Bureaucrats in the Making of Empire: A Drama from the Transkei, South Africa, October 1880." *American Historical Review* 108, no.4 (Oct. 2003): 1034–56.

Craven, Paul. "Law and Ideology: The Toronto Police Court 1850–80." In *Essays in the History of Canadian Law, vol.* 2, ed. David Flaherty. Toronto: Osgoode Society for Canadian Legal History by University of Toronto Press, 1983.

Crime and Punishment in Islington 1, no. 1 (2009). https://rebelhand.files.wordpress.com/2015/05/crime-punishment-inislington. pdf

Croll, Andy. "Street Disorder, Surveillance and Shame: Regulating Behavior in the Public Spaces of the Late Victorian British Town." *Social History* 24, no. 3 (Oct. 1999): 260–261.

Crone, Rosalind. *Violent Victorians: Popular Entertainment in Nineteenth-Century London*. Manchester: Manchester University Press, 2012.

Crossick, Geoffrey, ed. *The Lower Middle Class in Britain, 1870–1914*. London: Croom Helm, 1977.

Davey, B. J. *Lawless and Immoral: Policing A Country Town, 1838–1857*. New York: St. Martin's Press, 1983.

Davies, Andrew. "'These Viragoes Are No Less Cruel Than the Lads': Young Women, Gangs, and Violence in Late Victorian Manchester and Salford." *British Journal of Criminology* 39, no. 1 (1999): 72–89.

Davies, James Edward. *Criminal Law Consolidation Statutes of 24 & 25 Victoria, chapters 94 to 100, edited with notes, critical and explanatory*. London: Butterworths, 1861.

Davis, Jennifer. "A Poor Man's System of Justice: The London Police Courts in the Second Half of the Nineteenth Century." *The Historical Journal* 27 (1984): 313–15.

Davis, Jennifer. "Prosecutions and Their Context." In *Policing and Prosecution in Britain, 1750–1850*, edited by Douglas Hay and Francis Snyder. Oxford: Clarendon Press, 1989.

Davis, John. *Reforming London: The London Government Problem, 1855–1900*. Oxford: Oxford University Press, 1988.

Davis, Natalie Zemon. *Fiction in the Archives: Pardon Tales and their Tellers in Sixteenth-Century France*. Stanford: Stanford University Press, 1990.

D'Cruze, Shani, and Louise A. Jackson. *Women, Crime and Justice: in England since 1660*. Basingstoke: Palgrave-Macmillan, 2009.

D'Cruze, Shani. *Crimes of Outrage: Sex, Violence and Victorian Working Women*. Dekalb: Northern Illinois University Press, 1998.

D'Cruze, Shani. *Everyday Violence in Britain, 1850–1950: Gender and Class*. Harlow: Longman, 2000.

D'Cruze, Shani. "Sex, Violence and Local Courts: Working-Class Respectability in a Mid-Nineteenth Century Lancashire Town." *British Journal of Criminology* 39, no. 1 (1999): 41, 51–52.

DeGroot, Gerard. *Blighty: British Society in the Era of the Great War*. London: Longman, 1996.

Delap, Lucy. *Knowing Their Place: Domestic Service in Twentieth Century Britain*. Oxford: Oxford University Press, 2011.

Devereaux, Simon. "The Fall of the Sessions Paper: The Criminal Trial and the Popular Press in Late Eighteenth-Century London." *Criminal Justice History* 18 (2003): 57–59.

Doggett, Maeve. *Marriage, Wife-Beating, and the Law in Victorian England*. Columbia: University of South Carolina Press, 1992.

Drewry, Gavin. "Lawyers and Statutory Reform in Victorian Government." In *Government and Expertise: Specialists, Administrator and Professionals, 1860–1919*, edited by Roy McLeod. Cambridge: Cambridge University Press, 1988.

Dubber, Markus D., and Lindsay Farmer, eds. *Modern Histories of Crime and Punishment*. Stanford: Stanford University Press, 2007.

Edwards, Susan. "'Kicked, Beaten and Jumped On Until They Are Crushed,' All Under Man's Wing and Protection: The Victorian Dilemma with Domestic Violence." In *Criminal Conversations: Victorian Crimes, Social Panic, and Moral Outrage*, edited by Judith Rowbotham and Kim Stevenson. Columbus: The Ohio State University Press, 2005.

Emsley, Clive. "Crime and Punishment: Ten Years of Research (1) – Filling In, Adding Up, Moving On: Criminal Justice History in Contemporary Britain." *Crime, Histoire & Sociétiés/Crime, History & Societies* 9, no. 1 (2005): 2–19.

Emsley, Clive. *Crime and Society in England, 1750–1900*. London and New York: Longman, 1986.

Emsley, Clive. "'Mother, What Did Policemen Do When There Weren't Any Motors?': The Law, the Police and the Regulation of Motor Traffic in England." *Historical Journal* 37 (1993): 357–381.

Epstein, James. "Spatial Practices/Democratic Vistas." *Social History* 24, no. 3 (Oct. 1999): 294–310.

Feeley, Malcolm M., and Deborah L. Little. "The Vanishing Female: The Decline of Women in the Criminal Process, 1687–1912." *Law & Society Review* 25, No. 4 (1991): 719–75.

Finn, Margot. "The Authority of the Law." In *Liberty and Authority in Victorian Britain*, edited by Peter Mandler. Oxford: Oxford University Press, 2006.

Finn, Margot. "Women, Consumption and Couverture in England, c. 1760–1860." *Historical Journal* 39, no. 3 (1996): 703–722.

Finn, Margot. "Working-Class Women and the Contest for Consumer Control in Victorian County Courts." *Past and Present* 161, no. 1 (Nov. 1998): 116–154.

Forster, John. *The Life of Charles Dickens*. Vol. III of *The Life of Charles Dickens*. Boston: James R. Osgood, 1875.

Foucault, Michel. "Governmentality." In *The Foucault Effect: Studies in Governmentality*, edited by Graham Burchell, Colin Gordon and Peter Miller. Chicago: University of Chicago Press, 1991.

Foyster, Elizabeth. *Marital Violence: An English Family History, 1660–1857*. Cambridge: Cambridge University Press, 2006.

Frost, Ginger. "Claiming Justice: Paternity Affiliation in South Wales, 1870–1900." *Rural History* 24, no. 2 (Oct. 2013): 177–198.

Frost, Ginger. *Illegitimacy in English Law and Society, 1860–1930*. Manchester: Manchester University Press, 2016.

Frost, Ginger. "'I Shall Not Sit Down and Crie': Women, Class and Breach of Promise of Marriage Plaintiffs in England, 1850–1900." *Gender & History* 6, no. 2 (1994): 224–245.

Frost, Ginger. *Promises Broken: Courtship, Class, and Gender in Victorian England.* Charlottesville and London: University of Virginia Press, 1995.

Frost, Ginger. "'The Black Lamb of the Black Sheep': Illegitimacy in the English Working Class, 1850–1939." *Journal of Social History* 37, no. 2 (Winter, 2003): 293–322.

Gates, Barbara T. *Victorian Suicide: Mad Crimes and Sad Histories.* Princeton: Princeton University Press, 1988.

Gatrell, V. A. C., Bruce Lenman, and Geoffrey Parker, eds. *Crime and the Law: The Social History of Crime in Western Europe since 1500.* London: Europa Publications, 1980.

Gatrell, V. A. C. "Crime, Authority and the Policeman-State," In *Social Agencies and Institutions*, ed. F. M. L. Thompson. Vol. 3 of *The Cambridge Social History of Britain.* Cambridge: Cambridge University Press, 1990.

Gatrell, V. A. C. "The Decline of Theft and Violence in Victorian and Edwardian England." In *Crime and the Law: The Social History of Crime in Western Europe since 1500*, edited by V. A. C. Gatrell, Bruce Lenman, and Geoffrey Parker. London: Europa Publications, 1980.

Gatrell, V. A. C. *The Hanging Tree: Execution and the English People* Oxford: Oxford University Press, 1996.

Gatrell, V. A. C. *The London Hanged: Crime and Civil Society in the Eighteenth Century.* London: Allen Lane, 1991.

Geertz, Clifford. *Local Knowledge: Further Essays in Interpretive Anthropology.* New York: Basic Books, 1983.

Geertz, Clifford. *Negara: The Theatre State in Nineteenth-Century Bali.* Princeton: Princeton University Press, 1980.

Gillis, John. "The Evolution of Juvenile Delinquency in England, 1890–1914." *Past and Present* 67, no. 1 (1975): 96–126.

Gladfelder, Hal. *Criminality and Narrative in Eighteenth-Century England: Beyond the Law.* Baltimore: Johns Hopkins University Press, 2001.

Godfrey, Barry, and Paul Lawrence. *Crime and Justice 1750–1950.* Cullompton, Devon: Willan, 2005.

Godfrey, Barry, Stephen Farrall, and Susan Karstedt. "Explaining Gendered Sentencing Patterns for Violent Men and Women in the Late-Victorian and Edwardian Period." *British Journal of Criminology* 45 (2005): 696–720.

Godfrey, Barry. "Changing Prosecution Practices and Their Impact on Crime Figures, 1857–1940." *British Journal of Criminology* 48 (2008): 171–189.

Godfrey, Barry. *Crime in England, 1880–1945: The Rough and the Criminal, the Police and the Incarcerated.* Abingdon and New York: Routledge, 2014.

Goodman, Joyce. *Women, Educational Policy-Making and Administration in England: Authoritative Women Since 1800*. London: Routledge, 2000.

Goodway, David. *London Chartism, 1838–1848*. Cambridge: Cambridge University Press, 1982.

Gowing, Laura. *Domestic Dangers: Women, Words, and Sex in Early Modern London*. Oxford: Oxford University Press, 1996.

Gowing, Laura. "Language, Power and the Law: Women's Slander Legislation in Early Modern London." In *Women, Crime and the Courts in Early Modern England*, edited by Jenny Kermode and Garthine Walker. Chapel Hill: University of North Carolina Press, 1994.

Graham, Clare. *Ordering Law: The Architectural and Social History of the English Law Court*. Aldershot: Ashgate, 2003.

Green, S. J. D., and R. C. Whiting. "Introduction: The Shifting Boundaries of the State in Modern Britain." In *The Boundaries of the State in Modern Britain*, edited by S. J. D. Green and R. C. Whiting. Cambridge: Cambridge University Press, 1996.

Grey, Daniel. *Crime, Prosecution and Social Relations: The Summary Courts of the City of London in the Late Eighteenth Century*. Basingstoke and New York: Palgrave-Macmillan, 2009.

Griffin, Ben. "Class, Gender, and Liberalism in Parliament, 1868–1882: The Case of the Married Women's Property Acts." *The Historical Journal* 46, no. 1 (Mar. 2003): 59–87.

Griffin, Ben. *The Politics of Gender in Victorian Britain: Masculinity, Political Culture, and the Struggle for Women's Rights*. New York: Cambridge University Press, 2012.

Griffiths, Dennis, ed. *The Encyclopedia of the British Press: 1422–1992*. London: Macmillan, 1992.

Hammerton, A. James. *Cruelty and Companionship: Conflict in Nineteenth-Century Married Life*. London: Routledge, 1992.

Hammerton, A. James. "Pooterism or Partnership? Marriage and Masculine Identity in the Lower Middle Class, 1870–1920." *Journal of British Studies* 38, no. 3 (Jul. 1999): 291–321.

Hanson, Julienne. "The Architecture of Justice: Iconography and Space Configuration in the English Law Court Building." *Architectural Research Quarterly* 1, no. 4 (Summer 1996): 55–56.

Harris, Michael, and Alan Lee. "Introduction" (to pt. 2: "The Nineteenth Century.") In *The Press in English Society from the Seventeenth to Nineteenth Centuries*, edited by Michael Harris and Alan Lee. London: Associated University Presses, 1986.

Hay, Douglas, and Francis Snyder, eds. *Policing and Prosecution in Britain, 1750–1850*. Oxford: Clarendon Press, 1989.

Hay, Douglas, and Paul Craven, eds. *Masters, Servants, and Magistrates in Britain and the Empire, 1562–1955*. Chapel Hill and London: University of North Carolina Press, 2004.

Hay, Douglas, Peter Linebaugh, and E. P. Thompson. *Albion's Fatal Tree: Crime and Society in Eighteenth Century England.* London: Allen Lane, 1975.

Hay, Douglas. "England, 1562–1875: The Law and Its Uses." In *Masters, Servants, and Magistrates in Britain and the Empire, 1562–1955*, edited by Douglas Hay and Paul Craven. Chapel Hill: University of North Carolina Press, 2004.

Hay, Douglas. "Property, Authority, and the Criminal Law." In *Albion's Fatal Tree: Crime and Society in Eighteenth Century England*, edited by Douglas Hay, Peter Linebaugh, and E.P. Thompson. London: Allen Lane, 1975.

Hay, Douglas. "Prosecution and Power: Malicious Prosecution in the English Courts 1750–1850." In *Policing and Prosecution in Britain, 1750–1850*, edited by Douglas Hay and Francis Snyder. Oxford: Clarendon Press, 1989.

Hay, Douglas. "The Criminal Prosecution in England and its Historians." *Modern Law Review* 47, no. 1 (Jan. 1984): 1–29.

Hay, Douglas. "Women, Men, and Empires of Law." *Journal of British Studies* 44, no. 1 (Jan. 2005): 204–212.

Henderson, T.F. "Birnie, Sir Richard (c.1760–1832)." In *Oxford Dictionary of National Biography*, rev. by Catherine Pease-Watkin. Oxford: Oxford University Press, 2004.

Herrup, Cynthia. *The Common Peace: Participation and the Criminal Law in Seventeenth-Century England.* Cambridge: Cambridge University Press, 1987.

Hewitt, Martin, ed. *An Age of Equipoise?: Reassessing Mid-Victorian Britain.* Aldershot and Burlington: Ashgate, 2000.

"Historical Representations of Crime and the Criminal." *Oxford Research Encyclopedia of Criminology* (Aug. 2017). criminology.oxfordre.com/view/10.1093/ acrefore/9780190264079.001.0001/acrefore-9780190264079-e-205?print=pdf.

Hoegaerts, Josephine. "Legal or Just? Law, Ethics, and the Double Standard in the Nineteenth-Century Divorce Court." *Law and History Review* 26, no. 2 (Summer 2008): 259–84.

Hoggart, Richard. *The Uses of Literacy: Aspects of Working-Class Life with Special Reference to Publications and Entertainment.* London: Penguin, 1957.

Hopkins, Eric. *A Social History of the English Working Classes, 1815–1945.* London: Edward Arnold, 1976.

Howard, Pendleton. *Criminal Justice in England.* New York: Macmillan, 1931.

Howard, Pendleton. "The Rise of Summary Jurisdiction in English Criminal Law Administration." *California Law Review* 19, no. 5 (Jul. 1931): 486–506.

Hudson, Geoffrey. "Negotiating for Blood Money: War Widows and the Courts in Seventeenth-Century England." In *Women, Crime and the Courts in Early Modern England*, edited by Jenny Kermode and Garthine Walker. Chapel Hill: University of North Carolina Press, 1994.

Hughes, Helen MacGill. *News and the Human Interest Story.* Chicago: University of Chicago Press, 1940.

Hunt, Margaret. "Wife Beating, Domesticity and Women's Independence in Eighteenth-Century London." *Gender & History* 4, no. 1 (1992): 10–33.

Ignatieff, Michael. "Total Institutions and Working Classes: A Review Essay." *History Workshop Journal* 15, no. 1 (1983): 167–73.

Inkster, Ian, Judith Rowbotham, and Colin Griffin, eds. *The Golden Age: Essays in British Social and Economic History, 1850–1870*. Aldershot and Burlington, VT: Ashgate, 2000.

Innes, Joanna, and Arthur Burns. "Introduction." In *Rethinking the Age of Reform: Britain 1780–1850*, edited by Arthur Burns and Joanna Innes. Cambridge: Cambridge University Press, 2003.

Innes, Joanna. *Inferior Politics: Social Problems and Social Policies in Eighteenth- Century Britain*. Oxford: Oxford University Press, 2009.

Inwood, Stephen. "Policing London's Morals: The Metropolitan Police and Popular Culture, 1829–1850." *London Journal* 15, no. 2 (1990):129–46.

Jackson, Peter. *Maps of Meaning*. London and New York: Routledge, 1989.

Jennings, Paul. "Policing Drunkenness in England and Wales from the Late Eighteenth Century to the First World War." *Social History of Alcohol and Drugs* 26, no. 1 (Winter 2012): 69–92.

Jennings, Paul. "Policing Public Houses in Victorian England." *Law, Crime and History* 1 (2013): 52–75.

Jones, David. *Crime, Protest, Community and Police in Nineteenth-Century Britain*. London and New York: Routledge, 1982.

Jones, D. J. V. "The New Police, Crime and People in England and Wales, 1829–1888." *Transactions of the Royal Historical Society* 33 (1983): 151–68.

Jones, Gareth Stedman. *Outcast London: A Study in the Relationship between Classes in Victorian Society*. London: Clarendon Press, 1971.

Jones, Gareth Stedman. "*Rethinking Chartism*." In *Languages of Class: Studies in English Working Class History, 1832–1982*. Cambridge: Cambridge University Press, 1983.

Jones, Gareth Stedman. *The Languages of Class: Studies in Working-Class History 1832–1982*. Cambridge: Cambridge University Press, 1983.

Jones, Marjorie. *Justice and Journalism*. London: Barry Rose, 1974.

Joyce, Patrick. *The Rule of Freedom: Liberalism and the Modern City*. London and New York: Verso, 2003.

Joyce, Patrick. "What Is the Social in Social History?" *Past and Present* 206 (Feb. 2010): 213–248.

Joyce, Simon. *Capital Offenses: Geographies of Class and Crime in Victorian London*. Charlottesville: University of Virginia Press, 2003.

Kermode, Jenny, and Garthine Walker, eds. *Women, Crime and the Courts in Early Modern England*. Chapel Hill: University of North Carolina Press, 1994.

Kidd, Andrew, and David Nichols. *Gender, Civic Culture, and Consumerism: Middle Class Identity in Britain 1800–1940*. Manchester: Manchester University Press, 1999.

King, Peter. *Crime, Justice, and Discretion in England, 1740–1820*. Cambridge: Cambridge University Press, 2000.

King, Peter. *Crime, Justice, and Discretion in England, 1740–1820*. Oxford: Oxford University Press, 2000.

King, Peter. *Crime and Law in England, 1750–1840: Remaking Justice from the Margins*. Cambridge: Cambridge University Press, 2006.

King, Peter. "Newspaper Reporting and Attitudes to Crime and Justice in Late-Nineteenth- and Early-Twentieth-Century London." *Continuity and Change* 22, no. 1 (2007): 73–112.

King, Peter. "Punishing Assault: The Transformation of Attitudes in the English Courts." *Journal of Interdisciplinary History* 27, no.1 (Summer, 1996): 43–74.

King, Peter. "The Rise of Juvenile Delinquency in England 1780–1840: Changing Patterns of Perception and Prosecution." *Past and Present* 160, no. 1 (1998): 73–113.

King, Peter. "The Summary Courts and Social Relations in Eighteenth-Century England." *Past and Present* 183, no. 1 (2004): 125–172.

Koven, Seth, and Sonya Michel, eds. *Mothers of a New World: Maternalist Politics and the Origins of Welfare States*. New York and London: Routledge, 1993.

Koven, Seth. *Slumming: Social and Sexual Politics in Victorian London*. Princeton: Princeton University Press, 2004.

Lake, Brian. *British Newspapers: A History and Guide*. London: Sheppard Press, 1984.

Lambert, Alan. "650 years of the office of Justice of the Peace/Magistrate." *Amicus Curiae* 88 (Winter 2011).

Landau, Norma. *The Justices of the Peace, 1679–1760*. Berkeley and London: University of California Press, 1984.

Langbein, John. "Albion's Fatal Flaws." *Past and Present* 98, no. 1 (Feb. 1983): 96–120.

Langbein, John. "Understanding the Short History of Plea Bargaining." *Faculty Scholarship Series, Yale Law School*, Paper 544 (Jan. 1979): 292–94. (http://digitalcommons.law.yale.edu/cgi/viewcontent.cgi?article=1545&context=fss_papers).

Lee, Alan J. *Origins of the Popular Press in England, 1855–1914*. London: Rowman & Littlefield, 1976.

Lees, Lynn Hollen. *The Solidarities of Strangers: The English Poor Laws and the People, 1700–1948*. Cambridge: Cambridge University Press, 1998.

Lewis, Jane. *Women and Social Action in Victorian and Edwardian England*. Aldershot: Edward Elgar, 1991.

Lewis, Jane. *Women in England 1870–1950: Sexual Divisions and Social Change*. Bloomington: Indiana University Press, 1984.

Linebaugh, Peter. *The London Hanged: Crime and Civil Society in the Eighteenth Century*. London: Allen Lane, 1991.

Lobban, Michael. "Old wine In New Bottles': The Concept and Practice of Law Reform, c.1780–1830." In *Rethinking the Age of Reform: Britain 1780–1850*, edited by Arthur Burns and Joanna Innes, 133. Cambridge: Cambridge University Press, 2003.

Lock, John. *Tales from Bow Street*. London: Hale, 1982.

Macaulay, Stewart. "Images of Law in Everyday Life: the Lessons of School, Entertainment, and Spectator Sports." *Law & Society Review* 21, no. 2 (1987): 185–218.

Macleod, Roy, ed. *Government and Expertise: Specialists, Administrators, and Professionals, 1860–1919*. Cambridge: Cambridge University Press, 1988.

Magarey, Susan. "The Invention of Juvenile Delinquency in Early Nineteenth-Century England." *Labour History* 34 (May 1978): 11–27.

Martin, Jane, and Joyce Goodman. *Women and Education, 1800–1980*. Basingstoke and New York: Palgrave Macmillan, 2004.

May, Allyson. "Fiction or 'Faction'? Literary Representations of the Early Nineteenth- Century Criminal Courtroom." In *Crime, Courtrooms and the Public Sphere in Britain, 1700–1850*, edited by David Lemmings. London: Ashgate, 2012.

May, Margaret. "Innocence and Experience: the Evolution of the Concept of Juvenile Delinquency in the Mid-Nineteenth Century." *Victorian Studies* 17 (Sept. 1973): 7–29.

McGowen, Randall. "Images of Justice and Reform of the Criminal Law in Early Nineteenth-Century England." *Buffalo Law Review* 32, no. 1 (1983): 89–125.

McGregor, O. R., Louis Blom-Cooper, and Colin Gibson. *Separated Spouses*. Legal Research Unit, Department of Sociology, Bedford College, University of London. London: Gerald Duckworth & Co. Ltd., 1970.

McKibbin, Ross. *Ideologies of Class: Social Relations in Britain, 1880–1950*. Oxford: Oxford University Press, 1991.

McLynn, Frank. *Crime and Punishment in Eighteenth-Century England*. Oxford: Oxford University Press, 1989.

Merry, Sally Engle. *Getting Justice and Getting Even: Legal Consciousness Among Working-Class Americans*. Chicago: University of Chicago Press, 1990.

Merry, Sally Engle. "Legal Pluralism." *Law and Society Review* 25, no. 8 (1988): 869–896.

Mitch, David F. *The Rise of Popular Literacy in Victorian England: the Influence of Private Choice and Public Policy*. Philadelphia: University of Pennsylvania Press, 1992.

Mitch, David. *The Rise of Popular Literacy Rates in Victorian England: The Influence of Private Choice and Public Policy*. Philadelphia: University of Pennsylvania Press, 1992.

Nead, Lynda. *Victorian Babylon: People, Streets and Images in Nineteenth-Century London*. New Haven and London: Yale University Press, 2000.

Nelken, David. "Disclosing/Invoking Legal Culture: An Introduction." *Social & Legal Studies* 4 (1995): 435–36.

Nick Wikeley. *Child Support: Law and Policy*. London: Bloomsbury, 2006.

Nord, Deborah Epstein. "The City as Theater: From Georgian to Early Victorian London." *Victorian Studies* 31, no. 2 (Winter 1988): 159–88.

Nord, Deborah Epstein. *Walking the Victorian Streets: Women, Representation, and the City*. Ithaca and London: Cornell University Press, 1995.

O'Donovan, Katherine. "The Male Appendage – Legal Definitions of Women." In *Fit Work for Women*, edited by Sandra Burman. London: Routledge, 1979.

Old Bailey Online. https://www.oldbaileyonline.org /static/Crimes .jsp#simplelarceny

Outhwaite, R. B. *The Rise and Fall of the English Ecclesiastical Courts, 1500–1860*. Cambridge: Cambridge University Press, 2010.

Owen, David. *The Government of Victorian London: The Metropolitan Board of Works, the Vestries, and the City Corporation*. Cambridge, MA and London: Harvard University Press, 1982.

Paley, Ruth. "An Imperfect, Inadequate and Wretched System? Policing London before Peel." *Criminal Justice History* 10 (1989): 95–130.

Parker, Graham. "Review of Essays in the History of Canadian Law v. II, ed. David H. Flaherty." *Archivaria: the Journal of the Association of Canadian Archivists* 18 (Summer 1984).

Pearson, Geoffrey. *Hooligan: A History of Respectable Fears*. Basingstoke: Palgrave Macmillan, 1983.

Pellew, Jill. "Law and Order: Expertise and the Victorian Home Office." In *Government and Expertise: Specialists, Administrator and Professionals, 1860–1919*, edited by Roy McLeod. Cambridge: Cambridge University Press, 1988.

Pellew, Jill. *The Home Office 1848–1914: From Clerks to Bureaucrats*. East Brunswick: Rutgers University Press, 1982.

Pennybacker, Susan. *A Vision for London 1889–1904: Labour, Everyday Life, and the LCC Experiment*. London: Routledge, 1995.

Perkin, Harold. *The Rise of Professional Society: England Since 1880*. London: Routledge, 1989.

Petrow, Stefan. *Policing Morals: The Metropolitan Police and the Home Office, 1870–1914*. New York: Clarendon Press, 1994.

Petrow, Stefan. "The Rise of the Detectives in London, 1869–1914." *Criminal Justice History* 14 (1993): 91–108.

Philips, David. "A New Engine of Power and Authority: The Institutionalization of Law Enforcement in England, 1780–1830." In *Crime and the Law: The Social History of Crime in Western Europe since 1500*, edited by V. A. C. Gatrell, Bruce Lenman, and Geoffrey Parker. London: Europa Publications, 1980.

Philips, David. "Crime, Law and Punishment in the Industrial Revolution." In *The Industrial Revolution and British Society*, edited by Patrick O'Brien and Roland Quinault. Cambridge: Cambridge University Press, 1993.

Philips, David. *Crime and Authority in Victorian England: the Black Country 1835–1860*. London: Croom Helm, 1977.

Pinchbeck, Ivy, and Margaret Hewitt. *Children in English Society*. Vol. II of *From the Eighteenth Century to the Children Act 1848*. London and Toronto: Routledge and University of Toronto Press, 1973.

Poovey, Mary. *Making a Social Body: British Cultural Formation, 1830–1864*. Chicago and London: University of Chicago Press, 1995.

Prevost, Elizabeth. "Married to the Mission Field: Gender, Christianity and Professionalization in Britain and Colonial Africa, 1865–1914." *Journal of British Studies* 47, no. 3 (Oct. 2008): 796–826.

Prevost, Elizabeth. *The Communion of Women: Missions and Gender in Colonial Africa and the British Metropole*. Oxford: Oxford University Press, 2010.

Price, Richard. "One Big Thing: Britain, Its Empire, and Their Imperial Culture." *Journal of British Studies* 45, no. 2 (Jul. 2006): 602–627.

Procida, Mary. "Good Sports and Right Sorts: Guns, Gender, and Imperialism in British India." *Journal of British Studies* 40, no. 4 (Oct. 2001): 454–488.

Rabin, Dana. *Identity, Crime and Legal Responsibility in Eighteenth-Century England*. New York and Basingstoke: Palgrave-Macmillan, 2004.

Radzinowicz, Leon, and Roger Hood. *The Emergence of Penal Policy in Victorian and Edwardian England*. Vol. 5 of *A History of English Criminal Law and its Administration from 1750*. Oxford: Clarendon, 1990.

Radzinowicz, Leon. *Ideology and Crime: A Study of Crime in its Social and Historical Context*. New York: Columbia University Press, 1966.

Rappaport, Erika. *Shopping for Pleasure: Women and the Making of London's West End*. Princeton: Princeton University Press, 2001.

Readman, Paul A. "The 1895 General Election and Political Change in Late Victorian Britain." *The Historical Journal* 42, no. 2 (Jun. 1999): 467–93.

Reynolds, Elaine. *Before the Bobbies: The Night Watch and Police Reform in Metropolitan London, 1720–1830*. Stanford: Stanford University Press, 1998.

Roberts, David. *Victorian Origins of the British Welfare State*. New Haven: Yale University Press, 1960

Roberts, Elizabeth. *A Woman's Place: An Oral History of Working-Class Women, 1890–1940*. Oxford, UK and Cambridge, MA: Blackwell, 1984.

Roberts, F. David. *The Social Conscience of the Early Victorians*. Stanford: Stanford University Press, 2002.

Roberts, M. J. D. "Public and Private in Early Nineteenth-Century London: The Vagrant Act of 1822 and its Enforcement." *Social History* 13, no. 3 (1988): 273–294.

Rodrick, Anne Baltz. "'Only a Newspaper Metaphor': Crime Reports, Class Conflict, and Social Criticism in Two Victorian Papers." *Victorian Periodicals Review* 29, no. 1 (Spring, 1996): 1–18.

Rogers, Nicholas. "Review of James Vernon, Politics and the People: A Study in English Political Culture, c.1815–1867." *Histoire Sociale/Social History* 29, no. 57 (1996): 231–32.

Rose, Jonathan. *The Intellectual Life of the British Working Classes*. New Haven: Yale University Press, 2001.

Rose, Marjorie. *Justice and Journalism*. London: Barry Rose, 1974.

Rose, Nikola. "Governing by Numbers: Figuring Out Democracy." *Accounting, Organizations and Society* 16, no. 7 (1991): 673–75.

Ross, Ellen. "'Fierce Questions and Taunts': Married Life in Working-Class London, 1870–1914." *Feminist Studies* 8, no. 3 (Autumn, 1982): 575–602.

Ross, Ellen. *Love and Toil: Motherhood in Outcast London, 1870–1918*. New York and Oxford: Oxford University Press, 1993.

Ross, Ellen. "Survival Networks: Women's Neighborhood Sharing in London before World War I." *History Workshop Journal* 15 (Spring 1983): 4–27.

Rowbotham, Judith, and Kim Stevenson, eds. *Criminal Conversations: Victorian Crimes, Social Panic, and Moral Outrage*. Columbus: Ohio State University Press, 2005.

Rowbotham, Judith, and Kim Stevenson. "Causing a Sensation." In *Behaving Badly, Social Panic and Moral Outrage – Victorian and Modern Parallels*, edited by Judith Rowbotham and Kim Stevenson. Aldershot, Hants, and Burlington, VA: Ashgate, 2003.

Royle, Edward. *Chartism*. 3rd ed. London: Routledge, 1980.

Savage, Gail. "'The Magistrates Are Men': Working- Class Marital Conflict and Appeals from the Magistrates' Court to the Divorce Court after 1895." In *Disorder in the Court: Trials and Sexual Conflict at the Turn of the Century*, edited by George Robb and Nancy Erber. New York and Basingstoke: Palgrave- Macmillan, 1999.

Savage, Gail. "They Would If They Could: Class, Gender, and Popular Representation of English Divorce Litigation, 1858–1908." *Journal of Family History* 36, no. 2 (2011): 173–90.

Scott, James C. *Seeing Like a State: How Certain Schemes to Improve the Human Condition Have Failed*. New Haven: Yale University Press, 1999.

Scott, James. *Domination and the Arts of Resistance: Hidden Transcripts*. New Haven: Yale University Press, 1990.

Shanley, Mary Lyndon. *Feminism, Marriage, and the Law in Victorian England, 1850–1895*. Princeton: Princeton University Press, 1989.

Sharafi, Mitra. "South Asian Legal History." *Annual Review of Law and Social Science* 11 (2015): 309–36.

Sharpe, James. "'Such Disagreement Betwyx Neighbours,' Litigation and Human Relations in Early Modern England." In *Disputes and Settlements: Law and Human Relations in the West*, edited by John Bossy. Cambridge: Cambridge University Press, 1983.

Shoemaker, Robert. *Prosecution and Punishment: Petty Crime and the Law in London and Rural Middlesex, c.1660–1725*. Cambridge: Cambridge University Press, 1991.
Shore, Heather. *Artful Dodgers: Youth and Crime in Early Nineteenth-Century London*. Rochester: Royal Historical Society, 1999.
Smart, Carol, and Selma Sevenhuijsen. *Child Custody and the Politics of Gender*. London and New York: Routledge, 1989.
Smith, Bruce P. "English Criminal Justice Administration, 1650–1850: A Historiographic Essay." *Law and History Review* 25, no. 3 (Fall 2007): 609–615.
Smith, Bruce. "The Myth of Private Prosecution in England, 1750–1850." In *Crime, Prosecution and Social Relations: The Summary Courts of the City of London in the Late Eighteenth Century*, edited by Drew Gray. Basingstoke: Palgrave Macmillan, 2009.
Smith, Mary Roberts. "The Social Aspect of New York Police Courts." *The American Journal of Sociology* 5, no. 2 Sept. 1899: 145–54.
Spencer, J. R., ed. *Jackson's Machinery of Justice*. 6th ed. Cambridge: Cambridge University Press, 1972.
Spraggs, Gillian. *Outlaws and Highwaymen: The Cult of the Robber in England from the Middle Ages to the Nineteenth Century*. London: Pimlico, 2001.
Srebnick, Amy Gilman. "Does the Representation Fit the Crime? Some Thoughts on Writing Crime History as Cultural Text." In *Crime and Culture: A Historical Perspective*, edited by Amy Gilman Srebnick and René Lévy, 3–19. Aldershot: Ashgate, 2005.
Stack, John. "Reformatory and Industrial Schools and the Decline of Child Imprisonment in Mid-Victorian England and Wales." *History of Education* 23 (1994): 59–73.
Steedman, Carolyn. *Labour Lost: Domestic Service and the Making of Modern England*. Oxford: Oxford University Press, 2009.
Steedman, Carolyn. *Master and Servant: Lobe and Labour in the English Industrial Age*. Oxford: Oxford University Press, 2007.
Steedman, Carolyn. *Policing the Victorian Community: The Formation of English Provincial Police Forces, 1856–80*. London: Routledge, 1984.
Stevenson, Kim. "Fulfilling Their Mission: The Intervention of Voluntary Societies in Cases of Sexual Assault in the Victorian Criminal Process." *Crime, History & Societies/Crime Histoire & Sociétés* 8, no. 1 (2004): 93–110.
Stevenson, Kim. "The Respectability Imperative: A Golden Rule in Cases of Sexual Assault?" In *The Golden Age: Essays in British Social and Economic History, 1850–1870*, edited by Ian Inkster, Judith Rowbotham, and Colin Griffin. Aldershot and Burlington, VT: Ashgate, 2000.
Stone, Lawrence. "Literacy and Education in England 1640–1900." *Past & Present* 42 (Feb. 1969): 69–139.

Storch, Robert. "The Policeman as Domestic Missionary: Urban Discipline and Popular Culture in Northern England, 1850–1880." *Journal of Social History* IX (1975–76): 481–509.

Sutherland, Gillian. *Policy-Making in Elementary Education, 1870–1895*. Oxford: Oxford University Press, 1973.

Swensen, Steven P. "Mapping Poverty in Agar Town: Economic Conditions Prior to the Development of St. Pancras Station in 1866." *Working Papers in the Nature of Evidence: How Well Do "Facts" Travel?* no. 09/06. London: Department of Economic History, London School of Economics, 2006.

Takayanagi, Mari. "The Representation of the People Act 1918: A Democratic Milestone in the UK and Ireland." *OxHRH Blog* (February 6, 2018). http://ohrh.law.ox.ac.uk/the-representation-of-the-people-act-1918-a-democratic-milestone-in-the-uk-and-ireland

Taylor, David. *Crime, Policing and Punishment in England, 1750–1914*. New York: St. Martin's Press, 1998.

Tebbutt, Melanie. *Making Ends Meet: Pawnbroking and Working-Class Credit*. Leicester: Leicester University Press, 1983.

Tebutt, Melanie. *Women's Talk?: A Social History of "Gossip" in Working-Class Neighbourhoods, 1880–1960*. Aldershot: Scolar Press, 1995.

Thane, Pat, and Tanya Evans. *Sinners? Scroungers? Saints?: Unmarried Motherhood in Twentieth-Century England*. Oxford: Oxford University Press, 2012.

Thane, Pat. "Women in the British Labour Party and the Construction of State Welfare, 1906–1939." In *Mothers of a New World: Maternalist Politics and the Origins of Welfare States*, edited by Seth Koven and Sonya Michel. New York and London: Routledge, 1993.

The A to Z of Victorian London. London Topographical Society, 1987.

Thom, Deborah. *"Nice Girls and Rude Girls": Women Workers in World War I*. London: IB Tauris, 1998.

Thompson, E. P. "Patrician Society, Plebian Culture." *Journal of Social History* 7 (1974): 382–405.

Thompson, E. P. "Rough Music Reconsidered." *Folklore* 103, no. 1 (1992): 3–26.

Thompson, E. P. *Whigs and Hunters: the Origin of the Black Act*. New York: Pantheon, 1975.

Thompson, F. M. L. *The Rise of Respectable Society: A Social History of Victorian Britain, 1830–1900*. Cambridge, MA: Harvard University Press, 1988.

Todd, Selina. "Class, Experience and Britain's Twentieth Century." *Social History* 39, no. 4 (2014): 489–490.

Tomes, Nancy. "A 'Torrent of Abuse': Crimes of Violence between Working-Class Men and Women in London, 1840–1875." *Journal of Social History* 11, no. 3 (Spring, 1978): 328–345.

Vernon, James. *Politics and the People: A Study in English Political Culture c.1815– 1867*. Cambridge: Cambridge University Press, 1993.

Vincent, David. *Literacy and Popular Culture: England 1750–1914*. Cambridge: Cambridge University Press, 1993.
Waddams, S. M. *Sexual Slander in Nineteenth-Century England: Defamation in the Ecclesiastical Courts, 1815–1855*. Toronto: University of Toronto Press, 2000.
Walkowitz, Judith. *City of Dreadful Delight: Narratives of Sexual Danger in Late- Victorian London*. Chicago: University of Chicago Press, 1992.
Warner, Michael. *Publics and Counterpublics*. New York: Zone Books, 2002.
Webb, Robert K. "The Victorian Reading Public." *Higher Education Quarterly* 12, no. 1 (Nov. 1957): 24–44.
Webb, Robert K. "Working-Class Readers in Early Victorian England." *The English Historical Review* 65, no. 256 (Jul. 1950): 333–51.
Weinberger, Barbara. "The Police and the Public." In *Policing and Punishment in Nineteenth-Century Britain*, edited by Victor Bailey. New Brunswick: Rutgers University Press, 1981.
Weiner, Deborah. *Architecture and Social Reform in Victorian London*. Manchester: Manchester University Press, 1994.
White, Jerry. *Campbell Bunk: The Worst Street in North London Between the Wars*. London: Pimlico, 2003.
Wiener, Martin. *Men of Blood: Violence, Manliness and Criminal Justice in Victorian England*. Cambridge: Cambridge University Press, 2004.
Wiener, Martin. *Reconstructing the Criminal: Culture, Law, and Policy in England, 1830–1914*. Cambridge: Cambridge University Press, 1990.
Williams, Raymond. "The Press and Popular Culture: An Historical Perspective." In *Newspaper History from the Seventeenth Century to the Present Day*, edited by George Boyce, James Curran, and Paul Wingate. London: Constable, 1978.
Willrich, Michael. *City of Courts: Socializing Justice in Progressive Era Chicago*. Cambridge: Cambridge University Press, 2003.
Wollacott, Angela. *On Her Their Lives Depend: Munitions Workers in the Great War*. Berkeley: University of California Press, 1994.
Wright, Danaya. "Untying the Knot: An Analysis of the English Divorce and Matrimonial Causes Court Records, 1858–1866." *University of Richmond Law Review* 38, no. 4 (2004): 903–1010.
Wrigley, Chris. "The Labour Party and the Impact of the 1918 Reform Act." *Parliamentary History* 37, no.1 (Feb. 2018): 64–80.
Yngvesson, Barbara. "Inventing Law in Local Settings: Rethinking Popular Legal Culture." *Yale Law Journal* 98, no. 8 (Jun. 1989): 1689–1709.
Yngvesson, Barbara. *Virtuous Citizens, Disruptive Subjects: Order and Complaint in a New England Court*. New York and London: Routledge, 1993.
Zlotnick, Susan. "'The Law's a Bachelor': Oliver Twist, Bastardy, and the New Poor Law." *Victorian Literature and Culture* 34 (2006): 131–146.

Index